STANDING ROOM ONLY

Being a SPIRITED account of the BASEBALL in BOSTON

Between those years 2004 & 2008

by one

A. KNOEFEL LONGEST

Bartlett Park & Co.

Boston

Contents

BtPk

For Scott

STANDING ROOM ONLY

Ladies and Gentlemen, Boys and Girls,
Welcome to Fenway Park

It is a suspicion widely held among Red Sox fans that nothing in baseball truly exists, until it exists at Fenway Park. Other teams may, on occasion, meet in other cities and in other ballparks, far beyond the pale of New England; may throw pitches, call strikes, record hits, dispute outs, score runs, win and lose games, cheer and boo results, bemoan and celebrate and in general seem to *actually care* about games which have no discernable affect on either the Red Sox or the American League East divisional standings. Why exactly, one could not begin to guess.

Yet it is true. We have seen pictures. We are aware of the In-Game Update; we have come to terms with (if not acceptance of) the On-Screen Ticker; and we stare out across the misty outfield grass, in something very much like awe, at the haunting mathematical detachment that is the Out-of-Town Scoreboard. And yet these figures tend only to click downward, one by one, like coins through our internal counting machine—Angels 5-2 over A's, 4 ½ up, Yanks lose 7-1, Ichiro 3-5, O's lose 5th straight, Howard hits third, Santana 6 2/3, 1 ER, 8 K, now 3 back, Tigers win, sweep—into the various compartments of our ongoing mental ledger, where they are quickly tallied, recorded, filed away, and just as quickly lost beneath the next day's cascade of box scores.

Occasionally from somewhere among them an unfamiliar name will rise, from obscurity to recognition to distinction (*leading the team to…, leading the league in…, he is already a leading candidate for…*), yet so long as the bearer of this name does so at Safeco Field or Camden

Yards or Great American Ball Park he will remain a name. Perhaps attached to an impressive OPS or ornamented with some particular highlight, yet still distant, theoretical—a television character on a show we never watch. Until, that is, this name is announced over the grandstand at Fenway Park (*now batting...*); until it emerges from the visitor's dugout on the back of some gray road jersey, and the man beneath it saunters into the batter's box looking entirely too comfortable for his own good; until he clangs a double off the Green Monster, goes three-for-four, drives in a pair, and insists on getting a big hit in a close situation when any anonymous player would have had the decency to pop out to second. Only then do we begrudgingly assent to the reality of his talent.

Likewise the unsigned or traded or released Red Sox player who never truly departs, and who never actually signs with another team or wears another jersey until the day he appears in the wrong bullpen at Fenway, wearing the wrong colors, only to take the mound and bear down (one has to say, rather unsentimentally) on his former teammates; at which point the transaction—and depending on the particular stripe of away jersey, the *excommunication*—is officially sealed. Likewise the free agent who signs with the Sox, who wears red alternates in Fort Myers and opens the season in road grays, and who only enters our concept of the team when he appears in the home whites, lines a ball down past the Pesky Pole, turns first, and slides safely into second with the Fenway crowd rising to its feet around him. At which point he becomes one of our own, and is thus welcomed home, to Fenway Park. It is the all-validating, all-confirming context of baseball in New England, and its comfortable pale green familiarity is the filter through which we separate a deafening-loud spine-rattling stomach-clenching leaping shouting cheering spectacular panoramic floodlit actuality, from all that which is merely news.

SPRING

Promise

Seattle at Fenway
11 April 2007

To the Fens, then, and the parade of accustomed sights and sounds and sensations waiting to greet the river of Sox fans now cresting the Mass Pike overpass and flowing steadily onto the streets surrounding Fenway Park. An hour or so before first pitch and already it is dusk; the sky clear as it deepens downward from soft blues to pale yellows to rich oranges, smoldering to crimson between the building tops of Kenmore Square. The warmth of the day has disappeared in evening shadows, the air at dusk now crisp, cool, wintry, and the Sox fans bundled in long sleeve Sox shirts, faded Sox hats pulled low on brows, Sox bullpen jackets buttoned to chins, hands covered in knit Sox gloves and buried in the warm pocket of Sox *2004 MLB Playoffs* hooded sweatshirts, the hem of a white authentic Sox jersey hanging out behind, and a Sox fleece tucked under one arm (and beneath it all, one suspects, a pair of thick Sox socks). Eager, bright, happy and loud, we make our way down the overpass and bottleneck around a line already hugging the entire length of the Cask's new brick exterior, before gradually melding into the flooded delta at Brookline and Lansdowne. Where hawkers tower up through the crowd atop milk-crate pedestals, waving *Red Sox scorecards!* for *Just 2-bucks!* and plastic-sheathed *Globe here!* for a *only a quarter!* while at their feet stacks of the new *GameDay newspaper here!* disappear under the magic word: *free.* There are *Free 'K' cards!* compliments of your favorite Boston talk radio station; *Free Dice!*, which turn out to be red paper boxes in the shape of die, intended to be worn, as demonstrated by a pair of beery college-age fellows, as headgear; *Free headbands!* with Japanese characters placed on either side of a central

Legal Sea Foods logo. Farther up a tall, gaunt, grim-faced old man, yoked with a handmade double-sided board depicting (it seems) various images of eternal damnation, shouts out instructions on how to avoid such scenes and passes out red pamphlets offering the same (or attempts to, for there are few takers as many passing eyes find reason—*look kids, it's the Mass Pike*—to turn the other way). While perhaps twenty feet away, and despite the chill April air, three very tall, very slender young women in very tight hip-high skirts and very red knee-high stockings hand out club ads (no doubt advertising the very same damnation warned against farther up the sidewalk); which ads the trio run out of before reaching the corner of Lansdowne, and in whose wake there forms a slightly delayed and comically synchronized ripple of turning male heads. On one corner of a crowd-choked Brookline Avenue the intense glow of a key light shines on two fans in red alternate Sox jerseys (Nos. 34 and 38, respectively), who, having been pulled aside by a local news crew for a little impromptu *vox populi*, impart in as loud a *vox* as possible such insightful commentary on the general mood and tenor of the *populi* as, quote, *Go Sox!* and *Whooo-hooo!* and *Yeah that's right!* (Pause. Follow-up question. Long pause.) *Yeah! Go Sox! Whoo-hooo!* Opposite which a Japanese camera crew interviews one of the thousands of fans wearing a number 18 jersey in tonight's crowd, this a young Japanese-American woman who smiles and nods. While high above both interviews a giant billboard shows Ortiz, Varitek, and Daisuke beneath welcome messages in Spanish, English, and Japanese. Turning, twisting, swerving through the crowd, now headed in both direction, we make our way to the corner of Brookline and Yawkey and there find, like a tip of the cap from a familiar doorman, the sight of an old-fashioned peanut cart pilled high with stuffed brown bags, constant and familiar at the entrance to Yawkey, right before the turnstiles. A short wait, a quick fumble for the tickets, a *click-click* and an *enjoy the game*, and here we are—after days and weeks and even months of looking forward to- and planning on- and not being able to wait for-, after checking the rotation daily and the forecast hourly, after deciding on the appropriate luck-infused combination of Sox paraphernalia (the new 18 jersey layered between both '04 t-shirt *and* '04 sweatshirt, as to better absorb their talismanic properties), after coordinating meeting times and places, after *remind me to remember not to forget* the tickets, after a long drive, after fighting traffic, after looking for and finally finding (only to overpay for) parking, after crowding onto the Green Line, after waiting for the 39 bus because you dread the Green Line, after walking across the city because you can no longer abide the 39, after cramming into the Cask for a drink, after cramming out of the Cask for air, after all the tedious days and quiet nights which pass without notice through the cycle of our weekly routine we have come at last to the circled date on the calendar, to the time and place of genuine event, and after so often longing to be *there*, we suddenly find ourselves *here*—among the crowd on Yawkey Way. Listening to the high brassy sound of "On the Sunny Side of the Street" trumpeted out by the Hot Tamale Brass Band; air filled with the rich spiciness of grill smoke wafting high above, and the distinct nasal ping of each double-handful of yellow frothy beer passing below; moving unhurried through this familiar outdoor, free-flowing, front porch party all the way down to Gate D, where around its old brick façade dozens of complicated white stalks sprout from the media trucks parked on Van Ness, all clustered together and aimed skyward, ready to transmit tonight's events to the awaiting world. A bite, a drink, a laugh, one or two *hey there good to see ya*'s, and through the gate we go, down its uneven, patched-over decline straight into the bunched and slow-moving concourse. Weaving, excusing, turning shoulders sideways (the muscle memory of how to walk through a crowd returning unbidden), up a short ramp where a tingle of anticipation ripples up the back of our neck, greenish glimpses slip through the parting crowd, a few more steps, the crowd parts, and there it is: the pale green ballpark opens before us, the lush emerald of the outfield grass spreads out at our feet, and a low voice echoes out from the sky above, *Ladies and Gentlemen, Boys and Girls, Welcome to Opening Night at Fenway Park, America's Most Beloved Ballpark.*

Which, on this night, happens to be packed all the way up to its beloved steel rafters. Packed with young Japanese fans holding up signs in English; packed with American fans holding up signs in

Japanese; packed with fans who, no matter their age or nationality or language, all wear the red number 18 in all shape and size. On white replica 18 home jerseys, on blue 18 Matsuzaka t-shirts, on red 18 shirts with Japanese characters spelling (one assumes) DAISUKE across the nameplate. There are white t-shirts with RED SOX in English above Japanese characters spelling the same; red t-shirts with white die and large, rising-sun-filled K's; and yes of course *that* t-shirt, with that old familiar Red Sox sentiment in block blue on white, which caught up in the spirit of conviviality has been helpfully (sic) translated into Japanese. (The message apparently: *welcome, please join us in loving the things we love! and yes also to please kindly hate the things we hate!*) All items which have been spotted throughout the city with increasing regularity, along with the Japanese characters now in shop windows, newspaper ads, and across billboards such as the giant blue and orange sign above the right field bleachers, where the trademark rounded lettering of DUNKIN' DONUTS has (somewhat remarkably) been converted into Japanese characters. All in the name of what has been preemptively if unoriginally dubbed *Daisuke Mania*; all wrapped around the promise that *he* alone will be the difference (in the team, in the season, in the summer); all converging towards this night, and the moment about to take place before us.

Of course, the Highly-Anticipated Must-See Early Season Event (complete with National Media Frenzy) has become something of an April tradition here at Fenway. What with A-Rod's First At Bat As a Yankee at Fenway Park in 2004, the World Series Ring Presentation Ceremony (complete with Arch Rival Yankees Watching from Visiting Dugout) in 2005, and of course Johnny Damon's Return to Fenway Park As a Yankee, only last year. All dates circled in February; all moments preemptively referred to as *epic*; all ordinary early-season games heightened by the same crush of media and infused with the same grinning eyes-wide *it's going to be ridiculous here* buzz of nervy anticipation.

And yet it is worth noting, even as we shuffle through the ever-increasing and increasingly fluid crowd to find a suitable Standing Room Only spot (a bit like trying to find a nice firm spot to stand waist-deep in the ocean on a particularly wavy day), that the general hype surrounding Daisuke Mania has been quite unlike any previous must-see mania—more eager, less reserved, and we dare say a good deal happier. Part of which is due to the simple absence of Yankee involvement (the obvious and embarrassing constant in the previous three manias being their heavily anticipated booing and/or public humiliation of our New York rivals); but more so, and more positively so, because what we are anticipating is, unlike the rest, a genuine baseball debut. Meaning that apart from a few who made the trip to Fort Myers, none of us have ever actually seen Daisuke Matsuzaka—former International Prize Free Agent and current Red Sox rookie—in person (whereas we have seen quite enough of the Yankees, thank you); have never seen him walk out onto the field and take the mound; and, most importantly, have never seen him pitch. Add to this a winter of perpetual speculation, whereby our general curiosity has been stoked by reports steadily coming back to us from scouts and reporters and Japanese baseball experts who, like Marco Polo returning from an expedition to the Far East, have emptied their canvas pouches and awed us with the sparkle and spice of such exotic tales as the 250-pitch outings, the 17-inning shutout, and the half-whispered legend of the elusive physics-defying *gyroball* (an enigma of a pitch developed under the cover of obscurity by Japanese masters, no doubt in some distant baseball foothills; the mysteries of which are known by only a select few, and, depending on which reports one believes, either looks exactly like a fastball that takes an unannounced hard right turn and breaks *laterally* at least two feet and is therefore completely and utterly unhittable, or, conversely, does nothing at all but spin and is therefore completely and utterly fictitious). All this, along with the not insubstantial amount of yen required to have a man referred to as a National Treasure shipped overseas, has brought us here tonight expecting not simply a new pitcher, but a new *type* of pitcher. Something novel, something obscure, something slightly unfamiliar. Something, well yes, something quite literally foreign—foreign to both our baseball experience and our understanding of what is possible in the game. And to see it here. Live. In person. On the all-validating stage of Fenway Park.

It is therefore with a slight start of recognition that we see him there now, down on the field, suddenly and vividly before us; not wearing a suit or a warmup jacket or a red alternate spring jersey, but in the home whites, brilliant under the early evening floodlights. Beneath the rising swell of applause he jogs across the grass, then stretches behind-, climbs up-, and finally steps onto the Fenway Park mound. And as we glance around the grandstand to the crowd on its feet we discover a good many smiles, and a number of nervously folded arms, and several fans literally bouncing back and forth in anticipation as someone nearby (it may have been us) quietly says, *there he is.*

We really do see him there, but only just. It is a cold, clear April night at the ballpark, with Standing Room Only fans packed four deep behind the third base grandstand; giving us, from our vantage point among them and behind the old peeling blue seats, a wonderful view of the right field bleachers, the first base grandstand, and the various backsides of an entire section of Red Sox fans as they stand in anticipation before us. (Here again we notice the odd sensation of having a crowd—compact, loud, enclosed, jumbled and energetic and over-hyped—actually add to our delight in the moment; so often a distraction from the action on the field, here the crowd's unmistakable sense of *intent* casts an entirely apposite frame around the sparkling scene below.) And so it is through a slim crevice, opening up at intervals between it all (under one arm and over a head), that we manage to watch Matsuzaka take his warm-up tosses. Until finally even this slight window disappears. Which by eliminating all else, inadvertently focuses our attention on what is to be the real show of the evening: the brilliant display of flashbulbs popping throughout the grandstand. For even during his warm-up tosses there are flashes *pop pop* as he steps on, picking up *pop pop* into a flurry *pop pop pop* as he throws, catches and steps back on *pop pop.*

We have seen flashbulbs before, of course. For the first Ortiz appearance of the night, for any appearance of Jonathan Papelbon from the bullpen, for the opening pitch of a playoff series. But never before in warm-ups; never before with this frequency. And quickly we abandon our search through elbow crooks and around shoulders and turn only to the crowd as the low percolating chatter of anticipation grows steadily into applause (a slide image of Ichiro at the plate *click-clicks* between two clapping hands) and then a full clamor of shouts and clapping and yells and *pop pop* around the *pop pop* grandstands. He is there, somewhere behind a curtain of Sox fans, set on the mound facing Ichiro, and just as the noise rises to its peak we catch a fleeting glimpse of him stepping back into that slow arching pause before he disappears again and *pop pop* the stands *pop pop pop* explode *pop pop* in a wild eruption of *pop pop, pop pop pop* sparkling white flashes *pop pop pop* showering the entire grandstand and bleachers all at once as the cheer goes out, the last flashes *pop pop*, and a second, reactive cheer rises for what can only be strike one. And like that, *pop pop*, Daisuke Matsuzaka's career at Fenway Park has begun.

Denied a clear view of the play, we find ourselves forced to rely on other, more carefully trained senses to recognize (by the exhaling *oohhh-ahh* of the crowd) that he has thrown a ball. After a moment or two of audibly fumbling about in this fashion we hear, through the cheers, the familiar crack of the bat and an almost instantaneous burst of shouts (a line drive, nabbed) followed by steady clapping and then a second (over to first for the out) confirming round of cheers. We stare at the empty seat back before us, and—just as one can close one's eyes upon eating a fresh oyster and smell and hear and almost feel the ocean crashing over one's toes—record the first out in our scorebook, 1-3. (No doubt there is something oddly pleasing, almost gratifying, about discovering oneself the possessor of an ear so carefully calibrated to the rhythms of a Fenway crowd; this regardless of there being something considerably less pleasing, almost embarrassing, about long considering how many evenings have been spent recording 1-3's in order to obtain it.)

With the marquee match-up now concluded the fans of Section 25 take their seats along with the rest of the ballpark, and by doing so pull the curtains back on a spectacular panorama of Fenway Park. Where it seems a baseball game has broken out. Once again armed with the sense of sight, yet without a camera of our own to flash, we trust that the evening has been sufficiently recorded for posterity and go about trying to fix its images in memory by actually watching them happen. This works out rather well. Primarily because, as we noticed from the considerable photo-coverage after Daisuke's first start (it was *a frenzied playoff-like atmosphere* out there at Kauffman Stadium, KC, MO; or so we were told), the most striking images of his motion always frame the compact righty at a profile, and at the exact moment of his stride forward drop a shutter speed and trail the lens along his motion to intentionally streak the background, focusing the face and torso and making a blur of the firing right arm. The resulting image, which is a sweeping lateral rush, seems to be the choice Daisuke-shot among professionals. We can now see why. For it is at a profile that the curious particularities of Daisuke's motion are best appreciated.

He stands there at attention, glove at his side, looking in, perfectly still. A nod to the sign before a careful step back with the left foot, bringing both hands together and raising them (bent at the elbows) slowly above his head as he leans back, only to pause—he rocks back and forth on the left heel, once, twice, seeming to reconsider whether or not to go through with the motion (*perhaps...*)—but no, he must go on, and recommitted to the task he pivots, brings the left leg around and up, slowly rotates there, balances completely upright on the right leg, coiling back back back as the arms fall to the belt; then, suddenly, the right arm drops, hits some imaginary latch, a hidden trigger mechanism just behind his right knee, and all of a sudden every ounce of the slowly coiled motion is released—the knee buckles and the left foot gives a slight kick and the entire form uncoils and swoops down and rushes low across the mound, the arm a blur over the top and the ball escaping unseen and darting low over the lip of the mound, so low it seems to jump up to the plate and *snaps*, in the glove, for strike one to Adrian Beltre. The easy, relaxed rhythm returns as the right leg swings around in front and, in one of the motion's distinct features, does not land so much as bounce from the lip of the mound, springing off the right foot as it glides imperceptibly into the first backward step up, to begin again.

It is a wonderful motion, one which has drawn the obvious comparison to other Japanese pitchers who have employed similarly intricate timing mechanisms (inaccurately, inelegantly, yet almost inevitably referred to by American media as a *hitch*), most notably the original Imported Japanese National Treasure, former Dodger (and Red Sox) pitcher, Hideo Nomo. The comparison is unfair to both pitchers, as it obscures what is truly exciting about watching Daisuke pitch, which is not the calm, graceful yoga poses (for which Nomo was justifiably famous), but the explosive forward rush which follows. Both pitchers use the deliberate pacing of their windup to accentuate the contrast with delivery; yet Daisuke practically springs off the rubber, as if some object were propelling him other than simply the strength in his right leg, and altogether the complete, seamless movement of his motion seems to propel him plateward faster than any pitcher we have ever seen, Nomo included. We say *seems to* because we have no way of knowing, for sure, whether he actually does move faster from the rubber to release or if it only appears that way. It hardly matters though; not to us, and certainly not to the Seattle hitters for whom *seems to* is every bit as troublesome as *actually does*.

What he actually does, here with one out in the first, is force Adrian Beltre to ground out easily to short. He gives up a single to José Vidro, gets Raul Ibanez to hit a sharp but routine grounder to third for the final out, and marches off the mound after his first inning to another shower of *pop pop* flashes and another *pop pop* standing ovation.

With the ceremonial firsts (pitch, batter, inning) out of the way, Daisuke is given a less dazzling but more stable background to work against in the second. Again our expectations are for something slightly unknown. We couldn't exactly say what, of course; but if the ball were to, say, dissolve in midair, or spontaneously combust, or halt, or reverse itself, or otherwise do something no other pitcher in the history of the game has every caused a ball to do, and to do so in a way which is entirely visible and evident, *then*, well then we would give each other a knowing wink and applaud our new national treasure, entirely satisfied. The last thing we expect to see then are breaking balls left up in the zone (something we have seen quite enough of over the years) which is exactly what Matsuzaka throws José Guillén in the second. Guillén pulls the pitch hard to left and on a fast rising line, and it thumps hard off the wall for a ringing single. So then, whatever pitches he may throw, he can be hit. (*I mean you didn't expect him to get out every single batter he faced, did you? Well, no, of course not...but, I thought, I don't know, maybe?*) More surprising still is the ease with which Kenji Johjima, always the *other* Japanese player in this game, raps a clean double into the gap to move Guillén over to third with only one out. Daisuke gets Betancourt to fly into shallow left-center, and with Guillén tagging up Manny runs onto it and fires a good hard one-hopper to Varitek who fields wide of the plate and dives to tag Guillén, sliding across and tumbling over as both catcher and runner look up. Only to find the arms-spread safe sign, and hear a wave of indignant boos rain down from the Fenway crowd. (In truth he looked to have just gotten in just before the tag, but we boo anyway, on principle.) Daisuke gets Lopez to ground to short for the final out, limiting the damage to the one run, but in the process he has shown himself to be, however slightly, fallible. No longer merely an intriguing tale, the reality is that Daisuke will have to prove himself at Fenway Park through the results he produces on the field—just like everyone else.

Almost immediately he goes about doing exactly that. Beneath another shower of flashbulbs he forces Ichiro to fly out to center, Beltre to pop up to short, and ends the inning by striking out José Vidro for yet another first (Strikeout, Fenway) and yet another standing ovation. In the third he quickly adds a second and third, striking out Ibanez looking and Ritchie Sexon swinging, the two sequences in tandem—Ibanez frozen by a surgically precise breaking ball, Sexon woefully tardy on a (to him) unexpected fastball—show us in just a handful of pitches the factual basis for all the hype surrounding his arrival.

Johjima is up next, and this time Daisuke keeps the ball down and forces a fielder's choice to end the inning. In the fifth though, the Mariners get to him. With one out he gives up a single to Lopez, the ninth hitter, and after a dramatic strikeout of Ichiro (*pop pop*), leaves a ball up to Beltre who pounces and lines a slicing drive deep into the left-center field gap. It rolls all the way to the track before it is picked up and relayed home (too late) and then over to third (again too late), for an RBI triple. Vidro singles on the next pitch and Beltre jogs in from third, and although the inning ends with no further damage and the game is only now halfway over, the Sox and Daisuke now suddenly trail, 3-0.

*Meanwhile, in another part of the forest...*it is the game's other young right-handed phenomenon, Seattle's Felix Hernandez, who has quietly stolen the show. Forcing the Red Sox' hitters into one meager ground-out after another, and along the way mixing in a quick trio of strike-outs and two innocuous walks, he has, over the game's first four innings, surrendered neither a hit nor a single ball struck well in any direction. This alone is not particularly astounding. Fenway has seen many a young visiting pitcher swagger through his first four innings in quiet style, only to stagger off a few innings later, bedraggled and shell-shocked under a cavalcade of hits and cheers and Sox baserunners wheeling about the base paths. But there are signs, even early on, that this will not be the case tonight, and that this particular young visit-ing pitcher is getting by on quite a bit more than pluck.

The first and perhaps best indications of this come on a pair of strikeouts; one in the second, when a ferocious Hernandez curveball causes us all, most notably J.D. Drew, to blink at a called third strike; the other an inning later when Varitek sees the same pitch, swings at it, and misses by approximately five and one-half feet (or whatever the distance is from Varitek's shoulders, where the bat swung, to his shoe-tops, where the ball landed). This is not exactly a common sight at a Major League baseball game. When professional hitters swing and miss it is usually by inches, and even then only discernable to the naked eye by the snap in the catcher's mitt and a deflated glance back. Rarely is so much clear daylight visible between bat and ball. Yet over the first four innings several Sox hitters take similarly awkward swings, either high over or so far ahead of Hernandez's pitches as to produce visible wincing in the stands. And by the top of the fifth the truth is clear enough to anyone paying attention: our boys are simply being overmatched.

And then there is all that wonderful infield defense behind him. Almost from the beginning (with an acrobatic José López catch in the first) the Mariners infield of Beltre, Betancourt and Lopez has handled every ground ball with effortless composure, only to throw unhurried across the diamond to the intercontinental reach of their 6'8" first baseman, Richie Sexon. Betancourt (who has the curious but effective habit of circling each ball, even routine grounders directly at him, onto his backhand) has recorded three assists; Beltre and Lopez a pair each. This trend continues in the fifth when Drew leads off with a hard shot past Felix, the ball heading towards the outfield beyond second when Lopez comes streaking over and outstretched dives to make the stop, pops up and throws to first, a bit high so that Sexon's entire frame is called upon to stretch up, momentarily off the bag, then down with the ball an instant before Drew crosses. *Out.* We groan. (*Oh come on!*) We wave both hands to the side (mimicking the signal the umpire should have made, just in case he momentarily forgot how to make that particular call). And we give voice to our respectful disagreement with the umpire's ruling (*What the —!*), repeatedly. Drew, decelerating up the line, only shakes his head. Sexon and Felix both point to Lopez, who coolly wags his finger to signal *one out*. And still (not so coolly) shaking our own head we jot a dark question mark above the 4-3 on our scorecard; the image of Lopez dashing over to stop a sure single one of those plays which seems bound to resonate later on—one way or another.

Now then, it is always difficult to determine when the possibility of a no-hit bid is born in the mind of a crowd. On this night the term is first overheard after the fourth, when the Mariners jog off the field under a grumble of inactivity from the crowd, and a young man nearby turns to his friend and says, *Hey, we're being no-hit here aren't we?* Yet the realization does not seem to truly settle among the crowd until after the brilliant defensive play on Drew in the fifth, immediately after Matsuzaka has given up his runs; allowing the Felix No-Hit Bid to dovetail nicely out of the Daisuke Debut. Looking back the two stories share a tidy double bill, with the first act (or first four and a half innings) casting a clear spotlight on Daisuke in his home whites, who holds the stage until the moment he falls behind and both story and spotlight shift to the second act (or final four and a half innings) and to the young Felix Hernandez and his bid for the improbable. So that with two outs in the fifth it is the latter who has fully captured the Fenway crowd's attention, as a bellowing, heavily accented voice in the third base grandstand repeatedly shouts out, *Relax Felix! You're only throwin' a no-hittah! No presh-ah kid!*

He might have saved his breath. For throughout the fifth and into the sixth we are all able to focus our undivided attention on the tall young righty, and taking the time to study his movements and mannerisms we notice almost immediately that, at least so far as his body language will allow, he does not need to be told to relax. He's already there. Everything about him is loose, easy, none too hurried. Loose jersey, loose sleeves, loose pants, loose silver necklaces dangling below his collar. Only the arms—well-defined and slender and almost impossibly long—stand out. He is tall, and steps onto the mound in three easy strides, glove relaxed at his side, and has a habit of repeatedly punching out the right arm and ball in a quick, flicking motion, which kicks the hem of his jersey sleeve up a bit as the arm jumps out farther, freer, unencumbered. He rarely wanders to the side of the mound, and almost never steps behind it. And as he brings the right hand and ball into the glove he takes one nearly imperceptible breath in, drops both hands in the glove to his belt buckle, and exhales. Then nods. One shallow step out to the left begins the motion as he turns his left shoulder to the plate, sweeps the left knee up, drops head and shoulders down, nose to knee, balances in this compressed pose for one beat at the apex and then forward, easy at first and then all at once the right arm shoots back and cantilevers over the shoulder and planting left leg, a blur until an easy recoil sweeps it across his body, the right leg swinging casually out behind and turning him at the base of the mound to look, straight over his right shoulder, at the plate. A little flurry of arm-lifts and jersey-plucks follows on the lip of the mound, as all the folds of loose jersey shifted during the motion are shrugged back into place. With a tug at the right sleeve he raises his glove, receives the ball from his catcher, and turns back to the mound with his head down. All nice and loose, in no hurry to throw strike two.

It is the bottom of the seventh now (*what, already?*) and Youkilis is up. A quick glance at the lineup shows Ortiz and Manny up next; then, if no one reaches, Drew, Lowell and Tek in the eighth; with Crisp, Pedroia and Lugo to follow in the ninth. Given the quality of swings taken by the last six names listed (only Drew among them has made solid contact) it is generally believed and widely muttered around the Fenway grandstand that *this is it*—our last good shot at breaking up the no-hitter. It is then both en- and dis-couraging to see Youkilis's hard hit top-spin drive to left dip down and buckle Ibanez who staggers up, staggers left, and then entirely out of momentum lunges desperately forward to make the catch. A groan goes out as Youk hops in frustration and grabs his helmet with both hands on the first base line, with several fans echoing the gesture in the grandstand. On the one hand Youkilis has squared up a Hernandez pitch, something no other Sox player has done tonight, therefore allowing the first whispered hint that Felix may be tiring (unlikely, as he has thrown only a miserly seventy-three pitches through six inning); more ominous however is the fact that Ibanez's awkward but effective play in left has all the markings of the classic, desperately late defensive save without which no hitless bid would be complete. It is a sign, a tell, the mark of luck recognized even by those too pragmatic to officially believe in such things.

It is also an out, a resource in increasingly short supply after Ortiz flies to left (high and more comfortably played Ibanez). Which brings up Manny. The crowd at this point has honed its focus to the immediate task. With no thought of the score or baserunners or even runs, our one remaining wish is to see the Sox hit a ball in play which is not immediately caught and thrown to first for an out (or rather what we vaguely remember being called a *base hit*). And the type of raucous, pleading cheer usually reserved for a bases loaded situation goes up for Manny, who immediately falls behind in the count. The crowd grows louder, thumping out a Let's-*Go*, Red-*Sox!* chant, echoing throughout the ballpark as the clapping rumbles up to vibrate the entire ballpark just as Felix sets and steps into his motion. The chant ends. Johjima tosses the ball to the side. Manny undoes his batting gloves. And Felix, long arms hanging loose at his sides, walks quietly off the mound.

And no matter when one deems it appropriate to talk of a no-hitter, the seventh inning is unquestionably the point at which we all— home and away players, on-air announcers, print journalists, managers, assistant trainers, bat boys, principal owners, general managers, ushers, vendors, security guards, mere spectators and baseball fans alike— begin to count outs. After Manny's strikeout, the Sox are down to six.

By this point Daisuke has been lifted for middle relief (though not before a clever dig at first on a 3-6-1 double play to end his outing in style), so there is no other story. It is Felix Hernandez, 21-years-old, on a cool early April night at Fenway Park, taking a no-hitter to the mound as he steps on the rubber to begin the eighth. J.D. Drew, victim of a brilliant curveball in the second and a brilliant defensive play in the fifth, is the batter. And now Fenway rises and shouts. On the mound Felix drops his hands and glove to his belt and exhales, rocks back, pulls knee to nose and stretching out fires a fastball away, over the plate and, for one of the first times all night, slightly up. Drew smacks it hard back up the middle, Felix lunges down but just misses and Lopez again dives outstretched but this time the ball skips, once, under his glove and shoots out over the outfield grass for a clean base hit. A mirror image of the play in the fifth, only Lopez, now smacking his glove in frustration, just missed knocking it down. Already on its feet Fenway roars out a loud ovation, first for Drew and then, as Felix casually points out positioning to his outfielders, for the young righty who was less rattled than simply beat by both opportunistic hitting, and an equitable bit of tough baseball luck.

A third wave of cheers greets Mike Lowell's appearance at the plate and carries with it the dawning realization, apparent the moment the no-hit threat is lifted, that this is still a close ballgame. With Felix now hittable the 3-0 deficit which a moment ago was an afterthought suddenly looks manageable. Particularly with one on and nobody out in the eighth. And just as suddenly the fact that the man on the mound is only 21-years-old turns from a source of wonder to a source of hope. After all, *he's just a kid*—on the road, before an imposing crowd, facing a lineup with no less than seven former All-Stars, and having just watched his bid for history skip out into the outfield grass—and he could be rattled. We momentarily entertain this thought ourselves, and glance at our scorecard with a measure of optimism (one more base runner would guarantee Big Papi a chance) until at that very moment we are reminded of the loose flick of the arm, the easy step up to the mound, the single controlled exhale the exact same on every pitch; and even before Lowell swings, even before he flies out lazily to center, we know we are done.

We are. Crisp follows, already in the midst of an early season slump, he has been painfully overmatched all night. He checks his swing and knocks a rolling grounder to short, Betancourt scoops and throws and the inning, along with the Sox's only minor threat of the night, is over. In the ninth Felix returns, as we knew he would, and gets Pedroia to roll one to the mound for the first out, and Lugo to ground to second for another. He then works a pair of quick strikes against Youk, and, for his last pitch of the night, throws a devastating breaking ball at which Youkilis can only flail, striking out on what may very well go down as the worst swing of his entire career. The organist plays a slow dirge, the scorecard is (rather quickly) tallied, and we file quietly towards the exits and out into the streets. The sight of a disciplined hitter, known for his ability to make contact, swatting late and only in the general direction of a nearly unhittable pitch the only appropriate coda to such a performance.

April baseball is, in the wider scope of the season, almost entirely about promise. With the standings and statistics and observational data yet to amass the vast sample sizes required to give them weight and meaning, we are far more apt to look for (and therefore find) significance in the individual moment—to take one good at bat by a newly acquired player and imagine that same result repeated over and again (perhaps in the latter innings at Yankee Stadium, perhaps in deep October with bunting as backdrop), to take one bad night at the plate from an entire lineup and extrapolate it out into a summer of frustrating losses (*how many 3-0, 4-2, 2-1 games are we in for anyway?*), and, perhaps most of all, to take one outing from a new pitcher and no matter the circumstances or mitigating details or our knowledge of the game's precarious nature, to decide, on the spot, that *this is the pitcher*.

So it is. So it always has been. And so it will be for both pitchers in the aftermath of Daisuke Matsuzaka's memorable Fenway debut, even as we make our way through the crowd and home. For it is nearly impossible after witnessing such a night to trail out into a cool night air and back into the city with anything other than the firm belief that Felix Hernandez, at 21-years-old, is without question the most talented and promising young pitcher in all of baseball. (By the time we are back crossing over the Mass Pike he has started the All-Star Game, won the Cy Young, signed with a bigger club, won another Cy Young, raised the World Series MVP trophy, and given a wonderful little speech on a sunny afternoon at Cooperstown.) All of which we must force ourselves to preface with *on this night*. For *on this night*, he certainly was. Whether he can approximate that form from start to start, and stay healthy over a season of long innings is yet to be seen; but for now it is ours and the rest of the American League's lot to shake our heads and worry that this kid may in fact actually be *that* good.

As for Daisuke, he was not nearly *that* bad. He pitched well enough to win (the DAISUKE FALTERS storylines in the morning papers will be both unfair and entirely predictable), and should he continue to hold opposing lineups to three runs he will win a great many games at Fenway Park. Tonight he got beat on four or five pitches that missed location, and by a young pitcher who only missed once. Yet he showed flashes of real brilliance, composed himself nicely in the midst of a few tight situations, and, given the enormous amount of fan and media attention thrust upon this one start, displayed the remarkable and often underappreciated ability to perform at a high athletic level despite several thousand flashbulbs going off, mid-performance. Most of all what he showed—what he and Felix both showed—was promise.

Perhaps this is why tonight's game does not feel much like a loss. For as we slip through Kenmore Square crowd we have already added and forgotten the dropped half-game in the standings, so infinitesimal in the larger season, and moved on to the promise of Daisuke's next start. The fascinating motion, the array of pitches, the poise under a somewhat unhinged environment; all announce, if nothing else, the arrival of an immensely watchable character on the Fenway stage.

Beyond which there is the promise, so cherished by the April fan, of more baseball. The promise of more full counts with two outs and the runner on, and us up and cheering for a strike out; more rippling anticipation as Big Papi lumbers up to the plate; more leaping to our feet as a diving catch is risked and (*hey-hey!*) made; more standing ovations for an exiting pitcher; more tips of the cap; more curtain calls; more mobs around home plate; more new faces (Pedroia and Lugo) and stances and mannerisms to learn and know and cheer for; more opposing faces and stances and talents to learn and despise and root against; more wins; more losses; more walks from the ballpark with a brilliant game, only recently completed, sifting through memory to fix its most colorful moments in our scrapbook of the season. It is the promise, above all else, of more walks *to* the ballpark; of more early evenings on a crowded Yawkey Way; of more moments when you look up to see the Red Sox in their spotless home whites gain the top dugout step and shoot out in streaks of white like some wonderful baseball-loaded firework, flaring across the green grass before each slowly fades and settles to their natural position; the promise of more first pitches, more big hits, more rallies, more double plays, more moments (there was one tonight, right before Drew got his hit) where we stand with thousands and feel our pulse quicken and something within us tightens as the scene before us begins to shake with the promise that some amazing spectacle might very well happen before us *right now*, and then cheer like mad when it does. It is the promise, made by a cool April evening, of the first home run you watch clear the Monster in May, of the sun-warmed bleachers on a cloudless weekend in June, of the last out in a four-game sweep to start a three-day holiday weekend in July, of the condensation in your hand as you carry a cold beer on a hot

August day, of a late-night phone call telling you the Yankees lost a crucial game in September, and of flashbulbs sparkling brilliant across a sold out Fenway Park, thousands upon thousands of them, illuminating the clear Boston sky of some famous October night to come.

Some Kind of Holiday

Patriots' Day
Seattle at Fenway
17 April 2006

Try as we might, that first Patriots' Day pitch always arrives too soon. Of course, as a purely technical matter, it always arrives at the exact same time (11:05 am) on the exact same day (the third Monday in April) each and every year without fail; which would seem to suggest, again in a narrowly practical way, its being something which could be anticipated. So that if, say, one did not get oneself up and caffeinated and to the ballpark in time for the first pitch on Patriots' Day's day last season, or the season before that, or the season before *that* (about which one still claims extenuating circumstances), then one could reasonably be expected to set one's long and overly-elaborate pre-game schedule back a bit earlier than in previous years, and maybe perhaps get it together for once. Then again, not if the *one* in question is a baseball fan, and therefore a creature of regular, formal, some might even say rigid (though one prefers *dependable*) routine. Within which 7:05 pm and 1:05 pm are ever the North and South Poles, the times to which all other events either approach or recede from; and so when a butterfly flaps its wings in China and suddenly an otherwise normal Wednesday night game inexplicably begins at 7:35 pm rather than 7:05 pm, the effects are felt all the way around the world and we find ourselves, on the Friday previous, exactly one half hour late to lunch. Unbelievable, yes (this confirmed by one's lunch date), and yet understanding this effect goes a long way towards explaining the vast disarray caused within the daily routines of Sox fans (not to mention those butterflies in China) by that tiny notation, found only once a year on the Red Sox' calendar, of 11:05 am. Predictable or not, the mind still reels at its implications.

In one's seat no later than 1100. Scorecard filled out by 1055. Third cup of coffee, 1050. Call placed to best baseball friend recapping the various managerial crimes committed in last night's game, 945. (Second call placed to best baseball friend to remind him that if *we* were at work, and *he* were at the game, we would be so good as to answer his call, 955.) Survey of all box scores, injury reports and pitching matchups relevant to Red Sox's hopes and/or Yankee demise, 930. Second cup of coffee, 920. Solid rations (consisting of items rarely witnessed on the breakfast table of adults), 910. Fenway Park gates open, 905. Depart for ballpark, 815 (ETA 900). Shower, dress, groom, 805-815. Wake, 700-805. First cup of coffee, well, it would have to be the night before, wouldn't it?

To the carefully calibrated, routine-based baseball sensibility it all feels a bit off, disjointed, each step throughout the day arriving before we are ready for it, in the wrong light, and entirely too early. Too early for rubbing shoulders in a crowd; too early for the crank of the turnstiles; too early for sizzling franks and mustard and salty popcorn; and yes far, far too early for the substantial lines already queuing up at the beer taps on Yawkey (Patriots' Day being a Massachusetts state holiday established to commemorate the battle of Concord and Lexington, which proud moment in our nation's history is traditionally celebrated, in Boston, either by running a world-class marathon, or by going to Fenway and drinking oneself silly before noon). All too early, this year no less than last. And so this year, not unlike last year (or the year before), our carefully adjusted routine never does quite calibrate itself in time, and inevitably leaves us standing in line or out on Yawkey, or (as we find ourselves this year) filling in our scorecard when that first snap hits the catcher's mitt and we look up, slightly surprised, only to have missed strike one.

Slightly aggravated, we look down to finish our scorecard. Slightly surprised (and more than slightly re-aggravated), we look up again, this time at the crack of the bat, and find a high slicing drive trailing into the gap and Ichiro, as sleek and fluid and nearly weightless as ever, gliding around first and easing into second with a leadoff double. A few pitches later he glides (for he does nothing so crass as *run* or *jog*) to third on a José López ground-out; and moments later, when Raúl Ibáñez lofts a shallow fly to left, he sets himself, back heel to the bag and front knee crouched, like a sprinter in the blocks. The instant Manny makes the catch he's off, flying down the line as the ball darts in and Varitek stretches a leg to block the plate and Ichiro slides wide, behind and past Varitek, and as he sails through the far batter's box reaches out, almost as an afterthought, and brushes his left hand ever so casually across the plate. 1-0, Mariners. It is a stylish opening run— full of patience, balance, timing, and given a deserving finish by the Mariner's most stylish of stars.

In answer to which the Red Sox turn to their own one-name-only star, whose style is a bit more direct but no less affective, to equalize. Never one for fleet baserunning or crafty slides, Ortiz steps up with two outs in the bottom of the first and levels the score simply by demolishing a Gil Meche fastball. It clangs off the camera stand high above the center field wall, Papi circles the bases at a leisurely shuffle, and steps firmly on home plate with two fingers pointed skyward. Leveling the score, 1-1. And as we cheer we cannot help but shake our heads. For in the past twenty minutes or so we have seen two of the game's greatest showmen perform their signature acts to perfection. (And in such pleasing contrast, with Ichiro's subtlety balanced against Papi's raw force. Unique pleasures on their own, it is a rare indulgence to find them so skillfully paired—the sweet and the savory—in one satisfying inning.) At which point we steal a glance at the centerfield clock. 11:34 am, and we're off and running.

Both teams charge into the second with no regard at all for the sleepy-eyed fans still filing into their seats (or standing in SRO and undergoing massive difficulties trying to complete a scorecard and a cup of coffee at the same time), and immediately set about scoring more runs. Albeit by slightly more industrial means. In the top half of the inning the Mariners' Adrian Beltre singles and later scores from first on a Yuntiesky Betancourt double in the gap, causing the last ripples of excited, it's-a-holiday-and-we're-at-Fenway buzz generated by

Ortiz's drive to finally flatten out and subside. Only to return in the bottom of the inning when, with Trot Nixon on first, Varitek hits a grounder towards second, a sure double-play ball that López makes a mess of, fumbles to get the out at first, and leaves Nixon standing safe at second. After a Lowell ground out, Alex Cora doubles in the gap to score Nixon and retie the game, 2-2.

We pause, check our watches (11:55 am), and take a deep breath.

These first two innings have started us off at a brisk pace, lively and engaging; but it seems unlikely and perhaps unhealthy to keep up such back-and-forth swings too long, lest we run the risk of exhaustion in the later innings. Both teams seem to agree, and the game eases back to a steady jog as each pitcher settles into a more deliberate and sensible pace. For the Sox it is fill-in starter Lenny DiNardo, who has so far in his young career managed to become that rarest of Red Sox players about whom fans carry no strong feelings either way (earlier on Yawkey his name in answer to the question of *who's pitching today?* elicited only a blank stare and silence). He works quick and steady, and continues to allow runners to reach first and easy, double-play-ready groundballs to reach his middle infielders. A thin lefty who throws mostly breaking pitches and the occasional *gotch-ya* fastball (usually inside on the hands, and never to a dangerous hitter), DiNardo appears to somehow be in perpetual need of a double play ball, even in situations with nobody on base. Force of habit, it seems. He gets one in the third, another in the fourth, and would have gotten one in the fifth had there been anyone on, but gets out of the inning nonetheless and on the day gives the Sox their five solid innings.

His opposite for the day, Seattle starter Gil Meche (who seems to be perpetually looking back over his shoulder at a solo home run sailing out to the bleachers), manages to avoid any of the momentary but disastrous lapses in control which have plagued and unfortunately defined his career thus far, and after striking out Ortiz in the third (to end an arduous 10-pitch at bat) cruises steadily through the middle innings, and both he and the game reach the top of the sixth still tied, 2-2.

At which point the general pace of activity at Fenway reaches a kind of onset, early afternoon stasis. Here the realization that a wan, gray morning has given way to a wan, gray afternoon (the light not so much blocked as diffused by a high gauze of cloud cover) is expressed throughout the grandstands in a thousand re-zippered jackets and re-bunched shoulders and hands, already gloved, stuffed back in the front pouch of thick hooded sweatshirts. The movement to and froe within the aisles subsides to an occasional *excuse me, sorry, last time I promise,* and a full count or two pass with no more recognition than a few half-hearted claps from those looking up in time from the pile of peanut shells in their lap. It is the stage of general ballpark contentment wherein those who came to watch the game recline back a bit, one hand absently strumming their scorecard; where those who came to eat are sufficiently full; where those who came to drink are sufficiently drunk; and where those who arrived sufficiently drunk in order to become far more drunk than is typically acceptable before lunchtime on a Monday have now nursed the same beer for three full innings, with two untouched and gradually flattening beers beneath their seat. And within this quiet, milling atmosphere one can almost feel the apprehension settling in among us all (save perhaps the latter) that the brief flurry of runs in the first two innings might very well be it for the day; that perhaps that *was* the game, and we have experienced nearly all we will experience today in the way of baseball amusement. It is there—in the heavy shifts, the elbows planted on knees, the conversations wandering off to *what're you guys doin' aftah*—that palpable realization, still unspoken, that this is a 3-2 game waiting to happen.

As it turns out, the first sign that this might not be the case comes by way of former Red Sox slugger (and noted contrarian) Carl Everett, who steps to the plate with one on in the sixth to face reliever Rudy Seánez. Everett, who after a number of years away from Fenway has like many distant relatives returned looking both a bit thicker through the midsection and a bit slower through the strike zone, still bullies up close to the plate and gives confrontational little flicks of his bat in the general direction of the pitching mound; but the ferocity of his swing is long gone, making all the histrionics of twitchy juts and jerky glances at the plate look slightly ridiculous—like an aging boxer laying into an unmoved heavy bag. One suspects he could still hit a belt-high, middle-of-the-plate, batting practice fastball though; which, perhaps out of some misguided curiosity to prove this hypothesis (no other reason seems possible), is exactly what Seánez throws him. The ball hangs out over the plate, Everett pulls it down the line, high up towards the right field corner, and we all turn and lean and watch the ball hook, drop, and clank against the foul screen. And before it even reaches the ground Fenway lets out a low moan of shared disbelief (*Oh come on! seriously!*), as Everett, stocky and plodding and with what one almost recognizes as something of the old defiant swagger, trots around the bases and steps on home to give the Mariners a 4-2 lead.

All of a sudden realizing how difficult it will now be for the Sox to fulfill our prediction by winning 3-2, we begin to consider other outcomes. Though not long, as one is conveniently provided for us in the bottom of the sixth when Ortiz comes to the plate with one out, and Youkilis on first. Meche is still working for Seattle, and as his first and only mistake of record came on a pitch inside to Ortiz in the second, he now predictably works the big DH away away away. Ortiz shakes his head, frustrated at a strike call which runs the count to 1-2, then settles back in the box and crouches down. Meche gets the sign and nods, and the moment his catcher Kenji Johjima silently slides to his right, behind Ortiz's left knee, we stand bolt upright. (*Not inside. He wouldn't risk it.*) Here is Meche then, who has Ortiz down in the count; who with a two-run lead in the sixth needs only to *not* give up a two-run homer to the most dangerous hitter in the ballpark; and who to prevent this, and to finish his quality start in a respectable manner, needs only to avoid throwing a fastball anywhere near the inside half of the plate. Ah yes, but then again Gil Meche has not built a career of muddling mediocrity out of avoiding dangerous locations on dangerous hitters, and (with his reputation to protect) he boldly attempts to sneak an inside fastball by the big slugger. He does not succeed. His 1-2 fastball is on the inside corner and thigh-high on Ortiz, who rips out of his stance and launches the ball deep into the suddenly joyous right field bleachers.

If Meche were to have taken the ball and set it on a tee in front of Ortiz, he could not have put it in a more favorable spot for his opponent. The crouch Ortiz takes at the plate, the low bent knees and hunched shoulder and forward-tilted bat, all act to concentrate his rather large frame down and slightly back; meaning that the motion of his swing is designed to explode out and slightly up on the ball. (As opposed to say, Manny, who stands more upright and tends to hit down on the ball). Which is why balls down and in on Ortiz tend to fair rather poorly. They simply get in the way of his swing. And so when Meche puts one right through this spot there is no adjustment in the motion—no reaching out or pulling in or dipping down—and we see the Ortiz Swing as the heavens designed it to work. And when it works as it does on Meche's 1-2 pitch it creates some serious, diesel grade torque, the ball leaping off the bat, the arc high and majestic and almost unbelievably long.

The home run ties the game at 4-4, but it also let's loose the previously restrained pace of the afternoon, and the crowd now awakens (or sobers up, depending), cheers once again rise up for strike calls, and in the seventh both game and crowd kick into full stride—as down the homestretch we go.

With Tavárez now on for the Sox the visitors manage to somehow conjure up a run without the benefit of a hit (Bloomquist reaching on an absurd, Little League error by Cora, is then bunted over by Betancourt, steals third, and comes home on an Ichiro grounder) to retake the lead, 5-4. Foulke holds this score in check in the eighth with maybe his best inning in a year and half, striking out Johjima looking on a brilliant, vintage '04 changeup on the outside corner; which allows Ortiz to come to the plate in the eighth, with the remarkable opportunity to re-tie the game for the third time today. He nearly does, reaching up to get a Jake Woods fastball and power it high and deep to right, the swing even fiercer than the home run in the sixth and the ball seemingly higher and Fenway already celebrating this remarkable third home run and *what a story three times can you believe—*

when Ichiro, with one arm against the bullpen padding, leans over and at the last instant snaps the ball down a foot in front of the wall. Groans. Silence. Disbelief. (*Wait a second…what just happened?*) Equally incredulous, Ortiz stands a few paces beyond first, hands planted on hips, staring out in right field just as we at Fenway and around Boston and New England stand hands out and heads slumped. Because, of course, that was *not* how it was supposed to go. You see, Ortiz was supposed to hit his third home run, to tie it for the third time, and then yes naturally he would come up again in the ninth or maybe tenth and hit a walk-off and that would be it—game over, Sox win, Happy Patriots' Day. But the ball was high in the strike zone and Ortiz had to come too far up to get it, making the loft of the ball a bit too steep, the Fenway bullpens a bit too far, and Ichiro altogether too capable of getting back in time to make what for him alone was a routine catch. And so hands on hips we stare out and shake our heads, saddened at how close we came to seeing a truly memorable game.

Instead we are left with two outs and two strikes on Trot, who works a tough eight-pitch at bat into a full count, then doubles down the line to bring up Tek. There is a slight rumble in the crowd. And with the disappointment over Ortiz's near miss still lingering in the air Tek singles sharply up the middle. Suddenly (*what's this?*) we are reminded that there are methods to run scoring other than an Ortiz homer (for awhile there it seemed the only option), as Nixon turns third and sprints home, and the game is once again re-tied, 5-5.

Onto the ninth, with Foulke still on for the Sox and Papelbon warming in the bullpen and fans already muttering to each other, *how about this game, this is some game huh*, when with one out Beltre singles. Nothing terribly worrying, not with Bloomquist up; only Beltre takes off with the pitch and Bloomquist singles—a hit and run, wonderfully timed—to put runners on the corners. Another former Red Sox, Roberto Petagine, pinch hits and does exactly what he was brought on to do, which is not strike out. He does this by grounding hard up the middle for what looks like a sure single until Loretta dives, smothers it, and throws from his knees to get Petagine by a half-step at first. Beltre, indifferent to the dazzling infield play, jogs home from third and the Mariners retake the lead for the fifth (a check to scorecard confirms it, *fifth*) time today. Foulke gets José López swinging to end the inning, but after all the ways we have envisioned the Sox winning this close, highly amusing game, we now find them three outs from the rather un-amusing option of losing, 6-5.

Peña, Mohr, and Youkilis are due up in the ninth. If anyone gets on it would be Loretta. If any two were to get on, it would be Ortiz. Clearly then the idea is for Peña and/or Mohr to simply not get out, somehow. No one is expecting them to hit a game-tying home run, or even a double in the gap. All we really need them to do here is keep from being called out—to draw a walk, or take a pitch in the ribs, maybe trip over the catcher and draw an interference call. Anything other than strike out flailing at an outside fastball, which is exactly what Peña does; or strike out looking at the exact same fastball on the outside corner that was called for strike two a pitch earlier, which is exactly what Mohr does. So then, with two outs and closer Eddie Guardado looking perfectly comfortable out there on the Fenway mound, it is up to Youkilis.

Who immediately falls behind 0-2. At which point there is throughout Fenway a collective, irrepressible glance to the clock as our thoughts intuitively turn to the race. For the Marathon is still going, the top runners nearing the finish line, so *if maybe...let's see, it would be about...but we'll just wait and see first.* Youkilis takes a ball. 1-2 now, and the crowd seems to sense that it is almost over, that this wonderfully engaging game might end right here on this pitch, and the afternoon would be over just like that. Not 3-2 Sox, but 6-5 Mariners; all such drama lost on a hit-and-run and fielder's choice. Until Guardado throws and Youkilis swings and shoots a hard grounder up the middle that López goes deep in the hole for, backhands, turns and throws all while Youkilis is running, sprinting, charging head back and elbows out and digging hard *come on come on come on* and *bang-bang*, he's through the bag and whips his hands out wide to the umpire, who steps forward and throws *his* arms wide—*safe*. Yes and we too throw *our* arms wide—*safe!* Youkilis throws a right hook in celebration, pumping his fist as Fenway roars up onto its feet and bellows out the affectionate: *Yooooouuuukkk.* He's on, beat it by a step and *just* a step.

Immediately we look straight past Loretta, who is now up, to Ortiz, who is now on deck. For *if only...* if only Loretta could find a way on base; if only he could give Ortiz a chance with Manny behind him then, *oh then* we would have an ending, then we would have a holiday. Loretta takes a ball, 1-0. What drama that would be; and how perfect the casting, with Youkilis and DiNardo and Nixon and Varitek all in supporting roles, and Ortiz, of course, the hero. Loretta takes another ball, 2-0. That would be Red Sox baseball as we know it, the back and forth scoring, the desperate comeback in the ninth, Big Papi at the plate with the game on the line, photographers focusing in on tomorrow morning's front page. But we need Ortiz to get up for that to happen, and we need these unfamiliar names— Peña and González and Mohr and Loretta—to not mess things up, to not get in the way of the Classic Fenway Moment so successfully cast and set, and so beloved by an audience who knows its script by heart, and therefore knows how very close we sit to its immensely satisfying final scene. So then *don't you let us down here* Loretta; don't deny us the vicarious thrill of watching those celebrations pile around home plate, or the vicarious pride we take in those joyous post-game marches down Lansdowne; and most of all don't prove yourself to be a miscast understudy by doing something foolish like swinging hard and trying to be a hero instead of all that you are scripted to do in this situation which is simply draw a walk and let Ortiz get to the plate so that he can—

Guardado throws, Loretta swings, and the ball sails high out to left and over the wall and every Sox fan at Fenway and in Boston and in New England and across the country all raise both hands over our heads and shout out in unison, and for the very first time, *Loretta!*

We know the rest, know it by heart now, as Fenway goes up all at once and jumping, bouncing, hands outstretched and shouting, the sound reverberating out into the city as Mark Loretta rounds second, rounds third, and heads down the homestretch. And on a day which has seen so much variety of human strides—be it our morning walk through city streets, Ichiro's glide along the base paths, the marathon runner's steady pacing, Ortiz's casual lumber, the fan's unsteady stagger, Youkilis sprinting inelegantly but with every last sinew pushing for the bag and getting it, saving all, and Mark Loretta, at a jog—it is only appropriate that it end here, at the finish line of home plate, headfirst into a pile of teammates who leap around and affectionately pound our newest hero within an inch of his senses; from which pile he emerges a moment later, dazed and wobbly and, like the rest of us, grinning uncontrollably.

Grinning in the aisles, grinning down the slow-moving ramp, grinning onto a packed Lansdowne Street where the general scene—a cheerful exiting crowd, the Cask overflowing with a line around the corner, cars stranded on Brookline in a flood of unexpected pedestrians—is exactly that of 10:30 pm on a Saturday night, only with the of glow street lamps replaced by weakly filtered afternoon sunlight. Grinning at our luck, at the win, at it all being some kind of holiday. Grinning, most of all, at the scene around us. For here a group of happy young fans stagger out of Fenway, struggling to put one foot somewhere in front of the other as they head out to *the bahs!* While a mere half mile away elite runners from around the world sprint (after twenty-six miles) down Boylston towards a finish line in Copley Square. While miles back many a self-described runner also concentrates on putting one foot in front of the other (and wonders, perhaps, why it was ever so damn important to run the Marathon anyway). While farther afield grown men, with steady jobs and mortgages and health insurance, and today dressed in full British regimentals, march in formation towards a seemingly unoccupied bridge near Concord and Lexington. While the runners run; while the joggers jog; while those who thought they could run a marathon without training walk (*just for a bit*). While the patriots of liberty, with their tri-cornered hats and muskets, and cell phones set to vibrate within rough breeches, quietly shift into position behind a low ridge. And while we stand alone on the corner of Brookline and Lansdowne, amid a crowd of celebratory Sox fans, and once again check our watch. It is 2:18 pm on Patriots' Day in Boston. Time for a nightcap.

The Good Parent

Tampa Bay at Fenway
18 April 2006

Fenway. Late in the night, late in the game. Two outs. Two strikes. Bases loaded. And Papelbon on the mound, with a lead. Thirty-six-thousand fans on their seventy-two-thousand feet; their seventy-two-thousand hands pounding out a steady rolling clap of anticipation. All looking in. *Let's go now Pap!* All leaning in. *Come'on one more!* Ushers who have stopped ushering stand arms-crossed and try to look disinterested as they rock anxiously back and forth on their heels; vendors who have long stopped vending come out from behind their stands to peek through the crowd and clap along in time; two security guards stand at an abandoned gate, arms folded and staring up as one of them mutters a low, *come on' Pap,* to the television above. Cameras on their mounted perches swivel and train in closer to the scene; announcers lean on their elbows, voices high and quick to the moment; while in the press box reporters grab their notebooks and voice recorders and lean halfway to the elevators, ready to run. Above all—high above the crowd and the press box and the ballpark and the billboards and even the glimmer of the backdropped Boston skyline—are the lights, seven broad banks towering into a clear night sky, each one angled to the field and together throwing the enormous expanse of outfield grass into shining paths of alternating greens, a rolling emerald sea against whose waves the bright white of a single uniform glows brilliant as it bobs, a step forward and a step back, adrift like a buoy in deep center field.

It is Adam Stern, the young Red Sox outfielder still in his first full season in the Major Leagues, who just now looks up, stands from his crouched stance, and takes one, full, conscientious step forward. Then immediately glances across the field to the dugout; where Terry Francona, one foot on the top step, pushes his open palm against an invisible wall—*back up*. Stern takes a step back; then another; until Francona holds his hand still and nods—*right there*. Stern pats his glove, leans forward with both hands on his knees, and looks in at the lively but somewhat crowded scene before him.

There he finds four Red Sox infielders, one catcher, one tall young pitcher, four umpires, two base coaches, one visiting Devil Ray in road grays at the plate, and three more stationed around the infield, now stretching their legs and side-stepping into their leads. Sixteen figures in all—altogether far too many bodies for one baseball diamond—the effect always a bit claustrophobic, disconcerting, ominous (*something is wrong here*). And yet under closer examination, and within the context of the game, it reveals itself as one of those curious baseball situations which on its surface appears infinitely worse than it actually is. With the Sox leading 7-4, and one out away from victory, the chances of things going terribly wrong (for the Sox) are still relatively minimal; and short of a devastating home run or the extremely rare Fenway triple, Papelbon will have only to retire one of the next two batters to seal the win. Meaning that all things considered the Sox are far closer to victory than defeat. Though it does not exactly feel that way at the moment. Not with all those runners. For to fans in these situations the comfort of statistical probability is never quite as soothing as it ought to be. To begin with there are all those baserunners, so much closer together than ninety-feet; and there is Papelbon, who though he has not yet blown a save in his young career does not quite look his young indomitable self; on top of which, it has been *that* kind of game. The kind of game which follows no discernable pattern or narrative; the kind of game which switches direction and tone and even genre mid-inning, without reason and with no respect at all for the rules of dramatic structure; the kind of game which just might have the temerity to turn out badly for the Sox.

For six full innings it was as dull, as lifeless, as uneventful as one would expect from a nothing Tuesday-nighter against a last place team, the score still 1-0 Sox in the seventh when a good many Fenway fans were startled out of an onset doze only to realize that the Rays had not only tied the score, but (somehow) taken a 2-1 lead. Gradually blinking back to life, we were then fully awakened by three torrid Sox runs in the bottom of the same inning; were then fully dismayed when the Rays again scored twice to re-tie it in the eighth; and finally cheered, shook our heads, and slumped towards exhaustion after the Sox added three more (the big hit a Youkilis double) in the bottom of the eighth to take a comfortable, rest easy, 7-4 lead into the final half inning. So it was with one big communal exhale that we watched Papelbon strike out Joey Gathright for the first out of the ninth. (We were hardly bothered by the Carl Crawford single that followed.) And after Jorge Cantú ended a long at bat by swatting helplessly at strike three we involuntarily glanced towards the exits—gathering up programs, shaking hands, telling each other *good game* and *good night* and *drive home safely*. So then, two outs and a 1-2 count on Travis Lee, and Fenway standing for what is surely the final pitch of the game. Once, twice, three times. All balls, and Lee draws his walk. Causing Fenway to retakes its seat, momentarily. Jonny Gomes, representing the tying run, steps to the plate and takes a strike, then watches four straight balls from Papelbon and jogs to first. Crawford and Lee each move up—the bases now loaded, the go-ahead run at the plate—and Adam Stern, out in center, takes his one full step forward.

There he crouches down as Papelbon sets, and, without a single one of the sixteen bodies crammed onto the infield or the thirty-five-thousand fans packed around it so much as noticing, takes one small imperceptible step in, closer—the move involuntary, following the instinctive pull towards home plate, to the ball, and to the action which from out here seems a long, long way away.

Two strikes now on Damon Hollins, Fenway on its feet once again, and after a quick foul ball it seems as if our excitable young closer's temporary wildness served no other purpose than to add a bit more danger (and therefore a little more theater) to his now inevitable escape—like a magician adding an extra lock to the safe from which he will emerge with flourish and (strike three) *tah-da!* Then, just as suddenly, there is a glitch (a key frantically rattling in the lock) and the Fenway audience lets out a sudden gasp. Papelbon's third pitch has been a hard fastball up in the zone, thus far a pitch hitters have been lucky to even foul off; but after thirty-three pitches there is not nearly as much behind it and Hollins slaps it on a low drive to straightaway center, weak and floating and now dipping at an alarming rate towards very shallow center. Papelbon hops off the mound to look back, the runners all take off, and Adam Stern breaks in on a full sprint as all of Fenway and every player on the field and every fan watching on television focuses on an invisible point in shallow center where the ball will land and where Stern races in to meet it, leaning forward hard with glove out the ball dips and slices as he leans lower and at the last instant, risking all, dives stretching his glove out and down on the grass he tumbles over, rolls once, and comes up. Fenway Park holds its breath one beat. Stern springs to his feet, shoots his glove-arm into the air—the bright white baseball cupped softly within the very edge of his glove—and now sprints in, eyes wide, expression beaming (*I got it, I got it, I got it*) as on our feet we cheer and confirm to ourselves and each other yes: *he got it! he got it!*

The Red Sox win, we all sing about that dirty water, Papelbon wipes his brow and gives Stern a powerful bear hug on the infield grass, everyone not in a Devil Rays uniform cheers and smiles, and on the happy walk out the head-shaking conversation is about nothing but *what an incredible catch that kid, man oh man that was some way to end a ballgame.*

It is only much later on—perhaps on the way home, or the walk up the front steps, or as we drop our keys onto the kitchen counter—that the thought slips through our mind: *hey, wait a second, what if…?* It seems entirely possible that the thrilling rush shared by those who saw the catch wore off, like any other drug, at the exact same time for all of us, and that every Red Sox fan in the country paused at the exact same time (*hey, wait*), and muttered these exact same words in unison (*what if?*), like a chorus. For the next morning as we unfold our papers, click on our radios, and greet our co-workers and classmates and friends, our talk is less about the brilliance of Stern's catch, than whether or not he should have tried to make it at all.

Opinions vary from fan to fan, but the prevailing sentiment (based firmly on orthodox baseball strategy, and more importantly per his manager's direct orders) is that the catch never should have happened. This because Stern should have let it drop harmlessly in front of him, thrown it in, and let Papelbon worry about getting the next batter. The wisdom behind which decision is fairly obvious; even more so when we take into account that it ought not to have been a decision at all. For before the pitch Francona had mimed pushing and pulling his fielders into the defensive positioning commonly known as the No Doubles defense, which basically means everyone takes two big steps back in order to keep the ball, wherever it lands, in front of them. The idea is to play the odds and force the opposition to score by stringing together two or three singles, rather than turning the game on one big hit, such as a double. Hence the name: No Doubles. Of course, implied within this positioning, and sometimes forgotten by young and overly-eager outfielders, is that No Doubles also means No Triples, as well as No Inside the Park Home Runs Allowing Everyone to Score and Tie the Game Up on One Swing and Generally Ruining Everything for Everyone. So if nothing else Stern should have held up and kept the ball in front of him simply because he was told to do so by his manager, who after all is employed to make such decisions.

An even more compelling reason, and the one pointed out with a disappointed sigh and shake of the head by most Sox fans the day after, is the unspeakable consideration of: *what if...?*

Now it is, on the whole, pointless and unproductive and really rather bush league for fans to retroactively play the *What If?* game in baseball; which by no means keeps us from occasionally indulging in it anyway. Stern's gamble, high risk and high reward, is a *what if* situation far too tempting to resist, particularly as it is almost impossible to purely enjoy the play's substantial rewards without considering the entirety of what was risked to attain them.

So then, *what if…?*

If: the ball angles down a half-degree lower, or Stern is positioned a step back or a half-step in either direction, or hesitates just a fraction of a second longer, or takes just one step out of line on his path to the ball (*here* instead of *there*), or the wind is a mile-per-hour more from center, or a mile-per-hour less from home, or the grass is wet and Stern fails to get firm traction, or the ball has a millimeter deformation on one side and therefore slices two inches more to the left, or any other of the incalculable number of variables which would keep Stern and the ball from meeting at the exact same point at the exact same time occur, then the ball—instead of being cupped in its edge—glances off his glove, scoots under it, and goes skidding out into the wide open expanse of outfield grass recently vacated behind him. (While Stern himself rolls helplessly onto his backside.) Manny and Nixon converge as the ball rolls out to center and all three Devil Rays runners, off on contact and now jogging, come around to score to tie the game. Meanwhile Hollins, thin and quick on the bases, sprints around second and sees his third base coach wildly waving his arm home. (Stern, at this point, pulls himself to one knee and contemplates another line of work.) Nixon reaches the ball first and heaves it in to Loretta, who turns just in time to see Hollins halfway down the line; he throws plateward but Hollins slides in ahead of the tag and gives the Rays the lead on an absurdly improbable and perhaps even historical inside-the-park grand slam with two outs in the ninth. Devastated, Papelbon loses what is left of his control, walks two more, gives up a double and finally gets out of the inning with his first blown save, his first loss, and a tired arm. The Sox lose, but not before Nixon fouls a ball off his leg in the inevitably doomed rally attempt. The x-rays come back showing a fracture and Nixon goes on the 30-day DL. Meanwhile Papelbon, unaccustomed to the physical demands of coming back from a long outing (not to mention the mental demands of having blown a three-run lead in the ninth) looks shaky and vulnerable in his next save opportunity, which he also blows. Though he shows signs of recovery here and there he continues to struggle, and for weeks fights a losing battle to regain his old swaggering confidence before finally losing the closer job to Foulke and making a hopeful but ultimately rocky transition to the back of the Sox's rotation. Now acutely in need of a right fielder as well as middle relief, Theo Epstein makes a deal to *meet the immediate needs of the Major League club* and acquires Corey Koskie and Derrick Turnbow from Milwaukee for Papelbon, J.T. Snow, and two minor league pitchers. Koskie hits a home run in his first at bat but struggles the rest of the way; Turnbow gives up a grand slam in his first outing, is booed unmercifully, and develops elbow tendonitis in July, ending his season. The Sox mount a makeshift play-off run, but with their overworked bullpen and season-long questions in center and right the possibility of October baseball is never a serious one. They fade in September and miss the playoffs by three games. In the aftermath Beckett is criticized by the press for not coming up big in his late season starts; he pops-off in the papers, is then criticized for popping off, and by November is demanding a trade. Soon after, Manny says something about not caring if they trade him or not. Clement has off-season surgery on his elbow, Foulke has two more knee surgeries, and Schilling retires. Meanwhile the Yankees (having won the pennant by default, and Game Seven of the World Series on back-to-back-to-back home runs by Damon, Jeter, and A-Rod) trade to bring Andy Pettitte back to Yankee Stadium. He pitches three more years in pinstripes, wins a pair of Cy Young Awards, and acts as mentor to the staff's newest ace and the latest Yankee postseason legend—a young pitcher named Jonathan, whom they acquired from the Brewers, and who was once in the Sox system but was traded midseason 2006 for middle relief because he suffered a debilitating loss in confidence, because one night at Fenway he allowed four runs in the ninth and lost, and all because Adam Stern gambled and dove and tried to make a spectacular catch, but missed.

(A stretch, perhaps, but in the first hot flush of *what if?* this grim scenario appears not only likely, but practically inevitable.)

Which is to say that by every professional measure Stern's bravado in attempting the catch was, at the very least, imprudent. It was certainly brash; it may even have been reckless; and well (we hate to say it but) was a pretty clear example of the difference between the Major Leagues and Triple-A, which is often the difference between simply having the ability to play the game, and knowing how to use that ability as a professional. It did not have the best intentions of the team at heart. Therefore it was not good for the Red Sox.

And yet it was, at the same time, absolutely magnificent. Even beyond the tremendous amount of ground Stern had to cover to reach the ball, the catch was made even more remarkable by the fact that the ball took a late, tailing slice *away* from Stern, who caught it to his glove side and away from his body; plus the momentum he generated coming forward sent him tumbling over his glove and yet he was able, somehow, to hold on by the bare circumference of the ball. All this and yet what made the play so utterly thrilling, what made it a classic base-ball story rather than simply a highlight, and what will ultimately make it so indelible in the minds of fans for years to come (*you remember that catch, the one Stern made with the bases loaded…*), are the circumstances under which it was made. The sheer risk it involved, putting everything on the line including the lead and the game, is exactly what created the drama of the dive and the exhilarating thrill of the catch. And so it was the very aspect which made it inadvisable for the team, which also made it so enjoyable for us, the fans.

All of which serves as a choice reminder of something we all too often forget: which is that what is good for the team is not always what is good for those who follow it, and vice versa. For instance, it would be difficult to argue that Manny's bi-polar antics in the field are in any way beneficial to the Red Sox as a club; but there is almost no denying that they are part of the color not only of his intriguing character, but of this particularly intriguing team, and that without him the Red Sox would be (though one does not say such things among polite company) incalculably less interesting to follow. Ditto for his old teammate, Pedro, whose Mad Genius act began to grow old among fans in the years before his departure, but which nevertheless (though again, it must be said in a whisper) has been at times undoubtedly missed. The same goes for in-game decisions, where any fan would rather see Ortiz have the green light than not, no matter if the bases are loaded in a tie game and the pitcher has thrown nineteen consecutive balls a foot out of the strike zone. And even if Papelbon has two strikes on a hitter who is clearly sitting fastball, and good sound baseball logic tells us Varitek will want him to throw a breaking pitch in the dirt, it matters not to us. We want to see him crank it up and throw one right down the middle as hard as he can as we yell out *Come on Jon! Go get'em!*

None of which is at all relevant to the GM or owner or manager in whose professional interest it is to put together and manage a team that wins. All of which is vitally important to us fans, who, unlike owners and GMs and managers, watch our team play not with a professional interest but because we enjoy doing so. Or at least hope to. And while it hardly matters to anyone in charge whether our right fielder is exciting or compelling or at least mildly interesting to watch, it matters quite a lot to us fans who watch him play day in and day out. For it is still, to those of us who voluntarily look in to follow it, a spectator sport. And as hard as it is for the *go-team win-win-win let's-go-compare-OPS*'s fan to accept, spectacle matters. Distinction matters. Style, matters. Far more than we ever care to admit.

(Perhaps one is not entirely persuaded. In which case one would do well to be reminded that the Major League Baseball season is in fact still *one-hundred-and-sixty-two games long*, and as those of us who commit ourselves to watching the vast majority of these—rather than, say, a handful of Yankees games and the playoffs—well know, among those one-hundred-and-sixty-two games there tend to be one or two slow bits. Sometimes more. Which is why *no*, we do not mind saying that all things being equal we'd just as soon see the game played with daring and bravado and style, than not. Otherwise we'd save ourselves a great deal of time and trouble, and simply follow the box scores.)

And so when a young, athletic, overly-eager center fielder reacts to a ball off the bat and comes sprinting in, and his instincts tell him he can get there even though his manager and GM and the accumulated Baseball Wisdom of the Ages tell him to pull up and hold it to a single, we, in the bleachers and standing in our living rooms and staring up at a tiny set in a dark shop after closing, lean forward and hope like hell to see him stretched out diving across the grass and putting it all on the line in one thrilling instant.

Then again, we do not have to jog back into the dugout and face the manager, either. Stern did, and even after a terrific encore catch the following night (this time risking his body rather than the game, he makes a sprinting catch, crashes hard into the metal wall in left, and once again holds on) he is nevertheless sent down to Pawtucket midweek and veteran utility man Willie Harris recalled to replace him. It was a scheduled move, determined by details within both players' contracts, and all parties agreed that Stern's gamble and catch had nothing to do with the decision.

Still, there is little doubt that despite Francona's soft admonishments to the press, manager and player at some point sat behind closed doors and discussed the precise meaning of the phrase *No Doubles*. It is during a meeting such as this that Francona, so much the upbeat uncle at all other times, must play the role of disciplinarian father. We picture him sitting across from Stern with his hands folded, explaining to him in no uncertain terms that 1) his decision put the game unnecessarily on the line, 2) it might only take a few (and possibly only one) similar decisions to convince a certain GM that a certain outfielder still needs to learn a few things about how to play this game, 3) should that happen a certain outfielder will learn said things in Pawtucket rather than Fenway Park; and finally, just before Stern steps out of the office, Francona will remind him, 4) not to let the applause he received blind him to the fact that attempting it was still reckless and unprofessional and not to be repeated. Stern, head down and nodding (*sure thing Skip*), walks out, and jogs into center field where we, the fans, rise up and give him a long, loud, thoroughly approving ovation. Because we can.

Because in the end we are the good parent. The one who spoils them; the one who laughs when they act up; the one who might even encourage a few of their reckless impulses, if only because we give such effusive and overwhelmingly positive reinforcement when they so indulge us. Sure it may not have been the best idea to swing at that neck-high fastball on 3-1, but *man oh man* did it go a long way when he did. And yeah, maybe throwing a belt-high fastball to Giambi with a base open was a bit headstrong; but how satisfying was it to see the umpire turn and punch him out. (Of course like all Good Parent figures we reserve the right, when such hopes go horribly awry and Giambi doubles in the gap, to immediately boo and say *you should've listened to your mother* and pitched around him.) Perhaps it was slightly audacious to try and steal third with two outs in a tie game and Manny at the plate, but it hardly feels that way when the third base umpire sweeps the safe sign through a cloud of dust, and a moment later a single gives the Sox the lead. A lead we cheer with far greater enthusiasm than usual because of the dashing manner in which it was so singularly *taken*. And though we may, in the quiet calm of a morning conversation, over our coffee and newspaper, speak lovingly of patience at the plate and prudence on the base paths, in the roaring loud floodlight arena we sporting fans (perhaps Sox fans more than most) loathe even the slightest hint of timidity. A stance we reinforce each and every night with our boos—*boos* for the runner who held up at third, *boos* for the fielder who short-armed the ball at the track, *boos* (and usually bit more) for the batter who took strike three looking. For our cool, detached daylight talk is merely that—all talk. Talk in which we *appreciate* the smart play, and *admire* calculated play, and have nothing but the greatest *respect* for the coolly professional play; yet with our cheers we confirm the inescapable truth, louder than ever in the ears of the player, that we absolutely *love* the fearless play, the gallant play, the play in which the risks taken and rewards sought are placed at such a height that the desperate lunge towards them takes on something very close to baseball heroism. For this play more than any other, we do not merely applaud, but cheer. Let the executives worry about statistics and probability charts and *the best interest of the club* all they like; for us, if we are really honest with ourselves, the *how* of the thing matters nearly as much as the *what*.

And so yes, we want the Sox to win. Of course. And officially we always want what's best for the team. Then again, we rather have to say this, don't we? Good parent or not we must at least sound the part. And so we pull Stern aside and say in our best, most parental tone, that *in those situations it might be best to opt for caution and let the ball drop, to be smart, to be rational and to play it safe.* But we can only hold this expression for so long, and finally we smile and—like a parent who says no but slips extra candy in their kid's pockets anyway—cannot help but add with the sound of our most heartfelt ovations, *nevertheless kid, that was one hell of a catch.*

Manny, Drew, Lowell, Tek

Yankees at Fenway
22 April 2007

You simply never know what you may find when you come out to the ballpark. Could be that the ticket in your hand—hard won by means of a February raffle which itself won you the chance to wait online in March, all to buy this one April seat—only guarantees you admission to see your beloved team make a host of grievously unprofessional errors, run themselves out of several promising rallies, and ultimately lose a lifeless 6-1 game about which you will remember only that you were there, that you paid too much for peanuts, and that the Sox lost. (*Oh well, at least we had good seats*.) Then again, you may hold a ticket to some spectacular pitching performance, or a prodigious game-changing home run, or a fantastic catch you will forever describe in minute detail to anyone who will listen (always allowing for the very real possibility that you will be in line at the concession stand when the *how about that catch!* moment occurs). Better still, there is always the chance that you are in fact holding a ticket to one of those famous late-inning Fenway rallies, perhaps even capped off by a Big Papi walk-off that will send you leaping up and shouting, and spilling out onto a Lansdowne Street spontaneously transformed into a celebratory baseball carnival. Of course, it being a ticket to Fenway Park—and Fenway being an open-air venue in the sub-climate of New England— there is always the prospect that your have paid very good money for a ticket to stand in the back concourse and watch your very good seat collect puddles throughout a two hour rain delay, perhaps enlivened by some industrious grounds crew work (imagine the thrill of a rain-soaked tarp being rotated 90-degrees clockwise), immediately after which the game will be cancelled outright and rescheduled for a Tuesday upcoming, necessarily at 1 pm EST while you and everyone else in the city are necessarily at work, and while a friend-of-a-friend, who *honestly is not much of a baseball fan* but has the day off, will sit in the afternoon sun drinking a beer at Fenway, in your seat. More than likely though what you have is a ticket to something in between; a good game with a home run or two, maybe a strikeout to end an inning and hold the lead, some nifty infield play, a double in the gap that plates two, and a tip of the cap from the departing starter. (*Hey that was a pretty good game wasn't it?*) But there is always the possibility, however statistically remote, that the ticket you now hold as you wait in line on Yawkey is worth a great deal more than all that (examine it closely now) and is in fact your ticket to witness something utterly unique— not only in your experience, but the experience of the old ballpark itself. There is always a chance, that is, that you hold in your hand a ticket to *that* game.

The trouble being that in baseball you simply never know. Inclement weather, inopportune injuries, odd bounces, deplorable managing, lamentable middle relief, and shall we say *regrettable* umpiring, all conspire to keep live outdoor baseball from ever being something which should be counted upon to provide anything more than peanuts, beer, and the national anthem. Everything else being dependent on the weather, and (more so) pitching. And the sooner one learns this—the sooner one learns that it is best to *hope for*, rather than *expect*, tolerable weather and a decent game—the better. For you never will know, when you hand that ticket over and pass with a beep and a click through the gates onto Yawkey, what you're likely to find on the other side. And yet still, regardless, nevertheless, at any rate, and despite all that, what we do know and the truth so many of us carry along as we walk with enlivened steps through the Fenway concourse is: *there's always a chance…*

* * *

True, there is no real way of telling for certain how good one's chances are; but there are a few clues which may allow one to at very least venture a guess. For instance, if that ticket in your hand says *New York Yankees* on it, and the game time is 8:00 pm on a Sunday night (meaning nationally broadcast Sunday Night Baseball), and the newspaper tucked under your arm has the Next Big Thing in baseball featured in the pitching matchup, all of which is the case as we walk up to the ballpark tonight, then your odds are perhaps better than most. Though certainly not guaranteed. (Sox fans who held Saturday night Sox-Yankees tickets last August were just as giddy and hopeful throughout the proceeding week as those entering tonight, and had no way of knowing that they were being led only to one of the ugliest, most dour Sox losses in several seasons, and that they would shuffle out hours later feeling tired, bleak, and more than a little bit betrayed.) Still, by the looks of tonight's crowd the hope of *maybe*, and more specifically the hype of *Daisuke*, seem to have won out. Encouraged by the two previous night's games (which the Sox won 7-6 in thrilling, come from behind fashion, and 7-5 in a sloppy, back and forth matinee eventually won by David Ortiz and the Red Sox bullpen), and refreshed by the citywide exhale we all enjoyed over the first sunny and comfortably summerish afternoon of the year, the arriving crowd at Fenway pass through its gates in extraordinarily fine spirits; and by sunset we are a loud, happy, t-shirted baseball crowd, busy drinking our baseball drinks and eating our baseball eats, and finding our places at the ballpark before the Sox take the field and the flashbulbs begin to *pop pop* all about the grandstand.

Those flashes continue to *pop* throughout the first at bat (as with the Daisuke v. Ichiro at bat a week ago, tonight's first batter makes for an impossibly convenient photo-op; what with Daisuke v. Damon, Sox past v. Sox future, 18 v. 18 and so on), and though there are perhaps thirty percent less flashes per section in this First Pitch to the Yankees, as compared to the First Pitch Ever at Fenway, the effect suffers only by degree, and is nonetheless still an impressive sight to behold.

Made more impressive by Damon's promptly popping out to short to begin the game, followed by Jeter, who promptly flies out to right.

Two outs then, and after a walk to Bobby Abreu there comes a steady cresting of boos as *that man*, Alex Rodriguez, steps to the plate. And here we go again, Daisuke v. A-Rod, in yet another meeting of conflicting Red Sox mythologies, full of rivalry-defining implication, packed with the rich overtones of personality and origin and fate, utterly fraught with the entire overarching meta-narrative weight of—

Daisuke's first pitch drills A-Rod in the shoulder.

Fenway Park blinks.

And a beat later the stands echo out with sarcastic cheers for Daisuke and harsh, taunting shouts at A-Rod, who unstraps his elbow guard and jogs to first. As all around us in the crowded Standing Room Only sections behind third base the searching, cautiously rhetorical question of *you don't think that was on purpose, do you?* is passed about like a secret note. *Nah, of course not.* Not with a runner already on. Not with Giambi on deck. And surely not in his very first inning against the Yankees, in front of a Fenway Park crowd who wants nothing more than to see him thoroughly dominate this very New York lineup, which means not giving up runs in the first inning and not giving up, in any inning, unnecessary baserunners. So no, of course not. (*And yet...with such fine control...and of all the people to...yeah, but... nah...well, perhaps perhaps.*) In any event the pitch, errant or otherwise, comes back to haunt Daisuke as it is immediately followed by a Giambi double into the gap, scoring both A-Rod and Abreu. As does another presumably errant pitch in the third, which somehow finds Derek Jeter's elbow (*honestly, he hits* those *two*) and moves Damon into scoring position where he too is brought around to score by Giambi, this time on a flare over second which just barely ticks off the end of Dustin Pedroia's outstretched glove.

The play, which like all infield flares is agonizingly slow to unfold, is instantly bemoaned by a pair of fans standing next to us, two heavily tattooed guys from Maine who have apparently spent the entire drive down debating the relative baseball merits of our new and still unsettled rookie second baseman. Deriding and defending seems more accurate, as one of the two is clearly a staunch and quite vocal Anti-Pedroian while his buddy (who for what it's worth is quite a few inches shorter) is something of a Pedroia apologist. And therefore has already had his position bolstered in the bottom of the second when Pedroia— who has tonight attempted to break out of a dreadful April slump by the time-honored means of raising one's red stockings to one's knees— rapped a screaming double in the gap, cruised easily into second, and immediately reached down to give a little tug to each of his new lucky stockings. A fluke to the Anti-Pedroian, who instead seizes on this near miss afield as another plank in the platform of *his* second base candidate, Alex Cora, whose approval rating at Fenway has steadily risen at an inverse ratio to Pedroia's steadily falling batting average. Inevitably we are drawn in from our scorecard-keeping to swing the vote (Undecided as we are), but offer nothing more than that it was a very difficult ball (it was), and that Loretta would have had it standing up; which of course pleases no one.

Even less pleasing is the score, which after two-and-a-half stands at 3-0, Yankees; a surprise beginning given that tonight Daisuke is, thanks to the injury-depleted Yankee rotation, matched up against twenty-four-year-old Yankee rookie Chase Wright, making just his second career Major League start. Nerves would seem to be a factor then, and seemingly are as Wright walks the first two batters he faces, Lugo and Youkilis, to bring up Ortiz with two on and nobody out in the first; a situation which would seem to have Yankee fans peeking through their fingers at the accident to come. Only somehow Wright gets Ortiz to fly out, forces Manny to pop out, strikes out J.D. Drew swinging and walks off the mound with a little shrug. (As we make a small notation—*character?*—just below the K in our scorecard.) Wright pulls off a similar feat in the second, quickly retiring Lowell and Varitek before walking Wily Mo Peña (a rookie mistake), and giving up the aforementioned double to Pedroia. This time, with two in scoring position, he gets Lugo to ground out to short and again casually walks off the mound without a scratch. As if there was nothing to it.

Meanwhile it is right around this time, as Wright takes the last of his warm-up tosses in the bottom of the third, that we learn something remarkable about one of the two fellows from Maine standing next to us. It is the Pedroia apologist who, though in his early thirties and an avid Sox fan (and living only two hours away), informs us that tonight is in fact his very first game at Fenway Park. He says this almost apologetically (*I know, I know*) but our amazement is not so much at the tardiness of his visit, as its timing. *You mean to tell us that your very first game at Fenway is a Sunday night Yankee game that just happens to be Daisuke's first ever start against New York?* Correct. At which point there is an outside chance we become, by a certain measure, somewhat *overly enthusiastic* in our praise of such wonderful baseball providence; until like a veteran Sox fan he points to the storm clouds gathering in the distance, noting that while glad to be here, at the moment he is a little worried. You see the Sox are losing, and if they fail to come back, this being his first game and all *well*, he hardly wants to think he came all the way from Maine just to jinx the Sox. We nod. Of course. Naturally. A lot rides on the psyche of a fan at their first game, and superstitious or not no one likes to feel unlucky. We would all, like the Mainer at our elbow, prefer to feel even secretly as if our presence alone was enough to bring a touch of charm, and perhaps a bit of old-fashioned good luck, to those Red Sox bats. Even if only for a moment.

That moment arrives—rather emphatically—when Manny Ramirez steps to the plate in the third. And although we know Manny and the bottom half of the order are capable of doing their share, a quick glance at our scorecard reveals a somewhat troubling pattern. For down a narrow column just right of the lineup we have jotted the following descending sequence: 0, 1, 6, 1, 1, 1, 1, 1, 0; indicating the season home run totals for tonight's Sox lineup. This nearly team-wide power deficit is not exactly an emergency; but three weeks into the season is enough time to take note of it, and when Manny comes up we are not alone in calling out *What'da say Manny!* in hopes of his bending one of those numbers around. Wright falls behind 2-1 (*Come on Manny*), and on his next pitch Manny swing full and clean and stretches both arms straight into the follow-through as the bat falls behind him, and you don't even have to look. Gone. A home run; the crowd on its feet and cheering as Manny circles the bases, presses his helmet to his head as he rounds third, and puts the Sox on the board at 3-1. *So there you go*, we tell our Mainer, *you've seen a Manny home run at your first game at Fenway; and that's pretty lucky*, no matter what happens next. What happens next is that we look up from our scorecard (after the HR notation) to see J.D. Drew hit the next Chase Wright pitch on a long high drive out to the right-center gap, still going as Damon and Abreu look up, stop, and with the rest of us watch it land in the bleachers as all at once we shoot both hands straight up and give a happy, *hey-hey!* And nearby there is an exclaimed, *back-to-back!* and high fives and cheering as we note another HR in our scorebook and try to remember the last time we saw back-to-back; *Manny and Ortiz somewhere back there*, and will there be a curtain call or is that it for Wright when almost as an afterthought we realize that Lowell is in the box and look in to get out one quick *Come'on Mikey keep it going now!* among the steady cheers before Wright fires and Lowell reaches down and launches it, and on the crack of the bat our arms are straight up and we are shouting and making exaggerated wide-eyed faces of surprise at each other, *unbelievable*, as the cheers roar louder around us and hands obscure the field where somewhere below Lowell circles the bases, and we turn to each other and *can you believe that...have you ever?...no, never; I mean holy—yeah, back-to-back-to-back, wow!* There are intense, searching discussions swirling around us (amid the tumult of cheers which have never for a moment let off) about whether the Sox have ever done this, or when, though certainly no one can remember seeing it; hands are pressed to ears as cell phones are shouted into (*no, back-to-back-to-back, yeah*); text messages are received (*home run derby!*) from distant friends watching the nationally televised game; we abandon our scorecard to a period of greater coherence; and there is one quick *hey, wait, the game is tied* moment of lucidity before we suddenly remember the Mainer at our side and nearly miss the next pitch impressing on him, in somewhat florid terms, the utter magnitude of his baseball luck; *you realize you could come to every game for a decade and never see that again*; he knows, wow, amazing; *yes but what are the odds, on your first game, you might come to a hundred, five hundred more games without seeing something like that*—when someone nearby shouts *Let's go Tek!* Tek, right. We turn and lean among the still-standing, still-cheering fans and look in just as he swings, the ball leaps off the bat, and instead of shouting *yes* we are all of us suddenly shaking our heads and almost laughing as we shout *no way, no way, no way, there's just no way—yes!* as our night at the ballpark takes one big sweeping turn into the surreal.

After the cheers—after the low, happy groan of mock disappointment when Wily Mo Peña strikes out to end the inning, and after the long, exhausted standing ovation during which we half expect to see our first four-man curtain call—the conversation turns fully to a prolonged debate over historical precedence. First time ever by the Sox, definitely. Some say it has never happened before in baseball, ever, but *what about the Dodgers last year, was that three or four?* And at Fenway? Have you ever seen—? *Oh no not even close. Never.* And all the while we first complete, then admire, our scorecard—four scribbled diamonds, uncluttered by other runs, each with the little HR and one single RBI dot, all in a row. We hold it up, show the older man and one-time scorer (*back when I was a kid*) who has been peeking in over our shoulder all night, and we exchange a silent, appreciative nod. Some fans seem happy enough just to repeat the curious sound it has when spoken aloud, always with that last surprised pause, *back-to-back-to-back, to back.* Elsewhere, the game seems to have gone on without us (almost as an aside we realize the Sox have come back, tied it, and taken the lead; all *during*) but we are far too caught up in our revelry to notice.

Each fan who saw or heard it, no matter by what means or medium, will remember it in their own way; but for us, the experience of four home runs in such quick succession was something very much like baseball intoxication. Manny's home run served as the first drink, the clean easy one we took with relaxed gratitude (*hey, that's good stuff*); and Drew's the quick second round, the happy one, the one that tastes even better on top of the first and makes it really very easy (*this is gonna be a good night*) to say *sure why not* to a third. Lowell's of course was that magical third drink, the transformational one, the one that disappears without thought and has you slapping complete strangers on the back (*what a great night, honestly man*) and making loud semi-coherent phone calls to unsuspecting friends across the country. And then, in the middle of this celebration, in the middle of this party, when you've already had enough and the night is rolling along nicely under its own steam, here comes a fourth—the one you weren't even looking for, the one you don't even remember ordering, the one you really, really do not need—and when Tek hits it anyway it's lights out (*this is the best night ever!*), goodnight coherence, someone remind us to watch the highlights in the morning. For baseball fans, even for ones with a high tolerance for the improbable, this one was a bender.

The basking in which continues more or less unchecked throughout the entire fourth inning, until the buzzkill of a Jeter home run leads off the fifth and reties the score (4-4), and a first and third double play in the sixth brings in from third the go-ahead Yankee run (5-4) to provide the stiff, sobering cup of coffee which brings us fully back to the game. Only temporarily though. After a disorienting top of the seventh in which a tall left-handed pitcher emerged from the Yankee bullpen caused us to mutter *hey, this guy throws a lot like Pettitte*, and then turned out to actually be Andy Pettitte (who pitched 6 ⅓ innings only two nights before and whose appearance in relief seems to neatly summarize the desperation surrounding the current Yankee bullpen) gives way first to the stretch and *Take Me Out to the Ballgame*, and then to the bottom of the seventh and the tirelessly overworked Scott Proctor, who immediately gives up a single to Manny and a double to Drew. And no one is very much surprised (how could we be) when Mike Lowell hits his second home run of the night into the Monster Seats to retake the lead for the Sox, 7-5, and start the party up all over again.

There seems little doubt about the outcome now—it is our lucky night, after all—and so there is none of the usual fretting or head-shaking or unnecessarily dour little remarks (so much a part of the late-inning Fenway experience) when the Yankees put the leadoff runner on in the eighth, bringing the tying run to the plate and setting in motion a fantastic five-batter sequence in which Terry Francona and Joe Torre frantically attempt to checkmate the game from one another with a bewildering array of relief pitchers, pinch hitters and a pinch runner; all of which adds up to one Yankee run (7-6 now), two outs, runners at first and third, Donnelly on for the Sox, and pinch hitter Josh Phelps up for the Yankee. With Papelbon warming up in the bullpen beyond, this is it for the Yankees. And typically hand-wring-ing territory for Sox fans who as we look around are not only up for the moment, but almost spry with self-assurance—a crowd waiting for something good to happen. As luck would have it that something is a hard line drive right back up the middle, destined for the outfield and a tie game before Pedroia lunges to his right and snares it inches above the grass as he falls outstretched to the ground, pops up, holds his glove to the umpire who calls the out and sends Pedroia and the Sox sprinting off the field under a hail of wild applause—the lead safely intact and the game surely won right then and there.

Immediately we turn to the two fellows from Maine; but they are nowhere to be found, evidently gone early up the long road back to Maine (it is nearly eleven on a Sunday night). No doubt they are lis-tening though, and that the play has swung the Pedroia campaign a few votes in Maine, if not across New England.

The play itself had all the feel of finality, and for good reason. Papelbon comes on in the ninth and gets the first two outs, then walks Abreu (apparently only to intensify the dramatic effect, for there can be no other logical reason) to bring up A-Rod as the potential tying run with two outs in the bottom of the ninth. It had to end this way, of course; and does, as A-Rod hits a hard grounder to third where Low-ell (who won the game) fields and throws to Pedroia (who saved it), and the Sox win and sweep the Yankees in straight sets, 7-6, 7-5, 7-6.

On the way out—under a pleasant, tolerably mild spring night and among a pleasant, tolerably inebriated Fenway crowd—there is time to take full account of our considerable baseball blessings. Not only that of winning all three games (we are more impressed by the fashion in which the games were won than encouraged to believe that the Sox are so clearly superior to the Yankees; for all three games were close and lose-able, and besides that it's April and we know better), but also the fact that we were lucky enough to have added this particular game, no matter where we watched it from, to our store of baseball memories. (Over the course of the following week we will learn that *back-to-back-*

to-back, to back has happened only four times in the history of the game; and although a great many statistics are thrown around to underline its rarity, the only one necessary is this: 36,000. The feat happens roughly once every 36,000 games. This is a difficult concept to get one's mind around—like a 56-game hit streak or coming back from down 3-0 in a seven game series—and tends to leave us open-mouthed and shaking our heads. Further details only add to the disbelief. Such as: J.D. Drew hit the second home run both tonight and the last time it happened, only a season ago; Terry Francona's father hit one of the four the second time it happened; and the next time it happened the batter who ended it, the fifth man up, was Joe Torre. And there is no formula to calculate the odds of that.) For now all we know is what we have heard from others, that four home runs in a row has never been done in a Red Sox game. And this is enough for us. Enough to know that if you were, let's say, 112-years-old, and, beginning when you were six, had somehow been able to witness every single inning of every single Red Sox game, home and away, over the one-hundred-and-six year history of the club, you would have seen the four home run sequence now jotted on our scorebook exactly once. Tonight. The 22nd of April, 2007. The very date on the ticket in your hand.

Next time you'll get a rainout. Surely. You will click through the gates with the same buoyant expectancy only to see a drab, error-filled sleeper (such as the lifeless 7-3 beating the Sox take from the Blue Jays the very next night). It will be too hot, or too cold, or the person in front of you will talk on their cell phone and distract you throughout the entire game. Your favorite player (who has played something like a thousand games in a row without injury) will inevitably be out of the lineup with a strained calf muscle. And no matter how carefully you time it you will surely end up in line or in the restroom or on Yawkey when the only decent play of the ballgame occurs, the cheers echoing behind you as you search out a television for the replay. But not tonight. No, tonight you were lucky. Turns out we had the golden ticket all along, and by the end of the evening as we walk home among the loud and happy crowd, over the Mass Pike and past the Daisuke t-shirts in Kenmore, and call up our friends to tell them about it we will still have that golden ticket in our back pocket, the one which allows us to say forevermore, as we do now: *yeah*, we were there; we were at *that* game.

Force of Nature

Yankees at Fenway
1 May 2006

Exposed in the cold night air, head down, eyes winced, shoulders hunched over our scorecards, we brace ourselves against another icy gust of wind as it bursts through the ballpark, shoots down our collars and rushes clean through our jeans and sweater and thin, horribly overmatched spring coat. One bare hand, red with cold, holds down a flapping corner of our scorecard as the other jots in the new Yankee pitcher: 36 M. MYERS. Down below we watch him jog onto the mound, and the Fenway Park crowd, bundled beneath the lights in jackets and with hats pulled low, lifts its collectively frozen hands, cups them on either side of their collectively frozen mouths, and lets out a collective round of boos. More of a low, lethargic moan, the sound quickly dies out beneath another gust of wind as Myers takes his warm-up tosses and we quickly fill in the short, incomplete line for the departing Yankee reliever Tanyon Sturtze—0 IP, 1 H—who is responsible for the runner on first, Mark Loretta. The runner on second, Kevin Youkilis, is still the responsibility of departed Yankee starter, Aaron Small. It is the bottom of the eighth and game is tied, 3-3.

On the mound Myers blows into his closed left fist and steps on the rubber, facing in. And we rise to our feet (that is *we* the Fenway fans in general rise to our feet, for *we* in SRO are of course already on our feet and have been for several hours) as through the whipping wind the announcement echoes out, *Now batting for the Red Sox...the designated hitter...David...Ortiz.* Fenway Park lets out a full cheer, calling out *Come on Papi!* as down below Ortiz grips the bat and steps in, hunches over, wags his black bat low, and looks out to Myers on the mound. Myers sets, checks the runners, then jerks up and out and suddenly down, his left arm swinging low to the ground before the ball spins out and up, rising, and Ortiz takes ball one, high. We clap (three quick snaps), blow into clenched hands, and flinch our head away from another gust of cold, bitter wind as it rips through the grandstands and over the high, horribly exposed roof boxes. While out in center, high above the wall, the flag snaps against the wind pushing it in towards home. In protest, perhaps, for having been held taut in that direction for the entire game.

Gray and ominous throughout the day, the low clouds and blustery wind at game time threatened rain but instead have only blown hard, frigid air from straightaway center field into the faces of hitters and fans alike. It is the type of wintry wind that at a certain point takes on a recognizable character of its own (as if you'd be able to pick it out on the street if it blew by you, *oh, you again*); constant in presence, hostile in tone, and spiked with intermittent blasts which have a harsh, almost antagonistic feel to them, the gusts push us back when we walk up to find a better spot, slap us hard as we come around a corner, and tug at the bill of our cap as we look up to track a pop fly. Turning it from an element into a very real presence, stoutly set on resistance, as real and as daunting and as much an opponent in tonight's game as the entire Yankee roster combined.

Under the floodlights Myers resets, checks Youkilis, kicks, wheels and whips the ball low. Ortiz takes for ball two, inside. And we immediately re-cross our arms and re-tuck our hands to our sides and glance again at our scorecard, where evidence of the wind's very real presence in this game is translated into a dozen scattered asterisks—this evening's makeshift notation for an Assist to Nature.

They begin on the first column of the first page, a small mark atop the 8 by Giambi's name to indicate that his long drive to center, by all appearances headed in the general direction of Row FF of the bleachers, suddenly changed trajectory, dipped, was heeled down by the wind and caught by Wily Mo Peña, safely if not quite comfortably on the warning track. (Ortiz steps back in, wags his bat twice and cocks it behind his head; beyond him Myers sets, kicks and throws, spinning the ball low and across the plate; Ortiz follows it and nods. Strike one.) Another asterisks appears in the next column over, this one beside an 8 on Robinson Canó's ledger; another long drive deep to center, another gust and push, and another weak dip down into the glove of Peña, waiting on the warning track. (Myers sets and checks Youkilis, then snaps the ball low but wide, and Ortiz lets it go for ball three.) A handful of similar, smaller asterisks dot both halves of our scorecard, followed and overshadowed by one larger, darker, more forceful mark there in the seventh column, down by the name W.M. PENA. Who after having twice been giveth, now has a sure game-breaking double taketh away, the wind knocking his bases loaded smash flat and keeping the game tied, just as it had kept it from being untied so many times before. (Myers glances to Youkilis, rocks and throws the ball straight and in and Ortiz rips the bat through air—and misses—for strike two. Full count now, and Fenway Park again stands and pulls its hands from the depths of its jacket pockets and gathers up its collective voice to a low roar.) What we realize, looking over this constellation of mysterious, invisible influence on our scorecard, is that the wind has significantly changed how we are watching this game. Because at this moment we are not thinking *home run*, not thinking *double*, not even thinking *gap* or *triangle* or *left field wall* or even *line drive base hit*. Instead we are thinking *please Papi, get the ball on the ground*. Shoot it down the line or send it skidding between Jeter and A-Rod. Just don't get under it and try to hit it out because, well, because *you can't fight Mother Nature*. Others have tried—big, powerful guys like Giambi and Peña—and have only ended up shaking their heads as they jog back to the dugout. Over and over again we have felt the sudden internal leap of a well hit drive, immediately followed by the dull internal fall, and a low external groan as the ball fades and drops. Therefore we have (at some point and unconsciously) adjusted our Parameters of Baseball Reality accordingly; within which parameters, on this night at Fenway, a home run is simply not allowed. And so we stand up, and clap, and cheer, and hope like hell for a hard-hit grounder down the line.

Ortiz spits on his gloves, pounds them together with one hard pop, and steps back into the box. He wags the bat low in two gentle sways, pulls it back behind his head, crouches down and faces the mound. Myers comes set, kicks, wheels out and up and lets go a low waist-high pitch on the inside half of the plate and Ortiz—set, waiting, ready— takes a long hard cut and launches it, high and deep, rising up into the night sky above the crowd and above the roof and above the video board and above the John Hancock sign above it all, somehow still rising into the very wind we can feel flush against our shoulders as we follow it up and up and up and out it sails, over the glowing green out-field at its apex now miles above the still-taut flag, and the two gray fielders converging on opposite diagonals towards a point somewhere near the Red Sox bullpen, Bubba Crosby on the right, Johnny Damon on the left, the ball floats on farther and we glance down to the wall and up at the ball, down to the fielders racing and up again to the ball, up and down again and again because of course it *will not*, it *could not*, it *cannot possibly be*, even now as we hold our breath maybe *just maybe* and it falls floodlit through the night and Damon and Crosby both suddenly stop mid-sprint at the warning track before the wall and the ball sails down falling fast and from out of the cold night air is *caught*—caught clean in the glove of Jonathan Papelbon standing tall in the bullpen with his left arm and glove raised high over his head, and the ball safely within it, as thirty-five-thousand fans shoot both *their* arms in unison around him and—*yes! yes!*—we shout among the explosion of noise and continue to cheer with a sudden flush of warmth as in the echoing din of sound and light whirling below Ortiz circles the bases and (lefty specialists and the Yankees and Mother Nature be damned) touches home.

Picking Up the Signs

Seattle at Fenway
3 May 2007

There is a great deal of emphasis on language at Fenway Park these days. Always a ballpark keen on maintaining open lines of communication—namely those between fans and the home plate umpire, opposing players, and any Sox reliever with the temerity to fall behind in the count—there is lately an increased awareness of potential language barriers, along with a earnest effort on nearly everyone's part to try and overcome them. This awareness radiates out from the Sox dugout, of course, which is now trilingual, and if not quite the bustling cosmopolitan scene of, say, *Los Mets!*, is at very least a place where small cross-cultural gestures of cooperation (such as the Japanese phrases jotted on the armband of our Georgia-residing catcher) have become more and more commonplace. Then again, the Red Sox dugout is host to a full-time translator. Whereas the fans milling about a ballpark in which local New Englanders now regularly share an elevator with, or stand in a concessions line next to, or find their seats in the same row as Japanese fans, tourists, and media, have only our simple, improvised signs of welcome and approval to hesitantly try out.

Still, we do try. Already this season we have witnessed countless Sox fans (no doubt infused with the same spirit of hospitality as their club) manage pleasant, smiling conversations made up almost entirely of nods to the field and a shoulders-turned, thumb-back point to the nameplate of a Matsuzaka jersey. We have seen multi-national fans posing together for group photos; have seen gray-haired Bostonian ushers cordially, if somewhat hesitantly, return an informal Japanese bow; and once memorably witnessed a Japanese photographer, happily accosted by a group of loudish young men outside an elevator, send them away howling with a one word, bilingual joke (we did not hear what he said, exactly, but whatever it was included a gesture to his camera's impressively long lens). And we have stood by and winced at the inevitable, and inevitably awkward scenario wherein two Sox fans, well-meaning but quite beery-eyed in their oversized Schilling jerseys, greet a trio of young Asian fans in matching blue Daisuke jerseys with an exaggerated thumbs-up and say, in a thick Boston accent, *Daisuke, good*, only to have the young fans smile back and, the moment the two have left, turn to each other and say in noticeably less-accented English, *So do you want to go find our seats or what?* Mostly though what one sees communicated between Japanese, American, and Japanese-American fans at Fenway is the universal thumbs-up gesture of approval, and the similarly universal gesture of the simple, multi-lingual smile—just that basic recognition of a shared sentiment between two fans under the same dark blue hat, its message nothing more complicated than: *I see you like Daisuke. We like Daisuke, too. Go Sox.*

Which is precisely the message now being shared among much of the gathering crowd on a clear, breezy Thursday evening at Fenway. The game is a makeup of an April rainout between Seattle and Boston, and both the schedule and the Sox' rotation have aligned to produce (like a concert date added by popular demand) a rematch of the earlier Major Media Event that was Daisuke v. Ichiro. The fact that this second act came about by providence, and rather late, has considerably lessened the hype surrounding its arrival; and either that, or the fact that by now we have all somewhat gotten over the novelty of seeing a pitcher and batter who are *both* Japanese face each other, has left a few patches of grandstand temporarily unoccupied when the first pitch is thrown, by Daisuke, to Ichiro, under perhaps half the flashbulb exposures of their memorable first encounter. Therefore only a low, half-hearted groan is heard through the still-shuffling-to-their-seats crowd when Daisuke runs the count full and walks Ichiro to lead off the game. And little more when he walks Adrian Beltre, too. Not until

Daisuke's 2-1 pitch to José Vidro darts high enough to pull Varitek up out of his crouch is there something like a full-scale wince among the crowd. For this is definitely a bad sign. In his previous five starts Daisuke has pitched with confidence and effectiveness, save for the one inning per start in which he has suffered a bewildering loss of control and a subsequent loss in confidence. (Which is a bit like saying that of the dozen mussels you ate, only one was bad.) Each time he has regained form the very next inning, but the suddenness of these attacks, along with their odd regularity (almost always coming in or around the fourth inning), have been as difficult for Sox management to explain as they have been troubling for Sox fans to watch. The sight of Varitek having to leap up out of his crouch to snare an errant Daisuke fastball therefore acts as a signal to the crowd that not only is this habit repeating itself, but that it is upon us right now—not in the fourth, but in the first. All of which is confirmed by his next pitch, which misses low and walks Vidro to load the bases with nobody out in the first, as an uneasy silence falls over the Fenway Park crowd.

We shake our head without a word, and a moment later notice that we have done so in almost perfect unison with the small extended family who are our nearest neighbors this evening in the standing room area above left field. At first glance this small group consists of a husband and wife, their twenty-something son, along with an older uncle (brother to the husband) and his own slightly younger son. All of whom share a set of familiar, familial physical traits (all the males wear beards of varying growth and trim) as well as a common language which indicates that they too are a bi-lingual family, albeit of a slightly different sort. For throughout the first inning, as Daisuke works himself into trouble, they turn to each other and express their concern in a series of gestures and hand motions, single-hand signs built with finger placement and position, combined two-handed motions and quick, punctuating flicks and points; all casually flashed with remarkable speed and fluidity. They are each so skilled at this silent language that it takes a moment to realize that three of the five, including husband and wife and the older of the two boys, are also mouthing and sometimes even speaking the accompanying words, and that only the older, taller, uncle figure and the younger of the two boys are relying solely on the signs to communicate. They all interact with one another as a group, and after a minute or two it is clear they are a close, engaged, good-humored sort of family.

This is merely an impression, of course, for we are privy to none of the meaning behind their signs (our standard ASL vocabulary being limited to three official sentences, two of which are *What's up?* and *We're going to watch the baseball game*). Nevertheless we do manage to communicate, as Daisuke continues to struggle, through the shared language of nonverbal baseball despair—a language we suddenly discover ourselves (thanks in no small part to the Sox) remarkably well versed in. And so when Raúl Ibáñez grounds into a fielder's choice to bring in the first run for Seattle we each give a begrudging shrug (meaning, roughly: *at least we got an out*); and when Richie Sexson spins back away from an inside pitch that catches him somewhere on his 6'8" frame—a hit-by-pitch that reloads the bases—we give the same palms out, jaw open gesture of incredulity (*oh come on*); and when José Guillén doubles down the right field line and two more runs come in we share the same silent, brooding head-shake of frustration (*not good*) which is more or less the universal reaction of fans suddenly down 3-0 in the first. But this is not all. Not even close. For the *Standard Dictionary of Baseball Dejection* is Oxfordian in its dusty etymology and dense sub-meanings, and tonight it appears as if the Sox, and Julio Lugo in particular, are intent on delving into several volumes of it right here in the first. So that with one out and runners on second and third Lugo stretches for and just misses a grounder to his right, and we shoot a quick hand up (*honestly though, what next*) as another run scores. Moments later a little flare finds Lugo sprinting back into shallow left where he reaches up and back and has the ball just tick off the end of his glove and fall safely to the ground, and another run comes in. Lugo is charged with his second consecutive error, and we each cross our arms and shake our heads (meaning a sentiment or two perhaps best left unarticulated) at a scoreboard which now reads 5-0. There is head-shaking of a different sort a moment later when Manny, coming in towards the line on a soft flare, suddenly stops and makes an all-too-casual basket catch around his belt buckle for the second out (*only Manny, right*). This followed by a wry little smile and shrug when an Ichiro drive, easily the hardest hit ball of the inning, is caught by Crisp at the base of the center field wall for the final out (*yes, baseball is a bewildering game*).

Of course the communication skills involved in sharing a thrilling rally with those around you are somewhat less varied. All you have to do is cheer. Which we do, more or less constantly, throughout the bottom of the second as Mariners' starter Horatio Ramirez struggles, first with not finding the strike zone, and then finding far too much of it, and finally of just plain bad baseball luck. After walking Youkilis to begin the inning he gives up consecutive singles to Lowell, Varitek, and Wily Mo Peña, the last of these a lazy flare which finds an empty patch of grass between Ichiro and Guillén, to nicely balance out the Mariners' similar drop-shot in the first. Perhaps unnerved by this, Ramirez walks the struggling Pedroia to make it 5-2 and bring up Lugo, who with the bases loaded is presented a clear, immediate opportunity to erase with his bat the damage done earlier by his glove. He does just this, driving a ball into the opposite field gap; it takes one hop up into the Red Sox bullpen, scores two, makes it 4-5, and Lugo jogs into second having admirably repaid his debt to the scoreboard. After a Crisp pop out Ortiz lobs a two-out broken bat flair over shortstop and into the outfield grass for the second lazy, fortunate hit of the frame, which nonetheless brings Pedroia in from third to tie the game and complete the rally. And although anyone familiar with the rhythms of the game knows that these types of chance flukes and bobbles and near misses are essential to its balance, it is still somewhat maddening to look back and realize that: ten runs have been scored in an inning-and-a-half, and each team has hit the ball hard exactly twice. Nonetheless the game is now tied, and stays that way when the Mariners' defense comes up with a brilliant, diving double-play (Betancourt to López to Sexon) to end the Sox rally and give everyone looking in a chance to step back and breath.

Meanwhile, at some point during the early inning cannonade a warm, breezy afternoon has turned into a cool, windy evening, with the flag pushed straight in over the center field warning track (as it has been for the past two nights, over which we have watched outfielders dart hard back towards the track, only to drift back in with the flight of the ball and catch it harmlessly in the outfield grass). It is not, then, a night to be expecting home runs. More a station-to-station night, where flares and bloop singles and walks are the coin of trade, and where someone like Coco Crisp does his team an enormous service by drawing a one out walk in the fourth and then immediately stealing second. Particularly when Ortiz follows with a grounder to second that would have been a sure inning-ending double play, but instead leaves Crisp still in scoring position for Manny, who comes up next. Again, given the direction and force of the wind we are thinking *single*, *double*, something away from the left field wall and out of the wind; and we are thinking this right up until the instant Manny pulls his arms through a 1-1 pitch and launches it high up towards the left field wall at which point we all think nothing but *home run, home run, come on stay up there*, and then *yes, got it*, home run. And looking to our right we add another word to our ASL vocabulary as the uncle beside us makes a quick two-finger motion up and away (*gone*), and we nod before exchanging a congratulatory high five.

Here again we notice that, although the entire family before us seems to be made up of good solid fans of the game, none seems to bear the true baseball affliction more clearly than this uncle, who when we first came across him was very deliberately punching the selections on his paper All-Star ballot (a nostalgic and particularly endearing sight to fans who grew up offline). He is taller than his brother, with a bit less gray in his beard and a bit more wear in his Sox hat, and over the course of the first four innings we enjoy a lively discussion about the game at hand, and exchange those bits of reminiscence which are the traditional formal greeting among newly acquainted friends of the game; and do so all by means of our own rudimentary and wholly improvised gestures, a tremendous amount of patience and good humor on his part, a printed roster, and one carefully kept scorecard. So that we are able to communicate with each other, when a dubious strike is called on Youkilis, with no more than a raised level palm (*looked high to me*) and nod (*me too*); and with his height and better angle on the scoreboard he is able to help out with a flashed two-fingers-then-one (*2-1*) whenever we lose track of the count, which is often. In a lull between innings we trade stories. He shows us the pristine late-70's Dennis Eckersley card, carefully removed from a spiral notebook in his pocket, to which we nod approvingly (*nice, old-school huh?*), and from which he directs an index finger to himself, smiling (*yep, these were my Sox teams*); before we flip back through our scorebook and display four little black HR diamonds, all in a row, from which he looks up with eyes wide and points down (*you were here?*), and at which we nod solemnly (*yeah, we were at that game*). Thus acquainted we flip back in our scorecard to tonight's half-completed sheet, he returns the card to its place, and we both give an assured little nod of recognition before returning to the game. Two members of the same club, having exchanged the secret handshake.

By this point Daisuke has settled (as if nothing at all had happened in the first) into a nice easy rhythm, and the game along with him. Although not without a particularly ominous sign of things to come. It occurs just before the third inning, while we are hunched over making a series of amendments (not to mention an incomprehensible mess) on our scorecard, based primarily on a recently overturned ruling by the official scorekeeper. (During which interval there is a slight chance that the fans around us in SRO may hear bits of low, grumbling, half-muttered commentary on said ruling, not to mention a few thoughts on said official scorekeeper. For over this short three-game homestand we have waged a silent, one-sided debate with the official scorekeepers at Fenway, whose seemingly haphazard interpretation of the rulebook has more than once caused us to question our own understanding of exactly what is, and is not, a base hit. The best example of this came in the first when Lugo was initially charged with two errors, one of which we considered a hit. And therefore felt it only fair when an inning later it was announced that the scorekeeper had reconsidered, overruled himself, and taken back an error from Lugo while awarding a hit to the Mariners. We made the appropriate adjustments on our scorecard with a satisfied little 1B, only to find out later on that it was actually the error we agreed with that had been changed, meaning we now firmly disagreed with *both* rulings. And the one-sided debate, raged on.) Thus engaged we are not often distracted by the goings-on between innings, but immediately start up at the sound of a sharp loud *thump* echoing from somewhere behind the backstop, and look up to see the ball rolling away from the short wall behind home, Varitek jogging back to retrieve it, and there on the lip of the mound Daisuke, shaking his head and miming the throwing motion of his breaking ball.

Now, the sound of a pitched ball hitting the backstop at full speed, having eluded the catcher's reach completely, is not one that is often heard at a Major League baseball game. And is more than enough for us to note on our scorecard that Daisuke might not have *completely* regained his control just yet. He has enough of it left to get through the inning, however, and the next, at one point retiring ten in a row on the heels of allowing seven of the first eight to reach, his habit of suddenly losing and just as suddenly regaining form still very much intact.

It is not until later on, in the fifth, that the echo of this wild warm-up toss is heard on the scorecard in the form of a walk to Ibáñez, and a single by Sexon. Guillén, who produced the one crucial hit in the first (and incidentally was hit by Daisuke in their first meeting), is up again in a big spot, and his soft fly directly over second base looks harmless at first but as it begins to drop looks more and more like trouble, Crisp rushing full speed in and Lugo rushing full speed out until both players dive (causing an instant Damon-Jackson flinch among Sox fans) as the ball lands between them and they go sliding past one another. One run scores and Crisp and Lugo walk away shaking their heads along with the rest of us. Crisp in particular slaps his glove with disappointment. (Understandably. Over the past few nights the Sox's center fielder has put together a tidy little Gold Glove audition tape of outfield range and reflexes; the choice clip among them coming the night before on a fully-extended diving grab into right field—not the right field gap, but *right field proper*—to save a run in the ninth. In the second inning of tonight's game he recorded all three outs, the last on what has become for him just another routinely brilliant all-out diving catch.)

Lugo, however, must feel as if this particular game has singled him out for a night of personal torment; a feeling only sharpened by what happens after a Johjima groundout moves Guillén up to second. Betancourt hits a slow but otherwise routine grounder to short which Lugo sets up behind, before Guillén, slowing down, stutter-steps ahead of and at the last instant crosses over, directly between the ball and Lugo, who fields clean enough but whose timing (and perhaps concentration) is thrown off just enough by Guillén's interference to cause his throw to sail and pull Youkilis off the bag, the runner safe and the run scored. A cheeky move by Guillén—not exactly illegal, but certainly well within the category of *gamesmanship*—it prompts an interesting bit of non-verbal communication between he and Lugo as the former, now on third base, looks back and shrugs (as if to say *sorry, but you know how it is*), to which Lugo answers only with a quick head shaking glance (*whatever*) before looking down to sweep away an arch of dirt with his spikes.

Regardless of the means employed, the Mariners have now retied the score at 7-7; and after Daisuke strikes out López to end the inning we all peer out into the Sox bullpen, and the uncle to our side confirms who we see throwing by holding a palm level and raising it as high as he can (Snyder). The tall righty does in fact come on in the sixth and, as he has done quite a lot of lately, holds the scoring in check for two innings and gives us time to reflect on what has turned into a thoroughly entertaining game.

For though somewhat longish and prone to wildly disorienting swings of momentum, it has nonetheless been an irresistibly entertaining first seven innings of baseball—filled with odd and curious plays, and fascinating images such as that enigmatic glance between Guillén and Lugo. There was the long fly down the right field line, back in the third, on which Guillén seemed to have both a play and plenty of room to make it before inexplicably turning his glove over to attempt an underhanded catch, only to fumble the ball directly into the first row of the grandstand for a hilarious ground rule double. There was Lugo and Crisp sliding past each other, and the thumped warm-up pitch by Daisuke; Manny extending on the home run and Snyder with a snap throw to first to pick-off Beltre; Guillén's stutter-step in the fifth and later Sexon with another interference run (this time actually sweeping an arm down as if to scoop the ball up). Then, with one out in the bottom of the sixth and Ortiz on first, a hard grounder to the second baseman López stops Ortiz in his tracks, midway between first and second; López throws to Sexon at first for one, and up to Betancourt at second who, now only a few steps away from the still inert Ortiz, is in the process of reaching out to apply the tag when he is unexpectedly enveloped within the arms of the massive slugger, who accepts the tag with bear hug and a smile. This is baseball at its entertaining best— close, dramatic, ever-capable of surprise and always with the ready turn of fortune, and yet never without the sly, playful sense of humor that keeps it from ever taking itself too seriously.

All that, and a penchant for the pleasing statistical anomaly. Of which this game has had its share as well. Among them the odd appearance on the scorecard, down a column next to Seattle's lineup, of four single digits in a row, the last four batters in their lineup wearing the numbers 6, 2, 5, and 4 (needing only Vidro, who wears 3, to drop down in the order and complete the Straight Flush); the rare sight of three neatly aligned singles, not in a vertical column but horizontal, Mike Lowell having singled in three consecutive innings; and perhaps the rarest sight of them all, four straight hits (none of them home runs) for the free swinging, home-run-or-bust Wily Mo Peña. Only on a night like this, among so many other interesting images and storylines, does this sight register as a mere curiosity.

(It will be noted that each of these statistical oddities is revealed to us through the help of a good scorecard, a fact partially due to our placement in the ballpark. The new third base deck area at Fenway is yet another example of the wonderful architectural talents of Janet Marie Smith. Who has once again taken what was once dark and closed and made it open and airy, and done so without touching the essential feel of the ballpark. However, one of the quirks of this new area, shared with a good many rows in back Sections 27-32, is that the overhanging second level blocks from view each of the electronic info-centers in the ballpark, including the video board above the bleachers; which, aside from making guesswork of most high fly balls, has the pleasing side effect of taking one back to a time and place when the relevant information of the game was not within a single glance, and therefore required a bit more paying attention to. As it is, the experience is baseball without instant statistical prompting; and because of this it is an environment where a good old fashioned paper roster and a well-kept scorecard suddenly become quite useful. And yes, there is something of a nostalgic glean, familiar and pleasant, when a fan nearby leans over and nods at the scorecard to ask, *Is that right, Wily Mo is 4-4?* And the scorer answers, *yep, three singles and a double.)*

Yet for all this, ours is still a game without an ending, and a bad one (say brought on by more sloppy infield play) could easily spoil its rather significant charms. This seems unlikely in the bottom of the eighth when the lineup rotates to bring Crisp, Ortiz, and Manny due up against Seattle reliever Chris Reitsma. It seems a little more likely though when Crisp pops up meekly over the infield; and the first sense that this might not turn out alright after all comes a moment later when Ortiz, with a vicious home run cut, strikes out swinging. Fenway exhales loudly and shakes its head. Only momentarily though, as the silent disappointment over Ortiz is pulled under a rolling cheer for Manny, who is due up next. And once again we are struck by the sense of how very fortunate we are, as Sox fans, to have not only one star slugger in the middle of our lineup, but two. And therefore have the luxury of a dual climax, two consecutive chances for highly anticipated dramatic late-inning fireworks. One would be enough, of course, to feel lucky (there are certainly teams without any), but at Fenway it's *if at first you don't succeed*, there's always Manny coming up next.

Of course as fortunate as we feel there must be an equally striking sense of misfortune within the poor reliever who, having struck out one of the most dangerous clutch hitters in the league, finds himself facing one of the very best. And Manny, who is off to a slow start this April, is still without question one of the best, as he has shown tonight already and as he shows again on a 3-2 pitch with the crowd on its feet and begging for something loud and emphatic and thrilling and then receiving just that. Manny reaches out on another ball away, and this time drives it high out over the right field gap, and with our vision blocked by the overhang we watch only Guillén as he races back and looks up and stops and the ball comes down far back in the bleachers and, with two fingers swept up and out, gone. High-fives and smiles all around, and we are at last assured enough to asked the father in front of us how to communicate the one ASL sign we want to be able to know when this game ends. He shows us with a smile, and we thank him twice.

We all know, whether we realize it or not, the many ways in which it is possible to express joy to those around us, whether at a ballpark or elsewhere. Shooting our arms straight up above us works, as does leaping up and down, punching our fists in the air, and clapping with sustained vigor. For the most part, smiling will do. But we know other signs too, those of us who hang around this game. For instance we know how to signal with our index and pinky fingers and a slight wag of the hand (*two outs*); and how to mimic the umpire with a quick flick of the index finger to our side (*strike one*); and how and when to shoot a hasty point down the third base line (appealing for a called strike). We know exactly what sign to make when our man slides headfirst into second, our palms swept clean to both sides (*safe*), and when a relayed throw reaches Varitek in time for a slapped tag we jump right in with a fist punched downward (*out*). And we know all sorts of ways to dispute any injustice, real or perceived. Among them the double hand sweep to the side (*pulled him off the bag*), the hand pressed down over an imaginary ball (*he trapped it*), and of course the facing palms held anywhere from a few inches to an arms-length apart (*missed him by* that *much*). All these signs we pick up here and there throughout our time at the ballpark, and use them, without much thinking about it, to communicate with those on the field and with each other through the acquired, shared, and truly universal language of baseball.

This language is, like any other obscure dialect, not to be found in textbooks or traveling phrase books (though an *Essential Baseball*

Phrases and Expressions would be useful to many), but is as helpful and important as any of the multiple languages now spoken at our ballpark for the simple fact that it too removes barriers and allows us to better share the experience with those around us, regardless of the words we use to describe it. So that with a runner on first and nobody out in the ninth it hardly matters what language we speak in our homes—whether it is a thick Down East English, an island-influenced Spanish, a distinctly Yamanote-inflected Japanese, or standard American Sign Language—we all lean forward together the same way, and as J.C. Romero steps and throws our eyes all open wide at the ground ball hit to Youkilis, who throws to Lugo for one and back all the way across for two as our fists all shoot up (*yes, got him, one out to go*). We all stand the same with two outs, and clap the same for the final out to come; and when Sexon raps a hard grounder to Lowell and he knocks it down, stays with it and throws across for the final out and the Sox win, we all smile and cheer just about the same. Which allows us, in this season of new languages and fewer language barriers, to say goodbye to the family around us with high-fives and handshakes, and to use the one phrase of genuine ASL we learned back when Manny homered, communicating now one of the happiest phrases in the baseball phrase book by raising both hands up with palms out (*great*—), then lowering both hands and bringing two fists flush together (—*game*).

The Man in the Arena

Oakland at Fenway
10 May 2005

At times it can be a lonely game. It can leave you dust-covered and on your knees, propped up by one arm on the infield dirt before thirty-five thousand disappointed faces. And as you pick yourself up and shake your mitt out you will find no huddle to return to, no court to run back down, no bench to skate to and disappear behind; but instead will only have your position to walk back to, alone, as the judgment of a stark white 1 slides into place on the scoreboard to your right. It happens. And it happens to every ballplayer eventually because no player is perfect, and when each player's imperfections—whether they be in the glove, arm, bat, legs, or mind—are finally exposed they will not be given the comfort of the team to hide within but the isolation of the spotlight which falls hard to the runner, alone on the base paths (lying face down in the dirt); to the fielder, alone against the outfield wall (the ball bouncing on the grass behind); and to the pitcher, very much alone on a small dirt mound in the center of the field and beneath the glare of floodlights, with nothing more to hide beneath than the insufficiently narrow bill of a cap as baserunners circle victory laps around him. Every player who takes the field knows this isolation is a reality of a profession in which stark public humiliation is a very real occupational hazard, but only on certain nights do they experience it so acutely as Kevin Millar has on this Tuesday evening at Fenway, as he walks slowly back to his position, alone, after playing a harmless infield grounder into an Oakland run. Not once, but twice.

In truth neither error was terribly egregious, and a case can be made for Millar in both instances; yet the circumstantial evidence—

two runs on the scoreboard for Oakland, two errors on the scoreboard for Boston—creates an inescapable guilt-by-association effect within the minds of a Fenway crowd not inclined to consider much in the way of rebuttals. And so the plays stand as they are, and Millar stands responsible for them both. Each error began in his hands, each error preceded a run. Nevermind the details, in the eyes of Fenway Park each number on the scoreboard is and will continue to be his responsibility—from the top of the first when he is very much alone, all the way to the bottom of the ninth, when he is very much not.

This on a cool, clear evening at the ballpark—warm and shirt-sleeved and almost summer in the daytime sun, cool and sweatered and a reminder that it is *not quite yet* in the evenings—with the Fenway crowd and several of the players (including Millar) still in long sleeves. The sweaters are still in the top drawer of the closet; the boots still sit drying on the doormat outside; and the winter coat still hangs in the hallway, just in case. But we are getting there. The days are stretching out, the pre-game ceremonies no longer performed under the lights but under dusky twilight, so that this first inning situation—one out, Oakland runners on the corners—unfolds not at night but with the sun still descending back over the third base roof just as a quiet apprehension descends over the Fenway grandstands. At the plate the slow running (or rather, the slow *moving*) Erubiel Durazo stands in for Oakland. Millar, shaggy-haired and goateed, the odd juxtaposition of his rotund torso and thin lower legs reminiscent either of Babe Ruth, or the best player on the local adult softball nine (depending on how he's playing), stands back at first and creeps in a step as he eyes Mark Kotsay, inching off third. Durazo takes a strike and on the 0-1 pitch chops a hard two-hopper to the right that Millar dives to his knees to stop, sees Kotsay break for home, and balancing on one knee throws off-kilter and a bit sidearm towards home, a low hard throw that skips wildly in front of the plate, ricochets off Varitek's chest protector, rolls into foul ground, and allows Kotsay to jog in and tap home for the game's first run.

Groans. Shouts. *Oh come on!* Mouths open, aghast. Hands spread wide, palms up, imploring. *Are you kidding me?* Incredulous looks directed at fans to either side, wondering silently and then quite vocally (this fieldward) *What the 'ell was that?* Mouths close, hands retract, the glance burrows in the general direction of first base as incredulity turns to frustration. *Come on Millah!* And all across the Fenway grandstand and all through its bleachers there is a great crossing of the arms; a setting of the jaw; a furrowing of the collective fan brow. Not angry. Just, disappointed.

While in the hazy twilight below Kevin Millar, now shaking dust from his glove and walking alone back to his position, is charged with an error.

There is of course no such thing as a mental error on the baseball scorecard, regardless of the fact that there is very much such a thing as a mental error on the baseball diamond. A clear example of which we find here, where Millar's hasty off-balance throw surely undid the play and allowed the run (though it would have been a close play even with the best of throws), but where the real error was almost entirely one of selection. For when Millar dives and stops Durazo's hard grounder (an impressive and immediately forgotten reflex play) he suddenly finds himself with the ball in his hand, the runners on the move, and several options concerning how to proceed. He can (A) hop up and tag first, taking the safe out and conceding the run; he can (B) attempt a difficult 3-6-3, or even 3-6-1 double play, which would be risky (but conceivable given Durazo's footspeed); he can (C) throw home off one knee and attempt to cut down Kotsay at the plate, or even (D) steady himself on firmer footing and attempt a more plausible throw which still, given how hard the ball was hit, has a chance at preventing the run. Millar, obviously, choose poorly. Opting for C. Yet one of the interesting features of the play is that the most advisable option, just in terms of orthodox baseball theory, would be A, which still allows the run. It accepts an out in return, however, and by doing so cuts down on the chances of a big inning and therefore is well within the accepted school of thought in baseball's Opening stage (or first three innings; as opposed to its Endgame, or last three innings, where with the score still tied the proper choice would be either B or C). Given that Millar had less than a full second to consider all of this and make his decision we might grant him some leeway; given that he is a veteran Major League first baseman (for the defending World Champions, no less) and that such decisions should be instinctual for someone in his position, he is granted little more from Fenway than a low rumbling of discontent and a very lonely first base to return to. And if this rumble does not instantly turn to cheers a moment later when Millar leaps and snags a hard line drive which saves at least a run, and instead the crowd grumbles and mutters that his ensuing attempt to double-off Chavez at second was wide and pulled Rentería off the bag, and that he botched that one up, too, despite the catch—well that's just life in the big leagues.

Then again a run is still only a run, unless of course it is the only run, which this run still is four innings later after strong work from Athletics starter Kirk Saarloos and a pair of poorly timed double-play balls from David Ortiz combine to keep the score 1-0, Oakland, in the bottom of the fifth. By this point in the game it has become clear that the Red Sox best and possibly only chance of scoring on this night is to find a way to bring Johnny Damon (who is 2-2 on the night) to bat with at least one of his teammates (who are a combined 0-10) on base, preferably in scoring position. It takes four innings to do so but the batting order, a Rentería single, and a Bill Mueller walk finally combine to produce this very situation in the bottom of the fifth when Damon steps to the plate with two out and two on. He works the count full, and because he is always a difficult hitter to strike out and on top of that is in the middle of a terrific groove at the plate, he is able to swing five times in the at bat and make contact each time, fouling off the first four and lining the fifth into right for a single that ties the game at 1-1. It is nearly untied a moment later when Trot Nixon reaches out and shoots a low slider away into left field, slicing it towards the corner as left fielder Eric Byrnes sprints straight across and at the last instant leaps and stretches and catches with his entire body a flat plane parallel to the ground before tumbling over on the grass and bouncing up, ball in glove, for the final out. Byrnes runs off the field in exactly the same way he does everything from run the bases to shagging fly balls: at a full sprint.

An inning later the Athletics take the ball from Saarloos and end his impressive six-inning, one-run no decision. Not nearly soon enough for Sox fans, for whom Saarloos' short, compact build and efficient motion have been a bit too reminiscent of the erstwhile ace, Tim Hudson. Then again, his replacement appears to be even less encouraging, as Sox fans and Sox hitters take their first looks (with equal displeasure) at the Athletics' young rookie reliever and closer-in-waiting, Huston Street.

Street, who besides having one of those great baseball names which would seem obvious and banal in a baseball movie, but which in real life adds great color and vibrancy to a roster, has a distinct back-sliding windup, a curious 5-9 delivery, an explosive fastball, and is one of those rare pitchers who it takes opposing fans about three pitches to become adequately tired of seeing. After those three pitches he has forced Manny to ground out, takes only six more to strike out Ortiz, and only six more after that to strike out Millar and end the inning. He is a wonderful young pitcher, and we dislike him immediately.

Meanwhile, on the other half of the ledger Bronson Arroyo has continued to do what he is lately in the habit of doing, which is getting outs. Several of them. Through the first six innings he has allowed only one hit and one (notably unearned) run to go along with a few walks, a few strike outs, and a great many harmless fly outs and routine grounders. Only Bobby Kielty leads off the seventh by doubling high off the left field wall, Hatteberg follows with an infield squib he beats out despite a fine effort by Rentería, and suddenly Arroyo is in a spot. He does himself a favor by striking out Byrnes next, but now he and the defense behind him (including a certain dusty-kneed first baseman) find themselves faced with the exact same situation which caused all that trouble back in the first—runners on the corners, one out, tie game.

And here we go again. Adam Melhuse clips a slow-roller to the right side of the infield grass, Arroyo strides over (not quickly) to field, checks Kielty at third and then, taking the sure out, fires to first where Millar catches and immediately pivots, snaps a good hard accurate throw home that hits Varitek's mitt just as Kielty slides in behind the play, *safe*, for the go-ahead run.

Louder groans. Livelier shouts. *What the——?* Mouths gaping wider. Hands not only spread to the sides but now raised up, imploring to a higher court than ours. *Seriously?* Hands upraised come to rest (having heard no answer from the rafters) on top of badly mishandled Sox hats. Gradually the initial shock subsides. The eyes focus. The hands move farther down to cup either side of the mouth. And the voice, once lost, is regained. *Come on Millah you bum you're killin' us here!* And all across the Fenway grandstand and all through its bleachers there is an even more deliberate crossing of the arms, an even firmer setting of the jaw, and a furrowing of the collective fan brow into a look intended to convey the full damage done by the wound inflicted on its eternal fan soul. Beyond angry. It is fan, aggrieved.

Nevermind that there was nothing Millar could have possibly done to prevent the run (*whatevah, he's killin' us*), the image of his throw home and the runner scoring mirrors the play in the first too closely for us not to somehow (however irrationally) transfer the blame directly onto him alone. A mental trick which is validated a moment later when the sure out Arroyo played for is suddenly and somewhat incredibly waved off. Millar, it turns out, never touched the bag. Instead he straddled it, as first basemen are wont to do, with the kind of a quick sweep of the feet by which the tagging of first base is more *implied* rather than actually executed. Unfortunately however there is Brian Gorman behind first, an umpire apparently in an extraordinarily literal mood, who had his eyes fixed on the foot-to-bag relationship the entire time and is having none of it. Gorman waves his arms to the official scorer. The small red light on the scoreboard goes dark. And the white metal 1 beneath E on the Red Sox ledger is taken down, and replaced with a white metal 2.

Silence. Blank stares. A slow, deliberate, blink. Hands raised—not wide, not high, but to cover the face; to rub the eyes (as comfort against the sight just witnessed); to massage the temples (as comfort against the information just received); to move with a tug down the back of the neck and apply firm pressure (to comfort a suddenly overactive nerve thereabouts). Still, there are no shouts. No groans. No rhetorical questions. Only silence. The expression far too clenched, the lips far too tightly pursed for any sounds save the huff of deep, heavy breaths through the nose. Finally the arms are brought down long enough for one silent, dismissive swat of the hand (*you are released from our affections*) in the general direction of first base. Then re-crossed, set, and held indefinitely. The eyes are fixed in the same general direction, with the same intent, leveling to the figure below a cold, flat, lifeless stare of distrust. And so it is *woe to you*, Kevin Millar. Careful where ye tread from here on out. For hell hath found a new fury, in that of the Red Sox fan scorned.

In this case Millar, whatever his faults, deserved better. As did Arroyo. If anything both were victims of a wholly unprecedented interpretation of the rulebook (the call Gorman made could be called, if such things were called, no less than a dozen times a game and would break up half that many double plays), and more so of some clever base running on the part of Kielty, who timed his run just right, pausing at exactly the right distance down the line so that Arroyo had no play at third or home and was forced instead to go to first. As soon as he turned to do so Kielty broke for home and was quickly too far down the line for Millar to make a play, accurate or otherwise. Then again, there is not much in the way of scorecard annotation for clever baserunning, and it is similarly difficult to award a fielder's choice when no outs are recorded. And so with the game's rigorous zero-sum accounting system (nothing is ever given to the batter which is not taken away from the pitcher or defense) the only blame available once again falls to Millar, who is given his second error to go along with the second Oakland second run.

The fact that Scutaro and Kotsay both ground out and the error does not, technically, cost the Red Sox any runs hardly seems to matter at the moment (although it will matter a great deal later on). Not with the Sox trailing 2-1 at the stretch. And certainly not when they ground into inning-ending double-plays in both the seventh and eighth, and head, after some tidy work by both Alan Embree and Matt Mantei to hold things in check, into the bottom of the ninth down a run and facing the Oakland closer, Octavio Dotel. Where once again we rise to our feet, to cheer the opening of that miniature game-within-a-game that always is the bottom of the ninth, down a run. (Where what should matter, at least to those fans who are paying attention, is that a quick glance at the lineup shows us this game will not end without at least one more appearance by Kevin Millar, who is due up third in the inning.)

Dotel goes to work on Manny, out and in, all hard stuff, challenging him. Manny takes a ball, fouls off a strike, takes a ball, fouls off a strike, and on the 2-2 pitch takes what is easily Dotel's best pitch of the evening, a curling fastball that grooves the inside corner. Manny knows it before we do, and Joe West rings him up for the first out. We groan, and instantly turn to Ortiz, who has had something of a rough night himself (grounding into two of the Sox's four debilitating double plays), and who if nothing else needs to get on to avoid the disastrous scenario of bringing up Millar, still very much *persona non grata*, to represent the last out and final chance for the Sox. As it turns out, he does. Dotel challenges Ortiz as well, but either more cautiously or simply less accurately, misses badly, and ultimately walks him to put the tying run on and bring the winning run to the plate in the disheveled, dust-covered form of Kevin Millar.

And you know we should have seen it coming. The closer throwing nothing but hard fastballs, challenging hitters, wild on the corners and coming out over the plate trying to blow it by them; Millar, who invites such challenges (who must spend his offseasons day-dreaming about such challenges, if we are to judge by the zeal with which he attacks them), and who of course has a great deal on the scoreboard to make up for; and the score and situation *just so*. Millar takes the first pitch inside for a ball, then fouls off a hard fastball out over the plate, pulling it high up behind him. He swipes at the dirt with his feet, knowing he just missed it. (It is a miss we file away, to bring back a moment later when both we and Millar see that same pitch again.) Dotel's next pitch misses high and in and Millar bends back out of the way for ball two. And it is right about here that Fenway senses it, sees it laid out before us, lets the *what if?* scenario slip across our mind and feels that little ripple of anticipation climb the back of our neck. Suddenly the Lets-*Go!* Red-*Sox!* chant goes up, full-throated and thumping-loud, the lights seem to gleam a bit clearer off the helmets and shine a bit brighter on the Sox's home whites, the Fenway green surrounds it all, the noise throughout the ballpark rises to the point where you can feel physically feel it shaking within, and the stage is set. Millar looks in, wagging his bat, and rips Dotel's next pitch foul for strike two; then steps out, folds the bat under his arm as he refastens both batting gloves, and steps back in to take his stance—feet wide, open to the mound, red stockings up to his knees, dirt across both shoulders (from his adventures afield), bleached blond hair flying out one side of his helmet and detailed half-goatee above the collar of his red turtleneck. He huffs and puffs, and wags the red bat above his head; and we stand and wait; and both he and Dotel and everyone on the field and in the ballpark and watching at home knows that the fastball is coming and sure enough here it is from Dotel right back down the middle and Millar takes his cut and rips it on a hard line high and up and still going up higher and sailing on until it hits, deflects off, and rattles around the light stanchion high above the wall and a moment later the baseline sounds out somewhere beneath the ebullient roar of Fenway and we are all of us singing *love that Dirty Water, ohhhh, Boston you're my home...*

Cheers. Laughter. Shouts, louder than ever. *Hey-hey!* Mouths open, elated. Expressions beaming, delighted. Hands lifted straight up in the air, exultant. *How about that!* High-fives to the left, high-fives to the right; cheers raised for the team streaming down onto the field. As all across the Fenway grandstand and all through its bleachers there is a great clapping of the hands, a brightening of the eyes, and a triumphant raising of the voice to send the celebratory volley fieldward: '*Atta boy Millah!*

Yes, it can be a lonely game. No matter how well you play it, the game will eventually find your weaknesses and lay them bare beneath the floodlights and before a crowd and perhaps even on national television. So that if you are a burley, slightly awkward first baseman who at times tries to do a bit more defensively than he is capable of, it will find you out with a tough one out, runners on the corners situation. It will send the ball your way and make you look foolish and inept. And then, a few innings later on, it will do it again. Yet there is a justice built into the framework of the game. Because it requires each player to play both halves of the frame (disregarding the designated hitter, which is a sin against nature for this very reason), to field and run, to throw and hit, so too it gives every player the opportunity to make his impression on both sides of the scoreboard. So that if you are this very same burley, slightly awkward first baseman who has been doubly humiliated already, but who happens to have a penchant for your more aggressive sort of fastball pitchers, then the game will also give you an at bat in the final inning against the opposing closer. That is to say it will find out your talent, and expose it, too.

In the end, it will give you a chance.

Kevin Millar was given this chance on a pleasant late-spring night at Fenway. He was left alone walking back to his position as the first and then second Oakland runs jogged back to the dugout, with an error sliding into place on the scoreboard to identify for all the world his mistake. And had the game ended there he would have surely taken the consensus blame for the loss, surely. Instead he was given a chance, was given a bat to make up for his glove, and was given a pitch to hit. And that is really all the game can offer, the chance itself, the at bat and the pitch and that one last strike when it's 2-2 and you know the fastball is coming. Millar was given this and, to his credit, he did not miss. He put his swing on it, and because of that he circles the bases before us in a quick, clipped trot and leans down third with a smile and hops with both feet on home plate as the most popular man in Boston, pummeled by his teammates and wildly applauded by thirty-five thousand loyal and ever so graciously forgiving fans.

'S Wonderful

Baltimore at Fenway
13 May 2007

It has been a chilly weekend here in the shadows of Fenway Park. Where we have suffered through a depressing Friday night affair in which the Sox trailed the entire game, left the bases loaded three times, and lost, 6-3, with the biggest cheers of the night for nothing more thrilling than two bases loaded walks; then trudged through an unseasonably cold and unspeakably dull Saturday afternoon at the ballpark during which the Sox and Orioles not only conspired to play a lifeless low scoring draw (with no runs in the first three-and-a-half innings) *and* an artless, stumbling blowout (with seventeen runs in the last five-and-a-half innings), but took a full five hours to do so. In a game with no big cheers at all. And as Friday night games followed by Saturday matinees having a natural tendency to blend together as one, the cumulative experience has been that of one, long, dreary slouch before an interminable cycle of baseball tedium. (Would that this were an exaggeration. For in fact it is difficult to convey how impossibly little in the way of baseball interest, no matter how small or subtle or obscure, took place at Fenway Park over this nearly nine hour stretch of—of what we will not do the injustice of calling *baseball*. Imagine standing in a darkened crowd, hunched over a scorecard, with only one drink of stale coffee left as you stare out and watch the manager, pitcher, catcher, and infielders discuss—if one judges by the results—whether the next seven pitches ought to be in the dirt, or a foot high, or some combination thereof. Imagine this going on for several minutes and repeating itself a few dozen times at random intervals. Imagine a pitcher peering suspiciously over his shoulder at a base runner so slow and unlikely to run that he practically has his hands in his pockets as he takes the one indifferent half-step off first which constitutes *his lead*. Imagine this pitcher spinning wildly and firing to first as the runner, who barely deserves the appellation, casually shuffles over to place one foot on the bag and, hands on hips as the ball is caught and tossed back, says something to his first base coach which makes the opposing first baseman smile. Imagine a pitcher and batter staring at each other for several seconds among a deadened crowd. Imagine wondering how long this staring could possibly go on. Imagine the batter then calls time, steps out, re-adjusts his batting gloves and helmet (neither of which have budged since he adjusted them thirty seconds ago), stares at the label of the bat to see if it might possibly have moved up or down a few inches since last he checked (it has not), examines the handle to ensure that it has not suffered a fracture in the slight breeze over his head (it has pulled through intact), searches the batter's box for any obstructions which might have rolled like tumbleweeds across it since his last stepping out (there are none), sweeps it clean with his spikes just to be sure, plants his back foot, nods to the umpire that he is satisfied with the conditions, takes his stance, and stares out at the pitcher. The pitcher, as he has done this entire time, stares in at the batter. And we, as we have done this entire time, tap the end of our pen against our scorecard. The pitcher continues to stare in, only now seems to suffer an attack of acute short-term amnesia, for he no longer appears to know exactly where he is, why all of these people are staring at him as if he were about to somehow perform, why *on earth* he happens to be wearing knee-high breeches and stockings, or what he could possibly be expected to do with this curious little ball in his hand. He stares in. The hitter stares our. We tap louder. The umpire blinks. Finally the hitter calls time, steps out, re-adjusts his batting gloves and... And there goes the last cold slosh of stale coffee. It has been that kind of baseball—the game at its lifeless, grinding, tiresome worst. Watched among a lackluster crowd, within the dull chilled shadows of an uninspired weekend.) All of which has brought us, rather unenthusiastically, to today's game—a sunny Sunday matinee which through its first eight innings has managed the seemingly impossible, and somehow lived well beneath this weekend's already exceedingly low baseball expectations.

Down early the Sox have stayed down, their ceremonial pink bats (in honor of its being Mother's Day) not exactly winning any permanent places on the bat rack as Orioles starter Jeremy Guthrie has held them scoreless on only three hits, one of which was a fluke knocked down by the wind. Meanwhile the Orioles picked up a pair of runs off Beckett in the first, added one in the fifth, one in the seventh, and now give Guthrie the ball to take his 5-0 lead comfortably into the bottom of the ninth. (Not to be outdone, the loudest crowd noise this afternoon has been in response to—*for shame*—the wave.)

And so because it has been a game memorable for nothing else; and because we have stood in the cold shadows of the grandstand overhang all weekend; and because we have there endured fans calling for a double play with two outs and honestly asking if the reliever coming in is Daisuke; and because after the Sox went in order in the eighth a good many Fenway Faithful put their faith on hold in favor of beating the traffic, and a good many more inexplicably hurried to the exits after the *top* of the ninth (to which: *?*); and because when we fantasize about having season tickets our seats are always on the end of the last row of red seats in Section 30 (Row PP to be exact: right next to the isle, right in front of the ramp, in the sun on day games but under the overhang for rain, and with a perfect just-high-enough-but-not-too-high view of the third/pitcher/first axis); and because this is exactly where we now notice two vacant red seats among the scattered empties, we decide *why the hell not*, and walk down and take a sun-warmed red seat on the aisle so that on this otherwise dreary weekend we can watch at least one half inning, the bottom of the ninth, in the sun.

With a nod we ask the couple to our right if the occupants of our new seats have left permanently, and they nod back, *yeah pretty sure they're gone.* Alright then, a moment to get situated and spread out, and balance the scorecard and—and *good gracious these are fine seats*, even better than we remembered—and it feels quite nice and warm down here in the open, under the sun, a different day altogether. Which begs the obvious question: why anyone would ever, on a day like today, leave seats like these behind? And in the bottom of the ninth? And with Big Papi coming up? And on a Sunday no less, with the afternoon late and a long spring evening stretching out before us? Sure the Sox are trailing and will doubtless lose; yet still one has to ask: what could anyone claiming to be any kind of Sox fan have to get to, on a Sunday afternoon, that is preferable to watching Ortiz bat at Fenway on a sunny spring day? That is to say, beating the traffic *to what?* (Not to mention the fact that this is Boston, and therefore *there is no* beating the traffic.) Is it simply to avoid the crowd after the game? (Which if crowds are a problem, may we suggest that baseball at Fenway may not be the pastime for you.) Or is it simply out of habit? (In which case does one leave the symphony, or theater, or movies ten minutes before the final movement or scene? Does one go to see Romeo and Juliet for the first time and leave right before the tomb scene, whispering, *well I don't see what could possibly go wrong from here, let's beat the traffic*? Not to mention that in a play or symphony or movie the ending is not only repeatable but actually scripted, and therefore predictable. Unlike sports where you never can tell and therefore never really do know, as you hurry through an open gate to the parking lot, exactly what it is you are leaving behind.) Mysteries all, not to be troubled over today. Not while there is a bit more baseball in the weekend. Not while the Sox still have a few more outs to work with. Not as we turn our attention back to the game just in time to see Julio Lugo rap a grounder up the middle and Miguel Tejada, who has been death to grounders up the middle all weekend, scoop it up and fire close but in time for the first out of the ninth.

Coco is up next, and we glance up at the scoreboard to find that Guthrie has somehow thrown only eighty-seven pitches over eight-and-a-third. (Under the grandstand we were blocked from the pitch count, and while there are few limits to our scorecard nerdiness, tracking pitches just happens to be one of them.) This kind of economy is impressive but its immediate relevance is that Guthrie will almost surely finish this game, adding a nice little complete game shutout at Fenway Park to his resume, and no doubt making his own mother very proud.

This outcome looks even less in doubt when Crisp lunges at Guthrie's 90th pitch of the afternoon and pops it straight up over the plate. An exasperated sigh slips from the grandstand, and a long grumbling pause ensues as Guthrie, catcher Ramón Hernández, and third baseman Chris Gomez all converge and eventually give way to Hernández who settles under it, stares straight up, punches his mitt, and then all of a sudden takes two staggering steps backward (that wind again) and lunges for the ball only to have it kick off his catcher's mitt and land innocently on the soft green grass behind him. The ball lays there, perhaps three feet in front of the plate, and we all of us left at Fenway have a great big laugh—*hey-hey!*—and point, and clap, and maybe laugh once more a bit louder than necessary (as crowds looking for anything at all to cheer for are sometimes wont to do). Hernández, noticeably less amused, slumps his shoulders and gives a face one might give upon finding a stack of orange parking tickets stuffed in one's windshield, before leaning to pick up both mask and ball. (In retrospect all three Orioles misplayed the situation. As the third baseman and the only infielder with a play, Gomez should have called for it and made the catch; Guthrie, as a pitcher, should have gotten out of the way altogether; and even after calling for it Hernández, as an All-Star catcher, should have made the catch, wind or no wind.)

In any event the play extends our time in the sun by a few minutes, which: so much the better. And even if it doesn't spark a furious rally, even if it doesn't shift the balance of the game or alleviate the gloom of such a game and such a weekend, at least at least it gives us that much more baseball. Not to mention makes Guthrie work a bit harder for his complete game shutout. That is, until it doesn't. For by this point Orioles manager Sam Perlozzo has for some curious reason come out onto the field. There he has a word or two with his pitcher, holds out his hand, and for reasons known only to the heavens and Sam Perlozzo, takes the ball from Guthrie and gives him a good solid pat on the back. On his walk to the dugout Guthrie receives a rare standing ovation from the opposing Fenway crowd, a nice moment of sportsmanship which hardly obscures the fact that his departure still makes absolutely no sense at all, and leaves us fans turning to each other with parted hands, screwed up eyebrows, asking each other one form or another of the question: *What the——?*

For in no way was Guthrie either struggling or tiring. Statistically he was fine, with a comfortable pitch count and having scattered all of three hits. Observationally, he was better than fine, as the Sox had not only struggled to get hits off him but had struggled to get anything *close* to a hit. They simply weren't finding the ball. All of which is on top of the real mystery, which is how a dropped pop up a few feet in front of the plate signals to a manager that action needs to be taken? In this case drastic action. If Hernandez had caught the ball there's no question Perlozzo would have left Guthrie in for the final out of a complete game shutout; and so how the ball ticking off his glove changes who is the Orioles' best option to get the final two outs is beyond any of us. (The only possible explanation is that Perlozzo made the categorical decision, prior to the inning, to send Guthrie out only so long as no one reached base. A fine strategy which nonetheless is a clear example of the managerial dangers inherent in turning one's brain off a half inning too soon.) Not that any of it really matters; not with a 5-0 lead, and two outs to go, and only one runner on. But *still…*

The new Orioles pitcher is Danys Báez, who throws the first Baltimore pitch of the day not thrown by Jeremy Guthrie low to David Ortiz (looking surrealistic as the large and dangerous hitter waving about his pale pink bat) for ball one. Báez sets and throws again, and this time Ortiz puts one of the very few good swings of the day by a Red Sox hitter on it and drives it deep out over the outfield, and all of us are on our feet and cheering as it kicks off the center field wall, Crisp comes around from first to score easily, and Papi steps on second with a stand-up double. *And how about that, the Sox are on the board,* 5-1. So no shutout, and we had something to cheer about after all. Which is nice. You never want to leave the ballpark without standing up to cheer at least once. And with Wily Mo coming up (forgive us Wily Mo, but that defensive replacement for Manny in the top of the inning looks somewhat regrettable at the moment) that will surely be our last chance to do so.

It is not. Wily Mo swings his large pink bat and pulls a ball down the third base line, past Gomez and into the left field grass for a single, shallow enough to force Ortiz to hold at third; and more than enough for Perlozzo to stomach as he then marches back out onto the field, takes the ball, and sends Báez to the clubhouse for a barely needed shower. In his stead Perlozzo brings on the current Orioles' closer, Chris Ray, a twitchy right-hander whose name, interestingly enough, we only recognize because he is the same closer who a month ago gave up a five-run lead in the ninth at Yankee Stadium, including a walk-off grand slam to A-Rod. He is warm almost before this connection is made and quickly (everything happens quickly in these situations) runs the count full on J.D. Drew. Ray, who on mannerisms alone seems to be exactly the type of nervy, excitable pitcher you do not want closing out these types of situations, throws high and walks Drew to load the bases and bring Youkilis up. Incredibly enough, to represent the tying run. There is a great cheer—a rising, full bodied cheer—as for the first time all weekend Fenway Park stands, clears its throat, and finds its sporting voice. (And *oh yes, excuse me Mr. Usher, but you can take away all these seats now; we won't be needing them any more this afternoon.*)

In situations such as these, late in game, there are certain players who as a fan you simply trust—for whatever reason, knowable or otherwise—and in the brimming, optimistic tone of the applause now rising up you can hear that Kevin Youkilis is one of them. Right away he begins earning this trust by working the count full; at which point it seems highly likely that the next pitch will be either to his left elbow, left knee, or some major bone (say a rib or hip) in between. (Easily the most put-upon of Sox hitters, one of the quintessential Youkilian expression is his wincing in pain as he shakes an arm down the line.) Our bet is the elbow, and we're nearly right as Ray's 3-2 pitch zips up and in, just missing Youkilis' torso but nonetheless walking in a run (5-2). This brings up Varitek, who has been swinging the bat better as of late and surely knows that Ray does not want to walk the game away and therefore will give him a pitch to hit. Which he does; which Varitek promptly drills on a low liner into the right field gap; which sets off a wild burst of cheers and shouts as the thirty-thousand or so remaining fans all wave Wily Mo around third to follow Ortiz safely home; which makes it 5-4 with a runner in scoring position and which turns Fenway Park into what may very well be the loudest Mother's Day party on record.

Hinske is up next, playing first to give Mike Lowell a day off and having appeared so little this season that earlier we found ourselves stumped to come up with his uniform number when filling out our scorecard (like we said, there are very few limits). And we do not know whether to be immediately thankful or not when the Orioles opt to intentionally walk him to load the bases and set-up the force at home; that is until we see Cora stepping towards the plate. For this, surely, without question, has to be it; has to be how this inning and this game is scripted to end. As Cora—who has been the biggest surprise among the position players this season, who has every Sox fan repeating the mantra *something good always happens when he's in there*, who is hitting something like .450 this season and leads the team if not the league in Opportunities Seized—steps to the plate and works the count in his favor, at 2-1.

Here a quick glance around the curving grandstand and down the line shows our heightened expectations reflected in every standing body, in the little bouncing movements and expectant side-to-side swaying, in the loud, constant clapping and shouts from every corner. It is the kind of moment—late in a close game, with everyone standing and that much closer to the action—when Fenway Park, always an intimate setting by any standard, takes on an especially close, distinctly personal feel. Particularly near the end of a day game where in the golden haze of afternoon sun one can see the players on the top step of the dugout, can see the faces of the fans behind them as they stand and clap, and the teenagers up front thump the low padded wall in foul ground. The entire scene appears to be tucked in close around the field—the vast undulating sea of the grandstand crowd lapping at the field like waves against the shore, as if this whole active moving body was somehow leaning directly over the action, pushing in, crowding the plate and hedging right over the third baseman's shoulder. It is the old ballpark's greatest charm, this intimacy, never so charming as in these few brief moments in the sun. Cora takes a called strike. The count 2-2 now, and almost despite ourselves we are thinking of all the many ways this situation can end well for the Sox. A walk, a single up the middle, a low liner over first, a little flare down the line, a bleeder through the infield, a gap shot, a wall ball, a hit-by-pitch or even a wild pitch would get the job done and tie the game. And surely Alex will come up with one of these, now that he swings and makes contact and (*but wait*—) hits a grounder towards second, too shallow for a double play but which Markakis charges onto, fields clean, and with Youk plowing down the line throws home as every female in the ballpark lets out a piercing scream at the same exact moment Hernández catches and tags, and home plate umpire Gary Cederstrom steps into a cloud of dust and punches Youkilis *out*. A low bellowing moan echoes out from the grandstand as Youk leaps up and twists violently in the air, and coming down spikes his dusty helmet in the dirt. It goes spinning off towards the backstop, through the on deck circle, and past the slender legs of Julio Lugo—as lithe and unthreatening as the pink bat leaned against his shoulder—as he steps forward into the dust now settling over home plate.

Suddenly we are no longer thinking of all the ways the Sox can win. This despite the fact that with two outs and the bases loaded all the possibilities so recently listed would still tie the game if not win it; a sensible enough notion which is of absolutely no comfort to anyone at such a moment. Even less comfortable a moment later as the count runs full and Lugo begins swatting foul balls into the right field roof boxes. And on second thought *this is an awfully cruel game*, you know, when a team can come this far and still have it all go for nothing. (We let go a nervous exhale and a feeble, unconvincing, *come on Julio*.) That is to say that all this, and just look at all the ways the game can still end in disappointment. A lazy fly ball to right, a foul ball hanging over the dugout, a grounder pretty much anywhere near a middle infielder, a swing and a miss, a called third strike, a chopper up the middle. Any one of these would transform our few bright, cheerful moments in the sun into an *almost*, a colorful *might have been* at the end of an otherwise gray weekend, pleasant enough while it lasted but still a *not quite* and therefore merely decorative. Which hardly seems fair at all. But this is the deal, as we well know; just as we know that it is this same perilous balance, on the edge of both victory and defeat (and the time that it gives us, with no clock ticking away, to consider all the possibilities on either side) which makes the whole experience so wonderful and terrifying and above all else *fun*. Fun in the truest sense of the word; in the way we tend to use it around children but hardly ever around adults, hardly ever in connection with ourselves; in a way that is free from pretext, subtext, context; in a way that is not programmed; in a way that is not a means to anticipate or adorn some other greater moment, but is instead its own ends, its own benefit, its own reward for having waited for a moment, and then given oneself over its enjoyment. It is not what we as mature grown-up sophisticated urban or semi-urban adults would prefer to call *pleasure*. It is *fun*—fun the way you remember fun being. And it is all this, even before Lugo swings— when suddenly it is no longer fun but terrifying as he chops the ball hard to the right side of the infield where Millar comes in and fields on the run and leaning away from the play throws side-armed to first as Ray and Lugo and the ball all arrive at once and then...oh and then, and then it is just wonderful.

We all leap up at once and shout as the ball shoots clean through into foul ground and we realize that we will never again, so long as we are fans, forget Eric Hinske's number as that beautiful red twelve blazoned across a broad white background turns down the third base line and heads for home with the winning run—and *oh my oh yes*, Sox win, 6-5. And our boys, slightly out of practice on the walk-off celebrations (their first of the season) rush from the dugout and try to somehow mob both Lugo and Hinske at once before deciding on Hinske, who they pile around as the Fenway loudspeaker cues up "Dirty Water" and everyone who isn't still shouting sings along. And here we are, amid a scene of tremendous composition, attractiveness, and charm. There are the players, of course, who leap about their teammates in the foreground; and there is the great arc of fans in the background, standing and clapping and shaking their heads with smiling disbelief; and there is over it all that special hazy light of the golden hour which drapes the field, softens the shadows blanketed around it, hangs lazy in the air between, and burnishes this entire happy scene with the warm glow of a day well spent.

As for us? Well, we do our part, and cheer and laugh and exchange high fives with the couple next to us, and shake our heads at each other because, really, what can you say? Finally they do say something about the two people who earlier left these two seats open, and we shake our heads at that, too. (Here we would like to think that we are above indulging in a bit of schadenfreude by wondering whether they, and the thousands of others who left early and missed not only the best part of the game but the *whole game*, made good time to their Sunday dinners; and whether they reached their cars before or after they heard the deep, echoing cheers of a classic Fenway rally; or whether they merely listened to the whole thing, cheers and all, on their traffic-free ride home. Again, we would *like* to think that we are above such thoughts and many others along similar lines; but beneath our quiet smile, we know better.)

Quickly though we move onto other, still more curious topics; such as the plight of Jeremy Guthrie and that dropped ball by Hernández. And with these it becomes clear that as wonderful as the win was for the Sox, it has been an absolutely brutal defeat for the Orioles and their fans. Starting with Guthrie, who lost both the shutout and the win (though we suppose his mother is still proud); and Hernández, who must have been thinking of that error from around 5-2 on; as well as Báez, who ignited the flames, and Ray, who once again only fanned them; and of course Perlozzo, who not only mismanaged the entire inning from the moment the ball dropped to the infield grass, but did so with such creativity, with such *brio*, as to achieve a sort of landmark in the long and colorful history of dubious managerial fumblings, the likes of which we may not see again for some time.

Yet no team, not even with suspect pitching and spectacularly poor management, can blow a five run lead all on its own. For even with all this, the odds were still heavily with the Orioles. Which is why we are not thinking of their misfortune as we turn to leave, but instead only of Papi's drive, Wily Mo's single, Drew and Youk's walks, Tek's double, Lugo flying down the line and Hinske coming all the way around to score, and another famous Fenway win. And you know what? Come to think of it, that Friday night game wasn't so bad, really. It was a pleasant enough evening after all. And we had a few little rallies there; and the crowd, while not particularly interested in the game, was at the very least in good spirits. Even yesterday, looking back on it now, wasn't so altogether unbearable. Sure it was cold; but we were at the ballpark, and Schilling looked good there for a bit, and the Sox rallied to win so does it really matter that it took so long? Not now, not really. Just as it doesn't much matter that the vast majority of this game took place in the quiet afternoon shadows. After all there is a great deal to be said about the redeeming quality of dramatic timing, and a good eye at the plate, and a little speed on the base paths. And for hanging around until that last out, which on certain days never comes but instead allows the final inning to linger on, and stay with us as we shuffle out through Gate E into the twilight over Brookline and Lansdowne, with us on our stroll through the happy crowd, with us as we slip away from Kenmore and into our night, and week, and towards those long summer months which on such a day stretch out endlessly into the fading sunlight before us.

Our Guy Jon

It is a manifestly human game. Try as we might to stand at an impersonal remove, and view those who play it as mere performers whose
skills we appreciate, and whose feats we enjoy solely for their athletic
merit and value only in so much as they advance the cause of our particular team, the human moment nevertheless intercedes—unannounced, inescapable, and in the end entirely welcome. Summers and
seasons pass by without so much of a hint of it; runs are cheered for and
bemoaned, games are won and lost, and the players who occasion them
are traded, released, resigned, called up, sent down, debut, retire,
come, go, and play on in different cities, under different hats, to the
cheers of different fans. And the ones wearing our hats today we root
for and call our own. Perhaps with a little grown-up wink to show that
in reality, we know better. Until the moment arrives when we are once
again reminded (with a little wink back from the game itself) that we
are not really so clever or grown-up after all.

Earlier this evening just such a moment showed up at Fenway
Park, as casual and relaxed as a lazy fly ball drifting out to shallow left.
Looking back, it seems we had been needing it, though one could not
exactly say why. Perhaps it has something to do with that banner flapping wildly above center field; or the by-now commonplace scene of a
full house at Fenway, a lead on the scoreboard, the word BOSTON
comfortably atop the standings on the left field wall; perhaps it is the
unprecedented ease with which this particular season has begun; or
perhaps (yes *just maybe*) it is simply because have added yet another sea-

son to our own career stat line. For there was a time, however many seasons ago, when the game was always and entirely personal. These were the early days of fanhood, when our favorite players really were our heroes, when they were older than us (they adults and we kids, instead of the other way around), and when we didn't know anything other than the great things we saw them do on the field, which was of course not only all we wanted to know but so far as we were concerned all there was *to know*. We taped up posters of them on our walls, collected and traded for their baseball cards regardless of value (they were always worth more to us), and spent much of the autumn school term sketching batters and pitchers across a spiral notebook, careful always to spend extra time on the script 'B' on the hat, and blocking out a bold red '21' across the back.

Only somewhere along the way, we got wise. We heard more, read more, understood more. We found out that the players on our team did *not* all live in the same neighborhood (as we once imagined, since that's how our teams were drawn up), did not play harder when we were in the stands (as we always assumed they would, since we cheered so hard), and were shockingly capable of playing just as hard for some other random team as they once had for ours (as we once deemed impossible, so deep was their love for our particular club). And so we became savvy, shrewd, knowing. And the more we began to internalize this new set of facts, and the more the players themselves began to remind us (relentlessly at times) of their own flawed humanity, the more we came to understand that the best way to approach the game—the wisest way, the most mature way, the really grown-up savvy adult way—was to enjoy the players for their play, and leave it at that.

And so we did. And most of the time, on most nights, we manage it just fine.

Until one cold and blustery night at the ballpark when a tall left-handed pitcher stands on the mound to begin the top of the ninth, without having allowed a single hit. He is there below us now, upright and athletic, the floodlights glowing against home whites that extend all the way to his shoetops, dark flat brim of his hat low and level over the eyes, red sleeves extending to wrists, left hand and glove propped chest-high before him. He looks in as the cheers rise around him, steps back, kicks, uncoils his effortless motion plateward and fires the ball high and wide, for ball one.

The Fenway crowd surrounding him, already standing, claps out constant albeit somewhat anxious encouragement. Though technically a sellout it is no longer (and may never have been) a full house. With a brisk wind whipping throughout the ballpark on an already cold raw night, it has been at best a horribly uncomfortable night for outdoor sport; and many a fan has ducked their hooded head and blanket-wrapped shoulders down the ramp and out long ago. Those who remained cross their cold arms, and shuffle their cold feet, and alternately blow into or sit atop their cold hands, and have done so throughout eight uncomfortable innings either because it goes against their very nature to leave before the final out, or (more likely) because they realize, or someone near them has made them realize, the very special nature of what has been unfolding on the field below.

We are among a third group, and despite the fact that we seem to have chosen one of the two or three most exposed and therefore windiest and least comfortable areas of the ballpark on which stand, we have stayed simply because we enjoy watching Jon Lester pitch. In any weather. The tall form, the long stride, the nice easy movement into the windup and then that long gliding release to the plate—that fantastic motion which somehow makes an incredibly difficult physical event appear entirely effortless. Like watching a jet at the tip of a long white streak pass silently overhead.

Tonight that motion has traveled in a straight line, producing a casual assortment of ground balls, lazy flies, and the occasional strike out mixed in. (Even these last appear relaxed when coming from Lester, who rather than overpower hitters seems to simply place the ball in a spot their bats cannot reach. He throws, they swing, and nothing happens at all.) In the middle innings the Red Sox pile on five runs in a bunch—nothing overly dramatic, just a few hits and a few walks and one absurdly misplayed infield pop-up—and that is it for the suspense of the outcome. So that through the middle innings there is room for another story to develop, told with one zero after another lining the scoreboard and one single, significant white zero fixed way out to the right. It is that zero we have kept our eye on (and that one specifically; for while there are at least two digital reminders of the scoreline, we still find the heavy green metal and white painted zero to be the most satisfying, and somehow a more definitive expression of the situation).

Meanwhile the game appears on its surface more or less unaltered. The Red Sox fielders, Lester chief among them, appear calm, unperturbed, at times almost bored. More so in the later innings, until we realize that this of course is compensation. As the situation becomes more serious, as the fifth turns into the sixth turns into the seventh, and the whole thing begins to seem more likely to happen than not, the players involved appear to grow increasingly less associated with the roles they play in its success. None more so than Lester himself, who far from being an outwardly emotional pitcher to begin with is, in this context, almost supernaturally tranquil out there in the very center of it all. Bottom of the ninth, three outs from history, his presence on the mound is no different than it was before his first pitch of the night.

He has, however, thrown a hundred or so pitches since; and perhaps because of this Lester walks the first Royals batter of the ninth, Esteban Germán (current BA .103), on four pitches, and though a handful of *that's alright Jon* shouts call out they are heard far too clearly above what has been an uncharacteristically subdued Fenway crowd. Again, Lester's performance, brilliant as it has been to this point, has been a subtle one, rather more like watching a soloist than a full orchestral production, and therefore the reaction to it controlled, measured, appreciative—more or less what one would expect for a nice violin concerto. Then there is the game around him which has been, it must be said, awfully dull (the Sox' five runs were not exactly a cavalry charge, and they have threatened nothing else). More than all this though there is the cold. The distinction is always a vague one but there is coolness, there is cold, and there is the nasty, bitter, forceful cold—the kind of cold that cares not for layers, or gloves, or hats; the kind of cold that is coming for you no matter where you stand; that has a way of getting beneath tightly wrapped scarves and finding little exposed creases between your sleeve and gloves; the kind of cold that feels somehow *aggressively* cold. It is that kind of cold, tonight. And so no, we do not blame this crowd for its low, hunched murmurs and its quick, hands only-out-as-long-as-they-have-to-be claps. It is to their credit that they are here at all. And though it would take quite a bit of dramatic heat to thaw such a crowd, you can feel, as Lester jumps ahead of the number nine hitter, Tony Peña Jr., that we're awfully close. On his 0-1 pitch Peña chops a high-hopper towards third. Mike Lowell takes two quick steps in, fields chest-high and fires a hard but slightly nervy throw to first, well wide, Youkilis lunges all the way out to his toes—momentarily appearing as if he would rather dislocate several major joints in his leg than allow his toe to leave the bag—and hangs on *in time* for the first out. Its breath held and finally released Fenway roars, and beneath it we clap out hard and thick applause.

Two outs away.

It is here that we suddenly recall (curiously enough, for we haven't though about this for months) how close we as Sox fans came to missing out on this moment, as we think back to that long stretch of winter where the possibility hung in the air that Jon Lester might in fact be traded. Might be dealt, moved, exchanged along with Players to Be Named Later and Cash Considerations for another left-handed pitcher. It was news which, in the cold dark recess of the offseason, was received with a mature nod. *That's the nature of the game*, we said. *He's a good young pitcher, but hey, it happens, right?* Still, this very grown-up stance never quite took. No matter how strong the argument that such a trade would improve our team immeasurably (and there was room to argue, based on the total cumulative long-term effects, that it would not), we never could get over the fact that while the name to be acquired was enticing to imagine across the back of a gray Red Sox road jersey, so too was it more than a bit discouraging to imagine our missing out on the career of Jon Lester, who after all was a Red Sox guy through and through. Lester, Ellsbury, Lowrie—these, we said, were *our guys*. What we meant was that they were purely Red Sox guys, players who had been adopted into and raised within our own farm system, and developed into professionals among our New England family of teams and players. These were guys who had come to baseball maturity in places like Lowell and Portland and Pawtucket. And besides all that, we sort of, you know, well yes—we actually like watching them play.

The third batter of the inning is David DeJesus. Lester, now working from the stretch, runs the count to 2-2 before DeJesus, reaching for an outside pitch, shoots a little roller down the first base line. A routine ground ball. Youkilis fields and makes towards the bag, and when his hand reaches up with the ball to call off a charging Lester we are already cheering; and continue to raise those cheers steadily higher as the ball comes back to Lester and he returns to the mound. And like that, it is no longer cold. Hands come out and are warmed with vigorous clapping, legs warm the body by a nervous bounce from one foot to the other, and the icy wind is beaten back by the sound of a thousand unfettered shouts. Everyone is up, everyone is cheering. As the woman before us looks back at her friend with bright excited eyes, and holding up a single finger, silently mouths the words, *one more*.

And right here, we give in. With one out to go and Fenway echoing out its reverberating cheers and Jon Lester down there on the mound we cannot help but care, cannot help but allow ourselves to recognize that it is not just another game, it is not just another pitcher, it is not just a baseball player who we are rooting for because he is on our team. With one out to go we give in to the fact that the pitcher on the mound is in fact a person whom we admire and respect and feel great affection for, not as a pitcher, but as a young man and a person. So no. Not for a moment will we stand here and pretend he is like any other player, or deny that his story, that what he has been through and survived and beaten raises him immeasurably in our esteem and heightens the significance of this very moment. Not for one instant will we forget his battle with cancer. Not for one second longer will we pretend it does not mater. It does. Of course it does, immensely. Jon Lester, the young man and not the pitcher, was the one who at 22-years-old gave a heartrending press conference in which he sat alone before a room full of adults and explained the nature of his life-threatening disease, and the steps he would take to fight it. Jon Lester, the young man and not the pitcher, went through that battle away from the public eye and then, largely out of its reach, reclaimed his body and his left arm and his competitive spirit to the point where he could not only return to his profession, but thrive. And it is Jon Lester, the young man and not the pitcher, who we are thinking of when we finally give way to the deep humanity of the moment and cup our hands to our mouth and yell out with everything we've got *Come on Jon! One more!*

Alberto Callaspo steps into the batter's box for the Royals. A rookie. Fifty-seven total at bats in the Major Leagues. Now digging in under the bright lights of Fenway Park, beneath an echoing clamor of sound, at the center of the storm. And even before the first pitch is thrown, we know. Foul ball, strike two swinging, ball up, foul ball, and then it comes. Lester kicks and throws, Callaspo swings and misses badly, and quiet as an exhale *he's done it.* Fenway cascades its applause down through the cold night air. Lester holds both hands wide and for the first time all night shouts and smiles, and soon he is embraced and hoisted into the air by his catcher Jason Varitek, his teammates rush in to surround him (the façade down, the emotions forward, their happiness for a teammate and friend irrepressible) and all around them Fenway cheers on—for the performance, for the moment, for something very close to a miracle.

Every celebration is a bit different, a bit particular to the moment and achievement being celebrated. Some are wild, unhinged, almost out-of-body in their delirium of sudden joy. That had been the scene not so long ago when Clay Buchholz accomplished the seemingly impossible, and threw a no-hitter in his second Major League start. That celebration was something like an explosion, the tension ratcheted higher and the sense of utter disbelief more acute. Not this one. This one is composed, controlled, and perhaps above all else, grateful. You can see it in the crowd. We are not jumping about and mobbing one another (as we did after the last out of the Buchholz no-hitter, so enthralled were we by its spectacle), but instead stand and applaud—

loud and long, but still applause rather than cheering. You can see it in his teammates, too, down there below, who after they are done beating him senseless disperse out around and, one by one, each give him a solid congratulatory embrace. These are not hugs; they are big firm embraces—thick, solid, both arms around and one good slap on the back for a job well done. In them we see a clear reflection of this very human moment, the sentiment one which anyone who has followed this team and this player understands in an instant.

It all comes to fore with the skipper. Most of the players and a few of the coaches have filed away, but another figure lingers in the background, hands in pockets, chomping his gum, waiting his turn. Then, when a teammate steps away, the manager steps forward and Terry Francona takes Jon Lester's face in both hands and smiles, and pulls him in one aggressive tug into a tight embrace; one that last longer than the others, one with more intent to it, one in which you can tell by the angle of the head that the manager is saying something to his player and by the body language of the moment you can tell what that something is from every corner of the ballpark. When they finally release we glance at a television above us and see the emotion in the eyes of both manager and players, and suddenly, in the cold windy air high above, we too begin to blink.

It is a wonderful moment. Affectionate, parental, utterly genuine. The emotion all there, right on the surface, that overwhelming pride one takes in watching someone close to you rise up, not necessarily to achieve but to face a challenge and battle back. (Later on Francona will say, rather wonderfully, "He's not a great kid because he pitched a no-hitter. He's a great kid because he's a great kid.") And if perhaps we do not know the specific emotional bond between manager and player, we may guess at it well enough; for we feel something of the very same emotion. You see Jon Lester, the young man and not the player, is one of our guys. Someone we know; someone we cheer for not merely because he wears our hat but because he is so utterly deserving of our cheers. Which is to say that we care about him. We want to him to do well. And we are so grateful to see him pitch every night he goes out there, much less nights like tonight when he goes out there and achieves beyond even our expectations, that the big parental embrace Francona gives him before he tips his cap to the crowd is felt by all who share in his story.

It is, and always has been, a manifestly human game. We learn that as children, then somewhere along the way forget it because we believe ourselves too mature, too knowing, too sophisticated for something so banal as sentiment (for nothing is less sophisticated than to deeply and openly *care*); then, at a certain age, on certain nights at the ballpark, we are forced to relearn this lesson all over again by the likes of Jon Lester. Perhaps some do not. Surely to some fans the remove between the names associated with hits and runs and outs, and the men who create them is as permanent as it is distant. Perhaps to some it does not matter what a player does outside of his OBP or ERA, and perhaps the style in which he does it is likewise irrelevant. Perhaps it does not matter, one way or another, the respect he commands on the field or what caliber of person he is off it. We have tried this line ourselves, and found it of no use. Instead, we who have learned how often our better hopes in the men who play this game are disappointed, have also learned how valuable and enriching it can be when those same hopes are renewed and even exceeded. We have relearned, that is, how to care. Here as elsewhere this caring may be viewed by some merely as misplaced sentiment; as simplicity; as innocence, a childish state either willfully reclaimed or never fully shed. We can live with these accusations and many others. And not mind a bit, so long as they save us from the fate of growing cold, aloof, impersonal and unfeeling. We can live with them in the hopes that we may never grow so sophisticated and unsentimental as to see a night such as this as merely historical, to view a moment such as the one playing out before us as mere *accomplishment*, or to see the likes of Jon Lester as merely a ballplayer. No no, this is not the line for us. There is far too much warmth there for us to remain in the cold; far too much worthy of care for us to resist the caring part. So we will go on, all grown up and still blinking back tears because twenty-six outs were made without allowing a hit, still shouting out things like *'Atta boy Jon!* to someone we have never met, still feeling an overwhelming sense of pride in young men like our guy, Jon Lester.

SUMMER

The Perfect Game

Pittsburgh at Fenway
15 June 2005

(with apologies to Mr. Nick Hornby)

A game can be made memorable in any number of ways; perhaps in as many ways as there are for a game to be played. Often games will remain with us long after based on artistic merit alone (this the picturesque afternoon walk-off); other times on their rich baseball substance (that the flawless pitchers' duel); others still, particularly around this neighborhood, on the captivating narrative drive with which they carry us through another nine-inning comedy or tragedy or epic (this the relentless series of runs and rallies, errors and blown-leads, late pitching changes and rallies and blown leads and triumphant rallies back). Perhaps it will be an individual performance, or an individual inning, or even a single play of brilliance that will send us buzzing out of the ballpark, knowing that we will never forget what we just saw (saying as we go, *what a great game*, by which we so often mean, *what a great finish*, because the forgettable game which preceded it was wiped clean by the redeeming qualities of its finale). And then there are all those other reasons. All those personal bits. That we watched it with a very good friend; that we arrived late and missed the first run; that it coincided with some particular moment in that particular summer and thus distinguished an otherwise ordinary 8-2 loss on a Tuesday night as unique, special, cherished. There is no secret formula for how.

Yet the more time we spend around the game, the more we discover that there are certain definable elements we always find particularly satisfying to see, and that we look for (knowingly or not) each ballpark has us leaning back and breathing in a satisfied air as we nod and, looking around us, confirm to ourselves, *what a great night for baseball*. A particularly clever slide home has us shaking our head with a quiet *that's good stuff there*. A diving stop by the shortstop and throw to first has us describing it over the phone after the game to friends not nearly as excited about it as they should be (not to mention relating its difficulty point-by-point the next day to those with little appreciation for the finer points of infield play, and perhaps even giving little ersatz reenactments of it in our living room to those who we suspect are only being polite with their tired little, *no that's—that's great, really*). A sublime bunt rolls over the grass precisely equidistant from the pitcher, second baseman, and first baseman, as the runner on third comes home at a jog and we offer coolly appreciative applause along with the repeated one-word review of, *oh brilliant, just brilliant*. And an uneventful Tuesday night win in June is entirely forgotten, save for the long home run by Manny in the fourth that both tied the game and give the Sox the lead, and that we can still see sailing up into the floodlights even now, years later. These then are the baseball elements we find ourselves particularly drawn to, the plays and moments and situations which together map our very attraction to the game. So that as we stand and watch the early innings of a game unfold, and see one or two of these plays fall into place and then perhaps another, and looking over our scorecard realize that the game is now situated *just so*, we suddenly find ourselves standing up just a bit straighter, raising an eyebrow or two, and saying to no one in particular, *well now here we go, this is something*.

No game is perfect, of course. The furious and desperately late rally to win is preceded by seven slack, lifeless innings of the worst in baseball monotony. The bright promise of three crisp entertaining innings is instantly quelled an inning later by a dour, depressing, six run, two pitching change, walk-the-bases-loaded, full-scale bullpen meltdown. And the thrilling back and forth struggle filled with one acrobatic defensive play after another and played under a lovely summer sky is, four innings later, postponed by rain.

And yet somewhere in the deep subconscious of our baseball minds (there between the Opening Day 87' program and a signed Candy Maldonado card), we have an idea of what it all might look like, put together. What if the lively start and the thrilling finish appeared on the same scorecard? What if that scorecard had felt nothing but sunlight, warm summer air, and the unhurried markings of a comfortable hand? What if, in the middle of this very same scorecard, a play was circled and footnoted to be forever remembered as *that* play? What if *that* play took place in *that* game, on *that* night? What we are doing here, in these midday or late night wanderings, is creating a mental idea which, though we may not exactly refer to it as such, is something very much like a Platonic ideal—our own form of 'The Perfect Baseball Game.'

Of course as mortal fans living in the World of Becoming (not to mention the world of the hanging slider), we never have and never will see this form on dirt and grass. At best all we can hope to see are its shadows, flickering across the field below, which by their particular shapes and sizes only *suggest* the perfection which exists only in what the patron saint of this interior stadium once so eloquently called the *green fields of the mind.* There the fire; and here at Fenway, the shadows.

And what of them? What shapes and movements do we have in mind as we walk expectantly down Yawkey up the concourse ramp? What distant half-remembered plays do we hope to one game see repeated on our scorecard? What exactly, as we stare in with arms crossed and scorecard blank at the first pitch, are we looking for?

(And furthermore would one ever take the time to list, review, revise and formalize such preferences? So that when one is asked—even rhetorically, even by oneself—*what exactly, as we stare in with arms crossed and scorecard blank at the first pitch, are we looking for?* one could actually answer with) As many as possible, if not all, of the following:

1. *Tolerable Weather*. Not necessarily postcard perfect, or sunny or even warm. It just cannot be so cold, or so windy, or so damp as for the weather to make itself a presence in the game. Unlike football, where

shoddy conditions can enhance the mystique of a good game, in base-ball it serves only to make its play erratic and its fans uncomfortable.

2. *Tolerable Fans.* How to put this? Perhaps it is best to begin by saying that a good crowd can practically make a game all by itself. Active, engaged, dynamic, irresistibly spirited, and always with a spry sense of humor, the right crowd is the thirty-five-thousand voice chorus of live baseball; it enlivens the general ballpark atmosphere and height-ens every event on the field with its color and enthusiasm and wit. The wrong crowd, does not. In fact the wrong crowd (or even the wrong section in the right crowd) can blot the entire experience, often to the point of ruin, through nothing less than *becoming* that experience. Which is to say that while the great game is enhanced by a great crowd, it does not necessarily need it; and all we really care to remem-ber of any crowd is that it was awake, engaged, and perhaps lent a few moments of levity to enliven a slow middle inning. Being able to recall anything more than that about a crowd, is almost never a good sign.

3. *An Early Sox Deficit.* At some point in the first three innings we need to be reminded that the Red Sox might very well lose this game, and that they will not (as we tend to expect of them) simply roll-up the opposition just because we happens to be in the stands and there's tol-erable weather. So getting down early, while obviously not something one can root for, is at the same time not entirely a bad thing. The deficit should be more than a run so that the impression is clearly made, but less than five as to avoid the risk of losing hope (not to men-tion interest). A nice, early *and after one-and-a-half the Sox trail 3-0* is ideal.

4. *Brilliant Defensive Play.* At least two. Preferably to end an inning. Not only because it gives a wider berth for applauding and appreciat-ing the work itself, but because it is such a great exit cue—as if the brilliance of the play itself ended the inning (*and on that note...*), rather than its being the third out. (We are admittedly partial to clever infield/catcher work as opposed to acrobatic outfield play, but this is

a personal preference only and in any event with two outs and runners on we'll take what we can get, so long as it is done with style.)

5. *Multiple Lead Changes and Ties*. A pair of each would be ideal, but in general both teams need to lead at least once and there needs to be at least one tie (0-0 notwithstanding). A bit of back and forth is the lifeblood of all healthy sporting competition, no matter the sport, and aside from the 1-0 lead that is held precariously inning after inning, and the 6-1 deficit that is erased by one furious rally, we'd just as soon have the pendulum swing back and forth throughout.

6a. *The Sox Blow a Lead*. Not that one ever hopes for such a thing. But when this does happen (and let's face it this is bound to happen often enough regardless) it serves to remind us how fragile these small leads are, and how easily they can be lost. Now, just as with the early deficit, things need to stay proportional. Blowing a one-run lead hardly shocks anyone into such realizations, and blowing anything more than three is rather demoralizing and ruins the effect entirely. Two runs is perfect. Depending on who is pitching even a two-run lead can have a swagger about it, a blowout in the making, surely; and giving it back reminds us that two runs are but two runs, to be gained and lost and regained with a swing of the bat.

6b. *The Sox Hold a Lead or Tie / Get Themselves Out of a Situation*. The later the better. Best case scenario here would be bases loaded with a one-run lead, two outs, and the opposition's most formidable hitter at the plate. The potential for disaster in these types of situations is palpable throughout the ballpark, and so the subsequent escape from danger (the release of tension) is the same thrilling rush one gets from the clutch hit, only in reverse.

7. *A Bit of Baseball Strategy*. No matter the variety. Sacrifice bunt, hit and run, suicide squeeze, double steal, pitch out. Just about anything, really, so long is there is *a play on* at some point in the game. Those of us born with National League sensibilities love seeing the game played

well with legs and arms, but also like to see the brain come into play every so often, particularly if that brain belongs to the manager. Old-fashioned, perhaps, but our preference is to see the manager do a bit more than make out the lineup card and pull his starter after a hundred pitches.

8. *A Home Run That Either Ties the Game or Gives the Sox the Lead.* All Sox home runs are exciting, no matter the situation or score; but there is nothing quite like the thunderclap of a home run that changes the balance of the game in an instant. The roar is always a bit louder, a bit deeper, a bit more appreciative. It is tied and then, suddenly, it is not. Best of all of course is the home run which does both—which ties and unties the game with one quick, decisive swing. Down a run with a man on is the classic set-up for this (nothing really going on, bases empty; then a walk, light applause, next guy steps up and *bang*, every-thing changes). Two on and trailing by two is even better, and so forth.

9. *A Grievous Call by the Umpire, Ardently Disputed.* Not for everyone, surely. And we by no means recommend more than one per game and would just as soon it take place early on and not directly effect the out-come. (And fall short of genuine *shenanigans*, which is a different topic altogether.) Still, one has to admit there is something oddly invigor-ating about a healthy shout-out along the first base line. If we had to pick we would always have the call go against the visitors and be bla-tantly, criminally bad. In which case the opposing manager's sense of indignation is piqued, and more likely to stoke him towards apoplectic fits of hat tossing and dirt kicking, all to the greater delight of the Fen-way fans who (knowing the umpire blew the call) prod him on even more. A dubious wish, perhaps. But baseball is a sport with a keen, often dry sense of humor; and the old vaudeville duet of The Wildly Indignant Manager vs. The Incompetent but Unmoved Umpire is one of the game's most reliable crowd pleasers.

10a. *The Sox Blow at Least One Golden Opportunity.* Much in the same way as 6a, these situations can only be appreciated if complimented by later events, and even then only in retrospect. So that once 10b is accomplished, we look back and see that it was this situation which set-up the final dramatic resolution. If one were to orchestrate it the ideal scenario would have the two opportunities perfectly mirror each other—same number of runners on base, same number of outs, same score, same batter at the plate. That way when the opportunity comes around the second time we have the imprint of that first failure still firmly impressed on the mind, and know acutely just how wrong it can all go, making success all the sweeter when...

10b. *The Sox Rally*. Again, the later the better. The longer we sit and think on it—the longer we contemplate the failure of our pitchers to prevent runs, the longer we consider the seemingly impossible scenario of our hitters producing runs, the longer we have to calculate the dropped half game in the standings, to stare at the out-of-town and find the Yankees up by fifteen, to lower our expectations first to wild card status and then (if this goes on long enough) to wonder whether it will be next year or the year after before we can once again legitimately hope for the playoffs—and the less outs and therefore fewer opportunities we have of avoiding all this, the more satisfying the release when the Sox rally back and win it. There is simply nothing better, really.

11. *A Signature Play*. This is crucial. Surprisingly, all the of the above could fall into place, and in just the right order, and the game could still slip from our memory if not for that one, singularly thrilling play which gives it the mental stamp of individuality. Every great game needs that one play we can hold onto, and point to and say, *oh right, that was the game where...* It can be any type of play—a great at bat, a brilliant display of base running, a wonderful defensive play—so long as it has a bit of style to it and a distinct, unrepeatable quality which allows it to stand out as *that* play.

12. *The Sox Win*. Obviously.

This then, is what we look for. The Platonic ideal. The game as it exists in only the green fields of the mind. The envisioned and ever invisible form—Baseball, Perfect.

And it does not take many seasons of disappointment to learn that it is both unrealistic, if not unkind to the general fan psyche, to actually *rely on* any of this, nevermind the whole. One simply cannot get along as a fan if one sets conditions on the game which must be met or else (or else one ends up being a Christmas and Easter baseball fan, only showing up for Opening Day and October). No, the key phrase is *as many as possible*. Knowing that on some nights even one will be one too many for the game to manage. Usually, we are given at least the one. Perhaps two. Sometimes even three, on a really good night.

Then, one unsuspecting night in the middle of an unassuming season, it happens. We come to the ballpark just as we do on any other night; find our Standing Room Only spot and fill out our scorecard just as we do on any other night; the team takes the field, the umpire point, and the game begins just as every other game does. It opens well enough. It continues well enough. And then one by one, play by play, inning by inning, it all falls into place. And we find ourselves watching and scoring and experiencing that rarest of nights where we are allowed (with a peek over our shoulder to the fire) to see what it might look like, all together—on the same field, in the same nine innings, in something very close to the perfect game.

Perhaps it is a lingering baseball hangover from the Sox's first visit to Wrigley Field, or simply the lethargy built up over three lifeless games with the Reds to open the homestand, but not much seemed to be expected of this night. The Pirates are... Well, we don't really know who the Pirates are, exactly. (Somehow they have managed to remain anonymous in our baseball conscience, mixed in as they are among their more famous divisional relatives. That, and they have not been to Fenway, and therefore have not *really* existed, since the 1903 World Series.) Still it is a Friday night at Fenway, and the weather is cool but tolerably comfortable (1), and anyway you never know.

The game opens with lively start, two quick outs by Sox starting pitcher Wade Miller followed by an innocent looking infield single by Jason Bay (accompanied by the kind of *wow, that guy can run* reaction you get a lot of in interleague play), and then two not-so-innocent doubles which give the Pirates a quick lead (3), which they then add to with a nifty double steal (7) to make it 3-0 before the capacity crowd at Fenway has even had a chance to settle in.

In the second Miller himself settles in, retiring the side with only a hit-by-pitch mixed in and with a good deal of help from his second baseman Mark Bellhorn, who makes a fantastic charging play on a soft grounder, scooping and firing in one reflex motion to just get Bay at first for the final out of the inning (4). Properly inspired, the Sox orchestrate their own two-out rally in the second. Manny singles to lead off, followed by a Nixon fielder's choice and a Millar fly out. Then, with two outs and after a lengthy at bat, Varitek singles to center to push first and third. Bill Mueller then doubles to left, bringing Nixon around to score the Sox first run and, just as important, setting up second and third with two outs and Mark Bellhorn at the plate.

So you're thinking, at 3-1, a hit and we're tied and so *come on Bellhan! whadaya say kid! base hit baby!* But up in the count he takes a pitch here and a pitch there and (inevitably) runs the count full. And now all we can think is: *walk walk walk, don't strike out don't strike out don't strike out.* And he doesn't. Instead he takes that familiar hook swing and pops one high out to right, lofting up it sails over the low right field wall, bounces once in the bullpen, and ties the game and gives the Sox the lead—all at once (5, 8, 10b).

After which excitement the game cools. Only for an inning or so. Enough time for us to go to the restroom, grab something to drink (and to think to ourselves as we wait in line, hands in pockets, *not a bad start, this*), and return to our seats in the top of the fourth to watch:

The Pirates pull a run back with a walk, two ground outs that each move the runner over and a Freddy (we hardly knew thee) Sanchez single to center to tie the game (5). It stays that way, tied at four, for all of five batters as the Sox come up with another run in the bottom of the inning on a Nixon single and Mueller triple to retake the lead, 5-4 (5).

Another inning-long intermission follows in the sixth. Giving us another moment to relax, another chance to look around and find the Fenway crowd active and engaged and agreeable between innings (2), and another opportunity to reflect on an already fine looking scorecard. Here we find the action perfectly balanced, the runs evenly distributed, everything in proportion. Weight up front with the Pirates early rally, leveled by the Sox rally the following inning, space in the third, two counterbalancing runs in the fourth, with space on the other side in the fifth and sixth. Altogether a game with a pleasing shape. One worth admiring between innings, one deserving of the approving smile we give it, and one not to be passed over—as one would not pass over a favorite portrait or landscape—without a last, lingering look back before moving on.

On into the seventh and another very sparse, very Steel City type run as the Pirates go single, double, groundout to pull in a run through the back door and retie the game (5, 6a). Moments later they threaten to untie it as reliever Mike Myers hits Ryan Doumit to put runners on first and third with two outs and Rob Mackowiak up. On a 1-2 count, and with Fenway on its feet, Myers strikes out Mackowiak to end both the threat and the inning (6b). So that we suddenly find ourselves—as the shadows of so many baseball ideals begin to flicker across the field—standing up a bit straighter, raising an eyebrow or two, and saying to no one in particular, *well now here we go, this is something*.

With both starters replaced and the game tied at 5-5, and everyone involved aware that this is all shaping up to be something pretty good, the game moves into what will become its centerpiece inning—the top of the seventh. Timlin is on in relief for the Sox, and gets José Castillo to ground out for the first out before giving up a single to Humberto Cota. The next batter, Jack Wilson, grounds innocently back to Timlin who spins and fires to second (for what looks to be a sure inning-ending double play) and as Bellhorn straddles the bag he is already looking to first, already has his glove back and his hand in the position of one recording the out at second, while at the same time transferring the ball from glove to hand before firing over to first for two. And he is still in this same position when he looks down to the dirt behind the bag, and there finds a small white baseball resting at the feet of second base umpire C.B. Bucknor. Who nevertheless inexplicably pumps his fist to signal the force out. Immediately we look to the Pirate dugout, where manager Lloyd McClendon has emerged and now strides with purpose across the infield. True, he does not dispute the call as vigorously or with as much vitriol as he has every right to (at which we regret to admit our slight disappointment), perhaps because he had a bad angle on the play himself. Nevertheless he knows the call was blown, and so does Bellhorn, and in all likelihood so does Bucknor; so the whole thing is a bit ridiculous at the Major League level and by the time McClendon stomps off we are laughing (more at what he is going to think when he sees the replay, but still plenty good enough for 9).

Timlin, perhaps rattled by a play that very well could have ended the inning and very well should have ended in disaster (the fortunate out call was so quick, and such a gift, that we all instantly forgot that the play should have been two), walks the next batter, Matt Lawton, on five pitches. So now there are two outs with runners at first and second, and Freddy Sanchez at the plate. With the count 1-1 Sanchez lines a garden variety single to shallow left center that sends both runners off and has the Pirates third base coach immediately wheeling Wilson around third; Manny cuts it off in the gap and fires a quick throw home, clean through but a bit up the line and Varitek stretches a leg across the plate and backhands the throw just as the crowd crescendos and Wilson slides in feet-first, jackknifes wildly over his outstretches shin guard, and rolls onto his back in the dusty far side of the box. Varitek stands, reaches over, and tags him (he never did get to the plate) for the final out (6b).

It is one of those plays which we instantly question whether we saw it correctly; and it has Fenway cheering out in equal parts appreciation and bemused wonder over what exactly we are cheering in appreciation of. (*Wait, how in the...?*) Because the throw was off, and because

Varitek was so extended, and because the plate looked so wide and so white and so exposed, it seemed Wilson simply had to score. Making the immediate question *how did he not?* and the immediate answer *because Jason Varitek is a damn good catcher, that's how.* In replay the form is perfect: glove up, leg extended flush against the front edge of the plate, knee firmly planted (all textbook stuff). And yet the truly astounding and for the most part underappreciated part of the play is the catch; because while blocking the plate is one thing, keeping it blocked while performing a first baseman's stretch and backhanded dig is quite another. All this, and Varitek caught it clean, held his ground, and came up with the ball in his glove and his home plate untouched by the threatening Pirate. It is a play of distinctive brilliance, and reminds us of no other. A play that will be discussed at length (as it is already being discussed at length in the stands around us) tomorrow morning and on many summer days hereafter. For we know how these things work. Anytime there is a play at the plate, and maybe the catcher had to reach for the tag or had his knee in front of the plate or even just held on, the baseball mind will sort through its clutter of images and stories and find this one very near the top; and as the conversation turns (as it in-evitably does turn among fans) to the best-, the most-, the greatest-, we will cross our arms and with an eye to the field, and wait our turn to casually drop in *that* play—*you remember, that play Tek made one year against the Pirates*... (11).

And on that note, we sing.

As always, the crowd lets us know how things are going. The traditional middle-of-the-eighth singing of *Sweet Caroline* being, among other things, an excellent barometer of fan interest and enthusiasm. For on certain nights nearly the entire crowd will stand for the singing. Other times only a few uninhibited fans—typically drunk, typically coupled, always young—will rise and wave a crooning arm about and theatrically reach out (*reaching out...*) and press a hand to their chest (*touching me...*) and throw their arm around (*touching you...*) the person next to them who one presumes is either their significant other or a prime candidate for that position. While the seated crowd around them watches and laughs a bit, and taps their feet or bobs their heads in the general vicinity of the rhythm, and maybe mutters a word or two but only really adds their full voice, predictably, to the three downbeats of *so good, so good, so good.* This on a slightly below average night, with a slightly below average crowd. On a good night, more people than not will be standing, and if not actually singing along at very least swaying back and forth and moving their lips to indicate that they really would sing along, if only they remembered the words. On an even better night, everyone is up. Everyone is singing (even those who do so ironically, for it hardly matters in its effect). And a great many people including those who are not so drunk (but perhaps wish to be), who are not so coupled (but perhaps wish to be), and who are not so young (but may feel a bit younger at that particular moment) are *reaching out*, and *touching me*, and *touching you*, and making motions which are not at all consistent or even rhythmic but still manage to signify what we will go ahead and call dancing. This in the grandstands. In the concourses. Right out into the aisles. Yet the truest test is still to come; for when the visiting team retakes the field and the batter makes towards the plate and the music ends with a rousing *so good! so good! so good!* the great crowds—the happiest, the liveliest, the most spirited of all Fenway crowds—will not stop and applaud but carry on singing, acapella, for as long as they cares to. On a warm summer night, particularly on a warm summer Friday night, they have been known to carry on for an entire verse. The music stops, the crowd sings on, *good times never seem so good...*

And the happy self-congratulatory cheers roll right on into the ensuing Sox rally as Rentería

lines one off Salomón Torres down the right field corner and is cheered all the way around to third. John Grabow relieves Torres and gets Ortiz to pop out, then walks Manny intentionally to bring up the lefty Nixon. Faced with the lefty v. lefty matchup Francona makes the tactical switch to a right-handed hitter, pinch-hitting Jay Payton for Nixon and prompting McClendon to go to his right-handed pitcher, Rick White; which managerial workings bring everything all the way back around to the match-up the Pirates wanted in the first place— now righty v. righty instead of lefty v. lefty (7). And for once, it actually works. Payton takes a strike, then a ball, then grounds into an inning-ending 6-4-3 double play, wasting Rentería's lead-off triple and blowing a golden opportunity to break the tie (10a).

Foulke then comes on and makes quick work of the Pirates in the ninth, bringing the game to its final frame still tied, 5-5. Millar leads off the inning, and before things even get underway there is something mildly amusing about the sight of White, who is a burley character with a brushy goatee and wears the rarely seen (but impressively bold) 00 as his uniform number, facing in at Millar, who looks like, well, like Kevin Millar. And for a moment we feel as if maybe, in just the right light, if we could squint our eyes just so, we could easily be at some late night after work Beer League softball game; until White delivers, and this remarkably professional at bat begins.

White's first pitch is a ball, as is the second, and the third Millar fouls off for strike one. He takes a strike, leveling the count at 2-2. Then fouls another off. Then another. Takes a ball. Then fouls off another. And then yet *another*. And now the crowd is brimming up onto its feet with applause, recognizing the work being done, and away again Millar swats another foul, the tenth pitch of the at bat. At this point Millar has in a way already won, has hung in and battled and done enough work to deserve a hit. The game, as we all know, does not always reward such work, but this time it does as Millar digs in for one more and finds a pitch outside (the same pitch he had fouled off at least twice, only this time slightly over the plate), swats it down the right field line, and cruises into second with a well-deserved a double. And here we are, with *all the makings* before us.

Youkilis runs for Millar. Varitek lays down a beautiful sacrifice that White, indecisive for just that one decisive instant, misplays into a single. Setting up first and third with nobody out. Mueller is intentionally walked to load the bases. Bellhorn grounds out into a fielder's choice that cuts down Youkilis at home but still leaves the bases loaded for Johnny Damon who now faces a one out, bases loaded situation in a tie game. The *exact same* situation faced by Jay Payton an inning earlier. McClendon makes one final move to bring in the lefty Mike González, apparently to allow us more time to think about that

Payton double play ball. It is right there, the winning run, ninety feet away. And yet we know a ground ball is all it would take to ruin it; and we know exactly what that ruin fells like since we *just* experienced it back in the eight. So that there is a little leap of anxiety as Damon does in fact chop González's third pitch back up the middle, past the pitcher and into the infield grass it short-hops and rolls just short of the second baseman and shortstop and just far enough to bring Mueller sprinting in safely from third to break the tie (5), complete the comeback (10a), and end this nearly perfect night of baseball with a Red Sox win (12).

Go Johnny Go

Oakland at Fenway
8 July 2004

The situation itself—runner on first, two outs, tie game—is not inherently dramatic. Not in traditional baseball terms, where the majority of drama is based on anticipation, built step by step over the course of an inning. A seven-pitch walk, a pop out to second, a flare single, a strikeout, a stolen base—nothing overly exciting—in combination produce the classic second and third with two outs situation, the tension built in layers of expectancy as the runner moves closer and closer to home, with fewer and fewer chances left for him to reach it. And so as Johnny Damon loops around first and stops, steps back onto the bag, knocks fists with and then gets a pat on the back from first base coach Lynn Jones, he does not by himself present a terribly dramatic situation. Fenway, recognizing this fact, applauds but is not overly harried by his presence. We are encouraged by it, to be sure; but we also know that the road to extra innings is paved with two out singles that end up going nowhere. And we know that if this is really to be the evening's endgame there will likely need to be at least two more moves involved; a wild pitch to move Damon into scoring position at second, a flare single by Bill Mueller (now batting) to create first and third, a double to create second and third with two outs and Ortiz coming up (now *that* would be dramatic). Alone Damon represents only the possibility of something, and the potential to *possibly, maybe,* if one or two other things happen then *perhaps* become something more (become the *started it off by-* to Ortiz's *ended it dramatically with-*). And so it is with reserved curiosity that we watch Damon stand on first with his thick forearms crossed, one hand worrying the side of his beard, peering from beneath the low brim of his helmet across the infield to third base coach Dale Sveum. Perhaps he is getting the sign to steal. *Now there's something.* Damon has already flashed his speed on the base paths tonight, twice beating out infield singles, and perhaps he is looking to create something by himself, putting pressure on the defense and giving Mueller a chance to win it with a single. (Perhaps.)

Damon leans low, hangs down his hands, and takes his lead off first.

Where we must leave him, temporarily, as the scene around him needs scenery, the story before him needs backstory, and the handful of players who have had a role developing it need to be properly introduced. First among them is David Ortiz, who opened the game's scoring in the first by golfing a low fastball from Oakland starter Rich Harden deep into the Red Sox bullpen, as is his habit. Two innings later his sidekick, Manny Ramirez (Boo Boo to Ortiz's Yogi Bear), reached out and hit the same pitch, this time low and away to the righty, into nearly the same spot in the Red Sox bullpen, as is *his* habit, to put the Sox up 4-0 early.

The duel home runs restarted the open air block party Fenway has hosted at Oakland's expense over the last two nights (the Sox took the first two games of the series 22-3 on aggregate, with both games devoid of even the slightest moment of tension for Sox fans) and a cloudy, slightly breezing but nonetheless comfortable Friday night at Fenway promised to turn into a laid back and carefree celebration of our recent turn of fortune. Then did exactly that two innings later when Kevin Millar lofted a fly to left that Eric Byrnes just missed, both ball and outfielder clanging off the wall with the former rolling into center as Ortiz and Manny (Yogi and Boo Boo, up to their old tricks again) came around to score to make it 7-1. With a little over half the game played the route was on, and the semi-annual Maybe This Really Is The Year (For Real) Party had officially begun at Fenway.

Meanwhile Curt Schilling continued to work effectively if somewhat arduously through the first four innings, giving up hits but not runs. Mark Kotsay set the tone for Oakland's night by leading off the game with a long drive off the wall (its loud clap creating only a ripple of concern among the still settling Fenway crowd, which looked up from its hot dog and beverage sorting with a collective, *what was that?*). Kotsay ended up on second with a lead-off double, only to have given himself an excellent viewpoint from which to watch the next three Oakland batters strike out in order—swinging, looking, and swinging. The next three innings followed in similar fashion for the Athletics, who continued to have wonderful success reaching every base but home. (By the end of the night Oakland had at least one hit and had left at least one runner on in each of the first nine innings, totaling fourteen hits and ten men left on base. Sox fans, having endured a half season of such frustration, could have perhaps empathized with the Athletics' misfortunes had we not been so busy wildly celebrating our 7-1 lead.) This pattern was interrupted briefly but emphatically in the fifth by Byrnes, who after a long at bat in which he fouled off a number of Schilling pitches in a number of spots, both inside and outside the strike zone, finally got a fastball away and yanked it over the left field wall, just right of the foul pole. Byrnes— athletic, twitchy, constantly in motion—sprinted around the bases for Oakland's first run and was quickly dismissed by Fenway as an unpleasant but harmless foul at an otherwise good party.

Yet as so often is the case in baseball, the trickle of concern in the fifth turned into a leak in the sixth and seventh, before the floodgates broke in the eighth as Oakland put up four runs in the inning and leveled the score at seven. The decisive, equalizing hit came in the form of a Jermaine Dye rocket to center; but the crucial play (the ridiculous break of fortune which is a part of nearly every late-inning rally) came a batter prior when Scott Hatteberg, fooled on a two strike changeup from Foulke and with his entire body bailing away towards first, somehow managed to reach out with one hand across the plate and loft a soft flare over Bill Mueller's head at third. The ball seemed to be arching left of the line, but dropped down and kicked up a small puff of chalk before gently rolling into foul territory, scoring Oakland's fifth and setting up Dye for the equalizer.

Suddenly the scoreboard made sense. Oakland's fourteen hits had produced seven runs (Boston's seven had come on only seven hits), and the game which had in reality been played fairly evenly but had never really felt that way, was now in fact tied. And as a result the Maybe This Really Is The Year (For Real) Party in the Fens was put temporarily on hold (it's been an on-again, off-again sort of affair). Only to nearly start back up again (see?) in the ninth as Nixon drove a two out, 2-1 fastball into the right field corner and ended up landing on third (quite literally, as Trot appeared caught between sliding feet- or head-first and instead tried something in between, which was neither slide nor dive but more like *hurling* himself at the bag). Only McCarty's hard grounder down the line was absorbed by Hatteberg, who bobbled but held on and tagged first to send the game into extra innings.

Curtis Leskanic, who lately seems to be getting an awful lot of work for a guy designated to *emergency relief* status, came on in the tenth and worked the first 1-2-3 inning of the evening for the Sox, and the game and crowd both quieted down a bit. Then went silent when Varitek struck out and Reese grounded out to open the Sox' half of the tenth. With two outs in the tenth, and the game having downshifted significantly (the Sox's last run had come hours earlier), Fenway seemed to settle a bit in anticipation of a prolonged, frustrating grind into the farthest reaches of the scoreboard, and the latest hours of the night.

Which brings us back to Johnny Damon.

His first-pitch single past the pulled-in Athletics third baseman Adam Melhuse sends a ripple of applause through the crowd, but with two outs it is Bill Mueller who is the focus, because it is up to him to keep the inning going and therefore give Ortiz, looming in the on deck circle, a chance to do what he does. Damon, taking his lead off first as Oakland reliever Justin Lehr comes set, is similarly asked only to not make an out. But Johnny is having himself something of a week already (with eleven hits in his last five games) and on Lehr's first pitch he darts out towards second, halts a few steps out, and jogs back, bluffing all the way. Mueller, plain faced, human sized, batting from the left against the righty Lehr, takes the pitch low and steps out to get the sign. He gives an earnest look to Sveum (Mueller being one of those rare professional ballplayer who does everything in earnest, from getting the sign to taking infield grounders, which he fields with both hands and looks all the way in, all with the unassuming nature of one who uses both hands because that's the way he was taught), gets the sign and nods, steps back in, waves his bat around twice, and stretches it above his head so high it pulls his up onto his toes. The umpire leans in over the catcher's shoulder. (*And look at that...* Only now, briefly, do we notice the peculiar nominal overlap: the batter, Bill Mueller, stands before Athletics catcher, Damian Miller, who crouches before home plate umpire, Bill Miller. Which brings a smile.) Lehr delivers, this time a fastball low and away and this time Mueller reaches down and whips his long swing through it sending the ball on a low rising line into the gap in left-center. Damon breaks on contact, bursting towards second, eyeing third as the ball bounces once and rolls towards the wall. On the warning track Kotsay circles behind it. Damon rounds second. The ball short-hops, rolls, hops again, and at the last instant kicks up into Kotsay's midsection as Damon flies towards third, hair whipping behind him as he picks up Sveum, wildly waving him around. Crowd on its feet and waving along. Kotsay launches the ball in. Damon digs through third, heads for home. Fenway echoes to a roar under the floodlights. The throw to Crosby at short. He turns and fires home. Damon onrushing. Miller crouched. The ball darting over the infield, low and away from the plate. Miller catches, sweeps the tag across as Damon barrels in and crashes down on home plate in an explosion of dirt and hair and glove and dust and noise, all tumbling to the feet of umpire Miller who has lunged out on one knee with both arms and both hands stretched full length wide to his sides—*safe!*

Fenway erupts. Shouting, arms raised, high fives and congrats all around—the whole lot. For added effect Ortiz stands directly behind the umpire Miller, echoing his safe sign aloft, the High Priest of Red Sox Finales smiling down on Damon and his run. Behind him the Sox rush onto the field and mob Mueller, the unlikely and unassuming hero who would rather deflect the onrushing bench towards Damon.

His teammates will have none of that, of course, and they quickly have him surrounded and begin to absolutely pummel him; led by Trot Nixon, whose preferred method of offering his congratulation seems to be to corral Mueller by the shoulders, pull his helmet off, whip it across the infield, lock one arm firmly around his teammate's neck and, with his free hand, lovingly rabbit punch him in the midsection to his (Nixon's) delight. All while his teammates jump about and offer *their* congrats by pounding Mueller on the back shoulders and suddenly exposed head. Mueller, whose frame does not appear particularly well built to withstand a David Ortiz pounding, finally staggers frees along the first base line, smiling. Hair disheveled, uniform half-untucked— the humble anti-hero whose teammates would not allow him to escape the hero's spotlight.

Now a case can be made, without great difficulty, for the walk-off home run as the most dramatic play in baseball, and any argument against such a case would be hard pressed in the face of the walk-off's sudden, explosive, and rather obvious dramatic appeal. Nevertheless, the play at the plate must at least be given its due consideration. It has pace, clearly, and the visceral *bang-bang* quality that is key to all thrilling sports moments. On top of which it makes for a simply spectacular final image: the runner coming to a sudden stop at the end of his long sprint, face down and dirt-covered and most likely helmetless, the maskless catcher knelt over him applying the tag, both men in opposite uniforms looking up to the neutral black of the umpire who stands to the side and gives final, conclusive judgment on whether the game is to continue with a declarative punch, or end on the tips of his outstretched palms. Yet aside from even this elegantly composed, aesthetically pleasing scene, the play at the plate is unique in baseball if not in sport because of the balance between its distinctly parallel tracks of actions.

In all other team sport, where the ball is the end-all of every action, this type of drama is impossible. Be it football, basketball, hockey or soccer, if you keep your eye on the ball/puck you will not lose track of the game's focus, fixed as it is on a single inanimate object. Not so in baseball. In baseball runner and ball are of equal importance, and must be perceived in unison and in relationship to one another in order for the play and its considerable theatre to be understood and enjoyed. This creates a wholly unique experience for the sporting spectator. (Not to mention goes a long way towards explaining why baseball, more than any other game, loses depth when filtered through the medium of television. For even the farthest vantage points deep in the bleachers allow one to follow the two parallel scenes in tandem, and therefore experience the duel thrill of tracking their convergence; whereas television's multiple camera angles can still only provide its viewers with at best an either/or proposition. Watching the replay later on in the evening we see that this time the camera chooses the ball, cutting to Damon only briefly as he rounds third and then following the relay home to pick him up again as he splashes down to victory. It is, without a doubt, a thrilling moment of sport in any format; but it is also one of many which reminds us that baseball was meant to be watched live; and that it does not, as other sports such as football do, gain from television's angles and replays but instead suffers from its limitations.) Of course, neither of the two plays unfolding simultaneously are by themselves particularly dramatic—one is a man running, the other is a ball being thrown to a base—but it is the way in which the two push and pull against one another which ultimately holds the dramatic tension taut throughout the play, forcing us to constantly adjust our anticipation of its outcome as the two actions rush headlong towards a single, climactic point of convergence.

Consider the route the mind takes on the play. We start at home (as always) with Mueller, standing in the box with a 1-0 count. We glance out to Damon at first, recognizing him there and noting the length of his lead (rather short, actually), and then turn towards the mound, to Lehr. He delivers and we follow the ball in until Mueller changes its direction and sends it the other way, at which point we forget about both Mueller and Lehr and immediately pick up three others and note their position—Byrnes in left (playing too far towards the line for a play), Kotsay in center (rushing over with a chance to cut the ball off), and Damon (now bolting towards second). Eliminating Byrnes from the play we focus on Kotsay and the ball (keeping Damon in the corner of our eye), as he opts to circle behind instead of backhand it, which is the safe play right up until the moment the ball finds some unforeseen notch in the outfield grass, kicks up, and the instant it does we located third base coach Dale Sveum, waving wildly and altering the situation for Kotsay (who with the ball in his midsection must now hurry it into the cut-off) and Damon (who now kicks into high gear and digs around third), and at the same time bringing two more characters onto the scene—shortstop Bobby Crosby, out in shallow left to relay the throw, and catcher Damian Miller, mask off and positioned for the now inevitable play at the plate. As the ball comes into Crosby and Damon bolts home we lose both Kotsay and Sveum, and when the young shortstop wheels and fires home our perspective comes down to the final two players, one rushing at full speed, the other stationary, and rapidly telescopes in as ball and runner complete their out-and-back-again odyssey at a single point only a fraction of a second apart, both landing back at home plate, where it all began.

The entire circuitous adventure has featured roles for more than half the players on the field (six out of the eleven were directly involved), has covered the entire base path and most of the left side of the field, and has, of course, decided the outcome of the game. All in less than ten seconds.

When fans speak of the mathematical elegance inherent in the game of baseball, these are the plays they speak of. For here we have a long equation on which one side is a single object (Johnny Damon) moving at a relatively constant rate, describing an arc of predetermined length, and the other side is a set of multiple parts (the ball, Kotsay, Crosby) moving in multiple directions at various rates, which somehow add up to equal a whole that is only fractions of a second less-than or greater-than the object describing the arc. Or, to use our present example, the equation might look something like this: b (the ball's path from Mueller's bat to Kotsay) + c (Kotsay's field and throw) + d (Crosby's catch and throw) + e (Miller's catch and tag) < a (Johnny Damon's run from first to home). Damon becomes a dusty, helmetless out in this equation, and Fenway heads wearily and dejected into the 11th and points unknown. Only this is not how it worked out in practice. We go back, redo our calculations, and arrive at the same result (>). Have we forgotten something? We have. (...*finds some unforeseen notch in the outfield grass and kicks up...*) Ah yes, there it is. Seems we have left out f (Kotsay's bobble), which when added to the right side of the equation turns the < symbol around, makes Damon safe, makes the score 8-7, makes the Red Sox 46-37 instead of 45-38, and makes thousands of Red Sox fans very very happy.

Similar equations occur more or less consistently, if not so dramatically, in every baseball game; whether it is a double off the wall played into a bang-bang tag at second, a sac fly relayed into a play at the plate, or a crisp 5-4-3 double play in which the ball is spun around the infield to meet the sprinting runner at first in a flash of glove, bag, ball, and cleats. In each there is some slight imperfection in the equation, be it an unfortunate + (hesitation removing ball from glove), or an almost imperceptible − (stumble out of the box), which turns > into < and in the process changes the outcome of the play, the inning, and often the entire game.

These then are our quiet late night musings, reserved mostly for the drive, cab, T ride or walk home, and morning and day (and ensuing winter) to follow. None of which, not unbalanced equations or dramatic convergence or the incomparable merits of viewing baseball live, occupy our thoughts as we pass out the last of our congratulatory high fives and make our way along the long but buoyant exit from the ballpark. At which point in the evening our reaction to the play takes a more minimalist line, and the extent of our post-win analysis can be articulated with a little head shake, a little smile, a little exaggerated exhale, and the repetition at regular intervals of: *man, what a game.* Our fellow fans seem to concur (*no ——!*) and we go about voicing the same to a dozen or so friends (and the half dozen or so strangers) whom we greet after the game, each requiring no more commentary than the above three words. *Oh man*—head shake, exhale, smile—*what a game.*

* * *

Midsummer baseball is long and comfortable—the teams and faces and tendencies by this point familiar and somewhat predictable; but it can also be woefully redundant. One weak fly to left, one five-pitch walk, one routine 4-3 put-out as indistinguishable from the hundreds which preceded it as it is from the hundreds to follow. Innings pass with a runner stranded at first, a nondescript middle reliever takes over for the departed starter in a four run game, and a lazy 5-1 win goes into the books to be instantly forgotten. All the while we keep an eye out for signs, for the familiar staging pieces (the lead-off single, the two-out walk) which serve notice that *maybe*, if *this* or if *that* follow, then *per-haps* this inning could possibly amount to something after all. We take note, lean in a bit, waiting to see if the next step in the pattern will fall into place. Our anticipation builds with each step, leaning in farther on our seat as the runner is advanced on a pitch in the dirt, and farther still on a seeing-eye single up the middle. And after an intentional walk to load the bases we are on our feet and shouting.

Partially this pattern of wait-and-see comes out of a necessary conservation of emotional capital (it is simply impossible, and impossibly unhealthy, to allow ourselves to be agitated by every stray two-out single over the course of 162 games), but mostly it comes from our self-perceived knowledge of baseball. We think, perhaps understandably, that after watching hundreds of games and having seen the relevant situation play itself out thousands of times before, that we can predict its outcome with some regularity. In short, we think we know something about the game.

What we should know by now is that one of the reasons this game is eternally fascinating is because while it invites such assumptions (through its familiar, traceable patterns), it is at the same time ultimately unknowable. The game is enigmatic, as Damon's run—from first home with two outs on a single in the shallow gap—reminded us of once again. Through years of following it and watching it, of thinking about its multiple mysteries and discussing them to no end, we may learn a thing or two about the game, and we may understand something about its beauty, but we will never reach the point where we are ahead of it. For as long as it is played and as long as we are lucky enough to watch it the game of baseball will forever be able of surprise us; and every once in awhile—during the long summer months when we have become so comfortable in tracing the familiar patterns of the game as to actually try and predict them—it takes a burley and bearded center fielder tumbling onto home in a cloud of dust to remind us how magnificent those surprises can be.

The Good Fight

Yankees at Fenway
24 July 2004

A late July Friday night at Fenway: hot, muggy, stagnant air, packed in, overcrowded, blue hats damp with sweat, red shirts damp with stale beer, clammy arms nudge over, up, *hey watch it*, back, shoes shuffle half-steps on concrete, fingers up to wipe the brow, the heavy uncomfortable silence broken only by a low, clear, directionless muttering, *un-f—believable*, as we inch along the darkened concourse ramp, towards the exits and out. The Red Sox have lost (at this point it hardly matters how) 7-6 to the Yankees in the series opener, and the crowd, having shifted anxiously through a sultry, teeming night under the floodlights, now trudges its way in one grumbling mass towards the gates—weary, overheated, silent from having felt the creaking floor of our summer-long frustration finally give way beneath us.

By now the general disappointment felt among Red Sox fans (over the Sox, over the summer) has been growing steadily for months; yet over the past week—during which the Sox split against a free-falling Seattle team and lost two out of three at home to the last place Orioles—the tone of that disappointment has begun to slightly but unmistakably shift. That both manager and players were criticized daily, heavily, and in terms usually reserved for ruinous public officials, was not unique; that they were criticized not only for their poor performance on the field, but for laughing off it, was. That is for laughing in the dugout, in full view of the television cameras, during a miserable Sox loss. It proved too much. And the fan's message for a week solid, conveyed in any form possible (mostly booing), a collective, admonishing, *listen, this is no laughing matter; don't you know this is serious.*

This then the post-loss mood on Friday night as we slip out under Gate C and onto Yawkey Way, opting to take the long way around the park, counterclockwise up Lansdowne and against the crowd, watching the faces as they pass by towards Kenmore. Here, there is no laughter. There are no smiles. Instead there is shouting—large sweaty-faced men in red and white pointing fingers and barking at large sweaty-faced men in gray and black—and beneath it streams of quieter, more tortured expressions; faces twisted from fatigue and frustration, one after another. This post-game dirge is nothing new, of course. The gloom and shadows of Fenway after a bitter late-summer loss are regrettably familiar to most Red Sox fans, to whom the sulking expressions and deflated mutterings of this grim march often provide a kind of dismal low-grade catharsis—that of the empathetic group, the huddled communal suffering of a people devoted to an insufferable team. Not tonight. Tonight the expressions passing by on either side of us as we work towards Ipswich are not those of the dejected fan. They seem beyond all that—beyond disappointment, beyond frustration, beyond even the numbing sadness that comes with the death of any grand hope, sporting or otherwise. At some point this crowd has pushed past these gloomier, quieter emotions to something much more dire, and it is unsettlingly clear on the faces of the Sox fans around Fenway after Friday's loss that they are not heartbroken. They are angry.

It is this anger—the anger that begins where frustration can no longer reach—which needs to be understood as less than twenty-four hours later we are back at Fenway, on Saturday afternoon, sitting in our damp grandstand seat under a low, leaden gray sky, watching the grounds crew in their red polos weave across the outfield grass. It has rained hard throughout the night, the fat soaking torrents continuing throughout the morning before finally trickling off shortly after noon, leaving the city, its ballpark, and its fans cold and damp. Rumors and rumblings of long delays or even a postponement have circled the ballpark all morning. And as ushers struggle to wipe down seats with sopping wet towels for fans in slick parkas and damp sweatshirts and all-weather, three-season Sox jackets, and the anthem is sung by the Dropkick Murphy's, and the ceremonial fist pitches are tentatively thrown, the grounds crew continues to work. In the stands we sit and watch, feet growing cold in puddle-soaked socks, waiting. The umpires, both managers and the head grounds keeper meet on a soggy patch in left field, arms crossed, heads shaking, glancing down as they toe the soggy turf. The official start arrives and passes, and the grounds crew continues to work. For nearly an hour they work; and as they do the ballpark gradually fills to capacity, thirty-five-thousand strong now sitting under a cool grey sky, waiting. And if they be the thinking type of fan, they sit for an hour and think (about the season, about last night's game); and if they be the talking kind of fan, they sit for an hour and talk (about the season, about last night's game); and if they be the shouting type of baseball fan, prone to engage the Yankees fans pounding their chests and boasting (about the season, about last night's game), then they stand for an hour and shout. And if they be the drinking type of baseball fan, well, yes…until finally the grounds crew rolls off the tarp, the Sox take the field, and after an hour or so of thinking and talking and shouting and drinking, we play ball.

The game opens with a thunderclap, an immense booming drive by Bernie Williams that sends the first pitch deep to center, clearing the entire length of the field before Johnny Damon sprints back onto the track, leaps and crashes into the wall to make the catch. The crowd roars, all of Fenway completely alive to the game at first pitch. A thick, teaming, agitated crowd from the start, it becomes even more so in the top of the second as the Yankees open the scoring with a pair of singles and a Hideki Matsui double, then add a second on a Tony Clark fielder's choice that brings Jorge Posada in the back door to make it 2-0, Yankees. In the third they scratch out another run with a double (Williams), a single (Jeter), and a ground ball (Sheffield) on which the Sox turn the double play but concede a run in the process. Making it 3-0 Yankees, and bringing Alex Rodriguez to the plate.

At this point—down 3-0 in the game, down 9 ½ games in the standings, down however many championships and down several generations of disappointment and heartbreak—every Red Sox fan is left alone to his or her own thoughts, whatever they may be. And so it is that we find ourselves mouthing the words, low under our breath, *do not go gentle into that good night* (as the scoreboard operator hangs a three and Rodriguez steps to the plate) but *rage, rage against the dying of the light.* That Dylan Thomas did not have the 2004 Sox in mind when he wrote his famous poem (he was in fact thinking of his dying father), hardly seems to matter. The two oft-quoted lines stand out in literature and history as a kind of universal expression of the rallying cry, almost a proverb, an eloquent eleventh-hour plea for anyone pressed down by a difficult situation to struggle against it, to push back, to not give in but instead to stand up and no matter the odds or outcome, to fight the good fight. Oddly enough, in this moment at Fenway Park, the lines seem to fit. For throughout the season, but particularly of late, some of the harshest criticisms leveled against this year's Red Sox team (and one of the worst possible criticisms of any athlete or team) has been of their perceived lack of fight—*they play without energy, without urgency, without desire, they just go through the motions, just expect to show up and win, they don't seem upset, they don't seem to care, this team has no backbone, they got no g—d— pride, you know what it is with this team, the real problem is they don't have any heart.* Bitter words, gathering to a head for weeks, to the point where the disappointment of the fans in the team's performance seemed to be overshadowed by their disappointment in the team's reaction to that performance. This is why the dugout smiles and post-game laughter was criticized. Sox fans wanted their Sox team to be as frustrated and upset and as fed up with all of it as we were; we wanted the team to be as angry as we had been walking sweaty and tired and defeated down Lansdowne the night before; and more than that we wanted to see it. Pleas were made for someone, anyone, to get mad and *do something*—to knock over tables in the clubhouse, to throw water jugs in the dugout, to scream at a reporter or storm out of a press conference. More than anything else we wanted this team to pull themselves off the ground and dust themselves off, and lower their shoulders and get back in there and compete. If they were going to lose then fine. If they were going to fall in the standings and underachieve and miss out on the grand hopes we had laid for them then that was one thing. But if nothing else *do not go gentle into that good night, but rage, rage*—and for heaven's sake go down fighting.

Arroyo's 1-1 pitch is right at Rodriguez, no doubt about it. It hits him behind the left elbow, and brings the crowd to its feet with a cool, half-smiling, mocking cheer which quickly heats to an uneasy boil as Rodriquez stares and then barks back at Arroyo. Jason Varitek immediately puts himself between his pitcher and the Yankee third baseman, and continues to shepherd the latter up the first base line; but A-Rod continues to talk, then shout, then challenge and finally waves a hand at Varitek (*come on*), and at that moment all of it—the bragging and the boasting and the taunts and the jokes and the mockery and the embarrassment and the *1918* chants and the heartbreak of Game Seven and the aggravation of the offseason and the disappointment of the spring and the frustration of the summer and the anger of last night—every ounce of it comes crashing together and is smashed into Alex Rodriguez's face through Jason Varitek's glove and fist. We, Red Sox team and nation, had had enough.

The brawl which follows is confused and surreal and heart-stopping, as all brawls are, with both benches and both bullpens emptying into a pile on the first base line, players out and down, scrums, fists flying, numbers and faces unrecognizable—a nameless clash of white and gray. It lasts forever. It is over in an instant. Rodriguez pulled back against the backstop at one end, Varitek corralled by the shoulders near the Red Sox dugout, Yankee pitcher Tanyon Sturtze bloodied around the ear and pacing hard around home plate, and the ballpark as a whole staring in a collectively stunned silence, shaking its head as the shouts continue to ripple out from the grandstands. In the wandering, staggering, breathless post-brawl scene the umpires sentence out ejections (Varitek and Kapler for the Sox, A-Rod and Lofton for the Yankees), we finally let go a long steady exhale, and find ourselves, like more than a few Sox fans and perhaps even a few players, left with an unexpected but overwhelming sense of release. Here as elsewhere we would like to think of ourselves as reasonable, nonviolent people; but anger is not a reasonable emotion, and however ugly and brute the fight may have been it nonetheless broke free some rusted-over restraint within us, some lid that had heretofore kept bottled the steadily building and by now dangerously pressurized tension felt around the Sox and among everyone connected to them. The moment Varitek connected with A-Rod he broke that restraint off with a sledge hammer, and no matter how unsightly or inelegant or unprofessional the resulting release may have been to witness, it cannot overshadow the fact that it desperately needed to happen.

And when the game resumes, the Red Sox, seeming to feed off the heightened energy now churning through the ballpark, begin to fight back. Millar singles and Mueller doubles to lead off the bottom of the third—now every hit and every ball is greeted by a roar of triumph, every strike booed with bitter contempt—and it is the Sox who begin to scratch out runs; Bellhorn then Nomar grounding into force plays that each pull back a run to make it 3-2, and all of a sudden, we have a game.

Meanwhile the fight on the field has echoed back and continues on in the stands, creating a noisy, antagonistic, hostile backdrop to the action on the field as blustery Yankees fans stick their chests up and shout with points and chants; Sox fans nearby return the same in much the same language, only in greater number; Yankees fans return the same only louder now; and the shouts ring back and forth on both sides. From our spot in the ballpark, standing deep in back of the right field corner grandstand, we have a panoramic view onto this raucous, shouting, constantly moving sideshow, and watch as the familiar pattern repeats itself before us. Rings of fans pop up out of their seats in ever-widening concentric circles, facing in, then slowly settle back down, inner circles moving out again as royal blue security and dark blue BPD remove one or both of the belligerents. (We do not bother to look to see what goes on in the middle, for we have seen it often enough to know and far too often to care.) Eventually the surface of the crowd settles, however briefly, before another ring ripples out over to the right, and the entire process repeats itself. Now there's one up farther down the line; and another a moment later way over to the right in the center field bleachers; and so on, rolling on with rhythmic swell of spectacle, circles rippling out and fading, rippling out and fading, as if someone high above were tossing pebbles onto the smooth red-and-blue surface of the Fenway crowd below.

In the bottom of the fourth the major hostilities shift back to the field as Juan Padilla replaces the noticeably shaken Sturtze. (A curious figure in this drama, Sturtze needs one more glance before he departs. A Worcester native, Sturtze grew up loving both the Sox and Fenway. At one point his father, a retired police officer, had taken him to twelve straight Opening Day games at Fenway. How complicated must the emotions have been for him then, having had fate cast him as a villain in his own home, throwing punches against the uniform he once idolized, being booed from the very seats he once cheered in.) Padilla, visibly overwhelmed by the moment, immediately walks Ortiz. Manny doubles to put runners on second and third with nobody out, bringing Nomar to the plate. He rips the first pitch he sees up the middle and both Ortiz and then Manny come around to score, the Sox take a 4-3 lead, and the crowd roars with a depth and resonance that we had not yet heard this summer at Fenway. With the stands rolling and bouncing and the echoing cheers earsplitting after every single pitch (this in the fourth inning, in July), the Sox continue to battle. Nixon and then Millar each single to load the bases, and although Padilla and the Yankees slip out of the jam by way of a double play and a line-out, the fight (the real one, the one on the scorecard) has begun in earnest.

Then, after the respite of a quick fifth inning (during which a fighting mad Terry Francona is unceremoniously tossed for arguing a close play at second), comes the interminable sixth. With Arroyo still in, Enrique Wilson (who incidentally replaced Rodriquez after the brawl) reaches on an infield single, followed by a Posada double to left, and a Matsui double to right that brings both runners in and give the Yankees back the lead, 5-4. And for a moment it looks as if Arroyo might make it out of the inning down only a run as he gets Sierra to pop out, then strikes out Clark swinging; but Cairo singles in Matsui to make it 6-4. Williams follows with a single, and Arroyo's long and lively afternoon is finally over. Curtis Leskanic comes on in relief, offers none, and the inning deteriorates from there. Jeter walks to load the bases. Sheffield walks to push in a run (7-4). Wilson comes back up (again, still batting in A-Rod's slot) and singles in two more to make it 9-4. Finally the inning ends with Mark Malaska coming on to strike out Matsui with the bases loaded, but the storm of runs has already doused much of the ferocity from the crowd, and as we sit and let the five-run deficit soak in we notice how very grey, and very windy, and very cold Fenway has suddenly become around us.

All afternoon the weather has helped set the tone—the raw, brute air and iron-gray sky an entirely apposite backdrop to the raw, brute, hand-to-hand nature of both the fight on the field, as well as the inter-mittent skirmishes in the stands. Now, as the long top of the sixth ends with the score 9-4 and the very real prospect of falling an irrepara-ble 10 ½ games out of first settles in, the sky seems darker, the air cooler, and the wind once again blows gloomy thoughts through the minds of Sox fans everywhere. So then, *is this it?* Is this season of great hopes (of Schilling! of Foulke! of a new manager and a new hope and the best rotation in baseball!) gone already? Have we worried it away with injury reports and talk of regrouping and insanely pointless trade rumors? Have we talked ourselves so far out of overreacting that by the time we did react it was already over? Is the competitive portion of the Red Sox season, and the enjoyable portion of our summer along with it, really to end here, tonight, at Fenway?

The air and sky and scoreboard certainly seem to confirm this; but then Nomar singles to right, Nixon walks, and Millar singles again (this time off Paul Quantrill) to load the bases. And suddenly the air feels a bit warmer, and the wind not quite so sharp; hoods are pulled down and hands put together, and the chants and claps and yells begin all over again. Mueller responds with a loud sacrifice fly to center, scor-ing Nomar (9-5); Bellhorn doubles to left to bring in Nixon (9-6); and Damon singles to shallow left to score Millar and send Fenway into a teeming, raucous frenzy once again. Félix Heredia comes in and gets Mirabelli (in for Varitek) to strike out swinging before walking Ortiz to load the bases. Fenway rises and roars as Manny comes to the plate,

the *Maaa-ne, Maaa-ne, Maaa-ne* chant echoing around the entire ballpark, every section, from the front row to the back of Standing Room
Only. He walks, and Fenway begins to physically shake with the score
now 9-8. Nomar is up again for the second time in the inning. Scott
Proctor comes into the game for the Yankees, and at this moment
summer seems so very close to being reclaimed, no more than a single
away. Then, suddenly, Nomar strikes out. And we glance up to see
that the light banks high above Fenway have one by one come to life,
and that we have moved almost imperceptibly from afternoon to
evening.

And while the sixth may have been interminable, the seventh does
it one better by not only being infinitely long, but also infinitely difficult to watch. With Malaska immediately giving up a drive to Sierra
over the left field wall, pulling back a Yankee run to make it 10-8;
after which the Sox commit three errors but somehow give up no more
runs in a sloppy and remarkably unprofessional half inning of baseball.
(And here may be as good a place as any to point out that this game,
this classic battle which will surely take its place among the greatest
games in baseball's greatest rivalry, was for the most part not very well
played. Even without the ugliness of the brawl the game was mired by
unattractive baseball, full misplays and miscues, shoddy base running,
slightly *indeterminate* umpiring, and long grinding stretches of completely ineffective pitching. But the brute style of the game was itself
a distinguishing characteristic. Taking its keynote from the brawl, the
game was an inelegant but bitterly fought struggle, a bare-knuckle
affair remembered more for its intensity than its execution. If the classic 13-inning game in the Bronx on the first of the month was a symphony, then this was High Opera—soaring, desperate, surreal and
sublime, at once captivating and heart-wrenching and awful, and in
the end entirely wonderful.)

Within such a game it takes a stroke of inspired casting to bring
in Ramiro Mendoza, the down and out reliever from whom Red Sox
fans have come to expect only inconsistency followed by disappointment, and who comes on in the eighth and (naturally) pitches two
calm, quiet, remarkably relaxed innings of 1-2-3 relief. Retiring two-

thirds of the Yankees lineup in order, and doing it all as causally as if he was brought to Boston to do exactly that (which he was), and has done it comfortably each and every day all season long (which he most certainly has not).

Between Mendoza's two brilliantly uneventful innings was the Boston eighth, in which Ortiz walked with two outs to bring Manny up to bat and Mariano Rivera into the game. Manny eventually flew out on a ball hit hard towards the bullpens in right center, rising high and carrying as if it might have enough to get up and over before it was knocked down by the wind, blowing straight in over the right field bleachers, and caught by Williams on the warning track. (We will later remember that drive; for although we did not know it at the time, it was the first of a trio).

Into the ninth.

And if we are sitting on the outfield side of the ballpark we notice that the clouds above have thinned out, just a bit, and that the now setting sun glows faint but warm through narrow bands between them, creating thin unexpected brushes of light yellow and pink through the far grandstands. It is a wonder to see the sun at all. Not because of the gloomy darkness of the day (though certainly there's that), but because by this point we are nearly four hours into the game, nearly five hours past the national anthem, and nearly seven hours since the gates opened to let in the day's first fans. It seems impossible to now see even traces of sunlight at the tail end of such a dismal afternoon and evening; but there it is, glowing against the underside of the flat layered clouds, hanging behind the left field roof boxes somewhere out over the Charles.

Nomar leads off the ninth and promptly rips a low 0-2 fastball into the left-center gap for a double, his third hit of the day. Nixon is next, and jumps on a 3-1 fastball to sends it high and deep to right center, reaching for the bullpen before it dies against the wind, falls, and is caught on the warning track by Sheffield for the first out. Nixon pumps his fist down and furiously kicks the dirt beyond first. (That's twice now.) Millar follows, stepping to the plate beneath wild cheers from Fenway (by this point there are no problem children on the Red

Sox roster, no one that we want to trade, not in the eyes of the fans, not on this evening; every player in uniform is a fan favorite, everyone wearing the script-B is beloved). Millar instantly revives hope with a single that scores Nomar from third to make it 10-9, and now stands at first representing the potential tying run. Bill Mueller is next. He takes a ball high, then a strike, then a ball in and another ball low, and it is 3-1 with one out and we are immediately thinking that a walk would put the tying run in scoring position. (Then a single, then...) But first the 3-1 to Mueller, who we plead to with *nothing close Billy, be picky, take a pitch if you have to, Rivera's been wild, only swing at your pitch, get a good one if its there* (then, much lower, *please Billy oh come on you can do it, please*.) Rivera's next pitch is letter-high and out over the plate, Mueller's pitch all the way, and he drills it. On a line it rises out to right, up and back, into deep right center towards the bullpens, it could maybe (*but Manny's drive, but Trots drive, but does it have enough*), Williams drifting back and Sheffield moving over and the ball still going as suddenly Williams hits the wall and looks up and the ball sails into the bullpen and Fenway Park absolutely explodes, and for the next five minutes or so everything is a deafening blur of jumping and shouting and cheering and high fives and hugs.

It is the kind of sports moment that verges on delirium. The kind one hears stories about, in which moment of such sudden and intense animation fans have been heard to actually lose consciousness, their euphoria reaching such heights that they have trouble remembering anything that happened during the first few raucous moments after such an explosively dramatic finish. This was not the case with us (though it felt very, very close) for we remember everything that happened directly after Mueller's drive touched down; the look of every face, the sound of every cheer. And yet the overriding memory of the moment is still purely emotional, unconnected to sights or even sounds. What we remember is the sensation of being instantly, and momentously, happy.

It is an experience that is available to us in very few areas of life other than sports. We had, like everyone else, been incorrigible all morning and all day; even more so perhaps because we were disappointed in ourselves for once again allowing this game, and this team in particular, to force incorrigibility on us. Why had we not learned our lesson? Why had we allowed this game and this team to do it to us again, not by underachieving or trailing in the division but by pulling us in so deep that we allowed it all to affect us so much? Why had we not been able to keep them at a safe, emotionless distance? Bill Mueller and the moment he provided (that the team provided) answered that question with definitive clarity—*this is why*. Because the sport and team we love have an ability to cause us heartbreak and dampen our moods that is matched only by their capacity to cause us elation and lift our sprits once again. We cannot have one without the other, and so we choose both.

Yet this moment, and this night, and this drama, was not about sports in general—not about the greater game of Baseball, not about fans of other teams in other sports in other cities. No, this night was a family affair, about and for the Red Sox and their fans; and its significance and magnitude and ultimately its restorative effect on an entire community can perhaps only be fully understood by those within that family (other fans of other teams might view all of the above as an over-dramatization of a fairly exciting midsummer baseball game; but as Red Sox fans, we know better.) After so many nights when it could not be said, here finally was a good night to be a Red Sox fan. And as so often is the case with the Sox, when times are good they tend to be very good indeed.

Realizing this, and not wanting to let it go quite yet, the majority of fans (and by that we mean two-thirds, twenty thousand or so) linger long after the game to allow Mueller his curtain call and to watch the replay a half dozen times on the video board. (Where Mueller's celebratory trip around the bases and greeting at home reveals a fantastic look into his character as a player. He remains cool and composed as he rounds first, then second, Bill Mueller the professional ballplayer, and it is only when he rounds third and sees his teammates at home that the emotions come out, irresistible, two little finger pumps at them before he pulls off his helmet and lowers his shoulders and barrels headlong into the scrum, Billy Mueller the fierce competitor and loyal teammate. Perfect). Seven hours since the gates opened, and still no one wants to leave. Us included. We have spent the better part of our week at Fenway Park, most of it uncomfortably and irritably, but we can not yet bring ourselves to resign this night to memory and television replay.

Finally we turn and join the crowd. We exit out through Gate C and for the second time in two nights take a post-game lap around Fenway Park. This time the air is cool and crisp, not at all unlike October, and we work our way clockwise—Lansdowne to Brookline to Yawkey—following along the streets of a baseball carnival in mid-swing. Where we end up trailing a few paces behind a group of five or six guys—all broad-shouldered and wearing replica Sox jerseys—and watch as with raspy, hoarse voices they shout (*Yeeaah!* mostly) at the strangers flowing by them in the opposite direction. And of course the faces as they pass on either side are no longer twisted with disappointment and frustration and anger, but alight with smiles, laughing as they high five and give spontaneous shouts (*yeah go Sox!*) of their own. They are not, in all probability, the same exact faces from the night before, but they might as well be. Blue script-B hats pulled low and red alternate hats turned backwards; red **NOMAH** t-shirts and blue 38 Schilling shirts; groups of middle-aged men in polos and groups of teenage girls with visors; older couples carrying long umbrellas and foam seat cushions, and young couples carrying souvenir bags and holding hands; kids holding their parents hands and headed for the subway; older kids holding their IDs and lining up outside the bars. All are smiling (*this is why*), every last one.

As for the Sox, they recovered a game in the standings and perhaps a few believers in the process. This team, on its figurative deathbed all week and with its eulogy being rehearsed across the airwaves and the bars of New England, showed that it will in fact have a say in its own fate; and that win or lose they will not simply let the hopes of its spring fade away in the summer heat, and drift carelessly into a long cold winter. The team proved that much in the fourth, and again in the sixth. Varitek's spark may have won back the team in the beginning, and Mueller's drive may have won the game in the end, but it was the rallies back from defeat in the fourth and sixth and the emotion that fueled them that fully restored this team in the hearts and minds of its fans. It was there as Varitek shoved and as Kapler ranted in protest, as Damon pleaded after being called out at second and as Embree slammed his glove in frustration, and it was there as Nixon pumped his fist and kicked in disbelief, wanting to win so bad that the outward signs of emotion were uncontainable. It was with these bare uninhibited outbursts of the competitive spirit—reflecting so purely the emotions of those who follow them with such passion and seriousness—that the 2004 Sox proved to their fans (and perhaps themselves as well) that they will not go gently into that good night after all. And that whatever happens in the end, whatever their legacy is to be in baseball and Red Sox lore, it will never be that they were willing to go down without a fight.

Night at the Fenway Follies

Minnesota at Fenway
29 July 2005

Typically the conversation goes something like this: our friend, sitting next to us in the bleachers, stands and informs us that he is going to get a jump on the crowd and head to the concession stand and possibly the Men's. We, looking up from our scorecard, politely inform him that in American baseball it requires three outs to end an inning, and since the Sox have only made two, one still remains. Our friend tells us he knows all this, and that's why he said the thing about getting a jump on the crowd, it being hard to get a jump on the between-inning crowd, between innings. We politely inform him while we appreciate the complexities of the *getting a jump on the crowd* strategy, we also recognize (as doubtless he will agree) that there are certain principles one must adhere to in a civilized society and that one of them happens to be that you don't go to the concession stand and/or Men's while the Sox are batting. He thanks us (in so many words) for this information, but given that there are already two outs, and there are no baserunners, and the bottom of the order is up, and given that on top of all this the Sox haven't done [a phrase equivalent to *very little*] against Silva all night, he is going anyway. We remind him the man at the plate is the defending batting champion and therefore deserves a bit more respect than being dismissively referred to as *the bottom of the order*, if you please, and that he might miss something. He says like what? We say we don't know like something you wouldn't want to miss. He shakes his head and excuses himself down the aisle. We shake *our* head, shift our knees to let him pass (though perhaps not as far as we possibly could since one of them happens to catch our friend in the back of the calf on his way through), and turn back to the game. An empty plastic cup beneath our seat. An empty bag of hollow peanut shells beside it. And desperately needing (as we have since the second inning) to use the Men's but unwilling to move until between innings for the simple but entirely logical reason that although we do not know what we might miss, we know for certain that we do not want to miss it.

More than likely what we have refused to miss will be a lazy pop-up to second, or a routine fly ball to center, or a called third strike on a ball two inches off the plate; all of which (particularly this last) we have seen a thousands times before. Then again, it could be something else entirely—a gigantic jaw-dropping home run, a spectacular diving catch, an acrobatic double play, or better still, something we have yet to find a name for, something we have never seen before and may never see again. Something everyone will be talking about after the game and perhaps still talking about tomorrow, on one of those mornings in which fans greet each other not with *hello* or *morning* but *hey how about that play, that was something huh?* And we certainly don't want to miss something like that. So we sit still. We shake our heads at our friend's brazenness, at the cool ease with which he is willing to risk missing something, knowing that in all probability he will be back in a few minutes—relieved, replenished, refreshed—having missed absolutely nothing at all.

Other than a few casually reclined moments of this exceedingly comfortable summer night at the ballpark. Clear skies, lush temperatures, a soft breeze, the sun just now set and the lights just now beginning to glow against the fading twilight—if one could cheer for weather, this would be a night to do so. Certainly there has been little opportunity to cheer anything else. Scoreless in the fifth, and with the Twins' Carlos Silva and Sox's starter Bronson Arroyo both pitching as if they have some urgent appointment to keep after the game, there has not been a great deal in the way of distinctive brilliance (or for that matter, movement) in this first hour and a half of baseball. What there *has* been a great deal of is grounding out weakly to first, swinging at pitches out of the strike zone, and popping out to the shortstop.

Which perhaps explains why we take a bit more notice than usual when Bill Mueller, *bottom of the order* or not, chops Silva's next pitch off the dirt in front of home plate where it takes one long hop over the mound, skips between the converging shortstop and second baseman, past second, and rolls into the center field grass for a clean single—which is not really nothing, but then again is hardly something.

So then, one on and nobody out. Graffanino is next, and on a 1-0 pitch lines a clean single to right, moving Mueller up to second. And *well well well, look at us...* First and second, nobody out, and as Damon steps into the box the crowd ripples with a little murmur of applause, sitting up for the first time in anticipation of *the slim potential for the possibility of* something. But what? Single to score a run? Double to score both? Perhaps even a lighting bolt three-run homer? The file in a baseball fan's mind marked First & Second Nobody Out is an immense, overflowing affair, and instinctively we find ourselves thumbing through its numerous reference points to compile a handy list of its most popular outcomes, along with the relative likelihood of each. With this in hand, and with the game tied in the middle innings, we settle on a theme of modesty and shout out, *Come on now Johnny! Base hit.* (While secretly we hope for a double.)

As it turns out, what we get is something else entirely.

Silva's first pitch is a fastball inside, and Damon pulls his hands in to get through the swing and as he does catches the ball down near the handle, splintering his bat in two and sending the ball sailing gently out to right where it bounces safely in front of Twin's right fielder Jacque Jones for a single. Mueller and Graffanino have taken off on contact, the latter already nearing second and the former already rounding third (and the situation is so familiar, the combination so common, that we already click ahead to: *broken-bat single, Mueller scores, Graffanino to second*). Jones fields on a crow hop and fires hard to the plate, skipping the ball wild—once past the cutoff man, then again just beneath the glove of catcher Joe Mauer—as Mueller crosses home standing up and the ball shoots clean to the backstop. Instantly Graffanino bolts home. Silva scrambles to the backstop, grabs the ball and fires home, far too late, and Graffanino slides under Mauer just as the ball again darts past him, this time skipping clean through to the *opposite* backstop. And now Fenway is in an uproar, echoing great rolling cheers with every errant throw as Damon comes charging around third, then immediately comes charging to a full stop halfway down the line only to find himself staring at Justin Morneau, who has backed up the play and now stares back at him with the ball raised in a distinctive throwing position. Damon sprints back to third. Morneau throws to third. Damon stops, pivots, sprints hard in the opposite direction, not looking back but making a clear break for home as behind him third baseman Michael Cuddyer chases a few steps then throws down the line and—*thwonk*—the ball ricochets off Damon's helmet and lands on the grass in foul territory, and Johnny doesn't even break stride but raises a hand to steady his helmet just as he crosses the plate and all of Fenway nearly doubles over with laughter.

Surprised, delighted, and still laughing uncontrollably we shake our heads and look to each other with *what the hell was that?* and *hey just like we drew it up*, and *man oh man that was something huh?*

It certainly was. And it takes us a few seconds once the crowd has settled back in—still shaking its head, still pointing confused fingers this way and that, still laughing—to figure out how all of this is supposed to fit inside one tiny square on a scorecard. Going back through it (as we wipe away a tear), the play boils down to this: RBI single for Damon. Mueller scores. Graffanino scores on the throwing error by Jones. Damon scores on the throwing error by Cuddyer. (We would have preferred, aesthetically, to have a third error charged, but the official scorer ruled that once the ball got by Mauer the first time that Graffanino would have scored and Damon would have gone to third regardless, so Silva's errant throw was statistically irrelevant.) Which translates to: 6-1-3-5, 1B, E9, E5, with a dot for the RBI. A notation we have never had the pleasure of making before, and which it is unlikely we will ever have the chance to make again.

Where to even begin? Perhaps the first thing we notice among the many curios of this supremely curious play, is the long and adventurous path Johnny Damon ended up taking on what was in essence a garden variety broken-bat single to right. To start with the bat shatters in his hands. So there's pieces of wood flying about and the head of the bat spinning off with the now very light bat handle still in his hands, all before he's even left the box. He takes off, watching the ball sail over the infield and probably thinking *RBI single* like the rest of us, and keeps his eye on Jones as he loops out along the first base line, slows until Jones fires, then turns and sprints to second; rounding second he hesitates as he looks back to find the ball, stops, starts, stops, and as the throw skips past Mauer starts again and bolts towards third where he again slows and again picks up the throw, sees it again skip to the backstop, and suddenly digs hard through third and towards home before he spots Morneau with the ball and slams on the breaks. He now finds himself in the middle of the third base line, halfway between Morneau, who stands at the backstop with the ball (the two exchange a single cartoonish glance) and Cuddyer, behind him and awaiting his return to third. Damon takes a few hard steps back, sees the ball zip by him and hit the glove of Cuddyer, pivots hard, and runs like hell in the other direction, shoulders lowered and body leaning as he commits full steam towards home, anticipating a slide or a tag or a collision, or just about anything except what happens next, which is that something causes a rather loud sensation within his helmet (this within the sound of thirty-five thousand fans already cheering with delight). Suddenly he can no longer see. Seems the bill of his helmet has been forced down over his eyes. Still running full speed he settles it with his right hand just in time to plant his foot on home plate. And in the television shots of the Sox dugout after the play, he too is laughing.

Others are not. Neither during the play nor after. Among them the man at the center of all this nonsense (and our favorite figure in the play), Twins catcher Joe Mauer. The play, always comical in its slap-dash throws back and forth, turns into something closer to outright farce when we throw the spotlight solely on the catcher. Keeping in mind that his job description is to *catch the ball*, and with it protect the plate, we follow him throughout the course of the play. The ball is hit, the mask comes off, Mauer sets his feet and readies himself for a close bang-bang play at the plate. Only the throw is up the line and low, and rather than smother it he tries to scoop it like a first baseman and it skips under him and shoots through to the backstop. He turns to find Graffanino coming hard at him from the opposite direction. Mauer sets his feet and readies himself for a close bang-bang play at the plate. Only this time the throw is low and late, and as he blocks the plate against a sliding Graffanino the ball shoots through to the opposite backstop, and Mauer looks up to find Damon caught off third, sees Morneau throw behind, sees Cuddyer catch and chase, and finally sees Damon lowering his shoulders towards home. Mauer sets his feet and, for the third time in about fifteen seconds, readies himself for what will this time surely be a close bang-bang play at the plate. Just one bang this time, however, and that off Damon's head. And as the ball lands softly in the grass and Damon sprints past him Joe Mauer stands upright in front of a now terribly violated home plate, feet no longer set so much as his jaw. On the play he has been thrown to three times, has seen three runners run or slide safely behind him, has been at the epicenter of a long and complicated series of plays and misplays—and has not once touched the baseball. In the end he stands holding his mask, thick catcher's mitt planted on his hip and a decidedly unamused expression fixed in the general direction of his fellow fielders. Though we suspect one day he too will be able to look back on all of this and laugh. (Then again, perhaps not.)

Oh but *we* do, long and loud. Like a great punch line we will repeat the antics of the play to ourselves and our friends the next day, and it just keeps getting funnier (to us) every time. Even aside from the silent movie turns of Damon and Mauer, the absurdity of the play is heightened even more by it being so perfectly out of character for both teams. The Red Sox are and have been an offensive powerhouse, generating runs more regularly and more efficiently than any team in the league, and no team can put together a big inning faster than the Sox. Which is to say they pretty well know how to score runs, and therefore do not normally require much help from the other team to do so. But here are these very same Red Sox, a deep and dangerous lineup, going four innings without even a suggestion of run-scoring capability, and getting three on a broken bat single to right.

Likewise the Twins, who fully deserve their reputation as one of the most disciplined, efficient, and fundamentally sound teams in the league. Without the big star talent of other American League contenders the Twins have made the art of not beating themselves a key component in their formula for consistently fielding low-budget teams made up of either young or mid-range talent, which are always expected to be rebuilding for the future, and which in the meantime happen to be incredibly difficult to beat. It is not an exaggeration then to say that one would expect such bush league hijinks from just about any other team *but* the Twins. And the fact that it was not the bungling Rays, but the rock solid Twins who orchestrated such mirthful sloppiness...well, that just makes the whole thing that much more hysterical.

More than anything else though, the play delights because it is so delightfully unprofessional. Certainly we have seen errors at the big league level, some of which have been quite amusing (many have not); but it is rare, very rare, that we are able to witness such a string of slapstick miscues in a Major League ballpark. This is the type of play far more commonly found on the quieter, more intimate surroundings of the Little League diamond, where on hazy summer evenings kids zigzag around the base paths and heave the ball back and forth across the field, the runner (in jeans and an oversized helmet) starting and stopping along the base paths as parents and coaches yell *go! no no no, stop! now go go go!* But that all of this has happened not on some dusty cut-out Little League field in Methuen, but under the hallowed floodlights of Fenway Park in Boston, and was performed not by clumsy kids distracted by the amount of bubble gum they've shoved in their cheek, but by highly-skilled, highly-trained professionals (All-Stars no less) with agents and contracts and endorsement deals, is what made the play so rousing and, in a way, almost endearing. And so we file it away, in some recess among our tilting stack of favorite baseball stories, to be pulled out and retold later on, whenever good baseball friends gather around in need of a laugh.

A moment later and the fifth inning ends with Rentería flying out to deep center for the final out. The players jog off the field. The crowd bothers itself with *excuse me*'s and *want anything*'s. And our friend, hot dogs and drink in hand, shuffles back down our aisle. We turn our knees the other way. He sits and sets his drink beneath his seat, and once settled looks up at the scoreboard—now 3-0, Sox—and turning to us with a confused look, asks, *did I miss something?*

Stop the Presses

Minnesota at Fenway
31 July 2005

Broad shouldered and baby-faced, Jon Papelbon stands on the mound at Fenway Park and plants his back heels on a Major League rubber for the very first time. A Sunday afternoon game set to begin under pale, uninspiring skies, the crowd shuffles about as infielders take their final tosses around the diamond, the catcher stands and fires down to second, the second baseman feigns a tag on an invisible runner, spins and tosses to the shortstop, the shortstop pats the ball once in his glove and tosses to the third baseman, and with a point of the glove and a nod of encouragement the third baseman sends the ball back to the young man waiting on the mound. Tall and focused, a red 58 blazoned across his back, he stares in at Jason Varitek. In a moment his career—in the Majors, for the Red Sox, at Fenway—will officially begin. And yet he is not the story.

Far from it.

The story is elsewhere, off the field. Just as it promises to be throughout the afternoon, just as it has been throughout a week crammed full of off-the-field headlines, littered at every corner with off-the-field editorials, and all but choking itself on a riot of off-the-field exclamation points both in print and speech. It has been a week of Official Statements and unofficial counter statement and no comments; of Special Reports and Exclusive Special Reports, and Exclusive Special Reports Live from Fenway Park; a week of gossip and rumor, of gossip verified by *a source close to the team* (who could be a ticket taker or usher for all its worth) and rumor corroborated by *a source close to the story* (who could be just about anyone in Boston); of bold accusations and pleading denials; a week in which a great many people have insisted that certain things *have (!) to happen*, while certain other people have insisted that certain other things simply *cannot (!) be allowed to continue*; all while a great many people have claimed to know a great deal about jobs they have never held, about rooms they have never been in, and about the deepest, most personal thoughts of people they have never met. A week of bold speculation and outrageous deduction and truly creative theorizing; a week deafened by an incessant chorus of those who are *maybe not there in the clubhouse every day* but nevertheless are here to tell us *exactly what's going on down there* and *this is what has to happen there's just no way around it*; a week deadened by the opium of other people's money. It has been a week (in every way) full of it—full of talk and discussion and debate and disagreement and shouting and argument and quarrel and, only occasionally, of baseball.

Even then the baseball story has been who was *not* on the field, rather than who was, or what they did while there. Even now, as the umpire points to begin the game, we look on at best in a state of mild distraction, our minds already wandering off to what may or may not be going on in executives offices in New York and Tampa and Minneapolis, our eyes instinctively wandering up to the clock above center field. Now just after 1:00 pm. Only a few hours remain until the moment this entire week and our entire focus have been building towards—4:00 pm EST, Sunday afternoon, the trade deadline itself.

The young man on the mound is ready. Only we barely see him. For our attention is on the same figure it has held in view all week. And where is he now? Why, he is sitting on the bench, of course; with his hat off, his bat on the rack, and his braided black hair hanging down across his shoulders. We watch him there and wonder what he must be thinking (perhaps unnecessarily as so many this week have been able to tell us thought for thought), wonder if he will play today (as so many, so very far from the dugout, have told us with firm assurance that he will not under any circumstances), wonder if he will ever play on this field, in that uniform, again (since so many have told us that he absolutely *must not, should not, cannot*, and *will not* take up his bat from that dugout, ever again). Still, we wonder.

And still then there is Jon Papelbon, standing on the mound. He takes a step back and begins his windup, turns and raises his leg, pushes off—and suddenly we remember that there is a field, and a game on it, and that we can keep an eye on both throughout the day as we anxiously wait for our news—as Jonathan Papelbon throws both the first pitch of the game and the first pitch of his career, a 93-mph fastball on the inside corner, for strike one.

Strike two follows shortly thereafter, this time a 95-mph fastball low and away that Twins' leadoff hitter Shannon Stewart swings so far behind that it is hard to tell whether it should be counted as late for strike two, or early for strike three (it's a tough call). Papelbon, expressionless, holds his glove up and receives the ball back on the mound, steps on the rubber, and nods to Varitek. And because the game is the same everywhere, from Louisiana to Mississippi to Pawtucket to Boston, and because one gets the impression Jon Papelbon has been throwing mid-90's fastballs by hitters at each of these stops in his career, the next step is inevitable. Strike one, strike two, and with the third pitch of his career a fastball up in the zone that Stewart can only swat at, the swing flat-footed and all wrist and horribly late for strike three. Varitek tosses to third, the ball circles the infield, and Fenway gives out a surprised and smiling *hey-hey!* cheer and finds that there might, just might, be some entertainment on the field this afternoon to keep us occupied while we wait. Papelbon immediately confirms this as he works the count full on Luis Rodríguez, then throws the same shoulder-high fastball by him. Varitek tosses to third, the ball circles the infield, and Fenway smiles and shakes its head at one another. Joe Mauer follows and flies out to left on the first pitch he sees from Papelbon, who watches the ball drift into Kevin Millar's glove, and walks off the field having officially entered the name of *Papelbon, Jonathan* into the dusty multi-volume record of baseball history.

Which gives us time, between innings and perhaps even a little bit while the Sox are batting, to call up and check if there has been any news; to ask around the crowd if anyone has heard, well, anything. (The subject being entirely understood among this crowd.) Nothing? No news? What about rumor? Hearsay? Unfounded speculation? Not even an unnamed source able to speak with absolute confidence under the blanket of anonymity? No, not a thing? *Oh well*, then we suppose it will have to be back to the game.

Where Jon Papelbon opens his second inning of Major League work by immediately giving up his first hit to Terry Tiffee, and then immediately (as if by association) hitting Jacque Jones squarely in the foreribs to put two runners on with no one out and send a nervous *it was two good to be true* grumble throughout the crowd. It is short lived, however, as Papelbon settles in, takes his sign, and goes to work. He starts off Justin Morneau with a called strike, then another, and after a foul ball gets him to pop out to second. He repeats the pattern with Lew Ford who takes a strike looking, then another, and finally strikes out swinging on a high fastball. Michael Ryan follows and he takes a strike, swings through another (at this point Jon Papelbon has faced eight Major League hitters through two innings, and has been behind in the count for exactly two pitches), then swats at the air beneath a third for strike three. Ending the inning, and raising Fenway into a roar of an ovation as Papelbon walks off the field and the headline writers cry out: *Stop the presses! New headline*: DAZZLING DEBUT: ROOKIE K'S FOUR IN FIRST TWO.

With Brad Radke working steadily through the Sox lineup and Papelbon working a smooth third inning (adding one more strikeout to his total), no news crosses the wire on or off the field until the top of the fourth, when with two outs and the game still scoreless Justin Morneau sits back on a Papelbon fastball and launches it deep into the right field bleachers. (And as he circles the bases and Fenway settles into its quiet arms-crossed slouch, a new headline quietly scrolls across our mind: BABY BOOM: MORNEAU WELCOMES ROOK TO BIGS.) Papelbon allows nothing more in the inning though, and the Sox come up in the bottom of the fourth trailing by a run. Where with one out Ortiz steps up to the plate, to be followed by John Olerud. Both have long since proven their ability to hit a Major League fastball, and both do so here again. With the count 2-1, Ortiz pivots on a Radke fastball and sends it sailing out on a broad arch in the right field grandstand. Fenway stands and cheers, and is just settling back into its seat when it looks up to see John Olerud, again on a 2-1 count, turn around another Radke fastball and match Ortiz's home run inch for inch. Fenway rises back onto its feet for the second time in a span of few minutes and it's *Stop the presses! Again! Back cover shot of Papi high-fiving that new guy, the one who looks like a banker, and right across it run*: O'YES: ORTIZ AND OLERUD GO WAYBACK-TO-WAY-BACK. (*And jack up the font on the O's.*)

Now pitching with a lead for the first time (everything being for the first time, today), Papelbon immediately threatens to give it away and then some. After a quick groundout he walks Nick Punto on a full count, gets a second out from a Stewart pop out, then walks both Luis Rodríguez and Joe Mauer, throwing one strike in nine pitches (and none at all to Mauer). So then with the bases loaded and two outs, and the headline over Jon Papelbon's Major League debut still a long way from going to print, he delivers a first pitch fastball to Terry Tiffee—who just happens to be looking fastball all the way. Tiffee drills it out towards deep right, high and far (and all at once we see it blazed in 48-point block letters across our morning paper: SPANKED: TIFFEE SLAM RUINS ROOKIE DEBUT) with Kapler racing back to the track and looking up and finally—because Tiffee has not missed by much, but *has* missed, just—settling under it to make the catch in front of the wall. (As it turns out Papelbon would give up the home run he narrowly escaped one pitch later, on a solo home run by Jones to lead off the sixth; one pitch too late for the Twins but enough to tie the game, 2-2.)

Into the sixth, up around a hundred pitches, Papelbon works through a long, tough sequence of pitches to Morneau before striking him out. Lew Ford follows with a single, and after another long sequence that ends in a Michael Ryan walk Terry Francona comes out to the mound and tells young Jon Papelbon that he has done enough. Papelbon hands him the ball and walks off the field with Fenway Park already applauding as it rises full to its feet, as proper a standing ovation as any ten-year veteran ever received, for a kid who all but pitched like one. And like a ten-year veteran the young man brings his fingers to the bill of his hat (for what must be the thousandth time in his mind but just the first, ever, on a Major League field) and tips his cap to the adoring crowd. *Wow that's good stuff. Alright then let's run with this, back page, picture of kid tipping cap and the headline*: BIG PAP: ROOKIE STANDS TALL IN DEBUT.

When the ovation ends, with Papelbon shaking hands like a ten-year veteran in the dugout, there is still Lew Ford standing on second, Ryan on first, Nick Punto to be dealt with at the plate, and another rookie pitcher for the Sox on the mound. This time it is Manny Delcarmen, who pitched his first Major League inning on the road earlier in the week but now stands for the first time on the mound at Fenway Park, about a ten dollar cab ride from the Hyde Park neighborhood he grew up in. Perhaps understandably he appears twitchy on the mound, his nerves palpable. Yet he works Punto into a full count, then throws a pitch by him for the second out. Now with two on and two outs, Delcarmen is one out away from making his own headlines when Shannon Stewart smashes his first pitch down the third base line, and as is often the case in baseball Delcarmen is at first very lucky and then, suddenly, not. Mueller dives to his right and at full stretch makes a spectacular stop, pops up, takes aim at second, and throws the ball into right field. Ford comes around to score and give the Twins the lead, and after a walk to load the bases Delcarmen is lifted for veteran lefty Mike Myers. Delcarmen is applauded as he goes, because while his effort was not exactly dazzling (especially by comparison), he did enough, and when Myers gets Joe Mauer to ground out to short the damage is minimal. So maybe the other rookie appearance on this day was not front page stuff, but still, somewhere in the middle there... *Run an article on the local kid, short, to the point, just get a few quotes from former teachers and coaches saying what a great kid he was and how even though he was an athlete he always worked hard at school; you know, the usual; and let's run it in the back with a headline like, let's see, how about*: HOME BOY: HYDE PARK ROOKIE MAKES FENS DEBUT. (*Of course it's obvious. That's the point. How long have you worked here anyway?*)

An inning later and the situation nearly repeats itself with one on and two out, and this time Mike Timlin relieving Myers to face Lew Ford. After working the count full and fouling off several pitches Ford finally locks in and laces a ball deep into right field. Kapler, back in right after a half season away from Fenway, breaks as hard as ever on contact and sprints (also as hard as ever) in the wrong direction. Just as we remember him. And just as we remember him rushing headlong at the wrong angle, we remember him changing direction and hustling just as hard to recover ground and make the catch; and so sprinting into the gap he bends back as the ball slices behind him, over his shoulder, and at the last moment leaps and throws his arm back and makes the catch before crashing to the ground and rolling over once, on his back, where he comes to a stop on both knees. Hat off. Uniform dirty. Ball in glove.

Perhaps inspired by Kapler's indestructible grit (if not somewhat amused by his inexplicable lapses in perception) the Sox come out swinging in the seventh and create a situation of their own with an Olerud single and Varitek double. Millar is next, and just as Kapler's dive was characteristic of the way he often helped win games outside the box score, so too Millar, at the plate, works a typically Millarian at bat. Fouling off pitch after pitch, pulling everything inside a bit too hard, pushing everything outside a bit too wide, he stays in the box until he gets one near the middle and lofts it into center, deep enough to score the run and tie the game, 3-3. And as Olerud crosses the plate and Fenway cheers both he and (more so) Millar, we feel ourselves suddenly caught up in the flow of the game itself—in the thrill of Kapler's catch and the struggle of Millar's at bat, in the rookies stepping up and in the two deep rapid-fire home runs, and more generally with the back and forth swing of situation and circumstances and characters which is the mark of any truly wonderful game. So that all at once we realize, with a ripple of recognition trickling up our backs, that somewhere within the pleasures and thrills of this immensely entertaining game the time—and the clock we have watched all afternoon—has somehow gotten away from us.

It is after four. The trade deadline has passed.

So that after week of wondering and watching and talking and wondering some more, and waiting for news and commentary on the news, and even news on the commentary on the news, there is no news.

No news at all. Except, of course, the incidental news that the Twins have once again loaded the bases, and Timlin and the Sox are really up against it here in the eighth as our attention is once again drawn back to the place where it began, where it belongs, the place where the real news of baseball is generated—on the field. Where it is Tiffee again at the plate (he of the near grand slam in the fourth) who this time works the at bat a bit longer but ends it with a bit less drama, fanning weakly at a pitch outside the strike zone to end both the threat and inning. *Nice. If things work out let's run short piece on the bullpen; the old warrior shows rookies how to yada yada yada, we've run it a million times, with maybe something like*: HOLD-ING ON: TIMLIN's K PRESERVES TIE, SET'S UP—. (*Hold off on the rest; we'll let you know in a minute.*)

Headlines on top of headlines, the game has created enough news already to fill our entire morning paper, our daylong conversations, and the majority of our evening commutes. But it is not done yet. Not nearly. Even with the numerous stories unfolding on the field before us—all gratefully stories of what the Sox did rather than what the Sox said—we find that our boldest, front page headline has yet to be set. Because on this Sunday, the last day of such a hectic week, the story can only end one way, and can only be ended by one man. We glance down and find him there, still sitting in the right dugout after all.

For Manny Ramirez, the Red Sox left fielder and cleanup hitter, *is still* the Red Sox left fielder and cleanup hitter. As he has been for the last four season, and as he will continue to be for the remainder of this his fifth season at Fenway. And at the end of a week when this ques-tion—*will he stay or will he go,* and *does he want to stay or want to go*—was speculated upon and debated throughout New England, the argument has come back to where it began: that the Red Sox can no more make up their minds on wanting Manny than he can make up his mind up on wanting them. As it is, we are all of us—team, player, fans and media—stuck with each other; and so while we are all here together on a Sunday afternoon at Fenway, we might as well have a good time and try to win a baseball game. As Sox fans we might as well cheer, because that is what we do when a player with *Red Sox* across his chest comes up to bat. And Manny might as well do what he does, which is hit.

Both sides come to terms with this, and with each other, when with two outs in the eighth Rentería doubles to left center; which brings Ortiz to the plate, brings fill-in outfielder Adam Stern into the on deck circle, and leaves Twins' manager Ron Gardner to contemplate a now wide open first base. It does not take long. Twins catcher Joe Mauer stands, holds out his glove, and it is finally time for this long long week of talk to end with one final, finalizing act. Stern is called back from the on deck circle. And at the very first glimpse of him Fenway Park roars to a height it has not approached all day, as from top step the black helmet, the long black braids, the white jersey, and the Red Sox red of number 24 emerges on the top step, bat in hand. And after all the talk, and all the gossip, and all the rumors and speculation and shouts and boos and no comments and wondering about and speculation over and desperately waiting to find out *where will he go*—after all that—the answer turns out that he will go where he has always gone, to the right side of the batter's box at Fenway Park. Where the headline is once more: MANNY AT THE BAT.

Somewhere the announcer is saying his name, and number, and position, but it is all drowned out by the tumult of the crowd as Fenway, already on its feet in anticipation, now showers down a roaring, reverberating ovation. As for Manny, he stands outside the box with his bat under his left arm, looking down as he tightens each batting glove in turn—black braids hanging over his shoulders, the folds of his outsized white jersey hanging down over his arms, the folds of his outsized white pants hanging down over his shoetops—then takes the bat in his left hand as his left foot plants in the front of the box and his right hand presses his helmet to his head, the right foot follows as the bat taps the front of the plate, once, both hands to the handle and one good swing around and he is ready. Same as he ever was. He takes a strike looking; then a ball; then another questionable strike before fouling away a pitch off the plate (the same pitch which was called a strike earlier, with Manny protecting now). The next pitch is a ball on the outside corner of the plate, and Manny swings—head down, foot blocked, shoulder in, hip forward—and sends it bouncing up the middle past the mound and over the infield grass and towards second and, skipping once over the bag, clean through into center for base hit; Rentería comes around to score easily and the Sox take the lead and Manny lands on first pointing and smiling and we, wherever we are, jump up and down and high five each other and smile and cheer and everything that has been said and written about him all week long is forgotten, in one instant, as if it never happened. Replaced before Renteria even crosses the plate with *This just in*: MANNY'S BACK: SOX SLUGGER MAKES TRIUMPHANT RETURN, SINGLES IN WINNING RUN.

(*Alright clear the back page. Clear the front page. New story: Team decides to give Manny another chance. Manny eager for second chance. Team forgiving. Manny repentant. Team understanding. Manny revived, loves Boston and Red Sox and Fenway. Team glad to hear it. You know, the whole Prodigal Son Returns angle, play up the tension, get quotes from the team about how big a part of the club he is, quotes from him about happy to be back and all that, quotes from everybody saying they knew it would all work out in the end. The headlines practically write themselves. Oh we'll get a week out of this, at least.*)

All day, every day, all season long, we are surrounded by news—in the papers, on the radio, on television, on websites and blogs and chat rooms. It is on our streets, in our cars, and on our trains. It is on our televisions, in our radios, on our computers. Sometimes it is even in our phones. It is the static background noise which fills the spaces between the last out of one game, and the first pitch of the next. Only at times it grows so loud as to block out the sound of the game itself; it lingers far too long into batting practice to rush across one last bit of breaking news, and shows up too eager after the game, waiting for us the very instant we turn away. We wake up, and there it is, with stories more properly suited for the Business section somehow crowding their way onto the Sports page. We go through our day and talk with friends and fans, and there it is, not to talk about the seventh inning of last night's game, but about a *no comment* given an hour before it even started. Turn on the television, it is there. Tune in the radio, it is there. Pull up a website devoted to *baseball*, it is there.

Finally we go to the ballpark simply to escape it. We find a spot tucked deep within Standing Room Only and take up our scorecard for a few hours respite within the game itself. Only somehow it has found us there, too. Not content with the other twenty-one hours in the day it spills over past the first pitch, intrudes into a middle-inning rally, and finds its way into a tough situation close and late and with the game on the line. And it talks to us not about baseball but about contracts and clauses and deals, about terms and options and incentive packages, about agents and prospects and markets, about trades and about transactions and (mainly) about other people's money.

What we need, what in these situations we find ourselves desperately searching for, is something loud enough to drown out this noise. And nothing does this so effectively, so wholly, so satisfyingly, as thirty-five-thousand people on their feet and cheering. Cheering for something good to happen; and then, a moment later, cheering and shouting and laughing for something really exciting that *just happened right there in front of us, wow, can you believe that!* Beneath which the dull malcontent grumble of rumor is never heard—rendered small, silent, irrelevant—and disappears as if it was never there. Which is exactly what this Sunday matinee against the Twins, on an overcast day at the end of a stormy week, has given us. By providing us with so much to cheer about, so much to cheer for and so many (far more interesting) storylines to engage in and follow, it has in fact stopped the presses, and for one enthralling moment given us back the experience we came to the ballpark for in the first place—to be there, late in the game, with everything on the line, cheering on our team and pulling like hell for a base hit.

As for Manny, he was able to provide this experience by simply returning to what he too came to the game for—to be at the plate with the game on the line, to find his pitch, and to hit it. So it is no wonder then that the applause when he does just this feels so full, so rich, and that the good feeling it creates lingers with all of us long after the game. He played. We cheered. Fenway shook with the sound of a Red Sox run. And the Earth continued rotating right on around the Sun.

So that a half inning later (*Stop the presses!*) there is room for only one more headline (*Front Page!*) the last of the day (*All Caps!*) and our favorite of them all: SOX WIN.

In the Garden of Baseball Delights

(a triptych)

Cleveland at Fenway
31 July 2006

EXTERIOR, CLOSED

From the outside it has never looked like much—an unassuming brick wall, not particularly high, topped with pale green trim and marked only by the occasional corrugated steel garage door. Surrounded by concrete sidewalks, occasionally cracked and more often spotted with trodden black gum; and pinned in by five asphalt streets, occasionally clean but more often choked with wet newspapers and torn placards and broken white styrofoam cups. And that, really, is about all she is to look at.

Unlike the monumental Cathédrale de Notre Yankees it does not climb above the city and, in true High Gothic style, tower gloriously into the heavens, a status symbol of its club's power and its team's divine aspirations. Instead it is rather crammed in, twisted, turned, pushed flat on one side and ultimately hammered into place between an outdated railroad line, a roaring turnpike, a row of dark featureless clubs, and a parking garage. Unlike the magnificent Taj Oriole at Camden Yards it does not offer a series of lovely photo-friendly vistas, so typical of the game's now famous Early Renaissance period, in front of which fans may create postcard grade mementos of their visit. Instead visitors circle its perimeter for hours, turning one corner after the next as they look for (but do not find) a suitable backdrop for the mandatory We Were There group photo.

Perhaps somewhat embarrassed by these comparisons, recent efforts have been made to try and brighten the old girl up. A handful of small trees were installed on its sidewalks, and a handful of minor renovations were made to its exterior. The results have done much for the area (certainly more than the area has done for the health of the trees). And yet even with these improvements the environs skirting its exterior are still more often dark and loud and urban, than parklike; more often cluttered and defaced and littered, than clean. Despite all attempts to mask and adorn, from the outside the structure remains unimpressive. Still looks more like a warehouse than a cathedral; still fails to inspire either awe or flash photography; still looks incapable of enclosing anything more than the modesty its exterior suggests.

And yet. If you look close enough, and know where to look, you will find that among the bricks in the very center of this unremarkable image lies a small brass latch, slightly rusted from the elements but otherwise in fine working order. Lift it, and you discover that this plain exterior image is only the outer varnish of a triptych, two matching panels laid flat upon a third. And when we open these panels wide, and lay the entire work open, why what do we find within?

RIGHT PANEL

David Boomer Wells, heavy and disheveled, slouched back wearily on the Fenway mound with his glove held over his face. His shoulders lift and sag with an exhale as he reaches up into his glove, nods, looks back over his shoulder to check the Indians' Jason Michaels leaning off third. Wells pauses, pushes off, drops his left hand behind his back knee, strides forward, swings his left arm over in one long looping arc (the motion always oddly reminiscent of an elephant tossing up its trunk) and throws home. In the batter's box Indians catcher Victor Martínez follows the ball low across his ankles. The home plate umpire stands. *Ball four.* A low groan and spats of exasperated shouts echo out from the stands as Wells kicks dirt off the rubber. He shrugs both shoulders forward with a great heave, as if pulling on some immensely heavy jacket, and gives a tired little tug to his left sleeve.

It has been that kind of game, fitful and irritating. Two Sox runs in the first to take an early lead; three Indians runs in the second to take it back; two more Sox runs in the bottom half to immediate retake it; two more Indian runs in the third to re-take it back; a single Sox run in the bottom half to tie it; and another in the fifth to re-retake the lead, yet again. This the unappealing result of baseball without defensive supervision. So that even though the Sox lead by a run (6-5), and it is still only the fifth inning, there is nonetheless throughout Fenway a palpable and wholly justified apprehension about the way this game, not to mention this season, is shaping up.

A humid, airless night, the posted standings on the left field wall now show the Red Sox lead at only a game and a half (and a mere game in the more accurate loss column). This lead, which has fluctuated anywhere between a half game and 3 ½ games for nearly a month now, has over that same time become a kind of security blanket for Sox fans—something to hold onto after tough losses, and through our private moments of anxiety and misgiving—and we have become accustomed to muttering *well, we're still in first place* at even the slightest hint of foreboding. This tiny, bare-faced observation has put the brakes on many a doubt over the midsummer months (if nothing else it seems ungrateful to complain too much when one has technically won more games than any AL team outside of Detroit); and yet beneath it there has always been a queasy, apprehensive whisper of self-doubt: that *we've been lucky*, that *others have been unlucky*, that we are *not really that good after all* and that sometime, perhaps sometime very soon, the mask will fall.

Then too there is the now unavoidable recognition, with a glance above the scoreboard, that not only are the floodlights on at Fenway in the top of the second but have been on since the first pitch at 7:05 pm EST—a clear sign that the earth has continued on its oblong revolution around the sun and is now drifting farther away from its aphelion and towards its perihelion with the net result being that midsummer baseball is no more. That we are now closer to autumn than spring, closer to the World Series than Spring Training, and while The End is not exactly neigh, it is at very least uncomfortably within view.

Furthermore, today happens to be the 31st and last day of July, and just under four hours ago the closing bell rang on the MLB trade deadline, putting an end to a rather fruitless quarter of low volume trading. Despite all speculation to the contrary the Red Sox's investment analysts ultimately deemed the market prices too high, and held onto each of their considerable and soon-to-be appreciating assets. An admirable, courageous, and sensible act of shrewd baseball prudence which immediately set off a massive anxiety attack (it runs in the family) among Red Sox fans everywhere.

Certainly on the whole, given the number of unheralded faces on the roster coming out of Spring Training, it has been a pleasant surprise to find this team not only competent but talented, versatile, and increasingly satisfying to watch. With their mixture of young emerging prospects (Papelbon, Lester, Hansen) and rejuvenated veterans (Lowell, Loretta, Schilling) we have, thus far, been quite proud of the roster which constitutes Our Team. But there has always been a *but*, lying in wait; but *they need another left-handed bat;* but *they need a fifth starter;* but *they need a reliable long man;* but *they are not quite there, not quite yet;* but *they still need help.* With the market on all of the above still open the opportunity to remove one or more of those *buts* was always out there, serving to relieve stress through the pleasant notion that the Sox could, at any moment, instantly and unequivocally improve simply by trading for some immense new talent. (How exactly the Red Sox Baseball Operations team was going to manage this feat without destroying the farm system for a generation, we left entirely up to them. Naturally. All we knew or cared about was that it *was* possible. Why any of the struggling small market teams with a spare superstar on their hands were going to trade their most valuable assets to us in exchange for one of our unwanted spare parts—say, Wily Mo Peña and prospects—were, again, not details we could be bothered with. Such things could be worked out if a front office *really* wanted to win. And if they asked us—and their failure to do so was a pretty clear indication that they might *not* really want to win—we would surely offer the same answer we gave to all such negotiating puzzles, which was, is, and always will be, *uh, I dunno, we'll uh—we'll throw in a coupla' more prospects.*) At 4:00 pm EST the possibility of this seductively easy answer to all our problems was removed, leaving us with the now frightening notion that: holy sh—, *this* is our team. A handful of veterans limping towards retirement and a bunch of fresh-faced kids? A right fielder newly placed on the DL, a fifth starter with persistent back pain, and Rudy Seánez? (And by the way, just now, our catcher out of the game after limping home in the fourth.) And so whereas yesterday we were thrilled that our team had achieved so much with so little, tonight we openly worry that they may in fact have far too little to do much at all.

All of which is made infinitely worse by the sight of David Wells shrugging his shoulders and slouching wearily on the mound, flopping his glove to his side as he receives the throw back from Mirabelli. (Perhaps here it is worth mentioning, lest anyone assume otherwise, that we have always enjoyed David Wells's performance both as a player and as one of the great characters on baseball's stage, and that we fully embraced his addition to the Sox's roster. Which is precisely what makes it so difficult to watch as) Wells tugs at his sleeve again, and we in the stands fold our arms or dip our heads or pace about, or whatever it is we do when we fret over the fortunes of the Sox; because it is not just another start for Wells, or for the Sox. It is Wells's first start back after two months of rehab, his first innings of competition since a line drive off an already unsteady knee sent him sprawling across the Fenway mound. On that night Wells had fallen so hard and grimaced with such pain that we had assumed the worst—that this was it for Wells, a fine career unfortunately ended by injury. Reports of his rehab were encouraging, but it was not until he started to throw again that we allowed ourselves to even think about *what if*, and only when his start tonight was announced that we went a step further to: *if he can pitch, then maybe.*

Of course baseball being a game with a wry, slightly mischievous sense of humor, this first start back has perfectly aligned itself with the passing of the trade deadline. For emphasis, apparently. So that instead of new faces—instead of some rangy outfielder with power to all fields, instead of a compact lefty with a vicious bat-destroying cut fastball, instead of a lithe young infielder with otherworldly reflexes, a superb understanding of the strike zone, a professional maturity beyond his years and that special competitive spirit which not only performs under the bright lights of Yankees games and the playoffs but excels, and who *while we're at it* really loves Fenway and Boston and just everything about being a Red Sox to the point where he can't wait to sign his next contract for ten years, at a discount—instead of all that, we get the *Boomah*, slow and sweaty, trying to huff and puff his way out of one more half-inning without anything too disastrous befalling either himself or the Sox.

This then the source(s) of concern now clouding the faces throughout our section of the left field roof. Most notably those of a pair of young men standing behind its back row in red t-shirts (ORTIZ and RAMIREZ respectively, predictably), blue Sox hats variously tilted to the side or turned backwards, who from the first pitch on have shouted encouragement to the mound (*Let's go now Boomah!*), have turned away in disgust from Indian doubles off the wall, and have leapt up to punch the air with each Manny and Ortiz home run. Now, with runners on the corners and two outs and Wells facing Casey Blake, they look worried. In fact, they look distraught. Wells resets, shifts his weight onto his back foot as he comes set, checks the runner on third, then throws. The ball sails in, there is a soft pop, and we stare blankly into the sky as somewhere across it a ball silently rises up high above left field, floats gently down, and lands without a sound in the Monster Seats. And the entire scene before us, begins to sink.

Down it goes under the weight of the scoreboard, where the lead has fallen (8-6, Tribe), down under the standings where a half game will not hold up much longer. Down under the weight of our disappearing summer and heavy thoughts no longer supported by *just wait, it's still early*, or *this team is still coming together*, or *maybe they'll bring someone in*. Down under the weight of having watched the one positive, uplifting boost we have look forward to, our pleasant late summer surprise, give up eight runs on seven hits in 4 ⅔ innings and look every day his 43-years and maybe one or two more than his 248-pounds. Concern begets concern as we realize: there is no other option. Our team is on the field, and all of a sudden they look underwhelming and feeble and way, way too young.

So is this it then? Is this to be our lot, to hold our breath and hope that Julián Tavárez can overcome a lifetime of volubility in the next six weeks? Are we staking our best hopes on the backs of rookies? What if they aren't up to it; or, just as bad, what if they are up to it now but fold later on, when the pressure kicks in? Should we start checking the Wild Card standings now and just get it over with; or should we go a step further and simply look to next year, hope these kids mature and stay here and (honestly just tell us now) are we rebuilding here? Is that's what's going on? The aging veterans and the utility infielders and all the focus on pitching and defense and the farm system that is the keynote of every good Rebuilding Phase speech. What if this is it for this generation and when Schilling retires after next season and Nixon is gone and Wake retires and no one takes their shoes we are left with only Ortiz and Manny and an anonymous bullpen, and start loosing 10-9 games every night and more or less turn into the Rangers? We sit down, head between our knees, and concentrate on deep breaths.

Wells gives up a wholly unnecessary single to Peralta, and Francona shuffles from the dugout with his head down to pull him. Meanwhile, it has become noticeably muggier around the ballpark. The breeze has died off altogether and the crowd around us is fidgety, uncomfortable, annoyed. And we realize that we are thirsty, and have been for several innings. And the lines are ridiculous. And the wave pops up in the bleachers and the boos for its eventual fade blend seamlessly with the scattered boos for Wells. And we glance to the two fans in red at our side, who only shake their heads, as if they know it too that the inning and game and season and summer, and our night at Fenway, have all gone right to hell.

* * *

CENTER PANEL

Kyle Snyder, tall and slender with curly blond hair bunched around his ears, throws an offspeed pitch that Kelly Shoppach swings over and misses, strike three, for the second out (and second strikeout) of the sixth inning. Scheduled to start tonight, Snyder was bumped to make room for Wells's return to the rotation and now, after coming on in relief in the fifth, is out there primarily to save the arms of his teammates in the bullpen. We know this, of course, and have taken up a rare empty seat, and have kicked our feet up a bit (also rare), in order to more comfortably watch him work. A little breeze slips off the roof and over our section. We managed something to drink and a bite to eat between innings, and at this point more or less try and relax in the warm summer air and enjoy the game, regardless of the score or outcome. Snyder allows a single to Sizemore but we are no longer concerned, really, so long as this one does not get too out of hand we can move on to tomorrow. There will be other games.

Snyder sets and throws, Michaels swings and fouls it off, then takes a ball, fouls two more off and stands looking at a breaking ball that Mirabelli snaps up at his knees. The umpire turns and punches—*strike three*. We give easy, resigned applause as Snyder and the Sox jog off the field; and only a moment later when we jot the K on our scorecard do we notice (*well now that's interesting*) that Kyle Snyder just struck out the side.

He continues to work nice and easy through the seventh, retiring the side in order on two grounders and a fly ball, and between he and Indians' reliever Jason Davis—who came on for starter Paul Byrd and shut the Sox down in the fifth and sixth—restores a measure of composure to a thoroughly discomposed game. In the stands we take these moments to relax and breath; to go to the restroom without fear of missing one or more lead changes; to organize our scorecard a bit (ink rations were a concern by the fourth); to stand up and sing a bit in the middle of the seventh and once again, as ever, to *root root root for the Red, Sox*, when with two outs in the seventh Ortiz comes up, and doubles into the corner.

Manny is up, and the two fans in red beside us begin to chant *Let's-Go, Red-Sox!* *Let's-Go, Red-Sox!* until it spreads through our section, gathers with the same chant across the ballpark, and does not stop when Manny takes a ball but instead builds seamlessly into *Man-ny!* *Man-ny!* *Man-ny!* The two fans pace back and forth, cracking thick, loud claps on each downbeat, pushing forward into the aisle before each pitch as their enthusiasm and focused anticipation pulls them closer to the game. Their expressions are strained, electric, bursting; faces well beyond the point of merely *rooting*; voices for whom what is happening on the diamond below is absolutely crucial, desperately crucial, to their level of happiness if not equilibrium. Familiar faces here at Fenway, they are the faces and voices of Red Sox fans (bless their hearts) for whom it is nothing but glory and doom. So *come on!* it's *everybody up!* and *Let's-Go, Red-Sox!* They leap, pumping their fists when Manny walks and the chorus is taken back up, *Let's-Go, Red-Sox!* *Let's-Go, Red-Sox!* And when Lowell pops out there is a deep, leveling silence; but only for a moment. By the time Snyder takes the mound again you can feel it, that infectious energy, bristling with intent and now rolling throughout the ballpark. The rally has revitalized all of us, and for the next two innings Fenway is once again raucous, vibrant, alive from its highest light down to the last brick of its foundation.

(The pilot light at Fenway, it seems, is still lit.)

Over the next inning and a half Snyder continues to get ahead and continues to record outs. Tall and relaxed, he catches the return throw on the lip of the mound, turns and takes two long strides back up, slow and methodical and with a slight lean that somehow accentuates the slope of the mound, as if he were laboring up some steep backwoods hill, instead of a low mound of dirt. He sets, shoulders sloped to the right, and pushes off as his long arm fires forward, releasing the ball somewhere far out in front; it pops in the catcher's mitt, and leaves him standing on the lip of the mound with his glove up, preparing for the long hike back. In the eighth he strikes out Peralta swinging, then gets Héctor Luna and Shoppach to fly out. It is a joy to watch him work. Not only because of his pleasing motion, or because that motion is producing outs, but because there is real development here (Snyder is not just throwing well, he is pitching, changing speed and location, setting hitters up; it is a professional outing). And as we lean back and watch him work in the ninth, and nearly come out of our seat at a gorgeous breaking ball to strike out Marté, we are momentarily seized by one of those rare impulses to take a look around us, and appreciate all the good that we find.

For here we are, at the ballpark, among a full and enlivened crowd, the warm air cooled by an onset breeze, a cold beverage in our hand, enjoying the sharp work of a young pitcher. Having already slid fast and far into our own personal baseball hell we now find ourselves, only a few innings later, ascending it into a veritable garden of baseball delights. Standing among a swaying crowed in good voice we share a laugh with an old friend, chat with the two fans in red near us (laurels for Snyder; speculation over Varitek's injury), and as Snyder throws and Michaels pops up, high up over first, we are smiling before it even comes down. The line for Snyder: 4 ⅓ innings, one hit, six strikeouts, no runs. Which is something to cheer about, all by itself.

In a perfect world he would be honored with the victory he has earned. But standing here clapping we know that this is not always how the game works, and that it is best to appreciate the small joys within our reach—the warm summer night, a cool drink, the solid improvement of an unheralded pitcher, and good company to share it all within—knowing all along that each time we enter the ballpark it is this garden of baseball delights that we hope for, and nothing more.

LEFT PANEL

Until the bottom of the ninth, with the score still 8-6. The Indians' young closer, Fausto Carmona, is on the mound. We are standing, clapping, a nervous reserve reigning in the noise right up until Alex Cora swings at a 1-1 pitch and slaps it past a diving Marté and into left field for a leadoff single. Fenway bursts to life, clapping and chanting and shouting (you can no longer hear the two booming voices of the fans to our left; as with any real good crowd noise individual voices are enveloped within the whole). Youkilis comes up and looks at a strike, then in succession: takes a ball, fouls off a strike, takes a ball, then another, fouls off a strike, then looks at ball four and flips his bat to the side having worked another trademark professional at bat. Loretta comes up with the tying run in scoring position, only to quickly pop out to shallow center for the first out. A disappointed exhale slips out among the crowd, but it is gone in the time it takes to look from center field to the on deck circle.

For there is Big Papi, just now rapping his bat against his cleats and taking his first lumbering steps towards the plate. As Fenway Park rises to its feet and raises its collective voice around him.

And suddenly here we are—after a day of work or school or errands, moving about the city, checking our email and making phone calls, riding the T or fighting traffic, finding our seats, cheering the leads and bemoaning the deficit, raising our eyebrows at a Peña blast and lowering our head at Blake's long fly, we have grumbled at an aging star and cheered on an improving journeyman, and late on a summer night it comes down to this—bottom of the ninth, down by two, runners on first and second, Ortiz crouching over the plate. The count quickly runs to 2-0. Ortiz knocks his bat against the inside of his spikes as he steps out, spits on his hands, pats them together, picks up his bat and levels it over his back shoulder. The closer throws, Ortiz swings, and suddenly with a rush we are all of us on our feet straining forward with open mouths and wide eyes and laughing and swatting madly into the air we shout *go go go, get up, get up, get up* over and over again as the ball lifts into the night air and sails high above the floodlit field.

A Note from the Curator

An afternoon or evening within the brick and pale green walls of Fenway Park is not often, even by the most cantankerous of standards, a hellish experience. Yet on certain sweltering humid nights, when the past several weeks have been spent watching a solid division lead dwindle away to nothing, and the aging pitcher who is one start off the DL looks one start away from retirement, and you find yourself looking askance at the tender ages of half your bullpen (and with horror at the incompetence of the rest), and you are thirsty, and hungry, and your right fielder and catcher and set-up man and fourth and fifth starters are all on the DL, and in a crucial situation the only noise from the crowd is between pitches to cheer for (*honestly people*) the wave— then well, yes, the experience can, at these worst of times, approximate a kind of personal baseball hell.

Often it is a bit more tolerable than all that. And on certain nights (on most nights, truthfully) it is simply wonderful—a very garden of baseball delights. On nights like these when it is warm but not hot, and there is a soft breeze at your back, and more laughter in the air than shouting, and the whole Boston skyline lit up and draped beyond the bleachers, and maybe the Sox are not exactly running away with things but are right there anyway, in the thick of it, and you check your scorecard and see that the heart of the order will get one more turn; it is at times like these—these best of times—when you simply want to close your eyes and say a quick prayer of thanks. Because when you honestly think about it there is no place in the world that you would rather be, at this moment, than here at the ballpark.

Far less often are then nights when it is more—much, much more—than even this. These are the nights when the lineup and the ground balls and the walks and the doubles all tumble out in just the right order to bring the biggest star, the biggest name, and the most celebrated clutch hitter in the league to the plate with one out in the bottom of the ninth, with two runners on and the Sox down by two. And when the 2-0 pitch sails off his bat and rises up beneath the floodlights it does not dip or fade or slow but keeps going, farther and higher until it disappears into the rippling bleachers and you cannot help but shout *yes he did it can you believe it he did it again*; and all of a sudden life is a blur of noise and laugher and smiles and jumping and watching the pile at home, shooting our arms in the air and letting out a yell, and for maybe ten seconds—and just those ten seconds—you are lost in as close as a fan may ever comes to baseball paradise.

EXTERIOR, CLOSED

The heavy right panel is carefully lifted and laid across its front. The left panel is folded over and laid flat to meet it. The little brass latch is fastened over a now invisible seam. And we take a step back, to look at it sitting still under its gallery floodlights.

On the outside she still isn't much to look at. Just a brick wall with pale green trim, dressed up with a few arches and sidewalk trees. There are still cracks on the sidewalk; still grimy trod-upon gum between the cracks; still washed up newspapers in the streets. The old parking garage and chain-link fence and roaring turnpike look no better by street light than they do by daylight. And it all still looks (in any light, from any angle) as if it might just as soon be full of cardboard boxes, as baseball. And this, of course, is part of its wonder—part of its very particular form of magic.

Not because once we step inside it we are likely to find, in the remarkable range and intensity of experience, encompassing all the joys and heartbreaks of a season, a kind of baseball version of heaven or hell. Nor because of the more frequent times when we enter it to find, in the sheer vivacity of its colors and sounds and sights, that garden of baseball delights. But rather because it is one of those curious places (there are not so many) in which we are just as likely to find this entire range of experiences. Sometimes all in one night. A place where we are just as likely to shout at the top of our voice in frustration, as we are to shout at the top of our voice in delight; where we are just as likely to be uncomfortably hot (or cold) as we are to be ethereally comfortable; where we are just as likely to find ourselves grown thirsty, as were are to find ourselves having drunk way, way too much; where we are just as likely to see friends, as Yankee fans; where we are just as likely to be charmed by the kindness and generosity and good cheer of our fellow fan, as not; where we are as likely to sit for hours staring at nothing more interesting than the pit-cher cleaning his spikes, as we are to leap out of our seats and wave and yell at a small white ball sailing through the night air; where we are just as likely to dismiss the entire experience as a waste of time, as we are to have had the absolute time of our lives. All in one night. All in one place. All behind an unassuming brick façade, in the Fenway.

Good Night, Fenway

Tampa Bay at Fenway
14 August 2007

Alright, so this one has a happy ending. You see it's all about a young man who faces tremendous obstacles with courage and dignity, conquers a despicable villain, rises above adversity with his head held high, and upon his triumphant return home is given a true hero's welcome. Along the way he is joined by a tough and grizzled veteran, out for one last go around; a strong, silent leader (his captain); a fleet-footed teammate with a bubble afro and a quick bat (and a name fit for Hollywood); and, of course, the requisite gray-haired father figure, who steps in at the crucial moment and, with the ease of a hand on the shoulder, calmly saves the day. Just for good measure, there's even a cute kid involved. It's a feel-good story, you see, inspirational and uplifting and all that. The kind of thing you can bring the whole family to. And it only seems fair to let you know this up front, just as certain movies advertise themselves as *the feel-good story of the summer*. Particularly since this advanced billing is a luxury not often afforded to baseball fans, who after all have no trailer of the upcoming game to go by, and therefore rarely have any idea whether they are attending comedy, romance, or tragedy (until of course it's too late). It is then a rare pleasure to know ahead of time—as we know on this Tuesday night in August—that so long as the scheduled Red Sox starter makes it from the bullpen to the dugout, our story will be a good one. Tonight and tonight only, the happy ending is paid up front.

That this particular story will only get better throughout the night, that it has been perfectly cast and costumed (the grizzled veteran with a wad of chaw, the captain with a crew-cut, the distinguished father figure with specks of silver in his goatee), and that its ending will be as happy as its beginning, are pleasures we will discover only later on. Yet even here at the outset one can almost sense a slight unreality to the evening, set as it is beneath a pristine and luxuriously comfortable summer stage, lit by a golden late afternoon sunset, and told against a Fenway Park background so clean and clear and vividly attractive it appears almost *too* picturesque—as if we might reach out and discover that it is in fact entirely flat, the whole thing a Hollywood sound stage set for a baseball movie and propped up from behind. All wood and paint and set designer magic.

Alright then *places, please.* (We find ours here in the left field corner.)

Act One, Scene One: Fenway Park, mid-August, a few minutes past seven o'clock on a Tuesday night in Boston. Where it's: *lights, camera,* and *enter* Jon Lester, the hero, stage right.

With a flip of the collar on his red warmup jacket Jon Lester gives a nod and begins his long walk in from the Red Sox bullpen. At his shoulder is his catcher, Jason Varitek, and his pitching coach, John Farrell; but a few paces beyond the warning track these two drop back deferentially, and let Lester walk on ahead, leading the way across the outfield grass. It is, after all, the last leg of a very long journey. One which began last summer when Jon Lester was called up from the minor leagues and on June 10, 2006, made his Major League debut at Fenway Park in front of 36,920 fans. He recorded his first Major League win on June 16; threw a brilliant a one-hit complete game shutout at Fenway on August 8; missed his next start and went on the 15-day DL due to a mysterious back injury; and at end of August was diagnosed with anaplastic large cell lymphoma—cancer—after which he gave one of the single most courageous and dignified press conference Fenway Park has ever seen when he (alone) explained to the Boston media his diagnosis, outlook, and plan for overcoming it. He then traveled home to Washington state and underwent months of treatment, including chemotherapy. In early December he was declared officially cancer free. He began to workout, began to throw, began to pitch. He attended spring training in March of 2007, then joined the Single-A Greenville Drive and made his first post-diagnosis start on March 5; he was moved up to Triple-A Pawtucket in late April, made fourteen starts, waited, answered questions about a possible return, pitched, waited, answered questions, waited, and in late July finally got the call to rejoin the Red Sox and make his first start back on July 23 in Cleveland. And now, after three more starts both the schedule and the rotation have aligned themselves to bring him here, back to Fenway Park for the first time *since*, where he walks slowly and confidently across its green outfield grass with his head held high, and where all those around him stand and applaud and after so long a journey finally, gratefully welcome him home. And standing here cheering (and perhaps shaking our heads) we remind ourselves of one more date, and one more step along this journey. January 7—his birthday, on which date Jon Lester, Major League pitcher and cancer survivor, turned 23-years-old.

Now, a number of memorable ovations have echoed through the rafters of Fenway Park already this season. Not the least of which was the flashbulb ornamented home debut of Daisuke Matsuzaka; that an eager, peeking in, welcoming applause full of giddy expectancy. Later on there was the warm, deeply sentimental homecoming of Trot Nixon; his the heartfelt, slap on the back mixture of clapping and shouts as he came to the plate and tipped his tarry helmet. And then there was the thunderous reception (surprising even us) given to the Giants' Dave Roberts—briefly a Boston outfielder and now permanently a hero of Boston sports mythology—a roar that clamored over and above itself in one long resounding note of eternal gratitude. By comparison the applause Lester receives as he continues his walk is both less and more. Less in that it is quieter, less energetic, the applause made up of regular chest-level claps (none of the leaning forward, hands out thumpers), and is not interlaced with shouts of encouragement or welcome. A glance across the grandstand confirms that it is more than all this, revealing as it does that we are all of us very upright in our posture; our mouths not shouting or even smiling but pursed; our eyes not searching for a better view but fixed. This is new. With so many welcome back ovations raucous, energized, almost falling over themselves in their audible pats on the back, it takes a moment to recognize what is going on here; but when we do it clear that this particular ovation is quieter because it is infused not with gratitude, but with the deepest, profoundest sense of respect. Respect for what Lester has overcome, and for the courage and dignity with which he has overcome it. It is a sturdy embrace of an ovation (one firm handshake, the lean in, two thick claps on the back) and you can see it in the pulled back shoulders, in the nodding chins, in the quiet shake of the head, and in the eyes of so many fans who struggle in vain to blink back tears. In recognition of which Jon Lester, now approaching the first base line, lifts his Red Sox hat to the crowd, hands a ball to a kid in the front row, and as the applause lingers on above him descends the steps of the Red Sox dugout.

And if that were all, if we all gathered up our programs and cups and filed back through the exits, it would be enough. For tonight this *was* the happy ending. The anticipation of his first road starts, the circling of this date when his turn finally came around, the chorus of voices telling each other *boy that's gonna be a great moment*, the red 62 Strike Out Cancer bracelets being sold tonight to aide a cancer fund on Lester's behalf, the crowd gathered around the bullpen as he warmed up, have all led to this moment, to his official entrance—the hero's welcome and feel-good story and happy ending all rolled into one. Now that it has passed, and Lester takes his familiar sideways leap over the first base line (we'd almost forgotten about that) before stepping onto the mound, what follows must then necessarily be anticlimax. Surely. As throughout the day the consensus has been that while we all hope he pitches well, it ultimately does not matter on a night when his pitching at all is a kind of victory.

Does not matter to us, that is; but most assuredly matters to Jon Lester, who after all is a young pitching prospect and therefore must prove himself again every time he takes the ball. (And let us not forget: that being a Major League pitcher, getting Major League hitters out, is *hard enough already*. No matter the backstory.) For while everyone involved is conscious of the circumstances and therefore patient with Lester's return to the mound, there is nonetheless a question of whether in strictly baseball terms he is fully regained his form as a pitcher. Shaky in each of his first four outings, he has not yet shown the steady effectiveness which led him to an impressive 7-2 record before his injury and subsequent illness. And with his teammates having collectively idled away their comfortable midsummer lead of fourteen games down to an uncomfortable four, there is plenty of baseball pressure out there should Lester wish to add to the inevitable jittery butterflies of his return home. Perhaps understandably he walks the first batter of the game, Akinori Iwamura, on four pitches. After which he settles in, strikes out two, and walks off having recorded a scoreless first.

It is somewhere in the top of the second, on his way to his third and fourth strikeouts of the game, that we are reminded of something else about Jon Lester. That is: we really do enjoy watching this young man pitch. A tall lefty, with those incredibly long arms particular to pitchers, he holds his glove up before him and nods to the sign, takes a small step back, then sweeps the right leg up with toes pointed down, and coming to a balance point flows effortlessly into a long stride that brings his left arm over in one long smooth arc, the release clean as he follows through and the pitch finds its target. No hesitation, no hitch, no little idiosyncratic turn or twist or tap; simply up and over, nice and smooth, as if the entire motion somehow glides along over ice. It is pleasing to watch, so long as one is not in the batter's box trying to make contact with what it delivers. Again, it was not Lester's courage that first brought him to our attention, but his talent. Which he still has, and lots of. With an excellent curveball and a solid fastball, which is particularly effective when working in concert with his brilliant change-up, Lester's only vulnerability thus far has been throwing all of the above for strikes. When he struggles it is out of the strike zone, and while still able to get outs he can pile up pitches at an alarming rate and therefore rarely goes deep into games. When he throws strikes though, he has the potential to do great things. As he shows here tonight, overcoming the first inning walk to retire the next nine Devil

Ray hitters before giving up his first hit, a double by Carl Crawford in the fourth. After another single he gives up a long fly from Carlos Peña that brings in a run, but he recovers nicely, and cruises unharmed through the fifth and sixth.

Unfortunately for both Lester and the Sox this one run is holds up unthreatened thanks to the work of Lester's counterpoint for the night, Devil Rays' ace Scott Kazmir. Like Lester, Kazmir is also 23-years-old, left-handed, and full of promise (again, the casting touch deft). Unlike Lester he has, within the struggling Rays' system, been given a chance to develop that promise at the Major League level; a promise he has thus far (somewhat annoyingly) only seemed to fully live up to when facing the Red Sox. Shorter and more animated on the mound than Lester, Kazmir has the same smooth leg lift, the same clean line made by pointing the toes down; but the similarities end at their respective balance points, where instead of rolling over the top Kazmir sweeps low and dashes forward, vigorously. He throws hard, and though he too requires an excess of pitches to get through the lineup he is just as effective if not more so in the results. And after six innings he walks off the mound with a little shake of his left arm, having allowed the Sox only a handful of harmlessly scattered hits, and no runs.

It is up to Lester then, back out for the seventh, to hold serve. He records the first two outs, and with his pitch count rising everyone watching knows he needs just one more out to complete his night; and so there is a quick gasp when Brendan Harris hits a high drive to left, followed by a comforting exhale as Manny settles under it. He makes the catch for the final out and we are back on our feet again, rising to applaud Lester as he makes his exit walk. This time the cheers are louder, and there are shouts of *that'a'boy Jon!* and *nice work kid!* throughout, and the head-nodding appreciation this time is not out for what Jon Lester has overcome in the past, but how he has moved beyond it, and that his performance tonight allows us to all to look forward once again to the promise of his future.

After Lester's departure the houselights are brought up, just a bit, and overall there is a lazy Intermission feel to the stretch and the half inning which follows. With Lester and Kazmir having held a careful equilibrium over seven innings, the game (aside from Lester's emotional entrance and exit) has remained somewhat remarkably uneventful. A lazy pop up to left kind of night, comfortable and easy, the at-bats and outs and innings rolling along steady and unhurried. The type of night where one ends up noticing and interacting with the fans in the surrounding sections more than usual. Which for us, down in the left field corner and leaning against the wall (right of the partial Gulf sign), means observing a father and son team of Standing Room Only opportunists spend the evening gamely searching out empty seats and seizing upon them, only to be shooed away moments later by its occupants (undaunted, they re-take their survey posts and come running over with *hey Dad I found two good ones down here*, before they're off again); a scruffy-bearded Vermonter who, having recently graduated college is setting out tomorrow morning on his way first to California, then grad school in Seattle, and is not only undertaking the entire trip solo, but on motorcycle; and finally, shortly after the game resumes in the bottom of the seventh, a little girl in pink seated at the end of the row directly in front of us, who we had not noticed before but who now sits cross-legged with her father's scorecard in her lap and every so often leans over to make a small pen mark. To which our immediate reaction is *how sweet, she's playing scorecard*.

It is not until later on in the eighth, when Manny Delcarmen works the Sox into a jam and the little girl's father quickly steps away during a pitching change (Timlin for Delcarmen) that we realize, to our wonder, that she is not playing. Not exactly anyway. Her father, returning a batter later, smiles as he looks to the scorecard and checks the small marks she has made, and adds something like *good job*. And sure enough when Carl Crawford is intentionally walked to load the bases she marks down, with only the slightest paternal prompting, the appropriate mark on their scorecard. That is, *her* scorecard. At this, we are profoundly impressed. For those who admires the careful diligence of scorekeeping in any fan, much less one whose miniature Tevas dangle several inches off the ground, the image of such a young a fan not only keeping score but *wanting to keep score* is a necessarily hopeful sight. Made all the more so by what happens next. '

With two outs and the bases loaded and the game suddenly on the line, the crowd for perhaps the first time all night rises off its collective seat and cheers for a Timlin strikeout; and right on cue the little girl in front of us hops off her seat, looks out to the mound, and cheers. No looking about to make sure she is doing what everyone else is doing; no anxious reaching up for her father to lift her; she is not even standing on her seat (only a head taller than the seatback herself, the few empty seats in front of her cut a neat little alley for her to see through); and when B.J. Upton flails at a Timlin fastball around his shoulders for strike three she shoots her arm up with the best of them and cheers. At this point we have to ask and do. And her father smiles when he tells us that she is seven years old; that *yes*, she likes to keep score; and that although she has been to games before this will be her first time going all nine.

Which brings a smile.

For it is not just the fact that she is on her feet cheering while three rows up a little boy (at least her age if not older) lays across his mother's lap and sucks his thumb; or that she is still awake and involved long after many other kids older than herself have, after an inning of shirt-tugging and whining, been sleepily carted up the aisle in the arms of their departing parents. And it is not just that when Eric Gagne comes on to strike out the first batter of the eighth looking she expertly draws a backward K on her scorecard (which she does); or that when he later gives up a double she sits down with everyone else, then stands right back up with two strikes; or that when Gagne records the second strike out she rises up and not only claps but chants right along in perfect sync, Let's-*Go*, Red-*Sox*, clap clap, clap-clap-clap, Let's-*Go*, Red-*Sox*; or that when people exit her row she automatically lifts her knees (unnecessarily but politely) to let them pass; or that she does all of the above in a little pink sweatshirt and pinks shorts, with her faded pink Sox hat on (a small Fenway Park pin in its side), and her own red 62 Strike Out Cancer band around her wrist, and is, yes, just altogether completely adorable. For all of this makes her charming and one might even go so far as to say cute. But it is something else altogether which makes her encouraging and promising and even, for all those who care about the future of this game, somewhat inspiring.

Because while we know next to nothing about child development and therefore cannot honestly say if any of her scorekeeping or attentive following along is advanced for her age (though we suspect it is), we do know baseball fans. And we know exactly where she fits on *that* developmental scale. For she does not spend an entire inning text messaging, as the middle-age man a row in front of her does; and she does not chit-chat during pitches, as the college-age couple behind her do; and she is not off (or sending her father off) to the concession stand every other inning, as a good many fans of all ages do pretty much all night. What she does—*all* she does—is watch the game. So far as we can tell from the few innings in which we split our attention between her and the mound, she never misses a pitch. She cheers when the Sox do well, stands up when they need encouragement, and watches to see what will happen next. And this simple, fundamental act of following the game in an interested and engaged fashion puts her, in terms of fan development, at an extremely advanced stage not only for her age but within the ballpark as a whole. And because of this we find ourselves in the late innings rooting as much for her to make it through the whole game as we do for Gagne to strike out the side. Which he does, eventually, to send the game into the ninth with the Sox still trailing, 1-0.

Manny leads off, and as he twists his right toe into the box and gives the front of the plate one good chop we begin our encouraging cheers, *come on Manny*, with an optimism we perhaps do not entirely feel. This because we have learned throughout the summer that this Red Sox team, while more capable than many of its predecessors at attaining an early lead and far more reliable in holding it, is at the same time somewhat less resilient in overcoming even the smallest late inning deficit. In these situations—trailing close and late—they simply have not been able to produce the big hit when they need it. Or least it seems that way. Leading us to the impression that once down, this team typically stays down. (This feeling, only a vague impression among the crowd, is driven home with stark clarity to those watching at home as just before the ninth begins the television broadcast flashes a startling statistical confirmation: that these Sox, when trailing after eight innings, have a record of exactly 1-41. Those then, are the odds.) All of which is only reinforced by Manny, who strikes out looking and walks across the plate on his way back to the dugout; and by the time Lowell steps to the plate we have already begun to preemptively bolster our spirits with the familiar fan consolation of *at least*. At least we had a chance to welcome Lester back. (Lowell digs in.) At least he looked strong and threw well and despite all the emotions pitched a fantastic game. (Lowell takes a ball from Rays' closer Al Reyes.) At least Timlin came in and got a big out, and at least Gagne looked more like himself. (Lowell takes another ball. 2-0. We reflexively clap encouragement.) At least we have Lester's walk to the dugout, and walk off the mound to take away and remember this game fondly by, even if the Sox don't—and *pop*, with one good swing from Lowell the ball shoots up and everyone rises and in the corner we are shouting even as we look straight up and watch the white floodlit ball sail like a silent jet passing overhead across the black night sky and gone; and the little girl now lifted into the air by her father does exactly what fans of every age (including our own) now do: which is shoot our up into the air and shout something like *yeeeeaaaahhh!* It is the Sox's first run, and the first exuberant celebratory cheer of the game. And from here on out everything happens in a great rush and within a perpetual stir of noise and energy and nervous, bouncing optimism. It's a new game.

This raucous optimism rattles to a peek when Youkilis works the count 3-1, then full; and even when, to his incredulous dismay, he strikes out looking there is only a brief moan before the cheers are resumed for Varitek. The ballpark on its feet, Let's-*Go!* Red-*Sox!* ringing out, Varitek jumpy and tapping the inside of his heels. He falls behind 1-2 then fouls off a pair and takes another ball, and on the next pitch brings his big looping swing around and pulls a low drive towards the right field corner that has us leaning and looking eyes-wide (in that corner *it could be*) as the ball hooks and, just before the wall, bounces with one quick hop up into the seats—a double, and

Varitek jogs into second to represent the winning run. Everybody on their feet now, and Crisp up. Crisp, who in his last at bat failed to bunt Varitek over and effectively killed a rally before it started, and who now stands in and takes two balls, a strike, and another ball from Reyes. The count 3-1, and it all seems to be coming together, rolling to an inevitable happy ending until Crisp fouls off a change-up and runs the count full. Here, just for an instant, there is a doubtful pause and a quick, silent worry: *extras.* Ever since Lowell connected the inning has been a celebration of an eventual win, through which we have concentrated only on the lone run it would take to end it. Now suddenly we are confronted with the one strike it would take for the game to reset itself and have us sitting again for the indefinite drawing out of extra innings. (Mixed in somewhere is the realization that with two strikes Varitek will now be running on the pitch.) And for just an instant we worry that our young fan here—once again standing and along with the rest of us now vigorously clapping for that happy ending—might be dragged into extra innings and past her bed time, thus missing its finale. But this blink of foreboding is here and gone, swept away on the next pitch as Crisp swings and serves a nice easy backhand volley up and over the net of infielders, it bounces softly in shallow right and we are leaping and shouting and waving Varitek around as he digs past third and heads home, the throw from right low and up the line and with one hard skip pulls the catcher away from the plate just as Varitek slides with both feet across for the winning run. Sox win, 2-1, and amid the celebration the little seven-year-old Sox fan who has kept score and cheered through this her first full game is swept up into her father's arms, laughing and smiling, and gives us a good solid celebratory *Go Sox* high five before she is off to home and bedtime and what we can only hope will be a long and happy friendship with the game and with her Red Sox—both of whom, based on her own first complete game, will be awfully lucky to have her.

So then it's: cue *Dirty Water*, fade to black, and roll credits.

* * *

There is a tendency to distrust endings this tidy. Particularly when they involve young heroes overcoming great odds, strong silent leaders overpowering the opposition, and cute little kids doing and saying things that seem obviously and overly scripted. (*Come on, a kid that age would never do that.*) Freed from the usual clutter of real life stories these endings feel too clean, too pat, too neatly wrapped to be wholly accepted as true. And yet they happen still. Jon Lester, a 23-year-old kid, beats cancer, tirelessly works himself back to health and form, and is able to harness what ought to be overwhelming emotional distractions to perform an exceedingly difficult task well. In the same game his veteran third baseman, Mike Lowell, himself a cancer survivor and the first teammate Lester spoke with after his diagnosis, comes up with one perfectly timed swing to save the game. And a struggling center fielder who was booed in the seventh for not advancing the runner comes back, in the ninth, to single home the winning run. The End. No lingering backstory or ambiguity here. In fact it only gets more remarkable.

For all of the above is true, and so is this:

Last season Mike Lowell received a note from the family of the late Courtney Butcher, telling him the sad news that this 18-year-old UNH student whom he had never met had tragically lost her life in a car accident that April. That he had been her favorite player. And that unbeknownst to him he had, two nights after the accident, hit a home run to the exact seat in Fenway Park where Courtney, that night, was supposed to have been sitting. When the third baseman found out the news he sent his condolences along with an autographed jersey to be presented at the wake, then told the family he would hit a home run for Courtney that night, and did.

More than a year later the Butcher family, along with the family of another student who was lost in the crash, were the welcome guests of Mike Lowell for this Tuesday night game in August; before which he greeted both families on the field and gave them a personal tour of the Red Sox dugout. Then the ninth. As Courtney's father Jim Butcher told the *Herald* afterwards, "Right before the pitch I looked up towards the sky and said, 'Honey, we need something special from your guy right about now.' It was unbelievable." The Butchers, Lowell, and Sox head trainer Paul Lessard, a friend of the family, all knew it the moment it happened. "When Mike hit it," Lessard said, "I started crying, because I knew how much it must have meant to Jim."

They happen, happy endings. Maybe it is only when we are very young that we fully believe this. As kids (when our feet still dangle off our seat at the ballpark) the hero always comes out on top, your birthday is always right around the corner, and your team always comes through in the ninth. It is only when we grow older and grow up that we know better. We learn to roll our eyes, and question, and be skeptical. In time we learn that anything which seems too good to be true, probably is. We learn to hedge our better hopes against reality and history and the law of averages, and we learn that the frustrating ambiguity of life will keeps most days, and most games, from ending happily ever after. Which of course is exactly why we cheer and shout and raise our arms like children for the ones that do.

If on a Summer's Night a Pitcher

Baltimore at Fenway
1 September 2007

(with apologies to Mr. Italo Calvino)

You are now reading "If on a Summer's Night a Pitcher," a chapter in the book *Standing Room Only*. Or, perhaps more accurately you are now skimming the first few lines of "If on a Summer's Night a Pitcher" and are right now trying to decide whether to go on, whether you have the time, whether you might *just read a page or two*, whether or not you have time for even that, or whether you do in fact have the time and desire (however vague) to sit down and actually commit yourself to reading. A dilemma, surely. For one thing, how long is it? (You flip ahead. It is not so very long.) And what time is it? (You check your watch. It is not so very late.) And there are all those things—oh but don't let's think about *all those things* right now, all those things will be there regardless and besides there is this story, or something like a story, opening up right here before you, just waiting to be read. What do you say then? After all, you've come this far already. Yes? Are you sure? Good.

Please do try and make yourself as comfortable as possible. Realizing of course that your means of doing this may be limited if you are say, on the T, or waiting for a bus, or in a crowded café, or just about anywhere outside of your own home or maybe even only your own bedroom. Though perhaps you are already comfortable, which would be terribly convenient—if you were say at the beach, or before a crackling fireplace, or in some quiet park. Of course it is much more likely that you are at home and not alone, meaning not within an entirely quiet environment. Are those around you making noise? Are they using electronic media devices? Are they conversing at a volume you consider above a normal speaking voice? If so you could politely tell them that you are going to be reading and would they mind keeping it down; only, you know how this usually goes (a considerate nod, and a quick return to somehow *more carefully* making the exact same amount of noise). Perhaps you are alone, and the noise comes from outside your windows. Perhaps you are reading this in the city where it both takes place and was written, and there is a very large industrial vehicle backing down your very narrow street, or a very small dog barking wildly at this same very large industrial vehicle, or a cab idling outside and for some ungodly reason honking its horn even though the person it is waiting on is *right there* walking out the door. That, or the small dog is barking at the cab now honking at the beeping industrial vehicle. In which case there is nothing you can do, even politely. But do try and make yourself comfortable, regardless. Sit in a good chair, or couch, or across a good bed. Perhaps you'd like to order up or pour yourself a cup of coffee. Perhaps you'd care to order up or pour or mix or crack open something a bit stronger (this will help, with the noise). There now. Are you as comfortable as can be? Splendid. You've made the most of it and are now ready to enjoy a good read. (Oh, that phone. Perhaps—*but then*—oh why the hell not. You turn the thing off, just for a few minute, and feel better already.)

The question now becomes what do you know about this story beforehand? Surely by now you know that it concerns (at least in part) the game of baseball, and have carefully deduced from the front cover, back cover, and table of contents that it specifically concerns the Boston Red Sox Baseball Club, and takes place at their home ballpark of Fenway Park (4 Yawkey Way, Boston, MA). Just below the title you clearly read the exact date on which it is set. Does this date mean anything to you in particular? (Think back; what were you up to late in the summer of 2007? Ah yes, it was *that* summer for you.) Perhaps you do not recognize the date, but know the circumstances regardless. Perhaps you can tell by the opponent, or simply the general period of that particular season. (Perhaps you peeked ahead, and saw the significant name appear.) In which case you know in advance how this story will end. Perhaps you watched it happen, perhaps even live. What then? You remember it well, of course, and wouldn't mind revisiting it; but there are so many other options. Surely there is a replay of it somewhere on television, or a digital recording somewhere online, or something of that sort. Surely by now you could watch it on your phone while you wait in line at the airport. Yet you go on reading. Why?

Is it because the replay has been edited down to its highlights (or *the* highlight) and therefore cuts away the beginning and middle which both steadily create tension and build to the ending? Or is it because you have seen that particular highlight so often that it no longer carries meaning? Is it because watching it online at your desk keeps *all those other things* right at your fingertips, or perhaps even flashes them across your screen at odd intervals interrupting the action and ruining its effect? Or (perhaps perhaps) is it precisely because you do know what happens, and have seen it before, that you have gotten all you may ever get from its visual proof and desire something a bit more—*how to put this?*—engaging? Is that it? Is it because you have not yet found a downloadable full-screen high definition copy of this story which lets you know that it took place not only on Saturday night, not only over Labor Day weekend, but on one of the most hectic days in the entire city calendar and that your walk to the ballpark has wound past rows of double-parked moving vans, scores of eager young college entrants and their harried and overheated parents, and box-laden movers running relay legs between them; and that by the time you arrive at Fenway a large crowd has already pooled outside of Yawkey, spilling into Brookline Avenue, waiting for the gates to open; and that by the time the gates do open you have to cram sideways to excuse yourself onto a packed Yawkey Way; or that the grill smoke rises over it hazy against an orange sky, and curls beneath the vertical red and blue banners. Is it because the boxed widescreen shuts out the fact that on this night you can lean your elbows on a railing overlooking Yawkey and hear among the rising laughter a particular buoyancy, and whether from its being the weekend or the Sox being in first place or simply the subconscious realization that there are so very few warm summer nights remaining, there is within the very air around us the subtle yet undeniable sense of *special*, of a celebratory, holiday spirited crowd. Are you reading because you can now begin to feel this, too? Because you can be brought back to those lazy moments before the game begins when you are among friends, and in no hurry, and as you sip a cold drink you follow someone's point across the field see the familiar shape of Big Papi, all in white, out on the grass beyond first base as he drops his bat along the first base line, waves at the screaming fans along the wall, and jogs out idly to center. You are allowed to watch him there (we will not cut to commercial), to see him come to a walking stop in shallow center, and to smile when he spreads his long arms and smiling himself envelopes an opposing player in a friendly hug. Relax, go ahead and feel that slight low-level flutter in the area of your stomach when you take all of these elements together, as you too are struck by the elusive notion that *this is a special night*. Go ahead, wander down the left field line as the pregame ceremonies take place behind you, all the way down to the left field corner where you know there will be an open spot (because there always is, and because tonight we have saved a spot for you); and sure enough you find it there along the back wall just left of the GULF demi-sign. Where we welcome you to settle yourself into this spot (look over there, to your left, and see the famous pale green wall stretching out so long in perspective), to slip your bag off your shoulders and let it rest beneath a seat, to lean back against the cool shaded bricks and there, before you, find yourself at Fenway Park in Boston in that late afternoon sunlight, at the very moment our story now begins with the words:

If on a summer's night a pitcher...had been called up from Double-A at the last minute to make only his second Major League start tonight, you as a fan would not expect much from him. Even if this particular pitcher had shown flashes of promise in his first start (which this pitcher has) it would still not be fair to put the burden of expectation on him as you would a veteran. You would simply be curious to watch him pitch. And grateful to be at a sunlit Fenway Park, on such a night. A perfect night for baseball. Warm clear air, a high cloudless sky, a gentle breeze flapping the flag high up to your left. And when the PA system plays Sinatra's "Summer Wind," you would move your lips silently to the words, and let your eyes dip closed for a moment to let out a deep exhale. (*Lovely.*) When you open them the Sox are jogging onto the field under light applause, and the starting pitcher is stepping onto the mound. He warms up, you put your hands in your pockets and settle in, and a few pitches later the game begins with a lazy fly ball to left. Somewhere on the other side of the grandstand the sun is beginning its decent, and with a look high up the towers you notice that the floodlights are on to begin the game, glowing against a pale blue sky. The second batter grounds to third; Lowell fields and with a little stutter-step throws to first, while out over the John Hancock marquee in center the sky has deepened to a shimmering purple, with shades of hazy pink down near the bleachers. You check the digital clock on the video board. 7:14 pm. The next batter is hit by a pitch, a fastball on the back of the shoulder. In a few weeks the games will begin under nightfall, and summer will be over. Miguel Tejada hits a sharp line drive to second that Pedroia, shading towards the bag, has to dive back to his left and stab just above the dirt—a fine play that saves a hit and ends the inning—and you give your first light applause of the game. And after the Sox go down in the first you slip your hands back into your pockets, and in the top of the second take a better look at the pitcher on the mound, tall and slender with long red-sleeved arms stretching from his oversized white jersey.

With a thin, slightly exaggerated neck lifting above his red mock turtleneck, a trio of necklaces dangling about his collar which spreads immediately to narrow shoulders, and those long, gangly arms, there is something undeniably *avian* about Clay Buchholz, the prized Red Sox prospect now standing on the Fenway mound. The head and features just a bit too small beneath his flat-billed cap, as hawk-like his form tapers out below the neck and places all the emphasis, even while resting at his side but particularly when spread out majestically in flight, on those exceptionally broad wings of his. (This is true of a number of pitchers, come to think of it.) Then again, perhaps he is merely growing into his frame. You read somewhere that he is only 23-years-old, that he is a Texan, and that he is supposed to be pretty good at getting hitters out. Here in the second he falls behind in the count 3-0 to Kevin Millar. Decent enough fastball, you've heard. Throws a big looping curve. And the changeup, so much about *the great Major-League-ready changeup.* Buchholz works the count full and strikes Millar out on a changeup down. He walks off the back of the mound, slow and steady, and after each out holds his glove up by his shoulder just before he receives the ball back from his infielder. (Later on you will notice that he has a habit, while holding it there, of chewing on his leather glove strings.) His first pitch to Aubrey Huff is sliced out to left field where fellow rookie Brandon Moss, the stocky fullback of an outfielder playing in place of the injured Manny Ramirez, comes in and steadies to make the running catch. Buchholz takes the ball back and steps to the rubber with both feet (here another little habit, stepping on with both feet and leaning over, looking down, to settle them) then straightens up long and tall with a slight dip to the shoulders as he looks in. Glove and ball before him he takes the sign, nods, then brings both to his stomach as he takes a small step directly out to the side. There is a wonderful gathering up of limbs as he sweeps the left leg across and up, the shoulders and torso tilting first-base-side with a slight rotation; but then something unexpected happens right at the top of this long smooth motion. The right hand drops and as it does hits some imaginary release and—as if triggering the pedal on a mouse trap—sends the entire frame snapping over the top and the ball darts forward, too soon. Surprising both us as spectators, and Scott Moore the batter, to whom it is strike one looking. The entire motion seems to skip a beat (between the arm coming down and the ball coming forward), like a badly spliced piece of film. Each time we anticipate it, each time the arm comes forward a beat sooner than we expect. The swing a beat late; the pitch strike two. It is uncanny. This time we look for it, wait for it, here it comes and—we blink. The batter flinches. Strike three. And the rookie walks off the mound with his long arms at his side and an unflinching expression on his youthful face.

Before you know it Buchholz has worked the count to 2-2 on rookie J.R. House to lead off the third, and you find your concentration drifting for a moment to the surrounding crowd. It has, for the most part, been a quiet one. (In the distance Buchholz strikes out House.) A holiday crowd, out-of-towners come to the city for the weekend and thus easily distracted, they have made little noise throughout the first few innings and were only mildly ruffled to applaud the Sox lone run in the second. To our left is a young couple who, with only that odd single-seat row at the apex of Section 33 between them, have made the best of their dilemma and sat together, he in the seat, her on his knee; over there the Cambridge Lady with her wiry gray hair, multiple beaded necklaces, and dark-rimmed glasses who as she walked past you during the starting lineups gave Mike Lowell a coffee-house salute of three *snap-snap-snap*'s held high; behind her a pair of teenage girls in the middle of Section 32, one who lets out a piercing screech each time either Ortiz or Varitek's names are announced, then giddily looks about to make sure everyone has heard her, and her shy friend who during each screech ducks away in embarrassment; and farther back still the parents in SRO who together are capable of holding in place two out of their three young boys, while a third (not always the same third) wanders off at the end of the aisle; they corral him back just as one of his brothers wanders off, and so on. No one seems to be watching the game much. (Where Jay Payton just has missed a high changeup and, flipping his bat in anger, flies out to center.) Then again neither are you. It is there, in the background as you linger over the foregrounded audience. So that it is with a quick start that you notice Brian Roberts laying down a bunt. Shallow and dangerous but to the first base side—that is, to the side Buchholz naturally falls off to—and the thin rookie picks it from the grass and fires to first for the final out of the inning. The teenage girl cups her hands and lets out a scream, fans rise and head up the aisles, and the couple to our left glance briefly to the field, clap, and return their attention to each other's eyes, all despite being at the center of a sellout crowd at Fenway Park.

Perhaps it is that we Sox fans have grown a bit less attentive than is our habit this time of year. After all the Sox are in first place, as they have been the entire summer, and currently hold a five game lead over the second place Yankees. Less than a week ago that lead was eight, but a mid-week sweep in the Bronx and a frustrating loss to the Orioles on Friday night has pared it down and caused a slight, *slight* ripple of concern among some fans. Leading off the fourth Patterson grounds a changeup to the left side, Youkilis fields, and for a moment there is an anxious wince as Buchholz just barely makes it over to cover and tap the front of the bag, in time. You, however, are not the least bit worried about the lead. Neither are we, officially. Though there is that familiar fizziness in our stomach each time the Sox drop a game. Nonsense, you say; the Sox have gone through their struggles as every team in a long season eventually does, but overall there is less wrong with them than any team in baseball. True, we admit. (*Even so.*) Markakis flies to center on another brilliant changeup for an easy second out. Besides, you remind us, the only thing this Yankee team has done with any consistency is find ways to shoot itself in the foot anytime it appears even vaguely threatening. Also true, we admit. (*But still.*) You shake your head. And so on… This the quiet ribbon of debate that has threaded through New England workplaces and bars and between phones all summer long—one side telling the other not to worry, the other saying be careful about those words *never* and *impossible* when it comes to the Red Sox and Yankees. We are about to issue this very reminder when Buchholz throws a changeup and Tejada skies it high but harmlessly towards center, Crisp catches it standing still, and we both applaud the end of a lazy fourth inning and the postponement of this summerlong dialogue, here in the last lazy month of the season.

Of course even this casual ribbon of baseball debate will end soon, and with it comes an instinctual slowing down. The summer has gone by too fast once again. And with it another long, ambitious list of Things To Do This Summer, once expectantly scrawled out in a gray and drizzly April morning and now looked back on with head-shaking regret. A few items are crossed off. You did in fact make it to that beach you always meant to visit (though the weather that day was disappointing), and to that one restaurant in the North End you'd always heard great things about (where you were not disappointed), and you read four or five books on your always overly ambitious summer reading list. But what of the rest? You shake your head, both at this thought and at the sight of Buchholz, who now works with a 4-0 lead, walking Millar on four pitches to start the fifth. What about the Things You Didn't Have Time To Do? Or the Things You Had Time To Do But Not Time To Do Properly? What about all those Things That You Do Every Summer But For Some Reason Didn't Get Around To This Year, which are right above the Things You *Mean* To Do Every Summer But For Some Reason *Never* Get Around To. (Out on the mound Buchholz falls behind Huff 3-1, and you yell out *Come on Clay!* for the first time tonight. He walks him regardless, and pitching coach John Farrell visits the mound, also for the first time.) The list goes on. There are the Things That Were Planned But Ended Up Being Postponed, never to be rescheduled; and the Things That Were Postponed, Rescheduled, Then Re-Postponed and Ultimately Cancelled Altogether. (Oh and let us not forget the Things That Would Surely Have Been Done If Our Friends Could Make A Decision And Stick To It Already.) You shake your head. Meanwhile Buchholz throws three straight changeups to Moore, who swings and misses badly three times for the first out. You mention beneath your breath that Moore looks so confused at the plate that it's a wonder he's even swinging in the right direction. We agree. Now where were we? Oh yes, the Things We Really Wanted to Make Happen This Summer Before Money Became A Concern, which then became one of the many Things We Will Have to Do Next Summer When We Are (Surely) On Better Financial Footing. Here you feel compelled to remind us that we said the same thing last summer. We ignore this, and move right on to the Things Which Were Done But Done Poorly and Therefore Need To Be Done Again Next Summer, and the Things Done By Others Which Because of Scheduling Conflicts We Could Not Make and Would Like to Be Given Perhaps a Little Better Notice of, Next Time. And there near the bottom, starred and underlined, are the Things We Would Have Done Had The Weather Here In New England Cooperated and Just Once Gave Us a Break, Honestly. Buchholz works the count to 2-2 on House, who grounds hard to short where Lugo bobbles but recovers in time to get the force at second. So two outs and runners on the corners. All of which brings us to the inevitable question: where has the summer gone? There was work, surely, more than we expected and always jutting in at inconvenient times. And there were unexpected happenings—a surprise visit from a distant friend, a last minute trip to the island, tickets to a midsummer Sox game dropped in your lap. That and of course those things which together constitute your daily life, which continued on, filled with their typical share of difficulties and delights, small pleasures and nagging complexities, vexations, heartbreaks, and brief but practically life-saving flashes of unaccountable joy. And baseball. Suddenly Buchholz has fallen behind Payton 3-0 and is a pitch away from loading the bases. His next pitch is a fastball to get him over for a strike, then another in the same spot that Payton fouls off, and a third that he flies to right for the final out and the first surprising, rising cheers from the crowd as Buchholz walks off the field in the fifth. All summer long there have been these Sox, whose many delights and heartbreaks have both added to and complimented our own, and whose story is not quite finished, either. Not as you and the Red Sox look down and find on our list one more item: those Things That We Have Worked All Summer Towards and Are About To Realize Only Now, in the twilight of another beguiling summer.

The sixth begins quietly, a strike looking to Roberts then three straight balls. On the last of these Buchholz slaps his glove against his hip, the first outward ripple of discord in an otherwise harmonious performance. He seems to have sped up, getting the ball back hastily and right back on the rubber looking in. He gets a strike over, but his next pitch misses and sends Roberts jogging down to first. We lean back against the left field wall, look on with arms folded and wonder if we are both thinking the same thing. We are not. Like a good many others in this Fenway crowd, which has been deadly silent through most of the first five evening innings, you do not think about such things until they are slightly more imminent. And the sixth, being less than two-thirds of the way through, is far too early. We on the other hand cannot help ourselves, and admittedly begin thinking about such things from pitch one (so much so that the single to leadoff the game triggers a reflexive and utterly absurd little *oh well, not tonight*). We haven't wanted to say anything, and when we do now you advise caution. Three more outs. If he gets three more outs, which will bring him within ten outs altogether, then it will begin. And right then, just as we are both thinking this Buchholz spins and throws to first and Brian Roberts, flat-footed off the bag, flops headfirst back and Youkilis slaps the tag on his wrist and *got him*, picked off first. Like that, Fenway awakens. On its feet and cheering as Roberts jogs off and Buchholz steps back on the mound, the sound ripples forward from the back reaches of grandstand, builds on a strike to Patterson, holds its breath as the ball is lined out over center and then, when Crisp catches easily for the second out, bursts up again with a rousing cheer. It is as if Youkilis' tag on Roberts depressed the MUTE button on Fenway Park, and suddenly the surround sound of encouraging applause and buzzing anticipation envelopes all corners of the ballpark. Ten outs to go. (We've never seen one, we say. Neither have you. We've seen two one-hitters already this year but—*please shut up*, you say, quietly and with a halting glance add, *just watch*.) Buchholz's 0-1 pitch to Markakis is a big arching curveball that drops in like a yo-yo for strike two and brings Fenway to its feet. Still there after a ball, we are cheering and shouting *Come on, Clay!* when he steps back, winds, darts forward and lets go another roundhouse curve that loops up then down and ducks beneath the flailing bat of Markakis—*strike three*—as the cheers burst into the rafters once more. This time with long drawn out applause as we both shake our head, wondering just how this skinny young pitcher in only his second Major League start could throw with such ease and confidence.

Tejada leads off the seventh, and amid the ovation for Buchholz and the resumption of the story there is a jittery apprehension about the man at the plate. He has hit the ball hard twice, once to short and once to second; the latter having sent Pedroia lunging to his left in what was probably the closest thing to a hit so far. Buchholz starts him with a strike looking, then misses with two balls, one of which lands Tejada on his backside in the batter's box. We are both completely silent; you with your hands folded behind your back and us with one arm folded and a hand rubbing our chin, as we tend to do in these situations. The next pitch is away. Tejada slaps it hard back up the middle and the moment it skips past Buchholz into the infield there is a groan—thirty-five-thousand *oh no's* sounding one deadening low note—as it shoots out past second base and surely through until suddenly Pedroia comes bounding like some sort of jungle cat from the underbrush and pounces upon the fleeing ball, springs up and in one motion fire to Youkilis who stretched out at the other end with Tejada sliding headfirst through the bag catches—*in time*. Out by just a fraction Tejada bounces up and among the wild cheers throws an angry wave out to Pedroia, who has robbed the shortstop and his team of their one good chance. The count is 1-2 on Millar before we or anyone else have stopped shaking our heads at the play. Because it wasn't *almost* a hit. Past Buchholz at that angle with that speed, it *was* a hit. The only question was whether Pedroia could knock it down. And so there was not even time to consider the impossibility of an out until it happened, and the hit that *was* suddenly *was not*. Everything happens very fast now. Pitches go by one after another. Buchholz steps back, throws, and another sharp curve drops down on the outside corner for strike three. Two outs. Strike one to Huff. Strike two. Up on our feet for a foul ball. You are standing and cheering and perhaps now even smiling because this, right now, is happening. Huff swings, clipping the ball high in the air above first base where Youkilis drifts over and settles, and with the ball still in the air there is a loud, baying *You-uuuuk* that sounds until the ball lands safely in his glove. Buchholz walks off with the now continual applause and shouts before him, and a steady and at times inspired defense behind him.

You look over, and we exchange a silent nod before the first pitch of the eighth, you smiling and us taking a deep breath before turning to the field to cheer Buchholz, whose emergence from the dugout, whose ascent to the mound, whose nod to Varitek and whose every movement now brings the crowd to its feet in waves of applause. An announcement is made, *defensive substitutions for the Red Sox*, the rookie Moss from left field to right, the rookie Jacoby Ellsbury now in right. The crowd roars. The final warm-up pitches are thrown, the ball flies down to second, is relayed around the infield, and finally Mike Lowell turns his left shoulder to the mound and tosses it back to Buchholz (all night we have had a wonderful view of this little vignette, of Buchholz turning to face us with his glove held shoulder high, Lowell hitting it, and Buchholz catching casually and stepping to the mound). Moore and House lead off for the Orioles, and you make a comment to the effect that the umpire ought to point out to the mound to remind each to aim their swings *that'a way*. Buchholz nods. The crowd roars again. Quickly Buchholz is ahead 1-2 and we are pounding our hands together amid the din. Every pitch is an event now—every pitch two strikes with two outs and the bases loaded—and what has been an eerily quiet crowd for six innings is now, here in the eighth, piqued to a level approaching the fervor of a playoff game. Ball two; ball three; full count and then Moore swings, the ball flies out to center and Crisp settles under it. Another explosion of applause the moment it hits his glove. One out in the eighth. Strike one to House, swinging on a devastating curve. Strike two, swinging on a changeup down. On our feet again. Buchholz wastes no time, gets the ball, sets, nods, winds and drops another roundhouse curve in and House checks his swing, too late, strike three. Fist pumps and high fives. Two down in the eighth. The noise rises, louder still. It all happens incredibly fast now pitch after pitch and always with two strikes there is hardly enough time to even consider what is happening here, the scope of things, the implications and the sheer impossibility of what could possibly with any luck happen here before Buchholz throws and Payton chops a ball up the middle that takes one sharp bounce and jumps up at Buchholz's shoulder and with a reflexive reel back, hits his glove—right in the webbing—he lets the momentum of the bounce carry his glove up into the air, turns, head down (he can't believe it either), and tosses easily to first for the final out of the eighth as we both turn to each other for the first time all inning. Both smiling now. Three outs to go. This might actually happen, tonight. He just might…with just one good bounce of fortune he could.

Here we go then, headlong into the ninth. A booming chorus of "Sweet Caroline" carries us to the final inning with *so good! so good! so good!* and the applause rises from it as Buchholz looks in. Three outs away. You are sort of bouncing up and down in your place now as you clap, while we have our arms firmly crossed and unconsciously rock back and forth on our heels. Just three outs. We are both acutely nervous—stomachs fizzy, pulses thumping, hands clapping to stay busy and mouths muttering *come on kid, come on*, just beneath our breath. Buchholz starts Roberts off with a fastball away; strike one. Then after a ball comes back with a high fastball that Roberts flails away at for strike two. Another ball. Cheers, head-shaking, teenagers leaning over the backstop and pounding its green padding; and with two strikes and everyone on their feet a hard fastball in and right by Roberts's terribly late swing for strike three and the first out of the ninth. Roaring applause and shouts of *that'a boy Clay, that'a boy!* The stomach tightens, the pulse quickens. Two outs to go. (Only much later will you look back with wonder at the role Jason Varitek has played in this night, and this at bat in particular. After offspeed pitches all night in all counts, in the ninth, with the pressure on the Orioles hitters, Varitek puts down the one and jumps them with fastballs. Brilliant.) Two quick balls to Patterson before a strike looking. Again before we can settle the ball is through the air out of his hand and hit hard on a line to center—a quick gasp—but directly at Crisp who takes a step to his right and catches for the second out. One. Out. To go. We rub our hands together and realize that they have been held clasped in front of us, unintentionally prayerful. We glance over to find you looking bewildered, and you force an unconvincing smile. Fenway shudders up another decibel until the noise of thousands of shouts and motion of thousands of hands begin to create tiny physical vibrations within, and you realize, suddenly: the scene before us is shaking. There is nothing for us to do but watch. We shout out *come on Clay go get him!* before reclasping our hands. You continue to clap. And we both look into the crescent of cheering fans that hugs the floodlit field, the grandstand so close and the sound so immediate, the tall thin pitcher's uniform glowing so very white in the center of it all. Ball one, then a curveball away for strike one to Markakis. Two strikes away. Buchholz throws, Markakis fouls it off. One strike away now. Just one, more, strike. You smile. And for perhaps the first time all night you let the thought slip through your mind and maybe even mutter it to yourself, *this is going to happen*, as Buchholz winds and throws and a big looping curveball rises and falls and is caught clean by Varitek low around the knees and we all silently raise our arms and look to the umpire, who steps back and ever so slowly but unmistakably turns to his right, and closes his fist. Strike three and *he did it, he did it*, this kid just pitched a no-hitter at Fenway Park and amid our shouts and fist pumps the Sox stream onto the field and envelope Buchholz in front of the mound, and as we have been cheering for the better part of three innings we continue on; cheering as the pitchers running in from the bullpen join the mob; cheering as Buchholz finally breaks loose only to receive hug after hug from players, coaches, his manager, and comes staggering into the dugout skirting where his elbow is held by a sideline reporter. Suddenly her voice comes across the loudspeaker, and suddenly a young male voice with a slight drawl is heard and the crowd rises over it, washing out whatever short answer he has given. And we, still in our spots (we have not budged in over four hours now), glance up to the video board to find him there, skinny neck and all, shaking his head. The reporter asks another question, something about how he controlled his emotions in front of this crowd. We roar out again at the reference and Buchholz pauses, shakes his head, lets out an exhale, and suddenly looks very, very young. (It is the only instance all night in which he looks overwhelmed.) Finally he shakes his head again, and laughs as he says, "I don't have an answer to that question either." We cheer one more time; because of course, neither do we. All we do know, as you snap a picture of the scoreboard and all those gorgeous 000 000 000 0 0 0's, is that he has done it—that this young man has been able, all by himself, to reach back and take an ordinary game and an ordinary night and thousands of us ordinary fans along with him, and suddenly pull us all into the incandescent spotlight of history.

And with that, congratulations are in order, for you too have gone the distance.

By now you probably need to stretch out the legs, so feel free to take a short walk. Or simply stretch the arms and reposition the legs and let your mind rest a bit. Close your eyes, if it helps. It is always nice to step away (physically or mentally) after a long read, if nothing else but to take those last images linger with you awhile before you return to—to all those other things. For there can be, after a long read such as this, a very real sense of *stepping out of*. Not merely turning off or clicking closed, but of the need to bring oneself back out of the story. In this case away from the ballpark. To let the lights of Fenway fade back into the words on the page. To let the images of these players running and diving and leaping about our minds dissolve back into their printed names. To let that slight acceleration of the pulse settle back to a normal resting rate; to let our eyes adjust to the light of the room; to let the story become a chapter and the chapter to become part of a book, and the book something in our hands which we now let rest open in our laps.

Now why is this? Why this steady pulling back of mental and perhaps even physical engagement? This never happened with the highlights. Is it because we do not immediately turn our attention to another channel or another program, or because we cannot click onto another site or immediately go back and watch our favorite moment again and again until the feeling of it is gone completely? Is it because there have been no commercials? Or is it because (perhaps perhaps) the fact that great stories are not merely watched, but experienced. That our ability to engage in it is what makes it memorable to begin with, and therefore what makes the great story not a remembering, but a reconnecting to something that is in a very real way *felt*. Is that it? Is it that a told story allows us to feel the summer breeze against our cheek and the brick wall we lean against and the dampness of our hands clasped along with the clenching of our stomach as we sense the nervousness of a friend at our side beneath the lights and it all comes together in a way no level of high definition can ever duplicate? Or is it simply because:

If on a summer's night a pitcher, tall and slender with long red-sleeved arms stretching from his oversized white jersey and an unflinching expression on his youthful face—despite being at the center of a raucous sellout crowd at Fenway Park, in the last lazy month of the season, in the twilight of another beguiling summer—could throw with such ease and confidence and a steady and at times inspired defense behind him, with just one good bounce of fortune he could, all by himself, reach back and take an ordinary game and an ordinary night and millions of us ordinary fans along with him and suddenly pull us all—as the story is retold once again and once again we fall back—into the incandescent spotlight of history.

Swept Up

Anaheim at Fenway
2 September 2004

Fans of any team sport, though perhaps baseball fans more than most, simply cannot help but project. It is the natural reaction to that first forward-looking glance over the upcoming schedule, when the possibilities and problems of a season play out in our minds for the first time, where *that should be a win* and *that one could be trouble, we'll be lucky to get out of there with a win, that one over there should be cake,* and *this one, well if we don't get that one then the whole thing is lost, isn't it?* A steady undercurrent throughout most of the baseball fan's summer, these mental leaps become the waking dreams of fans involved in the complicated, multi-team playoff races which have become a September ritual since the Wild Card was introduced in 1995. Caught up in the multiple variables and endless solutions to these bi-divisional, bicoastal scenarios, the urge to play out the remaining schedule in our mind becomes almost impossible to resist. We compare schedules, home/road splits, pitching matchups, and read pages and pages of certified expert analysis, all of which brings us to the conclusion that there are endless possible outcomes to the season, and only a few of these are slightly more probably than any other. And so we project, and build our pennants in the air. We memorize the remaining schedules a half dozen teams; *if we could just-* and *if only they-* become our most common ways of opening a sentence; and as we look forward to a critical home series we catch ourselves—lost in a quiet trance at work the day before, or lying awake late at night on its eve—running the entire gamut of possible outcomes, the pendulum between blind faith and unflinching pragmatism carrying us everywhere from the optimistic (*two out of three, no problem*) to the realistic (*we get one, they get one, then flip a coin*) to the pessimistic (*hopefully we'll manage one*) and, more often than we care to admit, all the way to the apocalyptic (*we're getting swept*).

It is only on rare occasions, and even then only briefly, that we allow ourselves the flights of fancy which aligns our team with the best possible outcome, those obscenely generous moments when we envision our team cast in the most flattering of lights. Where rookies develop into superstars in a matter of weeks, superstars come bounding off the disabled list two weeks ahead of schedule, and relievers with long histories of incurable wildness suddenly develop an obsession with throwing first pitch strikes; all in a clubhouse suddenly infused with an aura of invincibility normally only seen by very young children (for whom atrocious umpiring and dastardly bad luck are the only possible detours from the inevitable victory/championship). *We sweep the three game set by playing crisp, mistake-free ball and dominating every facet of the game and our rivals, although playing a lesser opponent, lose two out of three including a humiliating home shutout of, say, 22-0.* Daydream stuff, of course. For over time we have learned that the game in general and the Red Sox in particular are not much inclined to comply with our grand designs, and we have found it much more useful, not to mention healthier, to simply dig our heels in and hope for the best. The three game sweep of a daunting playoff contender and the epic humiliation of our rivals are the domain of novice fools and barroom drunks, and September baseball is far too serious a business to indulge in such fantasy. Sobriety of heart and mind is the recommended path—better to be realistic and hope for two out of three.

And not be surprised when, after two romping home victories in a crucial late season series, the third game begins as this game against Anaheim does, with a two out Vladimir Guerrero double off tonight's Red Sox starter, Derek Lowe. Or much bothered when Garret Anderson follows immediately after with a hard shot down the right field line, the ball rolls all the way to the corner, Anderson pulls into second and Guerrero rounds third and jogs home with the first run of the game. Which we in the Fenway bleachers accepts as the Law of Probability in action. And offer nothing more in response than a low disapproving grumble, a disappointed head shake, then (recovering slightly from the blow) a dismissive shrug, a raise of the eyebrows and a conciliatory muttering of *well, they're due anyway*.

And oh yes (now fully recovered) *grab another round while you're down there*.

This from the very center of the center field bleachers, where over the past two nights something not unlike a baseball holiday has unexpectedly broken out. It began Tuesday, when on a lovely summer night in Boston the series opened with a first inning Manny Ramirez bomb to left. And it was *cheers to that*. The Yankees fell behind Baltimore 6-0 on the Out-of-Town, and it was *cheers to that*, too. The Sox continued to add runs, a now incredibly popular scoreboard operator inside the left field wall continued to hang big fat numbers over the Yankee scoreline (9-0, 12-0, 18!-0) until the Sox won 10-7, the Yankees lost 22-0, and the party in the bleachers spilled out onto Lansdowne street and points beyond, where it was *cheers to that* over and over and over again. Then, shortly thereafter (oddly the interval did not seem a long one), the bleachers were filled back up, the warm day cooled to a comfortable late summer night under the lights, pairs of little frothy plastic cups began to march up the aisles, the Sox began to score runs and the party started right back up as if neither had ever left off. And as another fine summer night wore on the party in the bleachers continued (as tends to be the case) to discover new things to *cheers to*. And so all game long it was *here's to* the now all-but-guaranteed rise of the Red Sox via a ten-game winning streak, or two, straight to the top of the Division standings from which they will summarily dominate all foes, American and National, for the next decade or so at the very least; and *here's to* the now all-but-guaranteed collapse of the Yankee dynasty via a ten-game losing streak, or two, and the sudden and complete loss of team morale which will inevitably cause a sudden and total loss of fan confidence, a drop in box office receipts and total revenue, a freeze on all free-agent signings, and provide them a nice comfortable home in last place for the foreseeable future; and *here's to* ordering playoff tickets; and *here's to* cold October nights upcoming; and *here's to* perfect warm summer nights, like tonight; and *here's to...to...*to all our new best-est friends here in the bleachers, the best-est section of fans in the whole ballpark if not the whole country or league or you know what we mean that's right *cheers! hey-hey! (wait...what? the seventh, already?)*, before it's *here's to* a final score of 12-7, Sox.

It is only natural that we would expected things to continue right on through the series finale Thursday night, particularly as it too opens up beneath another lovely late-summer twilight. Only there is Vlad, jogging in from third with the first Angels' first lead of the series; an early omen one would expect to introduce a (*ehem*) sobering effect on the Fenway crowd.

Perhaps it does elsewhere in the ballpark; but you know the bleachers are a funny place sometimes. Farther from the field, closer to each other, with steeper aisles to walk up and longer rows to scoot down, the bleachers tend to be an overly active, exceedingly chatty, relentlessly social place; filled with fans who are not so particular about where they sit or whom they sit with; who in general come to the ballpark to have a fine time; who in general *have* a fine time; who in general have absolutely no reservations about letting everyone around them know (at a high volume) exactly how fine a time they are having; and who have never been know to do themselves the injustice of letting a bad game get in the way of a good party. Particularly in the warm summer months. More particularly in the warm summer months when the weekend is in sight. Most particularly of all in the warm summer months when the weekend is in sight and the Sox have taken over the Wild Card lead and leapt back feet first into the Divisional race. As is the case, tonight. A night on which this bleacher crowd has shown up fully prepared to continue on with the week-long Fenway celebration, whether we're provided something to celebrate or not. (And cheers to *that*.)

And so it almost as if by the power of suggestion that Johnny Damon (who after all is the closest player to the bleacher) leads off the Red Sox's half of the first and promptly doubles into the gap. Two outs and a Varitek walk later and Damon remains at second, with Anaheim's rotund starter Bartolo Colón (latitude to Lowe's longitude) on the verge of stranding him there for good when Kevin Millar rips a high fastball down the left field line to level the score at 1-1. The Angels counter in the second as Adam Kennedy singles and later scores on a José Molina double which rolls all the way to the wall and puts Anaheim back in front, 2-1. (*After all, they're simply too good a club to sweep.*) Then, in the Sox's second, Bill Mueller wraps a drive down around the Pesky Pole to bring the Sox level (*cheers to that!*), again, at 2-2, and is followed by a Dave Roberts double off the left field wall and a Damon single in the gap, scoring Roberts and putting the Sox ahead for the first time, 3-2. (Damon, by the way, seems to have developed an intense aversion to the Red Sox dugout, and has spent the better part of a month stubbornly avoiding it by scattering hits all across the Fenway lawn; in this three game set alone he will reach base an astounding twelve times.) Only Darin Erstad leads off the Angels' third with a ground rule double deep into the triangle, is sacrificed to second on a ground ball to the right side, and scores on a ground ball to short to bring the Angels' even again, at 3-3. (*Lowe doesn't have it tonight, but we'll still take two out of three.*) Orlando Cabrera retaliates in the Sox's third with a broken-bat single to shallow left, moves to third on a top-spin ground rule double by Doug Mientkiewicz, and then on a Mueller sacrifice fly to right sprints in ahead (*just* ahead) of a rocket peg to the plate by Guerrero to put the Sox in front again (*cheers to that!*) 4-3. At which point Fenway takes a moment to catch its breath (and *hey can you grab another round while you're down there thanks man you're the best no really*).

Three innings and a little over an hour old this wild and wildly entertaining finale has seen twelve hits, seven runs, three ties, two lead changes and one appetizing early return (2-0, Baltimore) on the Out-of-Town. Both starting pitchers—Colón for the Angels and Derek Lowe for the Sox—have been predictably unpredictable, and the only question seems to be which will be pushed over the top and implode into a debilitating three-run inning first. (The only certainty, at this point, is that the game cannot possibly end 4-3.)

It is hardly shocking then to see Adam Kennedy line a low drive to right that somehow buckles Dave Roberts as he runs in for what should be an easy chest-high play but, after some awkward lunging this way and that, has it fall softly from his midsection onto the grass for an error. And it is only slightly less surprising to then watch Lowe compounds this mistake by immediately walking Molina to create a first and second situation, with only one out. Now with the game's third tie and Lowe's impending collapse looming a bare base hit away, Chone Figgins swats another low liner out over the grass in right center. Again Roberts charges hard, over and in, presumably to cut down the gap and keep the now streaking Kennedy at third but at the last instant he dives low and flat and sweeps the ball up inches from the grass, slides on his stomach, pops to his feet, and riffle the ball back in—just as Fenway catches sight of Kennedy, helplessly rounding third. Cabrera catches the relay, gently taps second, ends both the inning and the Angels' rally, and Roberts bounds off the field under a hail of applause having dramatically remedied the mess he helped create with an immediacy often only found, ever so delightfully, in baseball.

Roberts's startling catch and double-up of Kennedy, by stealing away a sure run and replacing it with the scoreboard's first zero, seems to jolt the game off its thematic tracks—almost as if it had mashed down on some distant remote control and switched us over to some alternate ending version of the game (the Pitcher's Version, perhaps)—and from here on the game is played out over an excruciating tightrope walk of dangerous base runners, threatening scoring chances, pressure defensive gems and very big pitches by two very big pitchers. None of us realize this at the moment, of course, as Colón wobbles precariously in the very next frame by giving up a single to Damon (see above) and gap double to Bellhorn, which quickly rolls towards the wall but is just as quickly cut down by Vladimir Guerrero sprinting across from right. He backhands the ball deep in the gap and riffles in a throw that sends Damon skidding to a stop on the third base line, holds him fast back to the bag and (eventually) prevents a run. Colón makes his first big pitches of the night later on as he strikes out Manny looking, gets Varitek to pop out and, after walking Millar to load the bases, strikes out Cabrera to end the threat. Yet the key component of the inning was the play, run and throw, by Guerrero in right—one of several remarkable plays made in the series by the Angels' remarkable new star.

(All series we have been fortunate enough to watch these games—the Angels' only visit to Fenway this season—from various outfield perches ranging between straightaway center and the right field foul line, providing a good view and plenty of time to observe Vladimir Guerrero in his natural habitat of right field. After which we can confidently say that we have never seen another player quite like him. Despite the fact that up until this year he has played in the farthest outpost of the foreign National League, we already know something of Vlad's talents. Seeing him perform is something quite different though, and we like to imagine what the reaction of a stranger to the game might be to his loping, quiet presence. They would not be impressed on looks alone, to be sure. There is the scraggly puff of black hair escaping at odd angles from a haphazardly crooked hat, the patchy black goatee, the tired, old soul eyes which seem preoccupied, understandably, by the array of persistently nagging injuries that hinder movement in every major area of his person. For he either has or seems to have: a case of chronic lower back pain so aggravating that it causes him to hobble along with his shoulders slightly forward, a dodgy right ankle which turns his right foot in as he favors it, a recurring or not quite healed injury to two fingers on his left hand, as well as some variety of ailment in his wrist, and neck, and perhaps his left elbow, and certainly his right shoulder which slopes a bit as he hobbles/limps out to his position. The total effect of this trainer's textbook is to cause the 27-year-old Guerrero to move around before and between pitches exactly like a very old, not very able man, for whom it is a constant struggle just to remain upright much less do anything remotely athletic. Between pitches he rather hangs forward, hands to knees, and dips his head, presumably thinking that another line of work might better suit him. Then the ball is hit. And with the crack of the bat this shuffling form snaps to—bolting from his stance and with remarkable grace and speed tracks down a ball in the gap, fields it cleanly, and in one smooth motion launches a throw of breathtaking force and accuracy that reaches its target, on target, a beat ahead of when experience tells us it could possibly arrive. With the runner either tagged out in the dirt or scrambling back to the previous base, the right fielder with the tired eyes shuffles back towards his position with a slight limp and a sloping shoulder. Extraordinary stuff. Even leaving aside his similarly remarkable work at the plate, as well as the fascinating Russo-Dominican name combination, his prescience in the outfield alone easily make him one of the most captivatingly watchable stars to visit Fenway this season; second only perhaps to the incomparable Ichiro.)

Colón, with the help of Guerrero, passes his test in the fourth and strands another runner in scoring position in the fifth. Leading up to and setting the stage for his counterpart Lowe's own moment of truth, here in the sixth. With two outs (both strikeouts) in the inning and his pitch count rising towards triple digits, and still holding onto a precarious one-run lead, Lowe gives up a long drive to Kennedy which sails out to straightaway center towards and eventually over the head of a backtracking Johnny Damon. For a moment it had looked, to the crowd and surely to Lowe, as if Damon would leap up and steal the inning away; but Kennedy's uppercut and the ball's lofting backspin fooled Damon just enough, causing that one crucial misstep forward before having to turn and sprint back, the ball clearing Damon's leaping glove to bounce on the track and give Kennedy more than enough time to reach third standing up. (As Damon walks back in and shakes his head a lone cry of *we still love you Johnny!* goes out from center field bleachers, to great applause and general laughter.) Lowe returns to the mound and settles in to face Molina, whom he has yet to retire. On a 1-2 count he delivers his one-hundredth and perhaps most crucial pitch of the night, a nasty sinker darting down and away from Molina who can only wave helplessly, striking out to end the inning, the threat, and at least a few lingering concerns among the Fenway crowd about the general stability of Derek Lowe himself.

There will be others, surely.

For the Red Sox fans' relationship with Derek Lowe, and his with us, has always been something of a struggle. We have alternately wanted him to be more like the pitcher we believe him to be and less like the pitcher we're worried he really is, and the same can probably be said of Lowe himself. The trouble is that not only does Lowe visibly emote these wishes and fears clearer than any other Red Sox player, but that those wishes and fears are the same exact emotions the fans feel for him, and at the exact same time. Simply put, Derek Lowe reacts to his pitching the same way we do. When he struggles he huffs and puffs and makes exaggerated *you have to be kidding me* faces, and has a tendency to at times over-dramatizes the issue; which, yes, is a fair description of the reaction many Red Sox fans emit at the very same time. When he triumphs he pumps his fist and shouts and makes wild *oh yeah baby* faces, and occasionally he gets carried away with it all; again, fairly mirroring the crowd around him and more than a few watching at home. No matter how much we would like to keep a controlled, studied calm (like Pedro) or a steady burning confidence (like Schilling), most of us tend to root for the Sox like Derek Lowe pitches, which is to say with very little emotional restraint. We see ourselves out there bemoaning every hit and cheering every strikeout, and this of course is part of the problem. We want the Sox to play every night like we know they are capable of playing, just as surely as Lowe wants to pitch every night like he knows he is capable of pitching. When either fails to meet that standard is when both have problems. As fans we have trouble accepting that the Red Sox at times fail to execute and fail to concentrate in part because we have set such high expectations for them—because, quite simply, we believe they can be better than they are. Failure becomes all the more aggravating then because of how very successful we know this team *could* be. The same dynamic, it seems, has at times troubled Derek Lowe. He has seen, both as a closer and a starter, how dominating he can be when he performs up to his elite talents, and it is perhaps that image (similar to our image of the team playing its best ball) that provides much of the biting sting for Lowe when he pitches poorly. Just as we invest our full confidence in him, he lets us down. And the moment we are ready to give up on him altogether for the last time, he lifts us up once again. (Does this remind us of any team in particular?) So that while Red Sox fans may embrace other players—Damon, Ortiz, Pokey—with a warmer, purer form of adoration; and may admire the talents of other Sox stars—Manny,

Schilling, Pedro—with a more respectful awe; no figure in this generation of Red Sox players so fully envelopes the entire Red Sox drama, high, low, and everything in between, more than Derek Lowe. Like it or not, he is the closest thing we fans have to a surrogate on the field, where all the joy and frustration and hope and doubt and wild cheers and head-in-hands despair that comes along with following the Red Sox can be seen in his singular presence, alone on the mound—the Red Sox experience, incarnate.

On this night, of course, he and we can do no wrong, and joy and hope are at there highest points in a very long time as Lowe returns to retire Guerrero leading of the eighth, then exits with the lead and in line for the win under a thunderous standing ovation from Fenway. Once again Lowe and the crowd mirror each other, the confidence of the one becoming lost in the reflected confidence of the other.

The Angels mount one final threat in the ninth, a lead-off shot down the left field line by Troy Glaus that is deftly held to a single by Manny and is eventually erased on a failed (and perhaps ill-conceived) first pitch hit-and-run by Kennedy, who misses a Foulke change-up that Varitek smoothers and pegs down to Cabrera to nail Glaus by a half step. Kennedy strikes out three pitches later and is followed by DaVanon, who pops Foulke's 1-1 pitch up into the September night air. Foulke points straight up, we point straight up right along with him, Orlando Cabrera follows both our directional aides (or, the ball) overhead until it falls silently into his glove and it's *cheers to* the dirty water, *cheers to* a 4-3 Red Sox win, and *cheers to* a late summer sweep we are still staking our heads at even as we celebrate long, long into the night

Fenway, as is often and perhaps overly alluded to, can at times be a magical place; and certainly it has played host to bigger, more improbable victories even within this very season than this 4-3 victory over Anaheim. But there have been very few stretches in recent memory where it has hosted a livelier, more joyous three night party than the one which ended so sweetly in the glove of Orlando Cabrera on this Thursday night in September.

Kicked off with a boisterous first inning blast by Manny on Tuesday evening, continuing on through the intoxicating swirl of reports from New York that circled throughout the stands that night (*did you hear, 6-0, no it's 9-0, I heard 12-0, 18, 19, you have to be kidding, no, really, 22, honest*) and passing through the extended party of Wednesday's rout and on, steadily building now, to the climactic euphoria of Thursday, the bleachers and grandstands and concourses of Fenway became places of many smiles and much, much laughter. This laughter, more than anything else, stands out among the other magical Fenway nights for it came about so unexpectedly. September is not traditionally a jolly time among Red Sox fans, and this one promised to be no more so, opening as it did with a difficult series against a streaking opponent, with the team having cleared the easiest stretch of its schedule and still embroiled in not one but two tight playoff races. None of which allowed much room for laughter.

But then how could we not smile to the point of laughter when Varitek threw out two runners in one inning, or when the Sox won a one-run game without a hit from Manny or Ortiz? There was no helping it; we had to laugh. We had to shrug our shoulders and pantomime disbelief to friends in the section over. We had to hold up numbers like three (*games back*) and nine (*wins in a row*) to strangers who understood and smiled back. We had to laugh because it really did happen; we really did rout the first two games; the Yanks really did lose 22-0 in Baltimore; we really have swept the talented Angels right when we desperately needed to; and if all of this is possible then why not more, then why not…? (That is, so long as we are projecting *why not go so far as*…?) And the talk goes on and on, out through the crowd and along the T and around the bars, among the novice fools and the barroom drunks and all the rest of us, too. And why not? Swept up on a rare night like this, anything at all seems possible.

OCTOBER

Washed Away

Baltimore at Fenway
1 October 2006

It is raining at Fenway Park—as it has most of the day, as it has so often throughout this most overcast of seasons. A few minutes past seven-thirty on the first dark evening of October, we stand alone behind the left field roof boxes, leaning on its green countertop, nursing a cup of coffee, waiting. Through a curtain of rain, hazy silver in the floodlights above, we watch the grounds crew in slick red parkas tighten spikes along the edge of the glistening white tarp. The Red Sox themselves have long since disappeared, along with the visiting Orioles, first into dugouts then one by one into their clubhouses and gone. Leaving the scoreboard in left field frozen with five innings played, the score 9-0, Sox, and the Orioles still without a hit. (To the left of this, and for the last month a sight to be avoided at all cost, are the divisional standings; where our fair city is listed not first, not second, but a distant third.) Below us the grandstand is a bowl of empty red seats, gleaming wet, broken only by a spare cluster of yellow, orange and red parkas, and the blue-and-white pinwheel umbrella tops of the few hundred who came prepared. A few hundred more sit scattered among the blue wooden seats sheltered beneath the upper tier and stare out at the field, or stand with crossed arms and watch a highlight reel playing on the videoboard above center. One clip is from a brilliant June afternoon against these same Orioles. Manny singles through the infield, Fahey charges in shallow left but bobbles the ball, the winning run comes wheeling around third to score, and a happy sunlit celebration around home plate glows out through the falling sheets of rain.

The rains began as soon as the gates opened at noon today, and left us to stand around or mill about the concourses until just before five, when they finally let up and the grounds crew began the slow and tedious process of readying the field. At 5:28 pm, after several thousand fans had left either for dry ground or football, rookie Devern Hansak threw a strike to Brian Roberts and the small crowd remaining gave a warm exuberant cheer. And for five damp gray innings there was baseball.

Then it began to drizzle, then rain, then shower, and finally poured long tilting sheets until the umpire waved play dead, the grounds crew wheeled out the tarp, and the players all hurried off the field. Hundreds of fans (perhaps half of the few thousand remaining) left shortly thereafter. Leaving the rest of us to stand and stare out at the tarp, and to consider not why they left (for that much is understandable), but rather the very reasonable question of why the rest of us have stayed. Why, in fact—on the last day of the season, with the Sox a dozen games back and eliminated weeks ago and the weather of a bad day only growing worse—have we bothered at all?

As it turns out many came simply because they had the tickets (the last game of the season picked up months earlier in hopes of a furious playoff race finale), because they had not made it to Fenway yet, and because, well, *it's now or never*. Others came out of a sense of obligation, season ticket holders looking to finish out the strip. Among them a man we met sitting alone in Section 42 of the bleachers, still in Sox hat and home jersey, still leaned back with his feet up on the rain-slick seat in front of him. Abandoned first by his three fellow season ticket holders (because of the standings), then by his wife and kids (because of the forecast), and finally by two friends made on the way into the ballpark (who left an hour into the first rain delay), he sits alone and cheers the last few innings because he goes to Opening Day and the last game every year, no matter what. Like others in this small crowd he is here to earn a kind of fan's merit badge, to reaffirm his vows of fidelity to the Sox, and to remind himself once again exactly why 27 October 2004 meant so very much.

By its reactions, and by the few small but lovingly crafted and proudly held signs in the right field bleachers, many more showed up today merely to say their goodbyes to old number 7, Trot Nixon; who has been with in the Red Sox organization since the day he was drafted (thirteen years now and longer than any other current Red Sox); whose contract is up at the end of the season; and who today is almost certainly playing his last game in a Red Sox uniform. This fact is so widely accepted that manager Francona has his right fielder leading off today, allowing him to step up to the plate in the top of the first and receive his ovation from the Fenway crowd. Nixon tipped his tarry helmet, dug in, and singled to center. Later on, when the heavy rains returned, Francona pulled Nixon from right field in order to give him his final, formal exit.

At first this scene—Trot jogging off in a dreary shower, to be applauded by a few thousand—seemed an unfair exit for someone who has given so much, to here be given such an incomplete farewell; but in the end it rather feels more appropriate than not, for Nixon has been a solid and hardworking favorite, every bit a Boston ballplayer, and is nothing if not a walking example of loyalty to club. So perhaps it is only fitting that his final damp salute is not given out to the midsummer tourists, the bandwagon fan, or the bright-lights big-game big-ticket opportunists, but to the few thousand diehards who stayed till the end, through failure and inconvenience and discomfort, just to acknowledge his years of grinding effort and by their applause, to thank him.

Before this exit there were others. Such as Mark Loretta's, subbed out ominously (*is this goodbye to you, too?*) to begin the fifth. And before that Ortiz, who walked in the bottom of the fourth and was immediately pinch run for. The crowd cheered, Ortiz lumbered off and ducked quietly into the offseason. And still the rains continued to fall. With Nixon and most of the starters out of the lineup and the delay lingering on and on, many of those who came to say goodbye have folded up their signs and left. No one could blame them. They have paid whatever debt there is to pay to their team, and this second round of rain has—like a manager taking the ball with a pat on the shoulder to say they'd done enough—ended the season of many a loyal Sox fan and sent them trickling out onto Yawkey and home.

As for the rest of us? Well, who's to say really?

Perhaps we hang around simply to see just a bit more baseball, regardless. No longer a matter of loyalty to team or respect for parting friends, those of us who rely on this game to provide the common, consistent thread of our summer now stay to hold onto its last fraying end for just a few hours longer. We are here then, to see one more ground ball sneak through the infield, to cross our arms and mutter *come on double play* and then feel that leap of recognition in the chest as the ball is hit just so—*there it is!*—to shortstop then flipped, turned, fired, caught and 6-4-3 we're out of the inning. We have stayed to cheer for a strikeout on one more full count, to shout *get in the gap* at one more liner into the outfield, and to raise our hands in shocked indignation at one more absurdly biased call by an umpire with an obvious agenda against us. We have stayed to wave one more hooking drive fair, to lean with one more outfielder stretching into a running catch, and to see one more ball ricochet down off the left field wall as a Sox runner cruises into second with a double. We have stayed, that is, simply to watch the game we love. Even if only for a few more damp and drizzly innings.

But it is not to be.

There are hurried movements down below as through the curtain of rain clubhouse boys move equipment and then, with a sudden downbeat, Carl Beane's familiar baritone comes over the loudspeakers to tell what few remain that the game has *been called due to rain*, and that the 2006 Red Sox season is now officially over. We look about for someone to exchange a disappointed shake of the head with—here along this same stretch of concrete where we have, over the past six months, crowded among so many baseball friends—but there is no one with whom to even share our disappointment. We are alone in the rain. Our coffee is empty. The game is over. It is time to go home. Carl Beane thanks the fans for a great season. The Fenway organist plays *Auld Lang Syne*. And we gradually make our way down the empty ramps, through the vacant gates (*should auld acquaintance be forgot, and never brought to mind*), and into the rainy October night, whispering the old familiar words (*should auld acquaintance be forgot, and days o' lang syne*) on our way home.

A Thing of Beauty

American League
Divisional Series: Game Two

Anaheim at Fenway
5 October 2007

Baseball memory tends to be mercifully selective. The game is so patterned with repetition that its familiar, nonessential events—the routine grounder, the harmless single, the innocuous two out walk—fade instantly to the background, gone before we even leave the park. So that we know, even as we bound down the crowded, cheerful ramps of Fenway Park during the first noisy post-midnight hour of an October Saturday, that we will not take with us the entire four hours of baseball we have just now experienced. All smiles and head-shaking disbelief, punctuated by the flare of a high five somewhere in the middle and the ubiquitous Let's-*Go!* Red-*Sox!* chant still echoing through the concourses, we have left behind in the detritus of our celebration outs, hits, runs, perhaps entire innings of this second game of the American League Divisional Series. The bit of trouble Sox starter Daisuke Matsuzaka got himself into in the first and again in the third, and once again in the fifth, have all melded together into one collective outing about which we remember only that *he struggled*. His opposite, in road grays and red hat, was the Angels' Kevlim Escobar, who pitched much better but was likewise done in by one bad inning—his the very first. Predictably what we remember clearest from both starters are their worst innings (this the pitcher's dilemma: while the batter goes 1-4 and we remember only the hit, the pitcher goes six strong and we remember only the one in which he faltered).

Likewise the scoring. For it is doubtful that the Sox's little two-run rally in the first will be immortalized in song any time soon. Pedroia grounded out, Youkilis walked, Ortiz singled, Manny flew out on a line (hit hard, but) to center, Lowell walked to load the bases. And were it anyone else at the plate we may have forgotten this next step, too. Only it was J.D. Drew, whose season-long struggles brought a low grumble from the crowd when he stepped to the plate, and whose easy single through the infield drove in two and causes a surprised roar—the backstory casting this one success in such stark, bittersweet relief. Here it is then (with a sigh): *the time he came through*.

The Angels' little three-run rally an inning later was no more distinct. A walk to Casey Kotchman to start the inning, a single by Kendry Morales that skipped under the glove of a diving Pedroia (perhaps we remember him slamming down on his elbow, wincing, the trainer coming out for a look), then a strikeout and a groundout to bring in a run. Daisuke struggling, piling up pitches. Nothing either new or particularly exciting.

Yet we remember the next two Angels runs distinctly; not because of how they came about—a Figgins single, a Cabrera double—but because they came under the disjointed background noise of Red Sox fans, cheering. As Figgins looks out at Daisuke a little ripple of applause comes from the right field corner, then spreads to a cheer along the right side of the grandstand. The Yankees, playing into extra innings in Cleveland, have lost. And there are happy cheers (some are standing) as Figgins lines his single to left and the tying run scores. Followed by a slight groan when Manny misplays the ball, chases it down, and Figgins lands on second. Then another cheer, this time from the changing number on the out-of-town scoreboard, where on the lone score of the day the Cleveland 1 changes to a 2. More applause, this time fuller and louder and ballpark-wide. The clapping finds a rhythm, and in a distant corner an old, familiar, slightly nostalgic chant rises up from the grandstands—almost as if the ancient steel rafters and chipped wooden seats had absorbed its particular sound (having been subjected to it so long) and stored it there, waiting only for the mere whisper of its name to come echoing back to us, years and years later—in a new era, among new fans, yet with the same old chest-thumping chin-out fist-pumping bravado: *Yank-ees Suck, Yank-ees Suck*, (Cabrera doubles, Figgins scores, the Angels take the lead), *Yank-ees Suck, Yank-ees Suck...*

Other moments are more particular, more closely tied to our own personal experience of watching this game. For instance we remember that the first inning and a half took a full hour to play. And we remember this acutely because we had been fighting off a chest cold all week and struggled early ourselves (though much like the Red Sox we too would rally after midnight). We remember that the 8:30 pm EST start meant a long night to begin with. We remember a little flair Garret Anderson hit in the third that landed between an on-rushing Drew and out-rushing Pedroia, but only because 1) it happened right in front of us, and 2) Drew slid, which is not something we remember seeing a great deal of in right field this season. Then there was the great sprawling stop Youkilis made on a hot grounder in the fourth; and the Angels intentionally walking Ortiz in the third, then again in the fifth to get to Manny and load the bases; and the Angels' catcher going headfirst into the front row on a foul ball (later we heard that a kid in the front row had nabbed the ball, fairly and astutely, away from the catcher; but from our section of the stands this was unseen and therefore spliced unevenly into our memory of the play). Then there was Mike Lowell hitting a long fly to center to tie the game. And the first ever *J-D, J-D* chant on record at Fenway Park, followed by the two-hundredth-and-eighty-third or so groan of disappointment when he promptly grounded out to first. We remember Crisp getting doubled-up in the sixth for not retagging second on his way back to first; Delcarmen hitting Vlad on the triceps; and the clubby hyperactive Oki Doki song playing as both the reliever and a gangly bullpen attendant with high shorts and an awkward, knees high stride raced in opposite directions across the outfield. Which in turn reminds us that this crowd *was* wearing shorts, in October; that it was 74-degrees at game time and a little muggy too; and that the seventh inning stretch came a few minutes before midnight (and that we spent it violently coughing into our scorecard). We remember looking down at the bullpen in the eighth and seeing Timlin and Papelbon throwing side by side, and experiencing both dread and hope (also side by side), until the latter stepped off the mound and strode head down towardss the door. We remember that the two guys in front of us exchanged a celebratory high five as Lowell fielded a grounder and threw across, and then, when the throw hit the dirt and Youkilis couldn't come up with it, were chastised by the guy behind them for *premature celebration*. We remember Angels baserunners advancing unchecked to second and third, and Chone Figgins looking very small as he stood alone at the plate after a called strike three ends the threat. And finally we remember that when the Sox came up in the bottom of the ninth our feet hurt, our legs ached, our cough had left us with a dull headache and without a voice, and that K-Rod was warming in the Angels bullpen.

All of which will be forgotten, eventually.

Over time the unique outline of this particular playoff game will no doubt begin to fade. The jotted notations on a scorecard will remind us of a few (time-conscious as we were throughout the night each inning on our scorecard bears its own unique timestamp), and the individuality of certain plays will preserve them longer, and keep them fresher in the mind than others. (Interestingly enough this is exactly what we do not want to happen with the J.D. Drew hit. We'd just as soon it become lost within a shuffle of crucial two-out hits. For now though, it stands out only because it stands alone.) The rest will blend in quietly with other playoff games, other Daisuke starts, other games watched from this particular corner of Fenway. For this is the nature of baseball, where the sheer volume of event in a typical season or series or even game overcrowds the mind with detail and leaves only a bare few moments (mostly personal) left to take with us. The dazzling pitching performance, the friend we watched it with, the key home run, where we went after, the thrilling play at the plate. As the years go by, even these begin to fade. We begin to condense. Two or three home runs appear more or less the same; two or three stellar outings take on a similar shape; and one walk-off celebration mirrors another until the two become indecipherable, become our stock image of the Ortiz Walk-Off, the Inning-Ending Strikeout, the Crucial Game-Saving Double Play. Leaving us with little more than the statistical record of who won, an inky scorecard detailing how it all played out, and perhaps a ticket stub or commemorative t-shirt to remind us that we were there to see it.

Beyond this, when all else is gone, we have with us those rare moments which occur every now and again in this game which are, by a combination their circumstance and style, suffused with such immense life and such singular beauty as to render them in every way unforgettable. And at 12:45 am on Saturday, 6 October 2007, on the last pitch of a long, summery fall night at Fenway Park, one such moment appeared instantly and incandescently before us.

No need for a scorecard here; the scene unfolds effortlessly before us:

Tucked into a dark, cramped Standing Room Only space behind the third base grandstand, we lean our arm against the cluster of cool steel pipes running up the brick wall at our back. On a slight concrete rise, a step up from the narrow aisle space between us and the rail above the seats, we can still see the Angels tossing the ball around the infield as fans shift and squeeze by in opposite directions. Glancing over our left shoulder we peer down onto Van Ness Street and find a long row of television vans silent beneath the glowing streetlights, their white saucer satellites aimed skyward. A breeze, luxuriously fresh, slips through the grating behind us and over our shoulders, cutting the stagnant air, heavy beneath the overhang, and as it cools our neck we close our eyes and shift from one aching foot to the other—both feet numb from having stood on a slab of concrete for over four hours, the pressure having now crept up our calves and brought on a dull ache just before the knees. Before us fans on the railing lining this particular grandstand section lean on their elbows. Among them two college-age guys, both in Ortiz jerseys (one red, one white), who have cheered the entire game and were joined around the third inning by two girls. The girls took a lot of pictures of each other posing in front of the field and then, right before the ninth, left. At our side, on the other side of the pole, is a young man who has stood and quietly scored the game on a folded up GameDay scorecard. We keep forgetting he is there. Then there is the fan somewhere in the section before us who every time a runner reaches first base has shouted *Now!* at great volume just before the pitch is delivered. On every pitch, for over six innings. After each shout he has received a fresh round of glances, from all directions and ranging anywhere from slightly annoyed to vaguely threatening. Also for over six innings. Oblivious to this (and much else) he keeps it up, each time laughing wildly and looking around to make sure everyone can see the source of such profound wit. We peer in. Because of the overhang, and because the grandstand is not well lit, the field before us is cropped into an exaggerated widescreen format. A clear dark line across the top, and the fading downslope of grandstand fans below growing lighter until they escape the overhang and are lit, along with the field itself, by the floodlights high above. Eminem's "One Shot" thumps from the loudspeaker, and the pair in matching Ortiz jerseys nod along involuntarily, *you only get one shot do not miss your chance to blow, this opportunity comes once in a lifetime...*

The Angels toss the ball back in, reliever Justin Speier takes one more warm-up pitch, the ball darts to second and Julio Lugo steps to the plate to begin the bottom of the ninth with his Latin beat intro playing and the crowd raising a hopeful cheer. Then instantly bolting up in applause as Lugo rips the first pitch into left for a clean single. We jot it down in our scorecard, and note that it is the first hit allowed by either bullpen. A glance to our right and we see Francisco José Rodriguez, K-Rod, throwing in the bullpen. Ominously, we can hear the hard *pop* of leather echoing out across the field after each pitch. Pedroia comes up and quickly grounds to short, moving Lugo up to second on the throw. Then a pause. We all stand still and wait. It goes on one beat too longhand then *yep, there he is*, manager Mike Scioscia steps from the dugout and we immediately turn to the visiting bullpen door, now swinging open. K-Rod emerges from behind it, sprints out across the outfield, and there is an unmistakable lull of apprehension within the crowd.

Once on the mound K-Rod appears more or less exactly the way we remember him. Though his body has filled out a bit in maturity he still has the same knees-bent crouch on the mound, still wears his straight-billed hat slightly too low over already goggled eyes, and still throws like someone on whose back right shoulder an infuriated cat has just now leapt, and which he must shake off by the most violent motion imaginable—and *right now*—by jerking his entire frame back, then hurling himself forward and to the left with such force as to send his entire body spinning in the opposite direction (and presumably send one imaginary infuriated cat spinning into the third base box seats). All to produce the same awesome combination of hard fastball and devastating slider. All with the same results; as he steps up, and strikes out Youkilis on four pitches. The low groans last only a moment though, and are washed away the moment the crowd turns its eyes to Ortiz in the on deck circle. Many stand, many more cheer. So much so that it is easy to miss the seated and wary head-shaking of those who have been paying attention and therefore realize what will happen next. Molina stands, holds out his arm, and the cheers instantly turn to boos. It is the fourth consecutive time Ortiz has been walked, the third intentionally; and it is quite enough to make clear the Angels' defensive strategy. They are not going to bother with Big Papi tonight. They will make someone else, anyone else, beat them.

Up next, is Manny.

He strides to the plate as he always does, circling behind the catcher, staring out into the grandstand somewhere just above the visiting dugout, searching (for something? for someone?) and then, after a pause (there it is), he turns to the batter's box. Right foot first, secure, then left as he brings the bat down to the plate with a tap and circles it back around. All this we see in profile, watching him from the first base side with K-Rod's back to us and the crowd surrounding them on its feet. The clapping is continuous, a-rhythmic, and rolling with a *Man-ny, Man-ny* chant rising and falling a few sections over. Red, white and blue bunting hang in crescents along the low back wall; extra photography wells have been added to each side of home, further tightening the space around the plate; and the ALDS logo, in bright blue, yellow, and white, covers the grass behind the umpire who now leans forward, hands to knees. The Angels infielders inch up. The outfielders shift into position. Out at second Lugo crouches way down, hands close in front of him, flashing peeks left and right. Ortiz glances over his right shoulder, takes two easy strides off first, turns and looks in. We clap among the reverberating echo of sound, our sleeves rolled tight to our elbows, scorebook pinned under our arm, we instinctively raise up straight with knees locked just as K-Rod kicks and fires and the ball darts in low. Manny watches it. Ball one. We relax a beat. The crowd around us takes a breath. And the entire scene repeats itself. Another *Man-ny, Man-ny* chant, this time louder, the applause steady now, the kids behind home plate thumping hands against the padded green walls. The fielders all lean as one; Lugo takes his lead; Ortiz steps off first. Manny taps the plate with his bat, windmills it to his back shoulder. The thumping noise vibrates the ballpark, causing the entire scene to shudder in the warm early autumn air. K-Rod comes set, looks down. He kicks, throws, the ball darts in, Manny swings and on the crack of the bat the entire scene before us erupts—a riot of wild leaping and thunderous noise and shuddering motion and laughs and shouts and delirious celebration and lost within it we punch the air and shout in disbelief and the Sox stream out from the dugout and the Angels and umpires jog silently off and down in the center of it all Manny sweeps around the bases amid a reeling vortex of light and sound and pure, uninhibited joy.

Suddenly we are cured. No more cough, no more cold. The fellow fan beside us whom we have watched the game with shouts a laughing, exuberant *my feet don't hurt any more!* Neither do ours. We are all of us, along with the entire ballpark of fans and onlookers and ushers and venders, completely awake to and enlivened by the moment. Below us Manny wheels around third, head low, leaps into the pile of teammates who instantly engulf him as they drift away from the plate, bounding over each other and pounding down on the game's hero. Eventually he is separated out, and as he staggers over, shirt untucked and dreadlocks hanging behind him, an echoed roar, deep and appreciative, comes up from the crowd. At this point we can only shake our head and watch, hands atop hat, knowing that we will never, as long as we have memories at all, forget what we have just witnessed.

Let us be clear: this one was all about style. The victory may have put the series in the Sox's control, but with a 1-0 lead and the Angels looking enfeebled and increasingly beatable the game itself was not of absolute dire importance. Tough as it may have been to watch, the Sox could have lost and still headed back to the West Coast with the series tied. And playoffs or not, this was still the *Divisional* Series—a crucial first step in the wider scope of the postseason, but a first step nonetheless. Not to mention that the game was in fact only tied. With K-Rod in and Papelbon used up we appeared to be heading for a battle of bullpen attrition, and the Sox easily could have come back to win in the eleventh or beyond. The situation then was not exactly desperate; nor were the means by which it was decided particularly unique. For we have seen walk-off home runs before, many times, including the last time the Red Sox won an ALDS game at home. So it was not what happened, or when it happened, that made this moment stand out; but instead *how* it happened—that is to say the absolute beauty of the moment itself.

Beauty may seem a problematic word to use here, applied as it is to a professional and therefore commercially exploitive sporting event; for surely we run the risk of being charged with overstatement and over-sentimentality. (That is to say, *it was a great home run and all, but come on.*) In its capital-B form Beauty can be made a heavy word, a mature word, a vaguely intellectual word best reserved for those areas of life already stamped with the culturally-approved seal of aesthetic, artistic Beauty. The latest Monet exhibit at the MFA. The latest Mozart symphony at the BSO. Here are local landmarks where it is acceptable to depart with the assurance that one has been in the presence of the Beautiful. (Both places, in fact, we go to expecting that very quality within.) But sport can be beautiful, too. Or rather, sport can produce moments of beauty, and it is perfectly alright for us to recognize them as such. The only difference being that we can't count on seeing it quite so regularly, that there is no gallery guide to inform us which figures are of principal importance, and while there is a program, it by no means outlines the scheduled performance in advance. Unfortunately. For we may go games, weeks, in some cases entire seasons without seeing anything even remotely approaching it; and in its place find only the mundane, the unappealing, at times even the vulgar. But still. If we keep showing up, keep tuning in, keep waiting for the dreary complexities of innings and outs and strikes to sort themselves into some kind of coherent meaning, it is possible, though exceedingly rare, for that outcome to arrive with such clarity, such harmony, its every element perfectly balanced and for one unconscious instant glowing brilliant with the fullness of life lived to the hilt, as to produce a single moment of incomparable beauty.

Manny's home run to beat the Angels in Game Two of the 2007 ALDS was one of those moments. Dramatically, rhythmically, aesthetically, it meets all the requirements.

First there is the swing itself, that perfectly balanced motion so wonderful to watch all on its own. This time its ease is amplified by the contrast set up between it and the spastic flailings of K-Rod, which on this last pitch to Manny is so exaggerated that it wheels the pitcher completely around in a kind of vicious pirouette. At the other end of this fitful twisting motion is the graceful sweep of Manny's swing. Back shoulder to back shoulder, it appears as one singularly effortless motion—like a long, slow, exhale. *Breath in*, pitch comes in, *breath out*, ball goes out.

Around this central pendulum, on which the moment literally swings, are the backdrop and foregrounded lighting which convene to both frame and concentrate its effect. As mentioned before, there have been other walk-offs at Fenway; some quite memorable. Yet in each there was that familiar home run down-beat, that breathless moment right after the ball is hit and each fan has shouted and risen to their feet and the ballpark waits and watches and hopes for it to go far enough, and the instant it does the celebration bursts up again, reaffirmed.

Manny's was different in two interconnected ways. First, its magnitude. The legend of how far Manny's home run ball traveled began to spread even as we were making our way through the concourse and onto the celebratory Lansdowne/Brookline nexus—*over the Coke bottles, way over...between the Coke bottles and the lights...close to the lights...way over Lansdowne*, and so on. For our own part we have no idea how high or how far it went, because we didn't see it. With our sightline cropped by the overhang we only saw it leave the bat. And although we would have certainly liked to admire such a ball, in retrospect it seems better to have had the view we were given; for it forced us to focus on the second, more stunning and ultimately defining characteristic of the moment.

That is the sudden, instantaneous shock of its arrival. The moment it hit the bat, we knew. Everyone. Manny, K-Rod, the umpires, the players on both teams, the announcers (who we later heard called it while it was in the air, *Red Sox win!*), and every fan in the ballpark or watching at home. There was simply no need to follow the ball. The angle and velocity with which it was struck left no doubt. And so there was only *one* crowd reaction, ballpark wide. All together now, every arm straight up, every voice full throated, the entire celebration full strength, all at once. It was as if someone had flipped a light switch; one moment everyone on the field and in the stands was standing in place, and the very next instant everything in view went absolutely wild with motion—the Sox players streaming onto the field, the Angels jogging off, the umpires sprinting off, the fans leaping in their seats and down the aisles, the ballpark shuddering beneath it all. We can still see the two images spliced together, like a pair of slides. Baited expectancy, *click-click*, riotous celebration. (One half expected to be able to flick it off again, *click*, and have it all switch back to nervous clapping. But then, why would we?) It was unlike any home run we have ever seen, at a moment unlike any other we have experienced, and in its totality it was without hesitation a thing of great beauty to behold.

A few days have passed now, and already the details of the game have begun to fade. The Drew single (*was it through the infield or a line drive?*), the work of Papelbon, the Yankees losing, and the warm summery weather; a good, exciting playoff baseball game, already replaced with another (this a sunny series clincher in California). And yet without any effort at all we can peer through the window before us on a cold, rainy Monday morning in the city, and see the scene open up (*... and the entire scene repeats itself. Another Man-ny, Man-ny chant, this time louder, the applause steady now, the kids behind home plate thumping hands against the padded green walls. The fielders all lean as one...*) just as it happened that night. Just as we suppose it always will.

For this is the great gift we find in a thing of beauty. That it lasts. Be it a piece of fine art, a composition of music, a great work of architecture, a vista of natural scenic beauty, or a single moment—big or small, private or public, sacred or secular—it stays with us and continues to enrich our lives long after it ends or we move on to the next painting, song, building or game. By arranging its elements in perfect harmony with each other, with not a single brushstroke out of place, it is able to raise itself above the discord of daily experience. And we guard it in memory because we know how exceedingly rare those moments are.

Perhaps there are those who would scoff at holding a home run up to such heights, or even loosely drawing parallels between the work of a Monet or a Mozart, to that of a Manny. To which our only answer (the only answer we have, the only answer we need) is to say that if one has found enough beauty in life outside of sports to satisfy the soul and affirm one's sense of harmony in the world, then one is very lucky indeed. For the rest of us, we'll take beauty where it comes, and not mind so much the where or when. On travels abroad to the farthest corners of the globe or on our walk to work; in the master galleries of the world's finest museums or in our homes; on the stage of the Majestic or in a movie rental; in the full orchestra of first night at Symphony Hall or in our headphones; at our work, with our friends, at the ballpark. It hardly matters. The rare moment comes to us unannounced and unexpected—sudden and brilliant and full of light—and if we are careful it can be ours to savor in memory. Where the swing will always be true, the ball will always fly clean off the bat, and that instant when our entire world snaps to life with the rush of pure experience will neither fade nor diminish, but instead grow constant—forever vivid, forever cheering, forever filled with joy.

Lucky

American League
Divisional Series: Game Four

Angels at Fenway
6 October 2008

It has nothing to do with luck. Baseball is a physical game played on a field of distinct mathematical proportions, on which specific forces are applied to a ball of definite size and weight, which reacts to the combination of those forces in a purely objective manner. So that when said ball travels at a certain angle, at a certain speed, with a certain rotation, and is then struck by a bat moving with definable velocity at a specific angle, the result will be to alter the path of the ball and create a new line with an altered speed and direction which begins at the intersection of the line of the ball and plane of the bat, and ends at a point somewhere afield; and that point will be either within other lines or not, and within the reach of fielders who themselves are running on other lines trying to intersect the path of the ball at a slight elevation and within a folded confabulation of leather. The play (single, out, double, foul ball) is the result of an equation—something which can be quantified, extrapolated and in theory predicted. All of which we know. All of which probably seems rather obvious. Yet in a month when one hears a great deal about decidedly *non*-quantitative forces such as *momentum, heart*, the *will to win* and (of course) *team chemistry*, and in a ballpark where those who once said the Red Sox *can't possibly ever* beat the Yankees now say the Angels *can't possibly ever* beat the Red Sox, it is probably worth reminding ourselves that the ball is after all an object, and therefore does not care who hits it, or what hat they're wearing, or whether or not they have playoff experience or struck out their last ten times at bat.

Not so the fans. Who are in fact defined by their caring a great deal about who is at bat, and what they've done in the past, and what their chances are of doing it again. (Those who watch but do not care are strictly speaking *spectators*, though they rarely refer to themselves as such and are prone to crowding under the very broad *fan* umbrella when, and only when, it is fashionable to do so.) The problem is that in the outcome equation there simply is no place for this caring, and therefore no place for the fan. For all our emotional investment, we fans are left with very little to actively do about it. Sure we can clap. If so inclined we can shout our sentiments fieldward. Rhythmically chanting the name of a player one wants to encourage is another option; as is baying the name of the opposing pitcher in a low, mocking tone for several innings on end. Yet even this rather short list (even sitting and trying to make this list) highlights the painful remove at which we fans sit from the object and outcome of our fandom. Yet over the course of a season great reservoirs of care and concern are built up around certain players, around a ballpark, around a team, and a portion of the emotional life (small at times, great at others) is unconditionally given over to ride upon their fate—to leap in the shared elation of their triumphs, and to risk sharing in the heartbreak of their defeats. Is it any wonder then that clapping feels inadequate? Does it surprise anyone that we shout at the radio and the television; that we will eat the same meal at the same bar (and make something of an issue over getting the same table) based solely on its talismanic effects; that during every playoff game we pull the exact same charmed 2004 sweatshirt over the exact same charmed 2007 road jersey; that we call the same friend in the middle of the fourth every game unless the Sox are trailing in which case *he calls us* in the top of the fifth; or that late at night we make the very serious and consequential decision to go ahead and turn our hat inside out *and* backwards.

Is it any wonder that when Jed Lowrie takes his stance in the left-side batter's box in the bottom of the tenth in Game Three of the ALDS, with the bases loaded, two outs, the Sox leading the series 2-0 and the ALCS one base hit away, that we are among the millions of Red Sox fans who turn to forces for which there are no mathematical symbols?

Dark at first pitch, the third game of the ALDS and the first playoff game of 2008 at Fenway Park has played out under a cold, windy, late October kind of night (a night which carries in its air the first reminder of what winter actually feels like). And while not always comfortable, it has managed to entertain. Populated with a wide cast of characters from both teams, highlighted by several outstanding defensive plays, made memorable through one hilarious mishap, balanced by a lead for either team and eventually one extended tie, the game now sits poised to culminate in this thrilling extra innings bases loaded situation. All of which has been somewhat dampened by the fact that it has taken absolutely *fore-ev-er* to do so. Thanks primarily to Josh Beckett, who having recovered from an injured oblique has proven only that either 1) he has in fact not yet fully recovered from an injured oblique, or 2) after two weeks off he has not yet fully regained the feel for his pitches, and has instead gamely soldiered through this important playoff start at something less than full strength. Either way he has struggled, and his four runs on seven hits over five innings are a tribute both to his impressive ability to grind out a short-handed start, and to the Angels' impressive ability to run and swing themselves out of one promising scoring chance after another. Which is how one ends up being out-hit, out-pitched, and tied, 4-4.

And how we arrive, four-and-a-half chilly October hours later, at the bottom of the tenth.

Jed Lowrie is at the plate. Thin, angular, athletic in a way that is somehow distinctly *collegiate*, the young switch-hitting shortstop steps into the left-hand batters box and sweeps his bat before him. Ortiz stands on third, Youk on first, Lowell on third. Two outs. K-Rod on the mound. And a great cheer from the Fenway crowd already on its feet.

Throughout this long game it has been, if somewhat sporadic, a good-to-great Fenway playoff crowd—up at every two strike count, standing through entire rallies—and like most playoff crowds has shown that special schizophrenic quality of going from tremendous enthusiasm to dead silence and back, all in one at bat. Here in the tenth it rises up to an entirely new level. It starts low, like any other rally cheer, everyone already on their feet through a long and tough at bat by Lowell, and cheering out *atta'boy!*'s for the walk. But then something happens which only ever happens in the playoffs; which is that everyone—not just the been-here-all-year fans but their flew-in-for-the-weekend colleagues, and the first timers, and the kids, and the friends-of, and the people venturing outside their suites for the first time and the last couple in the top apex of the bleachers and really simply *everyone*—cheers, shouts, and in general makes a raucous that is difficult to describe other than to say that it is the kind of sound which is loud enough to blend into one overriding enclosure of noise.

For this is it, surely. The series winner.

(The revelation comes as a surprise even to us. For all season there has been swirling around these Red Sox what can most tactfully be described as concern. Injuries, slumps, inexperience and a general lack of sustained momentum have combined to check any bombastic predictions, and after a full season of watching this Sox team we can come to no more encouraging assessment than to say that they are somehow *overwhelmingly competent*. And expectations coming into the playoffs have been muted accordingly. Drawing the Angels in the ALDS hardly helped matters, as Mike Scioscia's club has been the class of the American League pretty much all season. Yet here we are—up two games to none, coming back to Fenway for our all-but-ceremonial advancement to the ALCS. How did this happen? Certainly the Sox played well in Anaheim, and just as certainly the Angels played poorly. But more than this there came, sometime very late in Game Two, a feeling that this thing was meant to be. Our instincts were right: the Angels just *had a thing about the Sox*, they *couldn't find a way* to beat us in the playoffs, because *we've got their number* and so they just *can't get past us*. We knew it coming in, and felt even more assured of it coming back to Fenway. Even more so when Josh Beckett has one of his worst playoff starts ever, we get three runs on a botched single looping behind second, and here we are—thoroughly outplayed, with the ALCS a base hit away. Clearly it was meant to be. This then is where that special roar comes from, that wild gleeful raising of arms even after four freezing hours of joyful anticipation; because we know it is coming. We recognize the moment. And we know this is it, the momentary prelude to another front page, highlight reel, champagne soaked celebration.)

Lowrie swings, the ball flies lazily out to right, and there is a low and very brief gasp. Then silence. A groan. And the ball falls silently into the glove of outfielder Gary Matthews Jr. for the final out. The inning and rally are over, and we all quietly take our seats.

What follows are two innings remarkable only for the almost total lack of pleasure they provide the home fans. In the eleventh Papelbon slips out of an Angels walk-and-single mini-rally, only to allow a run on three singles in the twelfth. The Sox never put more than a runner on in the final two frames, and when Alex Cora grounds out to second they lose Game Three, 4-3, and we all go home cold and hoarse and very, very tired.

A bit under twenty-four hours later we are back again, standing again, cold again; hands in gloves and gloves in pockets again; hat tucked down and jacket pulled up to block a crisp wind again; shifting on a concrete slab from one sore foot to another and back again; nursing the last cold inch of coffee in a white Dunkin's cup, again. Among a crowd on its feet in anticipation again; waiting the Red Sox ALDS series win again. At the ballpark, late at night, and once again, cheering. This time for Justin Masterson to strike out Torii Hunter for the final out of the eighth. The Sox lead 2-0, and although the tying runs are on second and third we are but one out away from the ninth, from (presumably) Papelbon, and therefore one last step away from Game One the ALCS (again). Masterson throws, Hunter swings, the ball lofts out over second and lands softly on the outfield grass in shallow right, both runners come around to score, and with a chorus of sighs and shouts and even a few actual shrieks, the game is tied, 2-2.

Almost before this horrible bit of bad luck has registered within the hearts fans the Sox lineup goes down in order in the bottom of the eighth. Masterson returns in the ninth and immediately gives up a double off the wall to Kendry Morales who Howie Kendrick bunts over to third and who Reggie Willits runs for, and like *that* the Angles have the go-ahead run on third with one out in the top of the ninth, and the startlingly loud snap of K-Rod fastballs hitting the bullpen catcher's glove heard clear over a stunned Fenway crowd.

Now it is a well known baseball fan truism that the playoffs never really begin until one can sense that the end of the season is in the room. The feeling always comes slightly ahead of the really bad news (right before the crucial game is lost), when an astute fan can for the first time see a clear path to elimination. It is the *if we lose this, then...* moment. Which we all sense for better or for worse, but which is no more disheartening than in situations such as the one before us in the top of the ninth. If that run (Willits pinch running for Morales) scores, K-Rod comes in; if K-Rod comes in with a lead, we likely lose Game Four; if we lose Game Four, we go back West for Game Five; and if we go back West for Game Five it will be all in Anaheim's favor and—*my goodness*—we will have blown a 2-0 series lead and will have that to think about all winter and most of next season. (*If that run scores, then...*)

Manny Delcarmen is on the mound for the Sox and immediately falls behind Erick Aybar, 2-0. No longer silent, Fenway grumbles with discomfort at both the situation and its surrounding conditions; for it is no more physically comfortable, and possibly quite less comfortable than it has been all night, or was all last night. Clear and cold, it is one of those nights so perfectly dividing fall and winter that it almost seems as if one could determine which it is by choice. Seems so because this is exactly what we do, feeling very autumnal and crisp ourselves entering the ballpark and through the first two or three excited innings; then somewhere along the way (coincidentally at the very moment Hunter's single landed in the outfield), feeling as if it were awfully wintry, we begin to make all sorts of comments about the season running too long and starting the games earlier and so on, which complaints somehow never occurred to us back when the Sox were up 2-0 in the eighth. Now we are cold. And while a few fans shout out half-hearted encouragement those shouts are heard far too clearly among a more general shaking of heads, while most in view sit silently with their arms crossed with a look of deep, troublesome concern.

Because *we know* what's going on here. Oh you can't fool us, we see it plain enough. The narrow loss in Game Three, Beckett's troubles, the little flare falling for Hunter and now the Angels in position to take the lead at the very end and send the whole thing back to California. It all adds up. Clearly these Sox are unlucky, ill-fated, star-crossed, and (while we won't go so far as c—sed they are clearly without question) doomed. Obviously. There can be no other rational explanation. And since there is simply no recourse against the terribly unlucky break, the unfortunate call, the ill-timed string of singles falling in right where they need to, or (the unluckiest break of them all) the Angels' being lucky enough to have scored one more run than the Red Sox at the end of nine innings, there is nothing left to do but cross one's arms and furrow one's brow and shake one's head at the field, and wait for the final, impossibly unlucky blow to come.

Then something happens. When Delcarmen fires the 2-0 pitch Aybar squares—*squares to bunt*—and we don't even see Willits jetting down the line until the pitch hits Varitek's glove and suddenly there he is, Willits, frozen halfway between third and home. (Even watching the sensation is that of turning to find someone sneaking up on your shoulder, the start of wide-eyed surprise reflected on both sides.) There is a chase, Varitek running the fleet Willits up the line before he lunges to make the tag and goes tumbling gear and all over third; after which the ball tumbles out, but not before the out has been recorded. And Fenway Park roars up in delight. And *oh* how we laugh when Scioscia comes out to argue the tag, and *oh* how we shake our heads with amusement to think of how utterly foolish a squeeze in that situation was (and oh how interesting it is that Scioscia, so universally praised for his highly involved unconventional style of managing, always seems to find himself in these situations, having unconventionally managed himself right out of a situation in which it seems his team would have been far better served by his simply letting his talented players play), and *oh* how we cheer out with a big, full, deepbelly shout when Delcarmen's next pitch hits the glove and is called strike two. And when Aybar rolls an easy grounder down to Youk who fields and steps on the bag for the final out, *oh* how we cheer our mighty good fortune. (*What luck!*) That feeling—that things are meant to go our way, that the Angels cannot win at Fenway, that the Sox cannot help but win at Fenway, that coming back from down multiple games in a series is the exclusive domain of Red Sox baseball and not to be emulated by others, much less against them—is back. And we are a charmed lot once more.

The feeling continues into the bottom of the ninth, even after J.D. Drew strikes out looking. Shields is on the mound for Anaheim for a second inning and now faces Jason Bay, who takes a ball, then a strike. Nothing doing. Yet there is something about Bay, in these playoffs. This quiet, unassuming presence who is so often described as just *a good solid player*, is having quite a bit more than a good solid playoffs. Without question he has been the most important bat in the lineup, and without question the one most likely to strikeout in the third, fifth, and seventh, only to double in the tying run in the ninth. Shields throws, Bay swipes across the outside half the of the plate and suddenly the ball is lofting slowly down the right field line, low and slicing as Willits sprints in from right at a full charge, coming in and sliding at last towards the line as the ball drops fast and lands, fair and clean, inside the foul line and just before Willits's sliding glove. Bay jogs into second with a double, we roar to our feet around him, and the stage is set.

Then nearly unset a pitch later as Mark Kotsay laces a ball down the first base line, destined for the right field corner and only stopped by an outrageous leaping catch from first baseman Mark Teixeira. Low groans from the Fenway crowd, replaced almost immediately by the rising cheer for the next man up. One of the best pure reaction defensive plays one will see, Teixeira's diving catch saves the game, series, and season for the Angels. However momentarily.

Jed Lowrie is at the plate, again. Thin, angular, athletic in a way that is somehow distinctly *collegiate*, the young switch-hitting short-stop steps into the left-hand batters box and sweeps his bat before him. Bay stands on second. Two outs. Once again the series win is one hit away. Once again extra innings are a mere pop up away. Once again we stand and cheer.

And who among us knows the intimate calculus we fans use to pro-duce a feeling of either doubt or optimism in these situations? Before the series we were pragmatic; after Game One we were encouraged; after Game Two we were ecstatic and on our way to the pennant; three quarters of the way through Game Three we had won the champi-onship and were planning for a repeat; and twenty minutes later we were defeated and wondering what went wrong; one night later we were confident, deflated, and ecstatic in successive half-innings. Now, with Lowrie up, our fan intuition comes full term.

Perhaps because of how narrowly we escaped the ninth. Or how narrowly the Angels escaped last night. Or simply because we're at Fenway Park. Or because we knew even among our most wildly opti-mistic expectations that it would never be *that* easy against the Angels. Or because it should happen here in Boston and not way out in Cali-fornia. (Or because we have seen the sight of Papelbon in the bullpen so it pretty much *has to* happen right here.) Mostly though, at moments like these, it becomes personal. The feeling that it really is going to work out this time comes from such purely internal reasons such as the fact that we're having a good time with this team and in this ballpark. And because we want to see the celebration happen here, on the field at Fenway; and because we want others here to experience the same (which reminds us that we want it to happen because of the nice people we met in the bleachers earlier in the game, who got tick-ets offered to them last minute and found themselves happily at Fen-way.) And because it is Lowrie, who had a chance last night and didn't come through; and because one of the reasons we so enjoy this game of baseball is that it *always* seems to works out this way—to give a guy another chance; and because no one ever seems to come through and be the hero without having first failed, picked themselves up, and taken another swing at it. And yes, more than a little bit, it is because last February in the dead of another icy Boston winter we were, by mere chance, lucky enough to meet a Red Sox infield prospect named Jed, and had a nice long talk with him about baseball and Oregon and Fenway, and what it would mean to play in this town, in this ballpark, in October; and because this kid who nobody recognized by name or face was just entirely genuine and (for a person with his ability) exceedingly humble, and because he talked about how happy he was to see his buddies like Ellsbury and Pedroia doing well and it just made him work harder and try to do the best he could, and yes because he was just a totally earnest young man, who hoped to start the season in Triple-A and maybe get a shot at a late season call-up, but who when Lowell got hurt ended up getting called up early in the season and who turned out to be not only talented but completely undaunted by the Fenway stage, and who dove after balls and took extra bases and was just really easy to cheer for. And so no, it is nothing rational at all, nothing to do with the physical elements of the slider or the single but instead a feeling, gut-level and true as anything. Because we now at this moment think about that conversation in the winter where this bright and wide-eyed young man told us he was really excited about one day being given the chance to play at Fenway Park on nights just like this, and then we look down to find him there, taking his stance, steadying himself beneath the Fenway floodlights and before our roaring expectations—and because of all this we continue to clap and just this once say, actually say out-loud, not in a shout but in a low even conversational voice beneath the rising cheers: *Come on Jed, we have complete and utter confidence in you.*

And these words are still hanging there in the cold air, the cloud of frozen breath dissipating before our eyes as Shields throws, Lowrie swings, and the ball shoots on a quick hopper to the right and skips past the diving glove of the second baseman and bounds into the right field grass as Bay comes racing around, and the throw is made, and Bay slides in ahead *safe, safe, safe* at home as everyone at Fenway and watching leaps into the air with both arms raised and the Sox win on another magical night at Fenway Park.

* * *

Not, surely, because the kid we met over the winter was a really good guy; nor because it is so much more enjoyable to celebrate a series victory at home; nor because the Angels have lost three playoff series in a row to the Sox and just can't seem to win at Fenway. (In truth it was mostly because of Jon Lester, an ill-timed and poorly executed squeeze play, and because Jed Lowrie saw nothing but sliders the night before and was smart enough to anticipate seeing another. But these are rational thoughts, part of the mental process which happens much later on, long after the hot loud quick-beating emotions of the night have cooled.) So no, it was not because we *felt it*; but for now, as the Sox rush the field and "Dirty Water" blares out and everyone around us smiles and cheers, it certainly feels that way.

Just as it surely feels, to the young fan down around the Pesky Pole who had his hat inside out and backwards, that he really did give the Sox the little added edge they needed tonight. Just as it surely felt to the couple who landed tickets to this game, that it was meant to be because they were here together. Just as it feels to the fan who overpaid for a spare Standing Room Only ticket and now walks out with, their commitment paid in full. Just as the fan in New Hampshire knew all along the Sox would win because *there's no way they lose* on her birthday. As fans we allow ourselves these small indulgences because, well— because when it comes to influence, they really are all we have.

We know, deep down, that what takes place out there on the field is as physically disconnected from us as possible; that what we do, or say, or think, or feel has absolutely no impact on the outcome of the game whatsoever. And yet—and here we arrive at essential point—it does not work both ways. For the outcome on the field has a very real impact on what we do, say, think, and feel. Even if only while watching them, even if only while at the ballpark, even if only for those few moments on the way out when we personally feel a little bit victorious, or a little bit defeated. Which is why we allow ourselves the lucky shirt, the lucky bar stool, the lucky citation for disorderly conduct received while disorderly celebrating some famously lucky win and now carried in the Sox hat, for luck; and the belief that things work out just so because we are at the ballpark or we especially want this player to do well or this game to be won. We do it because we are not just spectators, but fans. It matters to us, what happens down there on that dirt and grass; and when our caring what happens opens us up to being dealt heartbreak and disappointment and a low, semi-nauseous regret over a good thing gone bad, then you better believe we're going to allow ourselves the indulgence of participation. And that when we bless the team by some little ritual of habit or dress or just the simple act of *believing*, and a moment later that runner slides across home and the champagne bottles pop and the players dance on the field, that we are going to allow ourselves to feel proud, to feel satisfied, to say that *we* won because *we* are the best team in baseball and yes, to allow ourselves the small personal joy of having felt as if we, even for only a moment, might be a little bit lucky, too.

Shadows in the Twinight

American League
Divisional Series: Game Three

Anaheim at Fenway
8 October 2004

In a sense there were two Game Three's—aligned back-to-back and the latter won by the Red Sox—which together settled the recently completed and still presently celebrated American League Divisional Series between the Red Sox and the Anaheim Angels. The first was a sunny, late-afternoon congratulatory gala, held in honor of the victorious Sox, who, after taking the first two games of the series on the road in California, returned home to receive their laurels at Fenway and before their adoring fans. The hero of this daylight Game Three was a tall, angular right-hander making his first career playoff start, and the quality and composure of his outing not only affirmed the confidence Sox fans had talked themselves into as the team flew back across the country, but also gave new currency to suggestions that this Sox team may in fact deserve the label which Sox fans have so reluctantly given them—that they *really are different*. As such this first Game Three evolved into something of a showcase for what may be called (not without hesitation) nouveau Sox culture, those widespread shifts in team philosophy, ballpark renovation, and general fan attitude which over the past three years have coalesced into the scene which now unfolds in the fading Fenway daylight before us. A trusting culture, infused with hope, comfortable in its bright and airy (and remarkably clean) ballpark, wide-eyed and smiling with a forward looking, future leaning stance. It is a culture, most importantly, freed from the dense gloom and shadowy apparitions of its own troubled past.

And yet there are still a few dark corners left at Fenway Park, if you know where to look, and as the twilight faded and the lights came up on the seventh inning, a second Game Three began to unfolded; this one at night, under the lights and deep within the much older, much grimmer recess of the collective Red Sox conscience. Turns out it had been there all along, lurking in the shadows.

In the beginning though, there is only light. A brilliant autumn sunshine pouring through the ancient rafters, rolling across the lush green expanse of outfield and hanging in a hazy, late-summer glow over Yawkey Way. The ideal lighting for a ballpark and crowd prepared for nothing less than the best party of the season. Here then, is Red Sox baseball in its party dress: the red white and blue bunting hung from the suites and along the auxiliary camera wells, a two-story high "Welcome to Fenway Park" sign covering the ramp wall outside Gate D, the broadcast dais (trimmed with bunting) on Yawkey Way, the luxury clubs decked out with flags and pins and pennants (the Sox logo ubiquitous, on everyone and everything), the media cafeteria converted into a secondary press box, the makeshift bleachers attached to the right field roof terrace, the souvenir programs and pins and hats sold from every corner and stand, the portable stage set in centerfield, the line of Marines in dress blues standing at attention along the left field warning track and behind them, in front of us, the American flag pouring down over all thirty-seven feet two inches of the left field wall, covering it. Enveloped within this scene both teams are announced and stand at attention along either base line for the anthem, sung by the Dropkick Murphys, and after the ceremonial first pitches and the announcement of *play ball* the Sox take the field and the first pitch of this daylight Game Three is throw by Bronson Arroyo, a called strike on the outside corner. Three pitches later Chone Figgins lofts a fly ball to left, caught by Manny for the first out, and the surprising capacity roar (a late-inning, full house roar) immediately signals that this game will not so much be watched as experienced, felt in the echoing shouts which will reverberate from its every pitch.

The full force of this brimming expectancy is held somewhat in check (simmering to a low boil) through the first two and a half innings as the Sox strand two runners in each of their first two frames. Yet on such a night, with such a celebratory air, there is an inevitability to the Sox's first runs. To the point where in the bottom of the third we mention that although a tie game, it somehow feels as if the Sox are up 2-0, already. Moments later, they are. Bellhorn works an 0-2 count into a 3-2 lead-off walk, Ortiz doubles off the wall, and like that Trot Nixon singles in the game's first run and a Millar fielder's choice brings in a second. An inning later (after an abrupt and highly inconsiderate Troy Glaus solo home run) Mueller and Damon both single, and another walk by Bellhorn loads the bases with no outs. A Manny sac fly brings in a third run and chases Escobar from the game. Another Ortiz double adds a fourth off reliever Scott Shields, followed by a crucial, uncharacteristic error by David Eckstein which plates a fifth and all but finishes the now reeling Angels. And in the bottom of the fifth, as the sun dips below the left field roof boxes and a crimson dusk settles over Boston, another pair of singles by Mueller and Damon (the two have reached base six times in their first seven at bats) sets up a Manny single which drives in another run, gives the Sox a satisfying 6-1 lead, and sounds the first celebratory *this is happening* strains among a now brazenly triumphant Fenway crowd.

All while Arroyo continues right along, one out after another. Thin by design rather than by youth, the tall righty has a distinctively fluid (and curiously soothing) windup; the left leg held stiff and rocked up, toes pointed flat, a quick move whips a nearly sidearmed delivery home, often spinning wiffle ball style breaking balls with bending side-to-side movement. A classic movement based pitcher, Arroyo works off his breaking stuff, mixing in a spot fastball—in and out, up and down—to set up the distortions of his curveballs and sliders. On the mound he gives the impression that all he is trying to do is throw a baseball which is difficult to hit, and nothing more.

This easy two-step approach, paired with the lazy, rhythmic delivery, seem fitting for what little we know of Arroyo the young man, the laid back Floridian (he was born, fittingly, in Key West) who plays a bit of acoustic guitar and who sometime late in the season, for no apparent reason, took to tightly braiding his sandy brown hair into corn rows. The style (which Sox fans, like all good friend of someone who has taken a radically different hair style, seem to have quietly accepted with the caveat that, *it's not that we don't like it, it's just that it will take some getting used to*) has in a strange way, by coloring him with a bit of peculiarity, placed Arroyo more firmly within the circle of his team. So it is on a team of eccentrics and individuals, where the only way into the group is by standing out from it. There under the bright October lights at Fenway Arroyo can be mistaken for no other Red Sox starter—he has neither Schilling's willful determination, nor Pedro's artistry, nor Wakefield's upright steadiness, nor Lowe's practically operatic sense of theatre—he is simply himself, a young pitcher rapidly establishing his own style upon the minds of his teammates and fans.

In the top of the sixth he works out of a two on, two out situation, and after the Sox go down in order in the bottom half he returns and walks Jeff DaVanon to lead off the seventh. There is a long pause (thirty-five-thousand shifting to peer into the dugout) before Terry Francona emerges on the top step and paces out towards the mound. Handing the ball to his manager Arroyo steps off the mound and walks across the Fenway infield under applause now steadily building to a low roar. Long after he has disappeared in the dugout the crowd continues to stand, continues to laud its young starter, continues to call for a bow which never comes. Arroyo remains seated on the bench, casually going over his outing with pitching coach Dave Wallace.

At the time it seems almost a shame, to pass up such a moment and miss out on a golden opportunity to celebrate. And we find ourselves wondering if perhaps Arroyo, in his inexperience, simply cannot hear in the roars how affectionately Fenway is requesting his presence on the top step.

It is only later that we realize he heard and understood our cheers clearly. He simply knew better. For eventually the game resumes, the cheers for Arroyo subside, and a few moments later Myers walks Casey

Kotchman on five pitches and is quickly pulled for the veteran, Mike Timlin.

Meanwhile, in the grandstands and bleachers of Fenway (and presumably in bars and living rooms across New England), a subtle shift in tone has passed over the crowd. As Timlin warms up pockets of fans remain standing, chatting, their laughter carrying back through the section while others make casual trips down the aisle for one last beverage run, stopping to point at and call out to friends along the way—relaxed, nonchalant, in no hurry. Others stand along the back rail of their section, cell phones pressed to one ear with hands held over the other, smiling and relaying the scene to Sox friends and family. Some speak of the ALCS, of plans for next weekend; others plan a post-game route for the upcoming night. Laughter, smiles, free and easy discussion as the game resumes somewhere in the background. The party, it seems, is just getting underway. And with it our thoughts, drifting a bit now, circle past the inevitable win and its relevance to the Sox and move straight on to how different this team looks from any of its predecessors, how it seems to play without the burden of backstory and in spite of all the chants and all the old inevitable questions. It is almost as if the changes in the team and renovations to its ballpark were of a piece, and that the structural changes which have made exterior life at Fenway more hospitable, more convenient, more livable for Sox fans have extended to the dugout, where this team has likewise made the interior life of its fans much more comfortable—lighter, airier, swept up and cleared away and cleaned of so much dusty historical clutter.

One word in particular continues to resurface, again and again. *Trust.* (In the distance Timlin retires Curtis Pride on a fly out to left for the inning's first out.) Somewhere along the way an understanding has been reached between this particular Sox team and the fans who follow them, and with that understanding a measure of trust. (Eckstein, meanwhile, lofts a soft single to right, just in front of Nixon, to load the bases.) The implications of which are practically self-evident for Sox fans. (Timlin strikes out Figgins; two outs.) For years fans of the Red Sox have held fast to the proclamation that no team, no matter how gifted or how favored, would earn their full trust until the very end (as Darin Erstad steps to the plate), and therefore no team would be able to show their true merit until they had achieved what we had not quite trusted them to do. (The count runs full on Erstad). Because of this we restrained ourselves from the true fan release that comes from believing in a team completely, of absorbing its glowing confidence and buying into its clichés. Every win and every run an affirmation. (Erstad walks, pushing across a run; the score now 6-2; two outs, bases still loaded). It is the release of opening oneself up as a fan and believing, without the slightest doubt, that *yes,* this really is the year. (Vladimir Guerrero steps to the plate.) This team earned our trust through a surging playoff run, and is now on the verge of galvanizing it with a convincing three game sweep in the ALDS. And so it seems they have done it at last. (Guerrero takes strike one from Timlin.) They have exorcised the Ghosts of Red Sox Past.

Guerrero slams Timlin's 0-1 fastball deep to right-center, soaring back we lose the ball and turn to Damon and Nixon as shouts of *no!* ring out and now they too look up. And stop. And watch. The ball lands, somewhere, and when it does the first of two Game Three's ends with the shock of a slammed door.

The stage is cleared. The hall emptied, the house lights dimmed, the floors hurriedly swept. The stage manager takes a look around, gives the okay, the crowd is ushered back to its seats, and the second Game Three begins in the dark of night and in utter silence, tied. In place of the anthem this second game (Game 3 ½), begins with "God Bless America," led *a capella* by a trio of Marines and accompanied by the majority of the thirty-five-thousand-plus somewhat stunned fans still wearily standing and gazing over the empty green field.

The bottom of the seventh begins. The bottom of the seventh quickly ends, with the Sox going down in order. In the top of the eighth the Angels, batting against Alan Embree, work a one out walk but manage nothing more after closer Keith Foulke is brought on to record the second and third outs. Two quick strikeouts by Bellhorn and Manny begin the Sox's eighth, then a burst of cheers for the quick arms-out safe sign when Ortiz beats out a grounder to deep second. Nixon follows with a walk. Mientkiewicz (a defensive substitution for Millar an inning earlier, at the end of the first Game Three) comes to the plate with two on and two out, and the thought of his being the hero hardly has time to form before he grounds into a fielder's choice, Amézaga to Eckstein, to end the eighth with a slightly defeated sigh.

Time between innings grows listless at moments such as these, and in it the crowd at Fenway no longer stands and chats but sits motionless, muttering remarks on bullpen options without taking their eyes off the field. Cell phone conversations continue along the back rail but now the free hands are shoved deep in pockets, the heads bowed, the feet pacing back and forth behind the aisle. A teenager in a red Schilling jersey and hooded sweatshirt leans forward, elbows on knees, holding his head in his hands. Not far behind him an older man in a Sox hat, two very young boys at his side, sits staunchly upright, arms crossed, shaking his head at nothing in particular.

And so the top of the ninth begins with Foulke still on the mound and immediately the concern deepening throughout the ballpark takes an even darker turn as Figgins singles to left, and Erstad follows with a double off the Monster to put Angels at second and third with one out and (*that man*) Guerrero back at the plate. He is intentionally walked by Foulke, who now faces Garret Anderson with the bases loaded and much more (so much more) on the line than merely the lead in this one game.

With Angels closer Troy Percival warming in the bullpen the next run, whichever team scores it, is accepted as the game winner; but this is only the beginning of Sox fans' worries as so much of the uninvited past seeps into the minds of this weary Fenway crowd. For we know and instinctively recognize that of course *this is how it happens*. This is how classic tragedies (in baseball as in life) are constructed. One is brought all the way to the brink, all the way to within sight of the desired goal and then just when the mind relaxes to consider the sweetness of success, all is removed, swept away, receding farther and farther back as the image of its fulfillment flutters like a shadow in memory. Sox fans understand this type of tragedy, understand it intimately and can therefore see the scenario play itself out—how the Sox lose this game after blowing a five run lead in the sixth, lose the following game on a fluke play or bad call or questionable managerial decision, then travel all the way across the country tired and weary and hounded by press and fans only to lose the deciding fifth, somehow (it hardly matters how). This, we realize with unwelcome ease, is a trauma worthy of the Red Sox history, dark and dusty and full of bitterness. It is a nauseating thought, chased back somewhat by Foulke working a steady series of pitches to Anderson, who he strikes out for the second out of the inning.

Glaus is next, and his heavy bat and long swing seem perfectly designed to loft any one of Foulke's harmless change-ups off or into or perhaps over the left field wall, forcing us to watch each pitch with a bracing half-turned wince. Only Glaus misses the first, watches a second, and checks his swing at a third. And thirty-five-thousand fans instantly look down the first base line to umpire Gary Cederstrom who holds his right hand up in a fist and rings Glaus up for the third out. Fenway erupts, deep and full as Foulke marches off and the game strides with purpose into the bottom of the ninth.

Unfortunately for the Sox it arrives to find Francisco Rodriguez (the still somewhat mythical K-Rod of postseason past) waiting on the mound for the Angels, ready for his second inning of work. It is brief. As K-Rod systematically retires the bottom third of the Sox's order in quick succession, coolly walks off the mound, and the game slouches into extra innings.

Foulke, having worked a tough two and two-thirds innings already, is finished. Leaving only two men in the Red Sox bullpen. One is Curtis Leskanic, and the other, Derek Lowe. All but forgotten, Lowe began the season as a key member of the rotation but has fallen out of favor so far, so fast, that less than a week ago there was legitimate debate among Sox fans and media whether it might not have been best to leave him off the playoff roster altogether, so remote was the possibility of a situation where his particular services would be of use. (The general consensus was that if Lowe made it to the mound this playoffs it could only mean that something had gone terribly wrong for the Sox.) And had Guerrero swung and missed instead of connect-ing, and had the Sox gone on to win the series outright, he might have sat at the end of the bullpen bench for a very long time. Only now here he is. Tall and utterly recognizable, the star closer turned failed closer turned All-Star starter turned exiled mop-up man steps from the bullpen door and jogs across the floodlit outfield. Where he is greeted with loud Fenway cheers, the collective voice a mixture of forgiveness and hope as Lowe takes the ball and faces Jeff DaVanon.

It is only fitting that he would.

For in so many ways Lowe is the perfect representative figure for this particular Red Sox moment. None more so than the way in which his presence on the mound encompasses both the Red Sox's inherent potential for spectacular success, and the widespread uneasiness that comes with their similarly inherent potential for truly spectacular defeat. And with his singular presence now on the mound the game seems to have reached a kind of reckoning point. It is in the very air among us: that whatever is to be decided tonight, good or bad, will be decided right here and now.

Lowe faces in, then immediately faces back out as DaVanon rips his first pitch deep towards center, soaring back as Damon races under it and at the last instant hand stretched up and back on the warning track he leaps and snaps the drive down for the out. Sighs and head shakes go out around the ballpark, and as with so many other Lowe appearances impassioned shouts ring out to the mound. Only here these shouts take on a new tone, as it's everywhere and only *come on D-Lowe, easy now, keep the ball down you're alright now, let's go D-Lowe two more!* And as Lowe falls behind catcher José Molina, 2-0, a nearly for-gotten chant goes up from the right-field grandstand. *Let's-Go, D-Lowe!* clap-clap, clap-clap-clap *Let's-Go, D-Lowe!* clap-clap, clap-clap-clap *Let's-Go, D-Lowe!*—this the heartfelt, slate clearing gesture of reconciliation between the fans and the tall, tumultuous righty with whom they have shared so very many celebrations, and so very many struggles. It does little good, however, as Lowe walks Molina on five pitches. But then Amézaga lays a bunt down the third base line, going for a hit, and Mueller charges in hard and reaching down on the run barehands the ball and a step later fires a bullet up the line to Mientkiewicz, cutting Amézaga down by a step. (This one of many astounding, momentum turning plays made late in these types of game which, although absolutely crucial to victory, are often overlooked among the shadows of the game's climactic moments.) Lowe then forces Eckstein to chop a bouncer to short, played between hops by Cabrera who fires a step too late behind the hustling Angel shortstop. First and third now, and two outs. Lowe pounds sinkers in to Figgins who clips an infield roller behind the mound, Cabrera breaks in and scoops and rips a throw across the infield to Mientkiewicz—*in time*—to end the inning as Fenway roars back to life one last time, showering cheers upon Lowe as he hops the first base line, and beneath the crowd rising to his feet steps into the dugout, absolved.

Bottom of the tenth now, and the night has drawn out long. At which point Fenway grows strangely quiet. Perhaps out of fatigue (it has been the kind of game where in the late innings hands begin to ache from clapping, voices strained from shouting), more likely from the thousands of quiet, personal, late inning pleas one senses being sent out to whomever or whatever we baseball believers send out our quiet, personal, late inning pleas. These scattered hopes go unanswered as Bellhorn strikes out, looking, and after Fenway rallies to its feet once again they once again fall flat as Manny strikes out, swinging. Two outs now, and with Rodriguez two and two-thirds innings deep and lefty David Ortiz due up Angels manager Mike Scioscia walks out and makes the move to his bullpen. Not to closer Troy Percival, but instead to the only left-handed pitcher he has, Game One starter Jerrod Washburn. (The move is too clever by half; and on our scorecard we still, days later, find Percival's name written in after K-Rod, not noticing and then not believing that Scioscia would put the season on the line with anyone other than his best pitcher.)

Washburn takes his warm-up tosses. Ortiz steps to the plate. Two outs, nobody on. And just as every Red Sox fan at Fenway, in Boston, throughout New England and across the country draws in a quick *here-we-go* breath Washburn delivers his first pitch, a hanging slider, Ortiz takes a deep uppercut swing and the ball goes shooting out high up towards the left field wall lofting higher up as Fenway springs to its feet the ball carries up into the lights and disappears into the Monster Seats and into a blur of hands and shouts and hugs and wild, wild celebration.

Moments later and the entire ballpark is still shaking, still bouncing as we spin and stagger upright again, realize our phone has been ringing nonstop for several minutes and give tired, laughing high fives to everyone within arm's length. Recalibrating a bit now we turn back to the field, where we find a leaping huddle of white along the first base line, the team still mobbing Ortiz somewhere deep within. ("Dirty Water" is playing, somewhere, but we only know this from habit, unable to actually hear it over the still deafening roar.) A few strained calls are made to close Sox friends and even closer Sox family, their shouts of joy hardly audible but comforting nonetheless (the point being to shout along with them, to share these few wild moments of bliss). Several minutes later and we are still celebrating. Still the pictures are taken by a once stranger and now kindred Sox friend, the jubilant scene of Fenway serving as backdrop. Still more high fives, and still more hugs. A friend at the game is remembered and called, and after yelling and laughing for a few moments he stammers to say that he *can not believe it*, either. Where is he? *In the bleachers*, still, where at some point in the celebration he has, for reasons unknown, removed all of his clothes. Why? Couldn't say. But he had to do *something*. (It has become that kind of night.) Eventually with the ballpark still teaming and the fans *still* holding close to the field, a final farewell is given to newfound friends, one last look to the still brilliant field before we file down the ramp, through the concourse, out into the fresh autumn air outside the ballpark—where the celebration has taken to the streets.

It is one of those nights, one of those good city nights where a crowd of thirty-five-thousand people stream through the streets towards bars and cars and T stops, shouting and laughing as we go, serenaded by drummers thumping buckets and cars honking in celebration at every intersection, and a brass band playing "When the Saints Go Marching In" on the street corner where a man with no rhythm wildly swinging his arms and legs in various directions, and the passers-by all cheer him on and laugh.

As always on these festive walks away from the ballpark, as the celebration carries itself far away form the orbit of Fenway, we pass by the stunned, head-shaking, slightly horrified expressions of those walking on the opposite sidewalk and in the opposite direction, taken unaware by the parade of loud and boisterous (and to them obnoxious, surely) masses decked in red and blue and randomly, perhaps insanely shouting spontaneous proclamations to each other, to cars passing by, to no one but the night air itself.

We have seen these sour, disproving faces often enough on such nights, and can all but read the judgment passing behind their eyes. *How ridiculous*, they seem to say. *How banal* that all these people should act so wildly (childishly even) over the result of a simple game. There are certainly more serious, more consequential events going on in the world today. How juvenile then is all of this, this insignificance, this misguided enthusiasm. *How ridiculous*, indeed.

It is an understandable reaction, and sensible in its way despite the fact that it nonetheless entirely misses the point. For it is not the object of our celebration that is at heart on a night like this, but our reaction to it. That is to say the celebration itself.

Of course we all realize that it is a game, and that there are more dire issues in the world today; but then none of these things have the capacity to send us jumping up and down in the middle of the night shouting at the top of our lungs and laughing to the point of tears. Would we prefer that they did? Probably. The world might in fact be a better place if the passing of a weighty piece of legislation caused millions of people to erupt in unison and stream out into the streets in celebration. This, however, is not yet the case (not in Boston anyway), and so in its place we must make do with a walk-off series winning home run in extra innings. Where else after all does life propel us to jump around and laugh and call every single person we hold dear to us and *know* that when we do, they too will be laughing right along with us? Where else do we walk the streets and wave at randomly passing cars who honk and wave back, just because we wear the same hat? Where else in the course of our city walks do we high five a uniformed on-duty police officer? Where else, in all our lives, do we spontaneously high five a complete stranger?

Baseball is a game, yes; but the experience of following it is not. It involves very real human emotions, formulated and expressed at a uniquely high pitch and in a clear, accessible, and above all collective form. That these emotions are genuine and true no matter their source may be inconvenient to the furrowed brows of those who disapprove of the enthusiasm with which they are expressed, but this hardly makes them any less genuine or any less true. Yes, it is entertainment. Yes, it is amusement. Yes, it is a pastime and recreation and at times even diversion. Yet the warm communal happiness of the victorious fan is not a watered-down version of happiness, but the very thing itself. The very thing we spend most of our days if not most of our lives looking for. And if the dour faces so startled and stunned by the unrestrained shouts walking the other way cannot see this—if they look and can see only bread and circus—then we can do nothing for them but to hope that one day (just for a change) they might step out the shadows of Lansdowne, drop the scowl, and find out what it feels like to cheer. For joy is joy, no matter which side of the sidewalk one walks.

As for this Red Sox team, playing these baseball games (Game 3 and Game 3 ½), the victory they achieved on this night was to provide more baseball for themselves and more opportunities for such moments as these for us, their multitude of fans. In the process we relearned (in Games 1, 2, and 3 ½) what we perhaps already knew: that this team *really is different*, that it is unlike its predecessors in several significant aspects and because of those differences we rate its chances of outpacing those predecessors as better than any Sox team in memory. But at the same time we were dramatically reminded (in Game 3) of the fact that this team is also, like every other baseball team ever assembled, fallible. It is bound to make mistakes, and the fact that these mistakes, like a fastball tailing out over the middle of the plate, are able to change the course of a game or series or season is a dynamic of the game itself, not one exclusively horded by the Red Sox as we are so often led to believe.

And so as we continue through the city and gradually slip away from the crowd, leaving its shouts and honks to echo in the distant streets and leaving us to our scorecards and our thoughts, we realize that what was ultimately discovered in the light of this curious twinight double-header was a kind of symbolic reconciliation between the ancient Red Sox past, and the nouveau Red Sox present; between the new old Fenway and the *old* old Fenway; between Thomas A. Yawkey and John W. Henry; between Ted Williams and Manny Ramirez; between justifiable doubt and true belief. And on an evening when the two sides were so closely aligned—like day and night, meeting in the twilight between—it seems as if this Red Sox team came to terms with its own past, and showed that if it is to be different from all the others in the only way which really truly matters it will do so not by exorcizing the shadowy ghosts of Red Sox past, but in their very presence. Despite them all.

Among the Believers

American League
Championship Series: Game Five

Tampa Bay at Fenway
16 October 2008

Arms crossed, jaw set, head tilted incredulously, we lean against an old green beam within the darkened grandstand of Fenway Park and stare out at the panoramic floodlit field below with all the slouching disinterest of students in the back recesses of a lecture hall—eyes forward, mind elsewhere. The kids up front in the shadowy blue grandstand slump and lean, elbows on knees, chin in hand, hats turned backwards; while those in the brightly lit red box seats sit upright and remain quiet (as those at the front of the class generally do), discretely more interested in shelling a bag of peanuts than in the pitches thrown before them. From somewhere deep in the right field grandstands a plastic novelty horn blows twice through the silence—*baaaawhn, baaaa-awhn*—but nobody turns to look.

(Somewhere beyond all this we are all dimly aware of the Red Sox, on the field, going through the motions of another half inning. This one the top of the seventh in Game Five of the ALCS, which like so many other half innings this week finds the Red Sox on their back foot, down several runs, with a runner on and with yet another relief pitcher quickly falling behind in the count. Trailing 3-1 in the series and outscored 29-3 in their last three games, the Sox have spent the week in a state of perpetual rout. As the season slowly slips away.)

Then, down in the little crux where the low first base wall banks against the foul line, a spectacularly overweight man in a blue t-shirt stands up from his front row seat, turns to face the crowd, and after looking over the grandstand with theatrical pause begins to raise and lower a fleshy arm to the beat of *one, two, three,* before throwing both arms in the air with a vigorous *hoaaahh!* In response a half dozen arms at most, all in the section immediately surrounding him, are rather unenthusiastically raised and lowered. He tries again. *One, two, three, hoaaaahh!* And again no more than a dozen arms lift up, a little less enthusiastically than before. He tries a third time. *One, two, three, hoaaaahh!* Ostensibly he is trying to start the wave (the logic of which, during a playoff game and from the infield box seats when the wave never ever starts anywhere but the bleachers, is dubious at best). Yet the few hands raised in response remain limited to his immediate section, along with a scattered few in the adjoining section. So it's more like a splash. *One, two, three, hoaaaahh!* Nothing.

In the background Manny Delcarmen walks the number nine hitter in the Rays' lineup, Jason Bartlett. Groans and rumbles in the stands, barely enough behind them to be made audible. *One, two, three, hoaaaahh!* Nothing. Delcarmen paces behind the mound, rubbing the ball. Off to the right, deep in the outfield corner, J.D. Drew looks down and casually sweeps the grass with his right foot. By now our rotund fan has grown visibly frustrated, flapping his meaty arms against his sides and pleading with those in front of him to *come on!* (The fans directly in front of him look more embarrassed than encouraged.) Delcarmen immediately falls behind Iwamura. Nothing, not even muttered disapproval, from the crowd. Our rotund fans looks around, bewildered. Then, an idea. Nearly an inspiration. The spirit (nevermind which) takes hold of him and while still standing, still in the front row, and still very much spectacularly overweight he reaches back with both hands, grabs two handfuls of blue t-shirt and in an instant pulls the whole thing over his shoulders and clean off—exposing one great mass of pale white hairy flesh to the glare of Fenway Park's enormously unforgiving floodlights.

Entire sections of fans blink to attention. Suddenly this great expanse of pasty white humanity is put in motion and, defying several laws of physics and structural engineering (not to mention good taste), mounts the red plastic seat before him and wildly waves his shirt above his head. Which motion causes not a few waves on the great white mass of flesh below. Which sight causes this Fenway Park crowd, for the first time all night, to go absolutely wild with applause.

Every postseason has its defining image, that one scene in which the details are so significantly arranged and framed as to instantly convey the story of the series itself. Dave Roberts sliding into second; Derek Lowe pumping his fist off the mound in Oakland; Drew's drive disappearing into the center field bleachers. All touchstones which by way of a certain clarity of narrative significance expand out to remind us what the series looked and felt like as a whole. In short, these are the images which come to mind first, most often, and which linger the longest thereafter. For better or for worse. And so it seems that this, of all sights, is to be our lasting image of the 2008 ALCS. In the far off background we have the left field wall scoreboard with its clusters of visiting runs above a long, repetitive row of zeros below; on center stage a Red Sox reliever struggles in vain to throw strikes and prevent a large deficit from becoming a blowout; and there in the footlights, at the center of half the ballpark's attention, a substantially naked, not *in*-substantially hairy, and (one must say) distinctly *Farleyesque* male torso balances atop his red front row seat like a circus elephant atop a ball, and yes now whips his t-shirt back and forth so energetically that it snaps at the wall behind him (it's a rather large t-shirt) as he gives it a *one, two, three, hoaaaahh!* And the Fenway crowd, so desperate to watch anything that is not a Sox pitcher giving up more runs, laughs out loud and cheers far more and far louder than we have all week. *One, two, three, hoaaaahh!*

Delcarmen walks Iwamura, Bartlett moves up to second with nobody out, and Terry Francona emerges hands in jacket from the Red Sox dugout and walks unhurried to the mound. He takes the ball from Delcarmen, and the light smattering of boos at his exit are quickly drowned out by a roar of recognition as Jonathan Papelbon emerges from the bullpen—the unexpected burst of genuine applause our Pavlovian reaction to the sight of our closer (an image so intimately connected with actually having a lead). Others, a good many in fact, remain unmoved. A woman several rows up shakes her head at the very thought, as if to say, *so it's come to this?* Two guys in the narrow Standing Room Only area behind her section shrug. One mutters, *why the hell not?* And a young man mid-section shouts out in rather florid language that, all things considered, perhaps Manager Francona would have better served his employers had he showed similar action in removing Josh Beckett from Game Two of this series, *eh, Tito?* Several heads within earshot nod in grim accord.

Only this—the raucous jig-dancing music, the sight of Papelbon lunging forward on the mound, the crowd up and genuinely cheering action on the field—puts an end to the burlesque show in the front row. And for a moment our attention returns to the baseball. However briefly.

With two on and nobody out Papelbon faces Upton, and although the at bat is long and hard fought, and although Bartlett and Iwamura steal third and second during it (causing several fans to call out for Papelbon to plant the next pitch in various regions of B.J. Upton's slight person), it all ends the same way every similar situation has ended this week. With Upton gliding safely into second; with Tampa runners high-fiving each other into the dugout; with another crooked number being hung on the upper register of the Fenway scoreboard; and with all us Sox fans shaking our heads in disgust. Down 3-1 in the series, the Red Sox now trail Tampa 7-0 with nobody out in the top of the seventh. And that, it seems, is that.

Immediately the rotund fan goes back to work. First standing up and flapping his arms (to attract general attention), then giving a coy little tug at the back of his shirt (promising, or perhaps more accurately threatening an encore), and finally pulling it all off again and once more swatting the shirt back and forth to the renewed cheers of several thousand people with absolutely nothing whatsoever else to cheer about.

At this point, we move. Turning our shoulders through the narrow passage we circle around the grandstand arch, merely to get away from this particular side of the ballpark. For if there are, as there now appear to be, only nine outs left in the Red Sox season; and if we are to sit and watch a promising campaign end in the most bitter defeat; and if we are to watch the heretofore lowliest team in baseball trounce our defending champions and celebrate on our own front lawn; and if we are going to further trouble our minds (as we surely will) with all sorts of dark thoughts about *the end of an era* and how the magical run of teams and games and seasons in this ballpark may be ending right here, tonight, leaving us to reminisce over our scorecards and ticket stubs and the *One night at Fenway* stories our friends are already tired of hearing—that is to say if we are going to sit here and sulk and feel sorry for ourselves over losing a baseball game—then we damn well are going to do so without being forced to watch a naked fat man gyrating in the foreground.

So we move along. Around the dark and crowded grandstand concourse. And in doing so encounter other fans who have gotten up from their seats and are also moving—not along, but out.

At first this does not seem all that striking. The Red Sox are losing badly, of course, and have all week looked so incapable of scoring runs that any deficit over, say, two runs, appears well beyond their reach. (This only assuming that any Red Sox pitcher, Papelbon included, could manage to go an inning or two without allowing the Rays to add another run, or two, or six, to their lead.) And so in purely baseball terms it all does look impossibly bleak. And were it an ordinary Tuesday night game in mid-June we would not think twice of those fans who choose to call it an evening and beat the traffic.

The trouble, and what causes us to glance back over our shoulder at those now stretching their legs down the steps to Yawkey Way, is that this is not an ordinary Tuesday night game in mid-June. (On the mound below Rays reliever Grant Balfour takes his warm-up tosses.) By concluding that the outcome is decided and the game lost, as one does when one leaves, then one has also concluded that the series and season are lost along with it. So: no more baseball. No more Red Sox. And no more Fenway Park under the floodlights. No more Pedroia stepping out of the box to tighten his batting gloves, Ortiz swinging the bat like a pendulum in the on-deck circle, Youk on the top step brining his right arm down in an imaginary chop, Francona on the seat next to him, chomping away. All this and our ability to enjoy it will, by the rationale of those fans conceding as much by their exit, end within the hour. And if one does in fact take enjoyment from such sights; if one truly looks foreword to April and Fenway for what happens on the field (that is to say if one actually does like watching baseball and not just being around a successful baseball team in a popular ballpark), then it seems to us that one would want to at least stay and be here at the ballpark as much as possible before turning one's back on the season, and conceding another October of *maybe* over to a winter of *maybe next year*. (A roar turns a few of the departing heads as Jed Lowrie lines a drive to right and it bounces in the gap for a clean double.) Two and a half innings, forty minutes at most, is all that is left. All that's available to us. All the commitment that remains for those who call themselves Red Sox fans. For many—not a great deal, but enough to notice—it is far too much to ask. Having seen enough they wish to see no more, call it a season, denounce the Sox (*to hell with those bums*), and off to winter and their winter sports they go.

Leaving a row of choice empty seats in the third base line grandstand behind, to us. Five of them in the next-to-last row of the ancient chipped blue wooden seats, they provide a welcome respite to Standing Room Only legs and a gorgeous panorama of Fenway Park unfolding right to left before us.

There at the plate is the Sox's captain, who still looks slightly off-balance at the plate but manages to work the count until eventually he latches onto a fastball and sends it out to center, with us rising up immediately behind it; only to immediately fall back as Upton sails beneath its path, reaches up, and comfortably pulls it in. Kotsay follows and he too works the count before shooting a drive high out to center and again we leap at contact (the offense so feeble this week that our reactions are now calibrated to register even contact), the ball headed for the gap until *are you kidding me* once more Upton glides beneath it, cool as can be, and brings it down at a canter.

Coco Crisp is up next (and suddenly one of those odd little numerical chimes we sometimes come across at the ballpark echoes faintly off our scorecard, which shows it to be: bottom of the seventh, the Sox trailing by seven runs, with seven outs to go in the season). Crisp lines a single to left that brings a sad little over-eager cheer from the crowd, moves Lowrie to third, and creates the best scoring chance of the night for Boston. Pedroia steps to the plate, and after getting ahead 2-0 takes a strike looking. Then another. He fouls off a fastball, then takes a ball to run the count full. At which point the Fenway crowd rises up to cheer out its encouragement. Not all thirty-five-thousand sold out seats, for empty patches remain—a strip of red, a patch of blue, uneven sections out in the bleachers—yet a curious thing has happened. When the thirty-thousand or so who remain stand up, all the empty seats disappear, covered by the Sox hats and jerseys and clapping hands which now beat out a vigorous *Let's-Go, Red-Sox* chant in the face of a dreadful week, a heartbreaking game, and a still impossible situation. Another foul ball and it grows louder still. *Let's-Go, Red-Sox!* clap-clap, clap-clap-clap, *Let's-Go, Red-Sox!*

Much later on we will look back at this moment and recognize it as the point when something ended and something altogether different began. But even here, in the moment, it is distinct enough to give us pause. And the subtly heightened significance of its message ripples through the grandstand with enough clarity for us to look around, shake our head, and take a private moment to realize what exactly is going on here. For directly in front of us is a couple, very well-dressed, comprised of a red-headed woman who holds her elbow close together as she claps and a man in a white sweater who does not clap at all but sort of rocks up and down on his heels. Farther up are a group of younger guys, one of them in an old faded red intramural t-shirt, who along with his friends only stops beating out the clapping portion of the cheer to cup hands to their mouths and better shout out the shouting portion. Then there is the peripheral sight of a middle-aged Japanese man in the row behind us, dressed in a dark business suit and crowding so far up in his row that he is all but hanging over our left shoulder. While over to our right four college girls stand with linked arms across the back row, their voices are heard above all others. And there are more, everywhere we look; ladies standing with Red Sox pins on expensive looking coats, stubble-faced guys standing in gray 2004 World Champion hoodies with their hats on backwards, a bespectacled man who looks unmistakably like a high school science teacher standing with his Red Sox hat on backwards *and* inside out. Suddenly we realize, with a ripple of familiarity, that these fans and the thousands who stand and even now fill Fenway with that incredible echoing din of shared resolve have, in this very moment, justified all that has been written or said about the passion and dedication and faith of Red Sox fans.

For the truth is that over the last few years the excessive amount of commentary on, aggrandizing about, and branding of this fan base has nearly turned the very idea of it into something uncomfortably close to another lifeless marketing slogan. While at the same time that slogan has seemed to be increasingly at odds with the reality of a more subdued Fenway Park atmosphere. More fans, at more games, have found the exits earlier than ever. And the more the fans' virtues have been touted—on shirts and stickers and signs and billboards and brochures and advertisements—the less those virtues seem connected to anything actually happening in the Fenway Park stands. As the proverbial Red Sox Nation, once an idea carried with pride by those it encompassed, veered dangerously close to being consumed by its glossy packaging and becoming what its detractors claimed it always had been—a meaningless, over-hyped cliché.

(*And yet...*)

And yet still there are *these fans*. A ballpark full of them. Down 3-1 in the series and 7-0 late in the game, on their feet and making a tremendous amount of noise for a full count, two out, second-and-third situation in the seventh, every bit as passionately as if the game were tied. True, part of this may be out of sheer want of activity. Our own guess is that it means more than all that. You can feel it. You can see it in the faces, and can hear it in the voices. There is something going on here. Something old. Something that is familiar, comfortable, known. So recently adjusted to the role of all-conquering Champions, so unaccustomed to defending the national popularity of a jersey and hat once worn in defiance, so often the apologists for a fan base diluted with bandwagoneers and sycophants and the fashionably faithful who simply *love* the Sox on Opening Day and in October (though rarely in between), and so lately the golden favorite of the national baseball media, Red Sox fans in this moment at Fenway Park stand and shout and roll along with the Let's-*Go*, Red-*Sox* chant having rediscovered our original voice, our natural cheering voice, and the one true *Vox of the Sox*—as once again we cheer the cheer of the underdog. This, and not the cool detachment of the returning champion, is the cheer we know best, the cheer which comes effortlessly to our hands and throats, the cheer that after all we were and perhaps still are known for, even now. And to look around us at these fans and see these hopeful faces and hear the deep pleading *dammit this is important* tone of the chants, it all comes back in a rush: 1986, 1998, 2003, midsummer 2004. And here we are, back again—among the true believers.

Balfour fires, Pedroia lunges out with a deep bent-knee swing and shoots a low drive over second and into right for a single, Lowrie jogs home for the run, and the Fenway fans whoop and cheer and smile and even high five each other just as if the Sox had scored some crucial game-changing run.

Sure it's only 7-1 now, and sure there are still two outs, and sure Ortiz strides to the plate painfully lacking the old swagger and the *you're-all-in-a-lot-of-trouble-now* smack of the batting gloves; but he is still Big Papi, after all, and we can stand and clap in the hope that maybe just maybe once more he could—

Ortiz swings, a deep catapulting cut from way back on his heel, and launches the ball high out to right on a soaring line (*but so many have and all those late season drives to the warning track only drawing us to our feat to drop our hands in disappointment*) it continues to rise as we watch right fielder Gabe Gross go back, back, back and still looking over his shoulder and *get up get up get up* and he slows and stops and looks straight up and then, only then, do we shoot both arms in the air and shout *yes, we knew it, oh we knew it atta'boy Papi!*

Like that, it's 7-4. And after a week of waiting and hoping and growing evermore frustrated finally, finally here at the very end, is a scene we recognize as Red Sox baseball—the long inning, the tough at bats running the count full, the clutch hit by our best hitter and the really big hit by our really big hitter, now lumbering around the bases and coming home with a stomp and a two-handed skyward point. And from this point onward, until the final ball of the night is thrown several hours later, no one at Fenway Park sits down and the old ballpark reverberates with a non-stop chorus of clapping, chanting, and cheers.

Those cheers linger from Ortiz's home run and continue on through a pitching change (Dan Wheeler for the visibly rattled Balfour, who can only shake his head), lap over a Youkilis' fly out to end the inning and carry on within the between-inning buzz to double-back with renewed strength for Papelbon on again in the eighth; then rising to chants of *Let's-Go, Red-Sox!* through strike one, strike two, and bursting open at a swinging strikeout of Willy Aybar; no lapse as he falls behind Dioner Navarro and only a moment's held breath on a fly ball to center, then *that'a boy that'a boy* as Crisp settles under and standing still makes the catch; those cheers feeding the loud strike one looking to Gabe Gross, up another notch at a terrible swing and miss for strike two, and the full-throated roar for an even worse strike three to end the inning and bring the Sox back up to bat. Where Wheeler, who looks no more comfortable beneath this enclosure of sound than his predecessor, promptly walks Jason Bay on four pitches to bring J.D. Drew up with one on and nobody out.

By this point the four college girls behind us have mounted their seats and, arms around shoulders, lead the chants of *J-D, Drew! J-D, Drew!* while several other chants ripple back from distant sections of the ballpark. A shout of *what do'ya say seven!* calls out as Wheeler throws and Drew takes strike one, looking. *Come on J.D. base hit baby base hit!* He stays in the box. *Whadaya say now kid!* That same easy sweep of the bat, that same balanced stance, relaxed at the knees, the bat comes back in both hands and then that one little bounce off the back shoulder and set. The pitch comes, Drew swings and the ball leaps off the bat, shooting out under the lights as Gross again goes back and again we all rise up with *get out get out get out*, still going as Gross turns and looks up and *holy sh— can you believe it!* High fives all around—to friends, to strangers, to the Japanese businessman behind us who gives an exuberant *double* high five, his face absolutely alight with surprise and delight—and it is many happy moments before we look up to see the score, now 7-6, and Jed Lowrie lofting a fly ball to left, caught for the first out of the inning.

We breathe, clap, look down to see not Varitek, but Sean Casey stepping to the plate as a pinch hitter. Casey, who has been something of a forgotten man on the roster this October, takes a strike, a ball, swings and misses badly for strike two and finally swings both late and very weakly for strike three. It is the second out of the inning, but more than that it leaves the Red Sox, still down a run, with four outs to go in the season.

Here the unwelcome thought—to have come this close, and come up short—is overrun by another, more to the point; which is that no matter the final outcome this rally has already fulfilled the only remaining wish we had for this team. Throughout the week as much has been made among fans about *how* the Red Sox have lost as about the actual consequences of the losses themselves. Being able to witness, stomach, and ultimately accept losing is a prerequisite of baseball fandom; but there are different ways to lose, with vast differences in how those losses effect the mood around the team and among its fans. To compete, to trade blow for blow, to hang on and lose by the margin of the better and on that day more fortunate team leaves disappointment, surely, but nothing to regret either for the players or their fans. Yet this has not been the case this week at Fenway, where the deficits have not only been lopsided but immediate and irreversible. All of which has been compounded by lackluster at bats, feeble pitching, questionable baserunning, and the general atmosphere of consigned defeat which has hung over the club all week. From the first early 2-0 and 3-0 deficits on the Sox have looked every bit the beaten team. Until now, when win or lose they have at least regained a measure of pride by battling back to push the issue, have furthermore made the situation uncomfortable for the (previously quite comfortable) visitors, and in the process have lit the fuse of a smoldering Fenway crowd. A loss at this point, disappointing as it would certainly be, would nonetheless be a dignified loss.

And still there are these last four outs.

With Mark Kotsay at the plate the Fenway crowd, perpetually standing, beats out *Let's-Go, Red-Sox!* through two balls, and on the 2-0 Kotsay swings and shoots a ball high out to left-center, Upton going back and tracking and again making up tremendous ground as the ball falls and near the track he reaches up and it hits off—yes *off*— his glove and tumbles to the ground, and a great thrilling roar goes out as Kotsay sprints into second and turning back to the dugout gives a *come on now!* pump of both fists to his teammates. It is (or at least feels like) the first mistake by the Rays, and first real break for the Sox, all week.

Crisp is next. He digs his back foot in the left side batter's box, a mere base hit away from completing the improbable. Coco Crisp, who singled in his last at bat but always, with his jerk of the chin and his fingers fluttering over the bat, looks nervy and over-anxious. Crisp, who never really has replaced the man whose shoes he was brought to fill; who through injury and personnel moves and a few brief, disastrously timed slumps has never fully gained the adoration of the fans; who although in his third season with the Red Sox is still somewhat skeptically viewed as one of *these new guys*; and who now takes a ball, a strike looking, another ball, and fouls off another before taking a ball to load the count, 3-2. All this with the ballpark raised up and echoing out a cavalcade of cheers around him; chants rising up, one fan beating out the chorus of a new chant all it takes to ignite the section and send the same chant sweeping down the grandstand where it melds with others in a strange confluence of overlapping noise; kids leaning over the backstop and beating out the chant with their hands low on the green padded wall; fans standing tight along the low wall that hugs the field, on top of it, in the pitcher's ear, crowding around the plate and batter. The next pitch is a fastball away and Crisp reaches out and swats it foul—a late, emergency swing just to stay alive. Nervous exhales all around, hands clasped prayer-like, eyes closed; then opened up again, cheers rising to the next pitch, another fastball and another desperately late swing to foul it off. More nervous exhales. Hands refolded. Heads shaking. (Somehow the nervous system sustains it all. The constant buildup to what very well may be the deciding pitch of the entire season turning the stomach and raising the heart rate to a thump and then, at its height—flinches. Resets. To do it all again. And again. And once more. Over and over, all ratcheted up by the sights and noise and visceral involvement of clapping and shouting over how many pitches, over entire innings on end. Where else in everyday life is the sensory and nervous system and emotional apparatus bombarded with so much, so consistently, for so long?) Wheeler sets, hands are clasped, the chants go out, *Let's-Go, Co-Co*, the pitch comes, Crisp hesitates and swings very late and just does get a piece of it to foul another off. Hanging in there, staying alive. Again it all reset, the chants go back up, the hands are reclasped, the nervous exhale escapes the lips as the pitcher comes sets, throws, Crisp swings and *again* late but enough to foul it back. Now another element, a different strain, as the sound climbs to a still higher level not out of renewed hope but by the addition of praise for the at bat itself, for the struggle undergone by Crisp already, for doing what we've begged the Sox to do all week—to hang in there and compete and *dammit give yourself a chance*. And compete he does, retaking his stance as Wheeler comes set for the tenth time in the at bat. The sound rises in anticipation, the sore hands are clasped, the exhale, the chants, the calls, the encouragement, the desperate hope of *come on Coco, come on Coco, base hit baby, base hit*, and finally the pitch shoots plateward and Crisp swings and this time, this time he connects—out over the field and on a low line and it's not *get up* but *get down ball get down get down get down* as it falls and lands softly in right beneath the shrieks of Fenway with Kotsay wheeling around and the throw from Gross bounces awkwardly short and the run—the game-tying, comeback-completing, faith-affirming run—scores as Kotsay sweeps clean across the plate. And there is much, much rejoicing.

Somewhere in the middle of which we glance to the field only to find that Crisp, assuming the throw to the plate, has made a mad dash to second only to be thrown out at second. The danger of which (had he been tagged out before Kotsay crossed the plate all would have been lost) barely registers among the now absolutely euphoric Fenway park crowd.

And on we go, tumbling into the ninth. With Papelbon used up the ball rests in the right hand of rookie Justin Masterson, who at 23-years-old is asked only to preserve the now historic postseason comeback by first retiring Bartlett and then the heart of a Rays lineup, and to do so without giving up even a single run which would of course lose the lead, endanger the game, end the ALCS and with it the Sox season, relegate one of the all-time great comebacks in Sox history to an unhappy footnote, and just more or less ruin it for everyone. Only this, and *oh yes*, nevermind the rollicking, foundation shaking cheers of the thousands of fans around you whose happiness now rests entirely in your hands. Not surprisingly perhaps, he gets far too much of the plate with his 1-2 pitch and the Rays' shortstop lines an easy single to center. Masterson comes back to force the perpetually on base Iwamura to fly out to left, but falls behind the perpetually-hitting-home-runs-over-the-Monster Upton, and walks him to set up an uninviting first and second, one out situation with Carlos Peña coming up. Here, for the first time since Pedroia's RBI single, the tenor of the crowd genuinely dampens, if nothing more than to a low anxious rumble, as (also for the first time, not only tonight but ever so far as we can remember) the chant of *Doub-ble Play! Doub-ble Play!* rises up to fill the void.

It is at moments such as these that the game has a way of working out which is very hard to explain. For no sooner do these chants go up and no sooner do we register the fact that we have never ever heard a crowd openly plead *as one body* for a double play, but Peña pulls a grounder to the right side and Pedroia is there waiting for it, shuffles to Lowrie who takes an extra beat to slide off second and set and throw, across and in time—*double-play.* Jubilation, laughter, and wonder. (When sports fans talk in terms of the mystical, this is why.)

Lefty J.P. Howell is on for Tampa in the ninth to face Pedroia, Ortiz, and Youkilis—the Red Sox three best hitters and by extension three best chances for plating the winning run. Beginning, as all good things this season seem to have begun, with Pedroia. Pedroia who last April was a not overly popular rookie second baseman fighting every day for his place in the lineup and now, eighteen months, a World Series ring, a Rookie of the Year award and a sparkling sophomore season later, is greeted in the batters box by a chorus of *de rigueur* M-V-P chants rising up around him. He takes a ball and on the 1-0 reaches for a low pitch and yanks it down to third where Longoria dives, the ball kicks off his glove (and we leap in anticipation) only to roll directly to Bartlett who scoops and fires across in time for the out. Amid the groans, Longoria pulls himself up and swats at his glove.

All week Longoria, along with Upton and to a lesser extent Peña, have been a golden trio for the Rays. Entirely comfortable on this stage and in this ballpark, they have been able to do no wrong, and for three games have launched batting practice grade home runs, jogged the bases, easily tracked fly balls, made ridiculously difficult infield acrobatics look routine, and in general have high-fived their way to pleasant little week at the ballpark. And oh how it has all looked so very easy; and oh how cool and calm and *poised beyond their years* they have looked doing it. Yet they have not yet done so under pressure. They have not done so under a roaring loud Fenway crowd. They have not done so against the run of play, against the momentum, or against a Red Sox lineup practically swaggering with confidence. And it is only here, late in the game and late in the week, that the nervy mistakes have cropped up at (for them) the most unfortunate of moments. First the Kotsay ball off Upton's glove, a catch he has made easily in the past but perhaps, just for a moment, heard the wall coming and flinched; then Peña rolling over into the inning-killing double play. Only Longoria, perhaps the most absurdly talented of the trio, remains untarnished. And even he has needed a fortunate bounce off the glove to remain beneath the halo of good fortune.

Now with Ortiz up, we Sox fans suddenly have all the makings before us. October, trailing in the series, tie game, bottom of the ninth, Ortiz at the plate. If ever a highlight were waiting to happen, this is where we would expect to find it. Only Ortiz takes not only ball one but strike one, then to our great astonishment (*what the—?*) he squares around to bunt the next pitch foul and before anyone can register why (*what was that?*) has swung at strike three and we are left with two outs and nobody on. And are still wondering *what the hell just happened* when Youkilis takes a ball, a strike, another ball, and yet another strike to level the count 2-2 without once moving the bat. Meanwhile Howell, a slight lefty with an easy, sweeping delivery and a relaxed, unhurried presence on the mound, appears entirely too comfortable in his work and in the raucous environment which has rattled his so many of his teammates. He kicks and throws the 2-2 and Youk fouls it off. Again the chants, the cheers, all carried along with the familiar baying *Yooouuuk* calls; and again another foul ball. And another. Just as with Crisp the rising noise is propped up by cheers for the at bat itself as Youk fouls off a fourth, and we shake our heads and take another deep breath and Youk takes a pitch for ball three. Full count now, and the *Yooouuuk* chants louder than before. The pitch comes and Youk swings and pulls a grounder to the left side of the infield just fair and rolling towards Longoria. The tall athletic third baseman charges and scoops on the run with his bare hand but instead of throwing pumps, once, and off the wrong foot flips across a low awkward throw without much behind it, it hits the dirt in front of Peña and with a roar of the crowd leaps high over his shoulder into foul ground and up into the stands, giving Youk second and the Red Sox new life once again. Longoria, beneath a chorus of shouts from the third base grandstand (which he is likely thankful to have lost among the general din), shakes his head, coolly blows a pink bubble, and saunters slowly back to his position. There he turns, shakes his head once, and tosses his gum into the grass beyond third base. Nobody in this game it seems, is perfect for very long.

Bay is up and before the cheers go out he has watched two intentional balls go wide; after two more he takes his free pass to first, and the stage is set: two outs, tie game, runners on first and second and—that man again—J.D. Drew, strolling to the plate.

It is a fascinating game, baseball. All season long and for several seasons on end we watch and follow and get to know the players who play under our hat. Along the way we cannot help but feel as though we learn things about them, get to know them, and variously trust or distrust them in certain situations. And then one night, in exactly the right situation and in the exactly the right light, we see them again in an entirely new way, as if for the first time. Drew takes ball one. So that here, in this situation, with our voices, hands, ears, adrenal glands, stomachs, heart rates, and entire nervous systems all pretty well shot to pieces from over stimulation and tension fatigue, we find J.D. Drew—he of the impossibly even and unaffected demeanor, he who has so often been criticized for not seeming to be effected one way or another by the game situation—to be, for those exact reasons, the very player we trust at the plate in this moment. He takes ball two. In part because we know that he is, no matter his demeanor, a fantastically talented hitter; but more so in this instance because he is such a remarkably composed figure, and seems the least likely of any player to swing himself out of a good at bat. He takes ball three. It is the strangest thing, that after all this (he takes a strike looking) we see J.D. Drew of all players, as a perfect fit. Howell sets. Drew taps the bat once on his back shoulder. We in the stands all continue to clap and peer in to the field and shake our heads and exhale deeply and mutter *come on, just once.* The pitcher kicks, strides out, throws; the ball comes home and Drew sweeps that beautiful swing across and connects, and ball leaps out into the night on a perfect line to right low and rising into the lights as we shout and wave and the ball flies out towards Gross going back under the ball he sprints and leaps and flashes the glove up and the ball sails clean over and *yes yes yes* we leap up *yes yes yeaaaahhhs* with arms raised *he did it he did it*—and like that the world around us tumbles into a great shouting laughing head-shaking roar in which every sight and every sound blends into one long ecstatic blur.

And for one night, Fenway Park is as magical as ever. Its confines as vivid and as extraordinarily intimate as advertised, its team as improbably dramatic as the legends surrounding them; its fans as loud and passionate and undyingly faithful as all the superlative piled at their feet have promised.

Finally, we let out a long and happy exhale. For every night when we come to the ballpark or tune in to watch our team what we hope for good competitive baseball, yes, but more specifically we are looking for that moment of tension when the game is on the line. Say, second and third, two outs, down a run—the classic close-and-late situation—with each pitch a potential game-changer. In a good game, a game we enjoy and feel satisfied with, there are maybe three of these situations. Most games have none. In a great game there are several, with three or four bunched in the last inning and a half. Tonight, there were twenty. All in a row. Holding the dramatic tension not only of the game but of the series and season for nearly an hour and a half, solid, without relent.

Leaving us so drained and numb and hoarse that it hardly matters what our chances may be in Games Six and possibly Seven in Tampa. There's not a thought given. The salient point is that there will be a Game Six, the season will go on, and this Sox team will not suffer the indignities of having folded at home, of having played its worst baseball at the worst possible time, and of having hung over the top step to watch others drench champagne on their home field. That dignified loss may still come, but it is going to have to wait.

In the meantime there is this night, which on the long walk home is filled with as much shouting, as much revelry, and as many honking horns as the ALCS *series* win last season. A night to remember and savor for its fantastic baseball drama and, perhaps even more so, for the atmosphere under which was played. That is to say for its fans. For the fans who stood late in Game Three, the Sox down 11-1, and cheered. For the fans who stood up at the end of Game Four, as the Sox were being pummeled 13-2, and pulled for the last Red Sox batter to hit a home run. And for tonight, for those who stayed to cheer the season out, regardless. Down three games to one in the series, down 7-0 in the game, down to the final seven outs of the season, two on, two outs, full count on Pedroia. An utterly grim, hopeless situation. *And yet...* And yet the crowd on its feet, full-throated behind a chant of *Let's-Go, Red-Sox.* Embracing the old familiar underdog cheer, the cheer *against* something, the push back that is both defiant and at the same time encouraging, hoping, believing; the cheer that not only earns but takes back and redeems the good old family name—never more deserved than in that very moment—of the Fenway Faithful.

Beyond Belief

*American League
Championship Series*

*Red Sox v. Yankees
20 October 2004*

One day, years from now, someone will ask you: *what was it like, back then?* Perhaps the question will come to you on some quiet summer evening, baseball on in the background, after an announcer makes a passing reference to teams facing insurmountable odds (*only one team has ever come back from being down...*), or perhaps the event itself will be referenced as a timestamp, the mention of a particular wedding or birth or move having occurred during *that* autumn, in *that* October. The speaker, knowing you, will perhaps mention to others that you were there—that you were a Sox fan back then, back when—and then someone much younger than yourself who has not yet heard all of your stories will turn to you and ask the inevitable question, *what was it like?* Your answer will come effortlessly (you have told this story many times by now, and know it all by heart) and as you begin to talk, as you tell them who Papi was, and as you hold up your heel and point to a tendon in your foot, your mind will slip back across more personal images, warmer and more vivid—images of pacing and cheering, of jumping and laughing and the spontaneous hugging of loved ones— as you remember the faces and names of those who you were with when it happened, and the voices of those who you called immediately after. Mixed in among these will be more universal images, those of Ortiz's follow-through as he launches the winner in Game Four, of Schilling's blood-soaked sock in Game Six, of Wakefield storming off the mound after a strikeout in Game Five. Johnny Damon's hair and Manny Ramirez's double point. Foulke's Texas glove and Pedro's red glove. Millar and Mueller. Trot and Tek. Cabrera to Bellhorn to Mienkewicz. Each makes a colorful appearance in your story, and by the time you have finished you are there once again, seeing each game in succession, remembering each celebration until you finish your story by whispering the same word you used at the time, the same word you have used ever since, as you shake your head and mutter: it was, *unbelievable.*

What will be left out of your story, the part which cannot be explained to those who did not experience it, is what it felt like, *before.* For although there are benefits to looking back over the arch of a story, in order to point out how significant certain events would eventually become later on, what is necessarily lost in the retelling is the view from within—the perspective one had from the dark center of the story, its ending unknown. It will, for example, be nearly impossible to return without premonition to that long and bitter night of Saturday, October 16, 2004.

Where hunched over elbows on knees in the nearly empty bleachers at Fenway, just after midnight, we sat motionless, unblinking, and watched the Sox fall down another run. Then another. Then a few more. Until the score was 19-8 in the game and 3-0 in the series and the breath of winter blew so close that we could feel it slip across our necks, as the cold reality of what was happening began to settle upon us. Not just because of what *was happening* (past continuous) here tonight and in this series, in this season; but what *had been happening* (past perfect continuous) for the last eighty-six years. For *they were doing it again.* The Yankees were winning. The Sox were blowing it. Despite all the changes and all the improvements and all of the supposed differences between this year and every other year before it, the outcome was coming out just the same. Worse, even. One could see it on the scoreboard, and in the thousands of empty seats around Fenway Park. Sitting there among those who remained, arms crossed or head in hands, the sense of hopelessness (so hard to convey in a story ultimately filled with hope) was nearly overwhelming. *So this is it then*, we thought and maybe even said out loud, *this really is to be our lot*. Like each generation before us we had come to learn this lesson late, come to accept it even later. As each run crossed and each fan turned and shuffled down the ramps, tossing a program in the trash along the way, one could feel this acceptance falling like a curtain over the hearts of the once hopeful. This was not just the belief in one season which was passing away, but for many, the very capacity to believe at all. *Never again*, we muttered. *Never*.

This then was the view from Saturday night, and with little change the view from the first eight and a half innings on Sunday night as the Sox came to bat in the last of the ninth (for the last time of the season, perhaps) trailing the Yankees, 4-3. But then something happened. Something small; something simple; something which happens in every baseball game played from the dustiest Little League field to the grandest stadium in the Major Leagues. A walk. Millar drew it, seemingly willed it from Mariano Rivera to lead off the ninth, and was quickly replaced by pinch runner Dave Roberts. Then Roberts stole second. Then, a few pitches later, Bill Mueller hit a single up the middle, Roberts came around to score the tying run and nothing in the game, in the series, or in the long and remarkable history between the New York Yankees and the Boston Red Sox, was ever the same again.

Looking back on this series of events, taking up all of ten minutes on an autumn night in Boston, we see how clearly it draws a line between before and after; between the old familiar story that we had come to accept (which ended sharply at the crack of Mueller's bat) and the fresh new story (which began the moment Roberts crossed the plate) that is being played out even now, continuing on into the future. And despite the chaotic drama and deafening noise and mad, joyous release which followed in its wake, there is nonetheless something quiet, almost elegant about the simplicity of the moment itself. Among all the convoluted stories and grandiose characters that have populated this rivalry over so many years, and among all the overstated endings to extravagantly overstated games, in the end it was three of the game's most basic elements—walk, stolen base, single—that came together in sequence (1, 2, 3) to change everything. Four balls, a steal, a single up the middle was all it took. Timing, of course, being everything.

The long story of Yankee domination and Red Sox failure ended right there, at the precise moment when Mueller's ball bounded into the wide outfield grass. A moment later, when Roberts swept across the plate, a new story began. Its first chapters would unfold over the following four nights, each straddling two days, bridging night to morning as they bridged their way from prologue to postscript. Each of the four contains its own story, its own history, its own memories for the players and fans who experienced them together; and in the future each will be chronicled in writing and on film, and passed on to another generation through our own well-handled tales. To detail them now, inning by inning, while they are still warm and while their story is still being told in the present tense (while we are still within *that* October) would be to diminish them somewhat. It is enough then to look back one last time at what they gave us; and more importantly what they took away, as collectively they tore down the last dusty monuments of a fallen empire, piece by piece, game by glorious game.

Game Four: The one, more than any other, that was about this team, about this particular group of players. With the season all but written off by the majority of media and fans the only real issue left to be decided seemed to be the legacy of this team. Would it merely be another in a long line of Sox teams that had fought hard and at times brilliantly only to come up short in the end to the Yankees (this the best case scenario), or were they to go down in infamy as one of the most spectacular collapses in the history of a club infamous for its spectacular collapses. All else was, at this point, a foregone conclusion. And so Game Four became an act of defiance for the players themselves, battling back in the ninth and fighting into extra innings if for no other reason than to say *at least*—at least they did not get swept. At least they would have that. A walk, a stolen base and a single produced the run in the ninth which suggested it, and an hour later David

Ortiz's game-winning shot in the twelfth stated it clearly: this team would avoid all that. Say what we would about them (as many already had), but they would not be swept. And as Ortiz jumped into the pile at home plate and "Dirty Water" played and Fenway shook there was among fans everywhere a collective exhale. At least they didn't get swept. At least they fought back and given themselves another shot. At least there would be one more day of baseball. If nothing else.

Game Five: And so it was with a sense of stolen time that fans filed back into Fenway on Monday afternoon for Game Five. These same fans had filed in three nights earlier on a cool and rainy Friday night, only to sit and wait and finally to be told that there would be no baseball that night, and then over the weekend realize that there may not be any more baseball at all. A cruel twist for a group of Sox fans who, already watching their season end one game at a time, seemed to have had even this last night at Fenway washed away by a cold autumn rain. Then a walk, a stolen base and a single held winter at bay for another night, and brought them all back to Fenway for one more day in the stands. And as the Sox once again fell behind and once again rallied back (this time from down 4-2 to tie the game in the eighth and send it to extra innings) and as the innings stretched on into the twelfth, into the thirteenth, one could feel a wave of instant nostalgia for the ballpark itself—for the experience of being there, or seeing its familiar face on the screen, or hearing its familiar call over the airwaves—pass over Red Sox fans everywhere. *Not here. Anywhere but here.* So much delight had taken place here over the last two seasons that it simply did not seem right for the end to come among these walls and in front of our own eyes. So that if nothing else Fenway could be left out of it, could be spared the disappointment of seeing the season end here, at Home. And so it was as Damon reached second and Ortiz fouled off pitch after pitch (Loaiza gallantly working him away, away, away, unable to get one by and finally letting one drift over just far enough) and at last the ball drifted out over second base and fell in as Damon raced around third and sprinted home. The Sox won, series and the summer continued on, and Fenway Park was saved once more.

Game Six: If Game Four was about the team and Game Five was about Fenway, then Game Six in New York seemed to be about a third, more personal and less tangible aspect of the Red Sox experience, one much talked about but rarely felt in such stark terms. It is something that has taken on a separate life among Red Sox fans, something which has been captured by advertising and promotional machinery and turned into a slogan (appearing on t-shirts and billboards and in television commercials) but which despite these corporate machinations has remained a steady and very real part of the Sox experience from the beginning, and never more so than on the night of Game Six. As Curt Schilling stepped to the mound in Yankee Stadium, and every Sox fan watching was forced to ask themselves: *do you Believe?*

On an evening when there seemed so much to disbelieve—that Schilling's ankle would hold up, that the bats would get to Lieber, that the momentum built at Fenway could hold up under the bright Stadium lights—the game, played under cool and drizzly conditions throughout, seemed to unfold as a series of revelations. The first came from the least likely, in second baseman Mark Bellhorn, who so many had stopped believing in long before, yet whose three run home run in the fourth would, with the run before it, be the entirety of the Sox's offense for the night. At first even the umpires were incredulous, doubting their own eyes until they convened and discussed and ultimately overturned their original call. *Believe it*, they seemed to say, the Sox were up, 4-0.

And there on the mound stood the figure about whom so much of the language of belief has centered over the last year, in whom no greater degree of faith was ever needed than on this night. Time tends to distort the kinds of courage Curt Schilling displayed in Game Six of the ALCS. We have been conditioned to understand that courage is never absolute, that each retelling of the hero's turn gives the story a somewhat mythical feel, making it one of those clearly apocryphal stories in which we instinctively distrust the details. That it *sounds made up* is our cue. We hear it and understand that the facts, in stories such as these, have been shaped and distorted and exaggerated by time, and that these legends never really happened the way they are told in posterity. Not exactly. And so an effort needs to be made not to mythologize what Schilling accomplished on the mound in Yankee Stadium, simply because it is unnecessary. In this case, the facts will do.

Near the end of the season Curt Schilling dislocated a tendon in his right foot. It was a season ending injury, which he nonetheless tried to pitch through in Game One of the ALCS, only to find himself unable to generate the necessary drive off his back foot as the tendon continued to pop in and out of place. He was scratched for Game Five, threw (poorly) for ten minutes before Game Three, and limped out of the bullpen under the concerned gaze of his manager and pitching coach. The physical structure of his ankle simply would not allow him to push off the mound, and therefore he was unable to pitch. Then, before Game Six, Red Sox team physician Dr. Morgan performed a procedure in which a tendon was intentionally pulled out of joint and succored to a bone in the pitcher's foot, anchoring it. It was by definition an experimental surgery, and neither patient nor doctor could be sure of either its temporary results, or long term side effects. The patient pitched seven innings. Against the Yankees. At the Stadium. In a deciding playoff game. He gave up four hits. He allowed only one run. He got the win.

These are the irrefutable facts of Game Six.

Yet we can already hear future generations questioning our memory when we reach this point of our story. Nodding along with us through the dramatic comebacks of Games Four and Five we can see them hold up a hand when we come to Schilling and Game Six. (*Whoa whoa whoa. Hold on a second. He did what?*) Still, the facts will remain the same, and the accomplishment of Schilling on this night will stand as one of the single most courageous (mentally as well as physically) sports achievements in any of our lifetimes. We can see the head shakes, the suspect looks, and to answer them we will only need to repeat the simple facts. The surgeon cut real flesh with a real scalpel. The pitcher pitched with real stitches off a real mound. The blood on his sock, was real.

Game Seven: The least competitive and most emotional, Game Seven was from its very beginning more about people than baseball. The Sox took an early 2-0 lead, never to relinquish it, and the remainder of the game became a series of small personal moments and widespread communal joys. Its heroes on the field included another pair of fallen figures; the first Johnny Damon, one of the season's most beloved stars who had until this night suffered through one of the worst weeks of his career, ending it (as seem so often possible in baseball) with the single biggest night of his professional life.

It was one of many such moments throughout the remarkable four day stretch, and each individual fan will perhaps hold one figure or one achievement above the others and will therefore throw a brighter spotlight upon him when his moment in the story comes about. For some it may be Damon's drives in Game Seven; for others it might be Schilling's courageous turn in Game Six. We have talked to some who will always remember Keith Foulke pitching his guts out and his arm off over two nights at Fenway. Others will always return to Mueller's hit in Game Seven. And millions will never be able to think of this team or this series or what they accomplished without picturing David Ortiz rounding the bases, and disappearing into a mob of red and white at home plate. Surely there are others. (For at least one, it is Wake.)

As for us, while we will always remember the images and efforts of the above there will among them be one figure who continues to come to mind when we think of what happened during these four days of baseball. Throughout the season we had come to see him as the embodiment of the Red Sox experience, and so it only seemed fitting that his personal triumph so closely mirrored the historic triumph of the team, and the vicarious triumph of its fans. It was Derek Lowe, after all, who most needed redemption; and it was Derek Lowe who was most completely redeemed.

Like all Sox fans, Derek Lowe has fought a long and never easy battle with his own personal baseball demons, and like the Sox as a whole he has been given up on and believed in and given up on again more times than seems possible—throughout his career, throughout each individual season. Like the historical Sox he has often had to answer questions about his mental capacity to succeed when it really matters, and has even been forced to deal with accusations (not always fair) about his own psychological makeup. It has been suggested that he is not of a stout constitution. It has been speculated on whether the pressure of playing in Boston and before the hypercritical glare of Red Sox fans might not be too much for him, or whether it is all too large a burden for him to handle. (It has been whispered that he might even be a little *self-destructive*.) All claims made about each and every Sox team over the last eighty-six years. Through it all Derek Lowe has mentally and emotionally fit this team and this franchise more closely than any other player of his generation; and this, of course, has been both the solution and the problem. And so it is entirely appropriate that not only would he take the ball and the mound at our lowest point (to start Game Four), but that three days later, on the night when an entire populace exorcized its own lingering demons, its own fears and self-doubt and worry, that he, the man who fell the farthest on the team which fell the hardest, should be the one to stand up tall in the middle of Yankee Stadium and with each pitch shake the last gray flecks of doubt off his shoulders, and onto the mound of ashes from which both he and his team had now so triumphantly risen above.

Surely there are others. Each and every person who experienced these games will have their own figures, their own images, and when they tell the story they may just as well include Trot Nixon sliding across the outfield grass to make a catch or Dave Roberts sprinting down across the dirt towards second. Whatever they may be they will surely be mixed in among the individual memories of the experience itself.

Who we were with and who we talked to first; where we were and what we did after; the sights and sounds and long sleepless nights which made up our own mental and emotion comeback. Yet in the days which followed one came to realize that more than anything else, more than any individual thread in the celebration, what happened as the innings wore on in Game Seven was an emphatically collective experience. Each story confirms it. Whether it is a group of old high school friends in Cambridge who, loud and raucous all night, say a quiet collective prayer in the late innings; or a mother on the North Shore calling her son in Connecticut to find him listening to a radio with his fellow prison guards, jumping up and shouting with each out. One conversation brings in a sister in Boston talking to her brother in Hawaii, celebrating with him across the continent; the next brings a son in Somerville calling his mother in Rhode Island, hearing her crying and she repeats the words *I'm so happy* over and over and over again. Until eventually one realizes that the same types of stories and the same types of celebrations (each filled with smiles, most filled with tears) are happening everywhere around us, all over New England and all over the country, and that millions of people feel the exact same joy you feel at the exact same moment. It is a little miracle, this realization, a breathless glimpse at the wider world that, so very isolated so much of the time, for one moment quietly reminds us that yes: *we are all in this together*.

That it took the Red Sox finally beating the Yankees to bring this feeling about might seem slight and shallow to some, particularly those outside the daily experiences of this specific culture, but this too is understandable. We've heard this claim before. And when we hear those in the national media talk of how none of this will mean anything if the Red Sox do not win the next series, *the* Series, we have to smile and accept the fact they too simply do not understand. Not really. How could they? How could they understand without having been there, without having heard the taunts and the jokes and the demeaning chants, without having stood with the Red Sox under the shadow of the Yankees game after game, season after season, generation after generation.

Never and *always* are powerful words (in baseball as elsewhere), and to be told, often with a look down and a smirk, not only that you will *never achieve that* and that you will *always be like this*, but that you have been a fool for having believed things could be otherwise—well, these words are not absorbed without consequence. Each person, regardless of their convictions, can only hear them so many times without bit by bit starting to break down, without starting to lose faith in *there's always next year*, without starting to believe in *always* and *never*. It is a terrible thing to have one's faith broken, in anything, no matter how superficial or contrived; and yet this is exactly what had happened to one degree or another within the entire culture of Red Sox baseball. Most of it coming at the hands of the New York Yankees. It was through them that we were told *never*, and so it meant everything that we would see it happen, this year, at their expense and in front of their own disbelieving eyes. And so *yes*, it does have to do with the Yankees; it has everything to do with the Yankees and it always has. Anyone who says otherwise does not understand what the looks on Yankees fans' faces meant to Sox fans everywhere. Not because we took vindictive joy in their bitter disappointment (as some suspect of us), but because these were the same faces that had smirked at us and the same voices that had told us they would *always*—, and that we would *never*, ever, do this. And the reason it meant so much to us—the absolute core of it all—is that we knew, at that moment, that we would never hear those words again. Not from them. Not ever. This is what we saw in their faces as the ninth inning began in Yankee Stadium. It was all ending for them, and for us. Winter after winter of hoping and being told not to hope; summer after summer of winning and being told not to enjoy it (*simmer down there buddy, it's only April*); autumn after autumn of being told how foolish we all were to have ever believed; winter following winter and coming back to where we started and doing it all over again, seeing and hearing it all over again—all the signs and the shirts and incessant *19-18* taunts, the laughing *why don't you give up already,* and the condescending *its never going to happen*—all those tiny little smiles and laughs and insults which add up year after year until Pokey Reese scoops up a grounder and throws to Doug

Mientkiewicz and millions of taunting, laughing, humiliating voices directed from one group of people towards another for eighty-six years all fall dead silent in an instant. Gone forever. Never to be heard from again.

As the Sox streamed out onto the field and jumped into each other's arms their celebration echoed throughout New England and in pockets across the country and around the world, as it doubtless will be for some time to come. It was over. They had done it, and nothing between the Red Sox and Yankees would ever be quite the same again. Which is of course what Sox fans had wanted all along. Change had come, and the realization was as gleefully accepted by Sox fans as it must have been bitterly difficult to accept for Yankees fans, who were now finally forced to accept the fact that one team was not made more talented or more noble or more worthy of praise simply by the city they play for, or the stadium they play in, or the pinstripes they wear. It was a similar lesson learned by Sox fans, that losing baseball games has nothing—nothing at all—to do with the scarlet letters stitched across a team's chest. (Pitching helps in this regard, as both teams learned.) And as one group celebrated the most dramatic and heroic triumph any of us have ever witnessed and another sat in shocked embarrassment the series of realizations on both sides led to a shared awareness, palpable to both, that something which had gone on long before any of us were around had just now ended. And that something entirely new and as yet unknown, was about to begin.

This is why years from now you will have some work to do when telling your story. This is why you will have to go back farther than Game Four. Why you will have to explain to them what it was like *before* '04. Why you will have to sit them down and take them through the years and the heartbreaks and the embarrassments. And when you do, be sure to tell them about Williams and DiMaggio; tell them about Munson and Fisk; tell them about 1978 and tell them who Bucky Dent is, and why. Tell them about 1999. Tell them what it sounded like to hear fifty-five-thousand people chant *19-18*. Tell them about Clemens, and why Clemens matters. Tell them about the 2003 season, and about the first Game Seven. Tell them what Aaron Boone did and what Grady Little did not. Tell them all about A-Rod. As you do, try to mix in some of the insults, some of the jokes, some of the snide remarks we heard over and over and over again. Try to explain to them why we came to expect fights in the stands during Red Sox-Yankees games. Try to get through to them what *always* and *never* meant, and what they had come to mean to us.

In the end it probably will not work, not entirely anyway; if for no other reason than your audience will already know how this period in history did not go on forever, but came to a very definite end. They will know the entire time you are telling them about Game Seven in 2003 that Game Seven in 2004 is only a year away. As you tell them about losing Game Three of that year they will know that Ortiz is still coming to bat in Games Four and Five, will already have seen the pictures and heard the stories of Schilling in Game Six, and will already know that Derek Lowe did not, in the end, waste away in the bullpen after all. Still, it is worth trying. Because while the story of the 2004 ALCS will always be remarkable in the pages of sports and baseball history, and while the achievements of its participants will always be remembered as some of the most determined and defiant of all time, the significance of those four days will one day be lost unless what came before it, and what was ended by it, is placed at the very heart of the story. It is its very center—those desperate times of *always* and *never*—and the joyous release which followed in its wake can neither be appreciated nor truly understood without it.

So when that day comes, years from now, when someone mentions a three games to none deficit and remembers that you were there, back then, and the questions are put to you about those four days, make sure you remember to tell them what it was like, before. You will likely have to repeat yourself. They will question your memory and your perspective on the situation and they will surely accuse you of exaggerating the more spectacular moments if not the entire story. Nod your head when they do. Tell them you were there. You remember every moment of it. And that yes, it was. And yes, they did. And yes, it all really did happen, just like that.

Beyond Belief and Back Again

American League
Championship Series: Game Seven

Cleveland at Fenway
21 October 2007

"All baseball fans believe in miracles;
the question is how *many* do you believe in?"

- John Updike

The trouble with the history lesson is that knowing the past is not the same as understanding it, and in no way guarantees our being able to use it in any productive manner. It simply means we know what happened. As Red Sox fans who stayed up very late this past Wednesday night found out, the historical record is not enough. Slouched head-in-hands in front of our televisions, watching the Indians celebrate their 3-1 ALCS lead beneath a cyclone of white dish towels, we inevitably recalled how three years earlier we had slouched in a similar pose, faced similarly long odds, felt similarly defeated, and that back then things seem to have worked out alright, regardless. We recalled this, momentarily, then promptly returned to muttering mild obscenities under our breath and bemoaning the Indians' ludicrous good fortune and yes, perhaps, maybe feeling just a bit sorry for ourselves.

So no, it was not enough to know that we had been here before and done what we hoped to do, if for no other reason than there were too many inconvenient facts cluttering up the comparison. For instance the fact that this was quite technically a different Red Sox team (only three regular position players, one starting pitcher, and one middle reliever remained from 2004); the fact that this current team had yet to show anything of the same fight or resilience of their predecessors; the fact that our players who were slumping now had slumped *all season*, rather than merely a few games; and of course the less tangible but vitally important fact that the 2004 team and what they did was special, unique, incomparable—quite literally a once-in-a-lifetime deal. By its very nature there could be no second act.

What was missing, both from our understanding of October 2004 and our inability to apply it to October 2007, was the sublime usefulness of the word *if*. It is true, the facts alone are not enough—not enough to predict with and certainly not enough to take solace in—but they are enough to get us to *if*. If this happens then... If that happens then perhaps... If things go this way we know from past experience that there is a good chance we might... And so on. It is an imaginative act to get past *if*—to understand the lessons of the past well enough to trace their patterns beyond the present and into the future—but once there it allows us to use the historical record as a kind of actuarial road map. Not knowing which road the season will take we can at very least see the different roads available, and know that there is a chance we might end up on the one narrow path which leads to safety. This knowledge alone is enough to bring our head from our hands and raise us from the distraught position of late Wednesday night. We remember that *if we can, then*...and thus equipped we breath in, exhale long and low, perhaps take back a few of the more inappropriate curses leveled at the Indians and their fans (inappropriate but hardly unprovoked), and look ahead to Game Five.

Where history will take us right up to the first pitch. After that it is up to the imagination. Up to us to complete the sentence *if only*... Up to each individual fan to be able to wake up on a Thursday morning in October with the Sox down 3-1 in the ALCS, completely outplayed, and still find a way (*if* we could- *if* Beckett can- *if* only-) to envision a scene four nights later in Boston in which David Ortiz, grinning wide in red commemorative hat and t-shirt, swaggers through a knot of media outside the Red Sox dugout and makes his way to the center of the infield, and with a swell of cheers rising around him plants the American League Championship trophy firmly on the Fenway Park mound.

In this regard it is always helpful to have a Josh Beckett. Undefeated and nearly unhittable in his young playoff career, Beckett took the ball for Game Five in Cleveland and immediately set about establishing a new tone for the series. That is to say, his tone. He gave up a cheap run in the first (Grady Sizemore's flair over third landed between three Sox fielders, he advanced on a single through the drawn in infield, and scored when Travis Hafner grounded into a double play), but retired the first two batters in the second and sent the very next pitch whistling over the helmet of Indians outfielder Franklin Gutiérrez, who gave Beckett a curious stare. Beckett stared right back; then, after a walk and an out, covered his mouth with his glove to offer Gutiérrez a few of his personal thoughts (*just between the two of us*) on his way back to the dugout. In the bottom of the fifth Kenny Lofton flipped his bat aside on a 3-1 pitch that happened to land in the strike zone, then flied out, and as he jogged out of the batters box was given a thorough shouting all the way up the line by Beckett; Lofton shouted back and made one or two strides towards the mound; both benches cleared and for a few lively moments met and shouted at each other near the mound.

Nothing tangible came of it, and while it must be said that neither message from Beckett was entirely called for within the framework of this one game (Gutiérrez had done nothing in the series, and Lofton's bat flip was at very least no worse than the posturing of our own left fielder), both were vitally important in changing the mood of the series.

For up until that point the Indians had enjoyed a fine time at their home ballpark, living it up in front of their highly excitable, towel waving fans. Beckett put an immediate end to all this in two distinct ways. The first and most obvious was by not allowing another run on only five hits through eight innings; but just as important in the end was his ability to make the Cleveland hitters first uncomfortable, then upset. Finally there were shouts and angry looks from the Cleveland dugout; finally there was head shaking and barks towards the umpire after another called strike on the outside corner; finally the Indians were no longer enjoying themselves quite so much and finally, for the first time all week, their home field advantage fell silent.

More so later on. Kevin Youkilis had opened the scoring with a first inning home run off C.C. Sabathia, the Indians' somewhat nervy ace, only to have that lead leveled a half inning later on Sizemore's flare. In the third Ortiz and Manny combined to break the tie for good, the latter on a long opposite field drive off the very top of the right field wall that proved controversial. Replays showed it hit off the top of *something*, but given that the yellow wall padding, which is in play, and the level wall beyond it, which is not, are on the same plane, it was difficult to tell. On the play Ortiz had scored; while Manny had, well, sort of lost his way and in the confusion never made it past first. The entire affair was needlessly drawn out (the national television announcers simply could not get over it), and ultimately made irrelevant by the two runs the Sox added in the seventh on a Pedroia double and a Youkilis triple off the glove of a diving Grady Sizemore and the arm of a tiring Sabathia. (Indians manager Eric Wedge seemed to do the Sox a favor here by sending Sabathia, who had thrown 106 unconvincing pitches, out for the sixth. Despite the starter's post-game assertion that he felt strong, and Wedge's similar claim that he was pitching well, the truth was Sabathia never looked entirely at ease under the bright playoff lights. A fact confirmed less by his mound presence than the televised shots of the big lefty on the Indians bench between innings, shaking.) Down 4-1 in the eighth the Indians bullpen finally showed signs of strain with a handful of walks, an error, and a wild pitch that broke the game open at 7-1.

In the end though this one was all about Beckett, who with each spectacular October start adds to the mythology already surrounding his postseason record. Much has been made of the tall, 27-year-old Texan's calm under the pressures of October baseball, and yet watching him work we find that calm is not exactly the word that comes to mind. Certainly he is composed, and in control of both his emotions and each of his pitches (when he throws his curveball for strikes and keeps his fastball down he is essentially unhittable), but his attitude is not relaxed. Instead he is fiery, aggressive, riveting, and when he lets loose between batters (usually into his glove) the burst of emotion is sudden and explosive. More than anything Beckett exudes a burning determination to succeed that is almost frightening in its intensity. He has a similar determination in the regular season, but it is far more pronounced in October, where he pitches as if every batter who steps to the plate represents a personal affront merely by attempting to hit his pitching. On this night, as on most nights, his ability to simultaneously stoke and harness that intensity proved more than enough to win the game, to save the Sox's season, and to send both teams back east for a raucous October weekend at Fenway.

Game Six, played on an unseasonably temperate Saturday night in Boston, was less a game than a large open air, baseball themed party. In the first inning Pedroia led off with a high chopper over the head of Indians' starter Fausto Carmona for an infield single, moved to second on another infield hit by Youkilis (the latter quietly having a remarkable series), and finally to third on an Ortiz semi-intentional walk to load the bases. So: bases loaded, nobody out, Manny and Lowell due up, and the Sox lineup right back in business. Only Manny struck out swinging, and Lowell flew out on the first pitch. Which brought up perhaps the last person in New England any Red Sox fan wanted to see at the plate with the bases loaded and two outs, the heretofore beleaguered and besieged outfielder, J.D. Drew.

Never a popular signing to begin with, Drew had spent the better part of his first season in Boston convincing everyone that he was in every way unfit to meet the demands of his role on the Red Sox. Or any role for that matter, save that of single-handedly souring an almost entirely sweet season. He had been booed, of course, but perhaps even worse than this was the repeated assertion that he had been spared our true ire by the overall success of his teammates. (The message more or less: *you better hope this thing works out in the end, because if not, just you wait...*) Here he took a ball, fouled off a strike, then took two more balls from the painfully rattled Carmona to run the count to 3-1. At which point every Red Sox fan in every corner of the baseball world likely entertained the same exact thought, all at once. *Walk. Please*, we thought and muttered and maybe even shouted, *please do not swing*. Just draw a walk and give Tek a chance.

Not an unreasonable request given that by this point we had watched J.D. Drew wear a Red Sox uniform for over six months, had watched him play 148 games, had watched most if not all of his 494 official at bats, and had watched with eroding patience as every last time he came up in a crucial situation such as this, he failed. Miserably. Not once during all that time and all those at bats had he done anything even remotely suggesting an ability to produce a decisive swing. Instead he had struck out swinging (occasionally he struck out looking, for variety), flew out to center, and grounded out weakly to the right side of the infield more times, to end more innings, than seemed statistically possible. What he had not done was put his stamp on the season in any positive fashion.

But there was still time. Even as late as this Saturday afternoon we had talked specifically about this kind of opportunity, the chance the postseason gives to erase and replace and restore a player's image and reputation. Particularly late in the playoffs, particularly here, where after all we had seen it happen before. (*You remember Bellhorn right*, we ask each other each time Drew's name is disparaged, how bad he was throughout the playoffs and how everyone wanted him out of the lineup; but Francona stuck with him and there he was, with a big home run early in Game Six. So who knows, one swing is all it would take. *If* it came in the right game, *if* it came at the right time, *if...*)

Carmona's 3-1 pitch is meant to be on the outside corner but drifts back over the plate and Drew, staying aggressive, extends his arm on the swing and drives the ball on a high rising line out to center that brings us all to our feet shouting and waving and leaning for it to just *get the wall*. Sizemore races back beneath it, looking up then backing off to play the carom, the ball hit hard but on a low, drifting trajectory and we are already leaping and cheering for the double off the wall when the ball sails out over center field, reaches the wall, and disappears. Like magic.

Joy and disbelief mix in equal parts as Red Sox fans everywhere turn with the same wide-eyed expression of utter astonishment, and repeat to one another in the same half-stunned, half-delighted voice: *Holy. Sh—*.

He did it. With one good swing J.D. Drew erased a season filled with bad swings, and as if to prove this the Fenway crowd continued calling for him until the player we had begrudgingly half-booed all season appeared on the top dugout step with both fists raised, and took this most unlikely of curtain calls. When he came up again with a runner on in the third the crowd stood, and to its own surprise began chanting *J-D, J-D, J-D*. To absolutely no one's surprise, Drew singled up the middle. This brought in Manny, made the score 5-1, and chased a thoroughly bewildered Carmona from the game after only two innings. Rafael Pérez came on for the Indians, and fared no better. Ellsbury singled to drive in Lowell (6-1); Lugo singled to drive in Drew and Ellsbury (8-1); Pedroia walked; Youkilis singled to drive in Lugo (9-1), then got caught in a run-down between first and second that ended with the ball clanking off his helmet; the ball rolled away and Pedroia scored (10-1) and the rout, and the party, and the series deciding Game Seven were on.

If in Game Five we had hung our hopes on the dominance of Beckett, and in Game Six had safely transferred them to the instability of Carmona, the Game Seven matchup of Daisuke Matsuzaka (who had not pitched well in Game Three) v. Jake Westbrook (who had) has left us with nothing to hold onto at all except the weakly circulating mantra that this young Indians club has been rattled beyond recovery. Clinging to this, we spend batting practice carefully studying the faces and mannerisms of the visitors as if to somehow espy a crack in the façade. An over-serious expression, a little hint of anxiety in the stance, some tell-tale mark of defeat. (Discouragingly, we find nothing of the sort.

In fact they look ridiculously bright and loose, almost playful, the middle infielders around second attempting circus double-play turns and laughing at their own exaggerated flips and leaps. Not a good sign.)

As it turns out, we were looking in the wrong direction. For it is the Sox hitters who, after a clean opening frame from Daisuke, look to execute the same double secret game plan from the night before; which is to calm the nerves (theirs and to a much greater extent ours) simply by scoring loads of early runs. Pedroia and Youkilis both single to lead off the first, and although Ortiz strikes out, Manny follows and scorches a grounder to the left that takes one explosive leap over Peralta and into left field for the game's opening run. Another single from Lowell loads the bases and, somewhat remarkably, brings J.D. Drew to bat once again with the bases loaded in the first inning. With the wry, baying chants of *Weeeeest*-brook, *Weeeeest*-brook, calling out from the stands and both the Cleveland starter and Cleveland season a long fly ball from total collapse, the sinker-baller gets Drew to ground into an inning-ending, sound-defusing double play.

This sets the pattern for the game's first act as two identical innings follow in the second and third. In each Daisuke stays ahead of the Indians hitters (who seem perpetually behind 1-2 in the count), and retires the side in order save for a lone innocuous single from Casey Blake in the third. Meanwhile Westbrook sticks with his Houdini act, continues to both give up multiple hits early and get crucial double plays late. And after three innings of what feels like a rout, the Sox lead by a mere three runs. In the fourth the pattern is broken by Westbrook's greatest escape yet, this time loading the bases loaded with one out and getting Pedroia to ground weakly up the middle where Asdrúbal Cabrera merely has to field, step on second, and throw over for the inning ending double-play. And with a clatter of broken locks around him Westbrook walks off stage right, unscathed.

Inspired by this performance, or perhaps merely persistent in their effort to make Daisuke work for every last strike, the Indians come back in the bottom of the fourth with a run on doubles by Travis Hafner (his first hit in a week) and Ryan Garko, the latter after a long at bat in which the rookie first baseman fouled off pitch after pitch. This new pattern of the Sox failing to score and the Indians scratching out a single run is repeated in the fifth as the Indians manage two singles and a sacrifice fly by Sizemore to make it 3-2; but now it is Cleveland's turn to feel aggrieved, as the inning might have been more had Kenny Lofton not been called out trying to extend a single to lead off the inning (replays seemed to show that he beat the tag). And like that, Westbrook goes from being an escape artists to a knife thrower, and strikes out four of the next six batters as he cruises through both the fifth and sixth, and brings us to the decisive inning in both game and series—the seventh inning, of the seventh game.

At this point on another warm, summerish October night at Fenway the game and series and season all teeter at a precarious balancing point. The Sox, having come back to force a Game Seven have carried that momentum like a cavalry charge into the depleted Indian lines, only to be turned away inning after inning, having gained runs but only at a tremendous expenditure of hits. Meanwhile the Indians have held fast, and after withstanding this initial charge have begun to make their own small advances. By all accounts the Sox should be leading the game by much more than the single run they now hold to, and with Hideki Okajima on for a second inning (he had replaced Matsuzaka in the sixth) the Indians look poised to make a decisive move to reclaim the lead and, with it, a stolen momentum. For Sox fans, it is a tragedy waiting to happen. And this Fenway crowd can feel it, sitting all too quietly as Okajima warms for the seventh.

A reassuring out leads off the inning, but then Lofton clips a flair down the left field line, high up and drifting back behind third where Lugo gives chase and Manny jogs over, a troubling combination which results in Lugo reaching back and missing while Manny looks on at a ball he probably should have called for and caught. Lofton lands on second, and the Indians are a base hit away from tying the game. They get it too, on a sharp grounder down the third base line that skips once and kicks off the jutting outfield wall, into shallow left field as a groan escapes the crowd and we all instinctively turn to third and pick up Lofton—not sprinting home as we had fully expected, but instead skidding to a low-crouching halt and now inexplicably scrambling back to third. No one seems entirely sure why. (Later on we will find out that he was held up by his fatally cautious third base coach, but in real time, watching the ball, it appeared that he must have tripped or stumbled around the bag. There seemed no other rational explanation.)

Timidity is a cardinal sin in October baseball, and the Indians dugout must know as well as we do what is coming next. So it is written—*waste not the late inning scoring chance, for thou shalt inviteth the inning-killing double play*—and so shall it be. As with runners on first and third Casey Blake grounds a hard roller to Lowell, who with the crowd pulling in an anticipatory breath calmly throws to second where Pedroia quickly spins and fires to Youkilis, in time for the double-play as all at once Fenway erupts in a loud exuberant cheer of relief. (And the people said, *Amen*.)

Still a close game after the stretch, Ellsbury leads off against the previously unhittable Rafael Betancourt and chops a routine ground ball to third which Blake (perhaps thinking about Ellsbury's speed, perhaps thinking about his rally-killing double play) short-arms and allows the ball to kick off his glove into foul ground. Ellsbury glides into second. And all at once it hits us: this *is* a tragedy we are watching, only not ours. In the Lottery of October Heartbreak we have opened our folded white slip and found it blank, and now look with a mixture of relief and empathy to the Cleveland fans who, so happy to be here a moment ago, have opened theirs and found upon it a single black spot.

The Indians tragic collapse and the Red Sox epic comeback now fatefully determined, all that's left is for the final blow to fall (*alright folks, let's finish quickly*). On the mound Betancourt sets. Pedroia wheels his bat round, wags it, and with one emphatic hack rips a fastball up into the Monster Seats and gives the Sox a 5-2 lead. Fenway Park goes absolutely silly with joyous celebration. And like that, we know it: *the Sox are going to the World Series.*

In the moment the events of the next inning and a half all go by very fast and with a blurry, intoxicated kind of zeal, filled as they are with bright cheers, a few happy projections, and a great deal of totally unnecessary but gratefully welcome Red Sox runs. (Here and after, we would just as soon not think about what this must have felt like for Indians fans.) In the eighth Okajima comes out for an unprecedented third inning of work and immediately shows exactly why that precedent has been set by giving up two straight singles (one a clever bunt by Sizemore). While technically endangering the Sox 5-2 lead, all this really does is provided an appropriately dramatic entrance for closer Jonathan Papelbon, who promptly blows three fastballs by a hopelessly overmatched Travis Hafner, gets a fielder's choice from Victor Martínez, and with two outs and two on gives up a frighteningly well hit drive to Garko which Ellsbury, sprinting back towards the gap in right center, runs onto and snags on the track before rolling off the bullpen wall. Inning over, and these good times never seemed *so good, so good, so good.*

Apparently unable to wait any longer, the Red Sox American League championship celebration begins an inning early, in the bottom of the eighth. With Betancourt still in Lowell doubles, Drew singles, Varitek doubles in Lowell (6-3), and after a Lugo out the two bats that have started the Sox off right for three straight games now end it, decisively. Pedroia with a ringing three-run double to make it 9-3 (the celebration through the pitching change, Jensen Lewis for Betancourt, as loud as Fenway has been all weekend), then Youkilis, who snaps a two-run homer off the Coca-Cola bottle to make it 11-3. And it's *Oh You Red Sox*, all over again.

These are happy, happy times in the Fenway stands. Whereas in a normal regular season game there is a law of diminishing return on runs past, say, a five-run lead or so, here in the playoffs each additional run brings only additional relief, comfort, happiness. For over the past six days Red Sox fans have lived with the statistical probability of our season ending here, one step short of its goal; and the internal wrestling between our better fan hopes and our better baseball judgment has taken its toll. Each successive game has lessened the grip of anxiety, but only by degree, and it is not until these back-to-back exclamation points from Pedroia and Youkilis that we give way to full release, and fall into the comfort of the unfettered cheer with the gratitude of a weary traveler towards a soft cool bed. (Why do the Sox continue to fall behind in the ALCS? Perhaps because it feels so very good when they come charging back.)

That would be enough, really. Enough to win the game and series, enough to celebrate about, enough to make for a very good baseball story. But the game and this team in particular have a way of outdoing themselves, particularly in these types of situations. And so with Papelbon on in the ninth we realize, as Carl Beane reads the defensive changes over the PA, one minor way in which the story could be improved. Coco Crisp, who played so poorly that he forfeited his starting center field position to Ellsbury (probably for the year, possibly for good), is announced as the new center fielder, with Ellsbury sliding over to left. He is cheered (everyone is cheered at this point) and there is a quick, fleeting thought that it would be nice if he could make one of the outs here in the ninth, just for the sake of closure. One of the nice symmetries in this story being that every player who had contributed to the 3-1 deficit has also contributed, in one way or another, to its erasure. Drew had been fully exonerated and, to a lesser extent, so had Lugo (who played a wonderful shortstop throughout). Schilling and Daisuke came back from poor starts in Games Two and Three to deliver qualities ones in Games Six and Seven. Even Gagne, the outcast, came on and retired the side in order to end Game Six. Everyone had pitched in to make it happen. Except of course for Crisp, the one sad little footnote in an otherwise happy story. Which is why it would be nice to see him make a put-out in the final inning. At least one.

As it turns out the first fly ball goes to left, to Crisp's replacement, and Ellsbury makes a nice sliding catch which only seems to exacerbate the need to have Crisp contribute. With one out we get our wish as Gutiérrez flies the next ball easily out to center, Crisp settles under it, and makes the catch. Hearty cheers for Coco, and all is forgiven. We ready ourselves for the final strikeout as Papelbon sets and glares, kicks and throws and the ball, instead of popping in Varitek's glove, goes shooting out in the other direction, far out over centerfield towards the dangerous triangle between wall and bullpen and all we are thinking is *stay in stay in stay in* when out of nowhere Crisp comes flashing into the corner and at full speed sweeps onto the ball and has it for the catch, out, game, and pennant.

And oh so many happy moments later David Ortiz, grinning wide in red commemorative hat and t-shirt, swaggers through a knot of media outside the Red Sox dugout and makes his way to the center of the infield, and with a swell of cheers rising around him plants the American League Championship trophy firmly on the Fenway Park mound.

What lessons do we take from this, the second furious ALCS comeback in four years? Perhaps a good place to start would be to say that some 3-1 series leads are sturdier than others, and when they involve needing to either beat the other team's ace or win a game on the road they may not be that sturdy at all, as Cleveland's clearly was not. Another might be that some pitchers who dominate the regular season are not necessarily capable, at this stage in their career, of dominating in October, as is clearly the case with Sabathia and Carmona. Still one more is that it is possible for a team to be fundamentally better than another and still find ways to make themselves not only look worse, but to nearly lose an entire series in the process. Of the three games the Sox lost in the series only one was lost decisively. Game Two was lost badly in extra innings, but was at one point a base hit from going to the Sox; Game Three was close, 4-2, decided on a single and a fielder's choice; and Game Four, the only real blowout for Cleveland, was the result of one atrocious inning that began only after a sure double play ball took an unfortunate bounce. Meanwhile all four of the Sox victories were blowouts (10-5, 7-1, 12-2, 11-2). So it appears that the best team clearly won the pennant, no matter the jumbled order in which they reached it. The lesson, we suppose, is that good teams are capable of looking very bad at times, but this does not necessarily make them any less of a team; it simply makes them unlucky.

Oh yes, and one more valuable lesson: Don't sleep on the Red Sox.

This surely is the one the Indians, their fans, and the rest of the American League will not soon forget. The statistical evidence here is quite enough, as we realize that since 2003 the Red Sox are an astounding 12-2 when facing playoff elimination. This number is difficult to comprehend (particularly given the somewhat unfortunate circumstances surrounding one of those two losses), yet it leads us nicely back to this idea about the lessons of history. For even though it was not because of 2004 that the Sox were able to come back in 2007, it nonetheless probably didn't hurt. As by then both the Sox and their fans had within the memory of 2004 enough historical background to get themselves to *if*. This wasn't the case in 2004, when no team had ever come back from a similar deficit and the Sox were asking themselves (as we were asking them) to do something with no historical precedence whatsoever. Not this time. This time the team and its fans could trace the patterns of history far enough along to find our way out of the gloom of 3-1, and back to the comforting mantra of *if*... If we could win Game Five, *then*... If we could get back to Fenway, *we might*... If we could force a Game Seven, *we could*...

They could, they did, they have. And now they and we are all headed back to the World Series. Having swept the Angels in the ALDS with considerable style, having stormed back from near elimination in the ALCS to force and then win Game Seven, we start to sense a very familiar pattern developing. And tracing that pattern out to the first pitch of Game One on Wednesday night we find ourselves once again at the impasse of *if*. Where we are freed by the comforts of history to speculate what we know from experience to be true; and with an eager eye to the World Series we repeat it to ourselves: *If* only they would... *If* only they could...*If* they can, well, *then*...

World Series, Game One

World Series
Game One

St. Louis at Fenway
23 October 2004

Among baseball fans, they are the magic words. The ones said in a low, hesitant whisper and rarely at that. Certainly not in the loose, alternate cap days of Spring Training, when among fans they are *that which shall not be spoken*. Perhaps now and again they will be floated out by eager fans in the bright, cheerful, effervescent days of April and May when some heady home sweep ends with a Sunday walk-off, and the bounce of optimism which carries us into the street mixes with a stomach full of cold domestic beer and the warm spring air and out it comes, those words heard loud and clear over Yawkey Way. Summer is different, the silky warm Fenway nights tempered by a series of drawn-out road losses, and the words only ever heard with incredulity and criticism and perhaps even resignation. And then not at all, as into August the heat rises and the humidity sinks over the grandstand and we pluck our shirt from our chest and fan ourselves with our scorecard, and by September the games have become rigorous, nervy affairs *to be got through*. As it all suddenly becomes very, very serious. Never in this clime will those two words be uttered by any fan who wishes to avoid a swift checking glance, a survey of Red Sox history recent and not-so recent, and (in all likelihood) a cautionary tale born of experience. Then one day the air turns crisp, the jackets and hooded sweatshirts and gloves are pulled on, the wins and losses together equal one-sixty-two, and with a rustle the calendar page turns over once more and there it is, *October*. The red white and blue bunting is hung, the field is painted, and the potent excitement of an entire month is distilled down to some extremely concentrated form in which every game is a season unto itself, every inning a game of rising and falling hopes. Here the words are often heard but never spoken, and it takes a tremendous, concentrated effort to shun them from conversation and even thought. They are, after all, right there. Almost. Just four games. Just two games. One game—just *one* game—away. And then, it happens.

And you find yourself at Logan late one night, weary from lack of sleep yet pacing baggage claim with a bounce of excitement; your only sibling arrives on a flight booked in the middle of the night; and the next morning you are walking out the door dressed for an October night, wearing new (special occasion, good luck) Sox hats, and with a rather large envelope zipped in a secure pocket and held close to the body at all times. The day is spent happily in Kenmore, Downtown, Harvard Square, Back Bay, and late in the afternoon back down on the Green Line where the conductor announces the next stop is Kenmore Square home of...and mocks our rivals and draws laughs from his passengers, then up into the now gathering crowd to several local establishments each one closer than the next; the sun setting between each ID check and entry; the crowd doubling and trebling in size and enthusiasm with each exit back onto the rollicking sidewalk. And towards the gates you go, removing the envelope from its pocket with great care, opening it, sliding out the two tickets and handing one, with unspoken ceremony, to your brother. Smiles. Heads shake. Printed on the ticket is *Game 1*, and this always an exciting prospect; but you have looked right past it to *the* words. With a silent understated nod you move to the gates, wait your turn, and with your mind racing to take in more and more detail and your entire body feeling lighter, a bit detached, almost like sleep, you *click* through the turnstile and onto a packed Yawkey. You turn to your brother. Together, you have arrived. And now the words can be said with sincerity and meaning, the way they ought to be said, the way we have wanted to say them since we first knew of their existence how many years ago.

Every sphere of life has its magic words, and so too baseball, whose two most enchanted words are said now as we pass into the crowd and can you believe it, here we are—at the *World. Series.*

One expects it to be different, and it is. The lights are brighter, the grill smoke richer, the beer colder; the faces filling Yawkey brighter and donned with even more numerous and far newer Sox hats. The voices filling the air louder and happier and more constant. Even the tall stalk of a young man hawking scorecards at the corner (the same tall stalk, hawking the same scorecards, on the same corner he has been at all season) seems to tower a few inches higher than normal, and call out *hey World Series scorecards here!* with a fuller, more dignified pitch. We nudge through it all to the open Gate D and down its patchwork ramp, into the concourse.

Then things begin to happen, things which do not happen on an ordinary night at the ballpark. We stand there and greet a friend, and while talking are interrupted by *hey isn't that*, as the club's confident young General Manager strolls by in the crowd, casual as can be. At the elevator we find ourselves flanking a dapper gentleman with a trim little moustache and wearing an immaculate pinstripe suit, a few inches shorter than both of us but with an immensely dignified presence about him; as one would expect given that he has won two World Series rings himself, is in the Baseball Hall of Fame, and is generally considered to be the greatest second baseman to ever play the game. On the way up we chide him a bit about his pick for the Series (he has the Cards in six), and share a laugh. It is no ordinary night. Reporters known by face linger about the ramps on cell phones, former Red Sox players pass through the crowd here and there, drawing double-takes. We are all of us part of a giant World Series mural wherein the entire baseball and Red Sox community has come home to celebrate. Among them are friends, closer acquaintances, those with whom we have gone through the season game by game, night by night, for this. There are smiles, hugs, and the like. Everyone moves with purpose, everyone speaks with that special kick to the end of each sentence that lets you know it is every bit as brilliant as they expected, too.

With no small ceremony we climb the ramp into the grandstand, and there find old Fenway all dressed up. Again the floodlights are most certainly brighter. The gleam off the players' helmets clearer, the bunting around the backstop and hanging from the suites balcony redder, whiter, bluer. And the ballpark itself crisp, sharp, startling in how vivid every detail leaps out from its pale green background. (Part of this is atmospheric, of course. It is late autumn and there is essentially no humidity in the air; meaning no diluting of smells or diffusion of far away objects through tiny particles of moisture, giving everything that characteristic crispness of autumn which the season is far too brief to ever grow accustomed to. So that is part of it. But there are other factors as well.) We should take a picture, and do. Right here is good with the Monster in back and sir, *would you mind?* Thank you we appreciate it. Oh that's great, but, actually, *maybe another.* Just in case. You think? Sure that works. *Thanks a lot.* Farther down there's the Pesky Pole (necessarily closer and glowing a brighter yellow than ever), and another picture is taken and this with an impossibly wide smile. Over there in center is a stage, the Dropkick Murphys we think, setting up. And finally to our section and our row where there are more friendly faces, and more *can you believe it*'s, and finally we take our familiar seats low in the center field bleachers among a now full house at Fenway where it all starts with Carl Beane's baritone voice calling out *Ladies and Gentlemen, Boys and Girls, Welcome to Fenway Park, America's Most Beloved Ballpark, for Game One of the World Series, between the National League Champion St. Louis Cardinals, and your American League Champion, Boston, Red Sox.* And we all cheer.

Both lineups are announced, one by one, every name its own event; the anthem is sung by an iconic rock star and after it the roar of a stealth bomber (unseen, of course) goes hurtling overhead and reverberates within. First pitches are thrown by the Mount Rushmore of Red Sox greats, *play ball!* is shouted out over the loudspeakers, the Red Sox take the field at a sprint, there is a nervous chill of anticipation as all is set as it should be, Tim Wakefield steps back, throws, and the entire ballpark lights up with a thousand sparkling lights.

Then a baseball game is played. We are sure of it. Pitches are thrown, swings are taken, balls are hit afield. Strikes, outs, hits, runs, errors, pitching changes; they all happen. Only they do not seem to happen individually, but instead as a rapid flicker of brightly lit baseball slides. Another run, *click*, another out, *click*, another hit, *click*, another close play at first. On and on, without intermission. More focused than ever on each pitch, literally leaning forward and concentrating, we somehow look too close and in the process miss something. All of a sudden the Red Sox have scored (there is much rejoicing), and scored again (ditto), and have taken a good size lead in the game before we even realize what is going on. It all seems to happen way, way too fast. In actuality it is merely the game as it is, as we always watch it, which is to say in sequence. Each pitch a slight adjustment of the situation, each out and hit and walk a subtle readjustment (one click on the knob) of this game's particular dynamic. Only there is no *slight* or *subtle* tonight. Every single pitch is *Game One of the 2004 World Series*. Gone then is the buffer of casual thought and easy conversation which smoothes an inning into one seamless narrative thread. Instead we bore in close; and by turning each pitch into an event, we lose the whole. So it is no wonder that (Damon doubles Cabrera is hit Ortiz hits a long euphoric home run Millar doubles Mueller singles him in) and *all of a sudden* the Red Sox have a 4-0 lead in Game One of the World Series.

At which point a fan behind us turns to his friend, both of whom we know from a season of conversing, and is overheard to say, *I feel like I'm going to wake up tomorrow and turn on the tv and realize this was the World Series.* We all agree. For as surreal as the experience around and immediately within the ballpark has been—as recognizably heightened—the game itself is shockingly familiar, known, almost ordinary. Sure there is the bunting; there is the logo far back behind home plate; and there are the two ladies, mother and daughter, who huddle within the very first pair of fur coats we have ever seen in the bleachers, their knees covered with a thick and expensive-looking knit blanket. (It is, almost incidentally, freezing out. Winter cold. And there are extra layers, hats, gloves, ear muffs, visible breath, and a great deal of blowing on hands throughout the bleachers and ballpark. All of which we have forgotten, in our considerable excitement, to either notice or mind.) And it is most assuredly a different crowd, even than other playoff games. Better-heeled, chattier, slower to react; all the familiar traits you always hear about Series crowds. So there's that. And there's our ticket which is roughly eight times the size of a normal ticket; and maybe a barely discernable patch on each player's uniform; and yes of course the fact that they are playing the National League Cardinals, in October. But that's about it. Otherwise, and most certainly when one only watches the ball in play, it looks more or less exactly like the same Fenway Park, and the same Red Sox running about it, as we saw in our very first game here (watched with similarly rapt interest, next to this same sibling, in seats not so very far from where we sit now). What is missing it seems is some sort of defining touch, some special lens or keynote capable of distinguishing what we are watching here from everything we have watched before. We need, that is, some constant reminder of this being the World Series.

And we find it, eventually but happily, in the very words themselves. It begins like this: *Let's grab another round.* Nod of approval. (pause). Perhaps we should rephrase that: *let's grab another round, at the World Series.* And that's it. From here on out the goal is to work those two words into as many sentences, with as much frequency, and each time said with the same slow lingering pleasure, as our imagination allows for. Want another dog, *at the World Series?* Sure, we'll have a dog, *at the World Series.* Hey that guy with the sign is getting thrown out. Not just getting thrown out, he's getting thrown out, *at the World Series.* Man this is turning into some game. Sorry, what was that? Pardon; this is turning into some *World Series* game. And so on. It is as if after being denied the ability to mention the words throughout the offseason and season we now, in their appropriate context, look to roll them over in our mouths a bit, to savor them as a kind of verbal nod to the palpable, irrepressible otherness of the night. What it becomes is our small way of actively celebrating both the event and our tremendous good fortune to being a part of it. That is it to say it becomes our way of doing what one is always told to do in these situations—which is to enjoy it.

Even when it brings bad news, as it eventually does in the top of the third when the Cardinals put two runs on the board (Larry Walker homers) to make it 4-2. Especially when it brings good news, as it once again does in the bottom of the third when the Sox *suddenly* (Mueller walks Mirabelli singles Bellhorn walks Damon singles Cabrera singles and Manny grounds out but brings in a run) add three more to make it 7-2. Even when the top of the fourth seems to take an awful long time (Edmonds walks Reggie Sanders walks Tony Womack walks to load the bases Mike Matheny sacrifices to right scoring Edmonds and Sanders scores on a throwing error by Millar and Womack scores on a ground out by So Taguchi) and for some reason so does the sixth (Taguchi singles and moves to second on an Arroyo error Rentería doubles him in and is doubled in by Walker) and the same fan behind us turns to his friend and asks, with legitimate inquiry in his voice, *Did we just blow a five run lead in the World Series?*

We did.

Somehow we managed it, and had it happened in any normal game we would surely be shaking our heads and muttering all sorts of unpleasant little epitaphs under our breaths; but somehow the brilliant shimmer of *special* cast over the game makes the whole mess of an inning slightly surreal, as if it were happening in some high budget baseball movie, rather than on the dirt and grass before us. It is the oddest thing. For there have been many a late summer Tuesday night in which we sat in this very seat and practically howled at some innocently blown two run lead. And yet tonight, by far the single most important game we have ever watched at Fenway, we sit silently in our seat, and blink. It is if the regal setting of the game itself has somehow absorbed our greater sporting passions, and left us staring mouth-open at the events which seem to move quickly and haphazardly before us. So that while the astounding inning and a half sequence which begins immediately after the stretch really does happen and really does register in our perception—we know, even as it is taking place, that this is incredible baseball drama—we watch and bemoan and cheer it all in something of a blur. As Bellhorn walks to lead off the seventh and (Cabrera walks Manny singles scoring Bellhorn and Ortiz reaches on an infield single that scores Cabrera to make it 9-7 Sox before Timlin comes on in the eighth and gives up a single to Matheny before he is relieved by Embree who gives up a single to Cedeño and is immediately relieved by Foulke who gives up a single to left and allows Jason Marquis who ran for Matheny to score on a throwing error by Manny before Walker hits a low liner to left that Manny *nearly breaks his leg* trying to catch but drops and allows Cedeño to score and tie the game and which causes the Sox to walk Pujols to load the bases with one out and a tie game in the eighth of the World Series before Foulke gets Rolen to pop out and Edmonds to ground out to end the inning and after an out and an infield error allows Varitek to reach first Mark Bellhorn comes back up) again in the bottom of the eighth, with one out and one on, and with Game One of the World Series now tied, 9-9.

Here the game pulls into focus. Slows. Takes a deep breath. Leans forward. You can almost feel the great eye of fan interest sharpening plateward, the television cameras panning in, the voices of the radio announcers rising an octave, and the players bearing in that much more on each and every pitch. They know as well as we do: a moment is coming.

For while every World Series game is necessarily historic, not every one is distinct. The 10-2 blowout and 3-0 pitching gem are memorable as viewing experiences, certainly, but are not exactly World Series memories in the Classical Mode. Very few are. Yet each Series contains at least one or two moments—either a key hit in a big situation, a great individual play, or some crucial relief performance to save the day—which, when they happen in the right situation, at the right time, and most importantly in the World Series, become part of baseball legend. And no fans are more acutely aware of this fact than Red Sox fans, who after all have not only been a witness to one of the very brightest, most memorable World Series images of all time, but also one of the very bleakest. Both are replayed *ad nauseam* and probably always will be; both are signature moments in the history of the sport; both happened late in close games (one of them involving the very foul pole we can now glance to our right and see). Tied in the eighth, it becomes almost inevitable that another such moment, good or bad, will happen before us tonight.

Julian Tavárez stands on the mound for the Cardinals. Mark Bellhorn stands in for the Sox. All season long it has been boom or bust for the Red Sox small, sleepy-eyed, straggly-haired second baseman, who has struck out more times than anyone in the American League but has nonetheless come up with some of the biggest hits of the season for the Sox. Most notably one extremely important home run in Game Six of the ALCS on a ball which just did clip the left field foul pole at Yankee Stadium. Here, after a strike looking makes it 0-1, he swings and pulls a ball high and deep down the right field line we are all up on our feet and shouting for it to stay fair come on and then, when it hooks into the seats—just foul—let out a collective groan and smack our hands together. Almost.

It is a ball which neatly sums up Bellhorn's entire season. All or nothing, hero or goat, gone or foul. All of which was, on this particular ball, made that much more gripping by our particular angle on the play. From straightaway center field our view to the right field foul pole is almost exactly perpendicular to the fist base line; meaning that on a ball hit straight down the line we have almost no depth perception as to whether it is off the line or behind it, hooking slightly or staying true. Even when the ball passes behind the foul pole it does so at a speed and distance from us which makes it hard to discern; and we end up relying on the fans in the right field corner to let us know— history, or strike two? For us to tell immediately, for the reaction to be instantaneous joy, a ball in that direction would have to actually hit the foul pole directly. (Rather like that other World Series home run here at Fenway, which was also down the line and high up and hooking slightly, but just...)

Between pitches the charged currant of *almost* lingers in the pulse, built on and sustained by the still crucial situation of the game itself as Tavárez sets for the 0-2. Bellhorn waits. We watch. The ball is thrown and Bellhorn swings and there it is again, just as before the ball sailing high and glowing white down the right field line, plenty high enough and all the speed and she just needs to stay fair *come on come on stay fair ball* as it soars out under the lights and races across the clear night sky—stops, midair. Falls straight down. And lands with one soft bounce on the outfield grass.

And so how *does* one celebrate a historic World Series home run? Is there a special cheer? Is there some sort of secret gesture or motion one makes? Are there different shouts, new ways of high-fiving, new facial expressions uniquely suited to conveying the special combination of joy and surprise when such a World Series moment literally falls out of the night sky? If there are, we know not. For all we can do when Bellhorn's home run hits the Pesky Pole is raise our hands as high above our heads as they will go, and open our eyes as wide as they will open, and shout as loud as we can shout a half-laughing cry of *Yeaa-hahahahha-ahhhh-ahhh!* Just as we always do. Perhaps we jump about a bit more, and high five more than the usual amount of strangers, and shake our head a few batters longer than normal, and throw our arm around our only sibling and say all sorts of semi-intelligible things about history and memory and the use of pattern as a dramatic devise in both the tragic and epic narrative structure, and so on. And yes find more ways to say the words *World Series*, in more sentences, than one would imagine possible over an inning and a half of more or less non-stop celebration. At the end of which Keith Foulke stands on the mound and we all stand around him clapping, shouting, calling for one more strike which is thrown, swung at and missed, and *all of a sudden* the Red Sox win Game One of the World Series, 11-9.

What then, after? Of course it all went by too fast, and was too wild (the game set the kinds of World Series records one don't necessarily want to own), and there will be a great many games in which the play-by-play details will be more accurately remembered than this one. Yet perhaps none which we will recall the experience so vividly, so presently, with so much still-living memory. It all has to do, it seems, with a sense of history.

For there are few moments in life that one walks into knowing, in advance, that history *will be made*. Election nights, perhaps. A wife going into labor (though that's hardly a date one can accurately print on a ticket). A coronation, maybe, but then there haven't been so many of those lately. Aside from which there are the major top-flight sporting championship. There is the World Series. Which we know is historical because we know, almost despite ourselves, its entire history. We know that Willie Mayes made a catch in the '54 World Series because we have been told how difficult that catch was a thousand times, and seen it replayed on a thousand highlight reels. We know who Bill Mazeroski is, and can picture him wheeling his helmet around as he sprints home. We know who has won it and who has gone a long time without getting close; we know that Don Larson did something no other player has ever done in it, and that Reggie did something no one ever even *thought* of doing. We know details about games played in the first decade of the last century because they were World Series games; know all about a crime committed during the Wilson administration because it was committed in the World Series; and we know the names of players who had mediocre careers with few highlights, only because one of those highlights came during the World Series. And we can picture Carlton Fisk waving his arms down the first base line as if we were in the stands watching him. Why? Because this is the oral tradition and visual history of baseball as it has been passed down to us. Because our mothers and fathers and older brothers love the game. Because a handful of superb storytellers have occupied World Series press boxes. Because its events determine which teams, and which names, and which moments will become part of the cultural baseball narrative. Because one-hundred-and-one years ago Bostonians and baseball fans and everyday Americans cared about who won Game One of the World Series in Boston. Because one-hundred-and-one years later we still care not only who won that World Series, but who won in (19)'08 and '12 and '24 and '26 and '55 and '69 and '75 and '81 and '86 and '90 and '93 and '01. And because one-hundred-and-one years from now Bostonians, baseball fans, and everyday Americans will still want to know and read about and actually *care* that the Boston Red Sox defeated the St. Louis Cardinals, 11-9, on the 23rd of October, 2004.

Which is why one takes the extra pause to examine the oversized ticket; why one takes long looks around familiar grandstands and bleachers for some special glean of *championship*; why we could not help but shake our heads and laugh when we said, we're here, *we're at the World Series*. Because of course as kids we had said, someday, we would be. Like all kids who love baseball do. For even then there is a sense that what happens at that level (so far above what happens even in the playoffs, and back then distinguished by being on *national television*), is somehow more permanent, more official, more proper than the ordinary Sunday afternoon at the ballpark. It is not something that can be explained or understood if one only peeks in through the flashbulbs now and again when the right team is involved; or if one spends the summer at the beach or by the pool and then (when those pleasures are out of season) gives up a slow night to watch the Big Game. No, it is not something which will mean all that much unless you have lived with it through several seasons. Not unless the word *October* means something special to you, and draws to mind visions of bunting, and cold nights, and mobs of players piling onto each other before the mound. It is a sense (the historical sense) which develops only over time, and with it the leveling realization that history is not something which is only read and recited but can in fact be experienced—that it is not always and ever a glance backward. It can be felt. And seen. And shouted at with great joy. And can leave one sitting with one's only sibling on a bench in an empty T station, very late at night, waiting for the Orange Line. Exhausted and elated, leaning back, hands in pockets, brand new specially bought good luck Sox hats turned backwards, muttering into the cold night air. What a game, huh? (Pause, smile.) What a *World. Series.*

Souvenir

World Series
Game Two

Colorado at Fenway
25 October 2007

It hardly seems possible for any seven game series, much less a World Series—with its inherent season-long accumulation of momentum and confidence and career years—to be decided within four hitters of its opening pitch; but this October, it happened all the same.

Two days after the Red Sox's furious revival in the ALCS, and eight days after the Rockies' tidy sweep of the NLCS (which achievement won them eight days of being asked whether the eight days off might make them a bit rusty, eight days to say no they didn't think the eight days off would make them rusty at all, and eight days of follow-up questions about how they plan to deal with the inevitable rust from eight days off), the 2007 World Series finally opens in Boston on a cool October night and under the light but persistent threat of rain. The rains have held off during the extended pre-game ceremonies, allowing Maestro John Williams to lead a detachment of the Boston Pops through the National Anthem and then a video tribute both to Williams's oeuvre and the Red Sox playoff run (Josh Beckett set to *Jaws* and so on), followed by a jet flyover, the now ubiquitous 1967 Red Sox appearance, a first pitch from Yaz, *play ball!* from a youngster, and, eventually, a first pitch strike from Josh Beckett to Rockies' lead-off man Willy Taveras. And with a deep, fortifying breath we fans ready ourselves for another long and difficult series.

Until Beckett strikes out Tavares looking, strikes out Kaz Matsui swinging, then strikes out Matt Holliday swinging to end the inning, and leading off the bottom of the first Dustin Pedroia takes one big looping uppercut swing at the second pitch he sees and hits it high and deep to left, it bounces off the top of the Monster Seats for a leadoff home run, 1-0, Sox—and that's it. Whatever shaky constructs we fans may have built up to support the idea of these Rockies as formidable (*they're a team on a roll you know*) and this Series as a tough one (*most experts are saying six or even seven*) come crashing down around home plate as Pedroia strides across it and elbow-blocks Ortiz outside the dugout. We cheer, we relax, and whether because of '04 or because we have the momentum or simply because we have the better team, deep down in our most instinctual baseball hearts we know: *we're going to win this thing, going away.*

This admittedly brash self-assurance is not dampened by the hazy veil of light rain through which we watch the next three innings, and is only encouraged by two additional runs the Sox tack on in the first, one more in the second, two more in the fourth, and the reaffirmation of our complete and total faith in Josh Beckett (at this point as close to a sure thing as there is in baseball) who breezes through the first five innings allowing only a run on three hits. So that by the bottom of the fifth we find ourselves, at 6-1 Sox, trying to make an argument for why this series will still be competitive and why we should not feel overly confident or assured or as generally pleased with our team and its situation as we undeniably do.

Just around the time we are piecing this idea together, Rockies starter Jeff Francis is relieved by Franklin Morales to begin the fifth. Where Julio Lugo leads off with a single, is then erased by a Jacoby Ellsbury fielder's choice, and when Pedroia pops up for the second out Morales is one out away from having stabilized both the score and game for the Rockies. Then, the deluge. In order: Youkilis doubles to score Ellsbury, Ortiz doubles to score Youkilis, Manny singles to score Ortiz, Lowell doubles, Varitek is intentionally walked to load the bases, and then, after a pitching change (Ryan Speier for the shell-shocked Morales), three straight bases loaded walks make it 13-1 and thus effectively end the competitive portion of Game One.

* * *

Game Two a night later provides both better baseball and, for a time, better conditions under which to enjoy it. This time it is James Taylor singing the national anthem, a 13-year old heart transplant survivor (accompanied by Dwight Evans) throwing out the first pitch, and Curt Schilling taking a long ceremonial walk in from the Red Sox bullpen to appreciative if somewhat tepid applause. Before crossing over into foul territory he gives a long look up and removing his cap tips it to the crowd, a gesture not typically included in the rigorous pregame routine we have come to know so well. (One of the indelible Fenway images of Schilling is that of him standing on the bullpen mound, absolutely still as he looks up at the scoreboard clock; the moment the digits roll over he turns to his catcher and makes his first throw. Exactly fifteen minutes before first pitch and not a second sooner, every single time). The tip of the cap is a sign. Easily the most history-conscious player we have ever watched, perhaps the single most *self*-conscious player we have ever know, he is as aware as we are that this is likely it—curtains for The Curt Schilling Show at Fenway Park.

If so it does not open on a promising note. Schilling's 1-2 pitch to Taveras leading off the game shoots up and in and nicks the back of his hand, landing Taveras on first where he remains after a Kaz Matsui fly out. Matt Holliday, broad-faced and broad-shouldered, a right fielder trapped in a tailback's body, is next for the Rockies and rips a hard drive down the third base line that Mike Lowell leaps at fully extended, only to have it kick off the end of his glove. A groan escapes the crowd as the ball rolls into foul territory, followed by a volley of sudden cries as we pick up Taveras rounding second and now bearing down hard on an unoccupied third. Lowell scrambles down the ball and throws to an onrushing Schilling, but ball and pitcher zips past each other with the latter awkwardly throwing out his glove, and the former rolling innocently to the vacant mound. Taveras lands on third, Holliday jogs into second, and we mutter to ourselves, *where was Schilling?*

Watching, it turns out. It was a quick reflex play and not one a pitcher is typically involved in, but there is little question that had Schilling covered immediately it would have been a close play on

Taveras who, if the bag were covered, might not have chanced it at all. Helton then grounds hard to first and Youkilis, playing back, takes the out and by doing so concedes the run. The Rockies take a 1-0 lead on a hit-by-pitch, a single, a physical error by Lowell and a mental error by Schilling. Not a good start.

The Sox go down in order in the first, and the crowd at Fenway grows quiet and uneasy. The Sox fans uneasy because Schilling has not come out looking particularly sharp, the neutrals quiet because of their neutrality, and both sets apprehensive that the three-game celebratory party spanning the last weekend of the ALCS and the first game of the World Series has suddenly (with a final tab of 36-5) come to an end. A few hopeful *Let's*-Go, *Red*-Sox chants blossom up in the second, only to fade out quickly within the otherwise silent and shifting crowd.

(It is both predictable and in all likelihood unnecessary to add yet another chorus to the old *World Series crowd apathy* song. Nevertheless a note on the peculiarity of each Series crowd is a baseball tradition we cannot ignore. And so yes, this year's Series crowd is, like many before it, undeniably older, richer, and (yes) whiter than their regular season counterparts. And has been, as we have come to expect, somewhat curiously inconsistent in their baseball interest. Before Game One they gave a loud cheer to a pre-arranged video montage and, moments later, quietly watched Jason Varitek stride across the outfield to the bullpen, foregoing the mandatory standing ovation the captain usually receives upon his entrance. Later they managed a good solid *Fraaaaan*-cis, *Fraaaaan*-cis taunt directed at Rockies starter Jeff Francis, only to later distinguish themselves by continuing the good solid *Fraaaaan*-cis, *Fraaaaan*-cis taunt in the general direction of Rockies reliever Franklin Morales. For an entire inning. They shouted out for Mike Lowell to *hit a grand slam* with runners on first and second; held up large and not so very clever signs in the middle of key at bats; crowded the aisles to get their pictures taken in the middle of innings; and yes, left early. All more or less standard, well-documented behavior for the oddest and most expensive crowd of the season. All as quietly disheartening as ever.)

Whatever its basis, in this situation the crowd's apprehension is justified. In their first seven playoff games at Fenway the Sox have scored at least one run in the first inning six times. The only game they failed do so before tonight, Game Two of the ALCS, is coincidentally the only one of the seven they lost. So there is reason for concern, and precedent for the discomfort we feel watching a young starter—this time Colorado's rookie fireballer, Ubaldo Jiménez—work his way through the Sox lineup, forever allowing runners but never runs.

His closest call and our best opportunity come in the third, when with two outs and nobody on Jiménez walks Pedroia on four pitches; then, with the Red Sox bullpen percussionists beating out a rhythm in fine tune, he runs the count full and walks Youkilis too. (The brainchild of youngsters Clay Buchholz and Manny Delcarmen, who during one longish September game found out, in the type of discovery only 22-year-old boys with too much time on their hands can make, that banging water bottles against the top metal ledge of the bullpen made a surprisingly loud clang, the bullpen percussionists have rapidly developed into a crisp well-conducted outfit, usually involving the entire bullpen in one long coordinated drumline. Undoubtedly adolescent behavior, it is also undoubtedly charming. And the sight of the two bullpens side by side in the World Series—the Rockies scattered and dour with hands stuffed in pockets, the Red Sox all in a row and concentrating on a clearly rehearsed routine of water bottle banging— is striking and perhaps somewhat telling.) The back-to-back walks by Jiménez give the Sox their first legitimate scoring opportunity of the night, and with Ortiz up the crowd rallies to its feet and its first concerted Let's-*Go*, Red-*Sox* chant (perfectly in time with their bullpen rhythm section). Jiménez, who is long and lean, wears retro white-wall stirrups, and throws more or less upright and very hard, comes right at Ortiz who opens up and launches a high drive to right that looks like it might be but at the last instant hooks imperceptibly foul. The crowd directly beneath the Pesky Pole waves hopefully towards the field but both the fans behind them, who had a better view, and Ortiz, who shakes his head as he slows up the line, know better. *Just* missed. On the next pitch Ortiz strikes out looking and as we shuffle back into

our seats a palpable ripple of apprehension runs through the grandstand, carrying along the faint but irresistible notion that it just might
be that kind of night for the Sox.

As it turns out, in yet another sign of how special this particular
October has become for the Red Sox, it is J.D. Drew, of all people, who
is the first to revive our hopes that it is not. With one out in the fifth
and the Sox still hitless Mike Lowell draws a walk and Drew, up next,
pulls a ball up and over the second baseman and into shallow right
field. A clear single, Lowell takes off for second and then, surprising
everyone including the Rockies, lowers his head, sweeps hard around
the bag and digs for third. Worried shouts go up from the crowd as
Matt Hawpe's throw comes sailing in from right and Lowell sprints in
and dives headfirst to the outside of the bag just as the ball is caught
and swept over, too late. A relieved cheer replaces the shouts as Drew
moves up to second on the throw, and all of a sudden the Sox are onto
a big inning.

And while the full scale restoration of J.D. Drew continues to
astound fans who ought to know better (the cycle of criticizing Terry
Francona for sticking with a talented but struggling regular only to
later praise him for doing the same has become something of an October tradition here in Boston), in this particular situation it is the veteran Mike Lowell who deserves credit for the decisive, game changing
play. Softly hit and only marginally towards the gap, Drew's ball was
a clean single but no more. The kind of ball on which a runner at first
instinctually runs out a few steps then slows and half-jogs into second.
Not Lowell, who running hard peeked over his right shoulder and,
finding Hawpe rounding the ball rather than charging onto it, kicked
hard through the bag to third. Hawpe, who has a strong arm, made a
good hard throw but to the wrong side of the bag, allowing Lowell,
who is not a fast runner but makes up for it by being a *smart* runner,
to slide wide and grab the bag safely with his left hand. A veteran
move all the way, it is the kind of baseball play we enjoy because it
takes that careful combination of perception and cunning and instinctual decision-making which separates the mere athlete from the genuine ballplayer. Lowell is one of the latter, and one of the best, and his

clear understanding of this game and how it is properly played earn the Red Sox their best scoring chance of the night. Fittingly, Drew's hit and Lowell's opportunistic baserunning are instantly rewarded as Varitek lifts a long fly ball to center, plenty deep enough to score Lowell from third and tie the game, 1-1. *Way to go Mikey.*

After Schilling works around a lead-off walk in the fifth, Jiménez returns in the bottom half and records two quick outs in Pedroia and Ortiz. At this point the Rockies rookie is quietly working on a remarkable performance, having given up one run on one hit through 4 ⅔ innings—in the World Series, on the road, against a team that has scored thirty-six runs in their last three games. But he is tiring, and as he tires he grows wild. He walks Ortiz, gives up a single to Manny, and with two outs and Lowell stepping to the plate he is suddenly in a jam. And for the Sox it is the right time, and the right situation, with the right man at the plate. Lowell sets his stance, pulls his hands back on an inside breaking ball and rips a low hooking shot over third it shoots down towards the corner, scoring Ortiz easily, chasing Jiménez from the game, and giving the Red Sox their first lead of the night at 2-1.

And that's it for the hitters. With Jiménez out and Schilling on his way, the remainder of this suddenly taut World Series game is to be decided by the opposing bullpens—by the men staring out at the field on one side, and, on the other, a group of young men currently testing out the audible banging-properties of various bullpen materials. Before it comes to this though Schilling returns for the top of the sixth.

It is, even going in, his last inning of the night and therefore very likely his last inning in a Red Sox uniform. He gets Matsui to pop up to short but allows a single to Holliday (his third in three at bats), then walks Helton. There is a long lull. Then, finally, Francona steps out of the dugout, hands in jacket, and walks to the mound. He reaches out, Schilling hands him the ball, and the ovation begins. And the player who hosted the most famous Thanksgiving dinner in Red Sox history; the wearer of the bloody sock and the winner of 58 games in a Red Sox uniform; the pitcher who has said much and done more; the man who is easy to be inspired by, easy to be irritated by, and impossible to ignore; the Big Schill, Curt on a Car Phone, *Curtis Publicis*, who came to Boston to win a World Series and did, now walks off the Fenway Park mound and steps over the first base line, and with the standing ovation rising throughout the ballpark removes his cap and waves it up with a flourish to the crowd and to his family high above. A few steps later he descends into the dugout, his night and possibly his Sox career over after delivering a big start in a big game, one last time.

In to replace one of the greatest World Series pitchers of all time is lefty reliever Hideki Okajima, the first ever Japanese-born pitcher to appear in a World Series game. Always a distinguishing moment to be the first of anything in 103 years of history, Okajima immediately sets about making certain it will be his performance, and not his nationality, that is remembered most. Working deliberately and efficiently he forces Garrett Atkins to ground out to first, then comes back to strike out Hawpe who flails helplessly at a pinpoint changeup, and Okajima walks off the field under a tremendous ovation and is greeted, on the top step, by Schilling. After a scoreless bottom half Okajima returns for the seventh where he continues spotting pitches and continues recording outs. Tulowitzki flies out to right; Torrealba grounds to short; and with two outs he works designated hitter Ryan Spilborghs into a 2-2 count before delivering what might be his single best pitch of the entire season—an absolutely gorgeous changeup on the inside corner, right at the hands, buckling Spilborghs knees— strike three and inning over. Spilborghs never had a chance.

Meanwhile two significant events take place in the bottom of the sixth and seventh, neither concerning the game on the field yet both significant moments in this particular World Series game and this particular October. With two outs in the sixth, a runner on third and Youkilis at the plate, the fan standing next to us suddenly and inexplicably and right in between pitches, goes nuts. He leaps into the air, pounds his friends on the shoulders, and shouts *touchdown! touchdown! touchdown!* over and over again. And only then do we notice the pair of thin white cords running from the sides of his blue Red Sox hat, down the length of his yellow Boston College sweatshirt, into his back pocket and by proxy to the events coming from Blacksburg, VA, where the second ranked Eagles are playing eighth ranked Virginia Tech. The Eagles, it turns out, have completed a last gasp third-and-twenty with eleven seconds left and won, 14-10. The BC fan to our right leans over the railing (we are on the Right Field Roof overhang, peering over the bleachers), finds a knot of burgundy and yellow clad friends down below, and with Game Two of the World Series as background raises his arms high and straight. *Touchdown.*

The second event of significance comes an inning later, when, with Manny leading off the bottom of the eighth, the air temperature at Fenway dramatically plummets. A seasonable 48-degrees and clear at game time, it has thus far been a cold but not uncomfortable night of autumn baseball. October weather. World Series weather. But all that changes in the seventh when within the span of a few pitches fans begin to bunch their shoulders and blow on their hands. Some fidget back and forth on their feet, others rub their hands together or tuck them across their bodies. Fans around us are still talking football, and suddenly we can see our breath. The baseball season is running out.

Under these conditions Okajima returns for the top of the eighth. (By this point the Rockies bullpen, uptight or no, has managed two and a third scoreless innings to hold the game at 2-1.) Already having thrown an inning and a third, Okajima has been precise enough to keep his pitch count down and with Papelbon warming in the bullpen now sets himself to work against the top of the Rockies order. He strikes out Taveras for the first out; then, against his seventh batter of the night and with the crowd rising to its feet, strikes out Kaz Matsui swinging to end a truly remarkable World Series performance. With Holliday coming up, Francona goes to Papelbon, and the ovation for Okajima's effort is instantaneous and heartfelt.

Of all the Red Sox players who exceeded expectation this season— from Beckett to Lowell to Pedroia—none has been greeted with greater astonishment or welcomed with greater delight than Okajima. After giving up a home run with his first Major League pitch on Opening Day, the pitcher who seemed destined to forever be *the other Japanese guy* has surprised us all. A memorable save in the first Red

Sox-Yankees game of the season (striking out Jeter for the final out) made his name with the home fan, and a dominating first half performance made him into an All-Star. His utility to the club has been almost incalculable, perhaps matched only by the tremendous affection the mentioning of his name inspires among Sox fans. With his awkward looping run from the bullpen and frenzied but oddly infectious theme song, his chunky red necklace and calm, almost serene mound presence (the casual walk behind the mound, the deliberate exhale between each pitch), and of course the fact that he has been unfailingly reliable in getting a close game from the hand of a tiring starter to the hand of a fresh Papelbon, has endeared him to the hearts of Red Sox fans everywhere. And on this night his two and a third innings of no-hit relief, taking a 2-1 lead from Schilling and handing it intact to Papelbon, is perhaps the first truly memorable pitching performance of this World Series. A pat on the back from his manager and teammates, and off the mound he walks under a tremendous standing ovation—pride of his club, pride of his country.

Four outs to go, and still plenty to do despite the fact that Okajima's performance and Papelbon's entrance have awakened Fenway from its shivering hibernation. As Papelbon warms and the Dropkick Murphy's "Shipping Up to Boston" blares out, a pair of fans on the roof deck dance an impromptu (and largely improvised) Irish jig, while in the bleachers below an ingenious cutout sign of Papelbon is held up, legs swinging in time below; and the guy to our right, a BC man and one of the touchdown celebrators, shakes his head and with his breath slipping out visible beneath the floodlights, says, to no one in particular, *this is incredible.*

Papelbon goes to work, and after getting two fastballs by Holliday tries a third, only this time the MVP candidate catches up and shoots it back up the middle for a single. There is a lull in the crowd, and a sinking realization of how very close this game still is. One good hit is all it would take (to even the score or, depending on how good the hit, the series as well), and with the Rockies' perennial All-Star at the plate the mood seems to tighten upon itself. For this is the critical at bat. Todd Helton steps in, Holliday takes his lead off first, Papelbon sets and then suddenly spins and throws to first where Youkilis slaps a tag on the diving Holliday and—*got him*—like that, it's over. The inning, the threat, the game, and in the ecstatic celebratory singing (*I've been inclined to believe...*) the Series itself.

For the time being only these first two prove true, followed closely by the third as Papelbon returns for the ninth, strikes out Helton, and gets Atkins to fly out to center. With two outs in the bottom of the ninth and Papelbon on the only question is *how* it will end, and five pitches later it does, in considerable style, with Hawpe swinging and missing for strike three, the 2-1 win, and the indomitable 2-0 Series lead.

As always, the crowd will carry us out. It is one of the curious features of attending a game at Fenway that although we all arrive at different times, by way of our own particular routes and at our own particular pace, we all leave together, shoulder to shoulder, shuffling along the same narrow concourse. It is a kind of recessional, this half-step walk through the ballpark, and as such tends to take on the specific tone of the game just witnessed. Tonight it is at first celebratory, buoyant, chatty, and then, as we continue on, quieter. On the field to our right the grounds crew in red sweatshirts and jackets jog across the diamond, cluster with long handled tools on the mound and around the batter's box, and begin their night's work of preservation. Down near the field a trio of smiling fans bunch together as a security guard snaps a flash in their direction. The concession stands to our left are empty. The old wooden seats of the grandstands proper are in disarray, half up and half down, their blue chipped slats and red iron bars having weathered another nine. Down below red plastic box seats gleam empty under the floodlights. Another couple has its picture taken over in the left field corner, the wall as backdrop. And a group lingering along the back is asked to move along. As the grounds crew continue to rake and sweep and unroll the tarp over in the outfield grass.

Closing time at Fenway Park. And as we continue around the grandstand and up the third base line—World Series logo stamped on the grass behind home plate, breath still visible, hands and feet and nose numb with winterish cold—one cannot help but feel as if a long and heavy curtain (necessarily Red Sox red) is being slowly drawn across the ballpark stage.

This is wildly presumptive, of course, given that the Red Sox still need two wins out of three, on the road, against the best team in the National League; and yet the impression remains nonetheless. Perhaps it comes merely from how very well this team has played over the last five increasingly crucial games; or from the by-now uncanny parallels between this October and October of 2004; or, more likely still, from the simple fact that this *feels* like an ending. A winter night, our breaths hanging visible, the summer players each taking their symbolic bows below—as a final act it has all the elements of resolution. And presumptive or not leaves one with the inescapable feeling that the entire production has taken its curtain call, and that our summer home must now be cleaned and prepared and ultimately closed up for the season.

Instinctively we slow down. Our half-step shuffle becomes an inching along. Although only to a point, as we are still a part of the larger crowd and therefore behind some and in front of others. Which means we must continue on, however reluctantly, up along the third base deck, glancing back to the field as our path scrolls along its length. Another flash before a smiling group. Closer to the stairs. We take one last look back to the brightly lit green of the field before we reach the stairs, Fenway disappears behind a pillar, and we are on our way down the steps.

Below, in the crowded Gate E delta, the descending flow of fans shift through a pair of long lines stretching out beyond a bank of retail stands. Where souvenirs, the attic bound ephemera of *occasion*, are being pointed to and paid for and carried away. (Which reminds us, as we excuse ourselves through their waiting lines, that we have purchased none. We have taken no pictures. We have bought no merchandise. And if we are correct in our bold impression of this being curtains on the 2007 World Series at Fenway Park, then it seems we will have arrived and left with no souvenirs at all. Nothing to hold, and nothing to show.) And still the crowd moves along, up the small steps to the open Gate E plateau where two tall hanger doors stand open onto Lansdowne and two security guards in blue jackets stare vacantly at the passing crowd. Gradually we are funneled down, half-step by half-step, the post-game press conference now on an enormous flatscreen television to our left, fans bunching in closer as we near the gate and the loud, full, slightly weary yet still heightened conversations echoes in the enclosed space.

And because the hanger door extends floor-to-ceiling and is double-wide there is no discernable threshold to pass over on the way out of the ballpark. We are in the exiting crowd, making its way in one concerted direction through the ballpark concourse and then, with a glance up to the night sky, we are outside, on Lansdowne Street amid the whirl of a crowd suddenly released and dispersing in a thousand different directions at a thousand different speeds, all at once. Turning, shifting, slipping this way and that, shoulders turned sideways. Stopping to let a pair of teenagers run by in one direction; scooting around a group of four stopped to say their goodbyes in the middle of Lansdowne; dodging a broad-shouldered fan in a Beckett jersey as he plows ahead, hat backward, shoulders lowered, one hand trailing back to tow his slender and slightly tipsy girlfriend through the wake; running flush into the red bullpen jacket of a fan on his cell phone who abruptly halts mid-step and turns to survey the crowd. Crowds huddled free-form around a sidewalk stand (*Sausages here! Half price sausages here!*) its intense white lights burning through the sizzle and smoke, highlighting the sweating sausages and franks, the bulky buns and mustards and relishes, and the fans using both hands to bring all of the above faceward as they linger on the sidewalk. Crowds across the street pressing up to the door of the Cask. Crowds moving up Lansdowne, crowds moving down Lansdowne; crowds moving up Brookline, crowds moving down Brookline; crowds not moving at all in intersection where Brookline and Lansdowne meet. People everywhere. Red Sox hats everywhere. Pouring around the Cask and its long line and flowing undeterred around two hopelessly stranded cars (their silent drivers wearily caught in the passing storm). Cresting the Mass Ave.

overpass, gradually turning downhill towards Kenmore where the tall t-shirt stands on either side of the street rise up above the crowd, their red blue white and green shirts flapping and swaying in the night air (*T-shirts, ten dollars! Only ten bucks!*) as fans bunch beneath them along the way. Still moving with the snap and clang of makeshift drums first heard and then seen, arms moving back and forth across overturned white plastic buckets and tin cans while fans look on, or clap along, or dance berrily past. Dividing off at various points along Kenmore Square, the vast majority of fans still flowing along the right side of the sidewalk, past the drummers, past the t-shirts, away from the ballpark. Finally we reach the copper awning of the Kenmore T stop where a small mob has congregated at the entrance and where more fans branch off and gather in the back (this the *entrance* to the stairs, to the platform, to a train one hesitates to even think about). Thinner now as we walk on among a still identifiable Sox-clad group, out of Kenmore Square and yet not quite in Back Bay, down through two blocks of no man's land buffeting the Charlesgate overpass. Along the way fans branch off—left here, right there—walking backwards a foot off the sidewalk, one arm raised. Cabs running either direction pick up couples and groups of four and whisk them off to points north and south. The pubs lying on the outskirts of Kenmore (with outskirt names like The Crossroads and The Other Side) absorb some; the hotels lying similarly (The Commonwealth, The Eliot) others still. And by the corner of Mass Ave. we find ourselves at a typical Boston intersection, late on a typical Thursday night, among no more than the one or two Sox hats one finds just about anywhere in Boston. The only detail distinguishing the fact that a World Series game has been recently played and won a little less than a half-mile from here are the two clear plastic bags held by a couple to our left, each stuffed with red and blue souvenirs, and the fellow with his arm raised into the street and searching down Mass. Ave. towards the Charles. A moment later a cab rushes to a stop at the curb, the couple pile in, and off they go.

There is a break in the traffic, and with a glance both ways we walk out across the street to the Back Bay side of Mass Ave. Where we find, on the last half-block leading up to the Comm. Ave. Mall, that we are no longer among the crowd. That the post-game celebration has tapered out and ended. And that now, we walk alone.

Though not necessarily empty handed. For somewhere along our walk we were reminded that in fact we have souvenirs. Immense stores of them. And that these particular souvenirs (*souvenir* in the original french sense, as 'a remembrance'; *souvenirs* as Proust would have them) are made of far sturdier stuff. Are brighter, broader, lighter; do not fade or fray or gather dust, or become lost beneath a pile of winter clothes; are decidedly un-official; and are absolutely one of a kind.

They are the memories of our time spent here at Fenway, with our team, and with this wonderful game of baseball. That great store of experiential clippings—the images, sounds, stories, moments, afternoons, nights, weekends, scorecards, crowds, cheers, family and friends—all taped and folded and stuffed into our own mental scrapbook, lovingly compiled over the years and now cherished as something very much like an heirloom. These, are our souvenirs. Of all the days and nights spent in our wonderful old summer home. Of the way it looked from a ramp behind home plate, empty on that cool March morning however many years ago; of the way it looked here tonight, all lit up and packed full and dressed in red white and blue for the World Series; and of so very much in between. Of so many satisfying days filled with the ease of having returned to something known, comfortable, and welcoming. Of so many magical nights invigorated with the sparkle of *event*, the wonder of *spectacle*, and the transcendent beauty of a beautiful game played with talent and conviction and spirit. Of such a ballpark as this. Of such a time as ours. And of such life, in these precious few moments so fully and so exuberantly lived.

APPENDIX:

The Intrepid Fan's Guide to
Standing Room Only at Fenway Park

Or

How to Plan, Navigate, and Quite Possibly Enjoy
the Standing Room Only Experience

*(including decidedly candid advice on matters of decorum,
etiquette, native customs, expectations with regard
to general civility, cordiality, sociability, &c.)*

PART ONE:

Right to Home

There is always something a bit cavalier about going Standing Room
Only, even under the best of circumstances. The we'll-figure-it-out-
when-we-get-there mindset required of those without an assigned seat
in a pre-determined section cannot help but put a slight spring of
adventure into the step of those who, passing through the gates with
only a spare SRO in their back pocket, set off to find *the perfect spot*.

This spring is felt less acutely, one must assume, in ballparks where
instead of *the perfect spot* one sets off to pick out which of the several
thousand empty plastic seats spread generously throughout the ballpark one would like to watch the game from. For even in ballparks
which occasionally sell-out there are still empty seats to be found here
and there (left from the out-of-town season ticket holder, the family
who couldn't make it, the group who came late and left early and so
on). And the practice of buying SRO only to seek out available empties
is so widespread throughout the league that it has become nearly syn-
onymous with Standing Room Only itself—the *0* more a theoretical
designation (or wishful thinking on the part of the ticket office) than
a genuine restriction. So that in most places and in most ballparks the
term has come to designate merely the least expensive ticket available,
and nothing more.

Not so at Fenway. Where entire seasons are sold out in one swoop;
where season ticket holders unable to make the game give their tickets
to friends (or sell them); where some arrive late but hardly anyone
leaves early; where the announcement of new Standing Room Only
areas warrants headlines usually reserved for the announcement of a
new terminal at Logan; and where the emphasis in SRO is always and
emphatically on the *0*. Here that spring of adventure becomes a rush of
determined purpose, as the Fenway fan without the benefit of an
assigned seat well knows, or quickly and often rudely finds out, that
more SRO tickets will be sold than there are available SRO spaces.

Which means there is the distinct possibility that one will end up (if one does not plan accordingly) wandering about the aisles, peering to the side, being told *that spot is taken* by slightly brusque SRO settlers, being told to *move along* by slightly perturbed Fenway ushers, being nudged, bumped, jostled, and in the end seeing far more of the shoulders and necks and backsides of one's fellow Sox fans than of the actual Red Sox themselves.

However (*take heart!*) this regrettable SRO fate is not unavoidable. It simply takes a bit of forethought, a general understanding of the terrain (forthcoming), a little basic SRO etiquette (ditto), and a healthy and preferably indefatigable dose of the aforementioned cavalier spirit. These requirements are not for everyone, of course. Some fans prefer to forgo all of the above by simply and rather un-adventurously going in with an assigned seating ticket and sitting down. Others, either by choice or by necessity, go a different route, and with a sense of purpose stride through the concourses with eyes always on the lookout for a better spot, as headlong and headstrong we go all in for Fenway Park's version of Choose Your Own Adventure.

On the surface it all looks simple enough. Standing Room Only at Fenway Park being officially limited to certain designated standing areas, all of which are found along a ring of walkway directly behind the blue grandstand, stretching from the right field corner all the way around to the left field wall. That's it. (Or almost it. There are quite technically SRO sections on the Green Monster and Roof Boxes, but these require separate ticketing and therefore are far more easily navigated than regular old *all I could get was* SRO) And were this ring one generously wide, unobstructed aisle, with comparable vantage points and amenities (or even the same climate) throughout, then it really would be as simple as picking a spot and standing there to watch the game. Yet like so much else at Fenway Park, this walkway is something of a patchwork between at least two eras, and therefore nothing if not particular.

The first and original template one comes across is Old Fenway, designed in baseball antiquity and long before anyone ever came up with the phrase *fan friendly*, it actually predates SRO (at the time general admission occupied what is now the bleachers). This then the narrow walkways, the child-size seats, the cramped quarters. All of which discomfort (on a good day it is called *charm*) is alleviated only by the sporadic and unexpected renovations of New Fenway, the more recent modifications undertaken by the Sox which have lately introduced into the SRO experience such modern marvels as Open Space, Fresh Air, and in certain areas a pleasing luminescent element, rumored to have been discovered in California and transported in stock cars to Fenway, called (we believe this is the correct phrasing) "Natural Sunlight." All of which makes a lap around the grandstand concourse at Fenway a virtual stroll through the *Ballpark* wing of the Museum of Science and Natural History. Only nothing is labeled, and there is no gallery guide. And as such calls for a guided tour; which tour we shall begin (nevermind the funny looking headphones) in the far right field corner.

Now, it stands to reason that the worst seats in the ballpark would not be much improved by one's moving all the way to the back of the section and standing on a slab of concrete for the entire game; a fact predictably true of the right field corner SRO. Here all that it is undesirable about this most undesirable section is made more so its by being without even an undesirable seat to sit in—the already considerable distance from home plate greater, the overhang more pronounced, and the game therefore more dramatically reduced to a high-ratio widescreen format that has one constantly ducking down to find anything above a low line drive. In fact the only real point of recommendation to this particular space is that, being one of the least attractive in the ballpark, one will generally have more elbow room with which to endure it. (A bit like wintering in Maine in order to avoid all the tourists.) That is until later on in the game, when a steady stream of under-prepared and under-motivated SRO ticket holders, having found no purchase in the better and therefore more crowded areas, begin to trickle down into the corner only to settle in, with a shrug and a disgruntled word or two about the attitude of certain Fenway Park ushers, right next to you. These spots will fill up eventually,

but in general there is more movement here than elsewhere and therefore a better chance of being able to leave and come back to the same
unoccupied spot. (Unless it is a Yankees and/or playoff game, in which
case scratch that.) Ultimately it is an area for stragglers, late arrivers,
those who tire quickly of crowds but inexplicably buy SRO tickets,
and for ticket holders sitting in the cramped corner grandstand to
occasionally stretch their legs. In order to avoid all this it is best to
arrive a bit earlier, plan a bit better, and move onward and upward
towards home.

Along the way one finds that the right field corner and right field
grandstand are of a piece, all the way up to about the Red Sox dugout.
Which means the narrow aisle trimming their top row is narrow
throughout. About 1 ½ average adults wide, it is roughly six inches
narrower than would be required for two fans to comfortably pass each
other in opposite directions without the always awkward and often
confrontational exchange of raised eyebrows, weak half-turns, and
stressed *coming through* looks. (Occasionally two tourists from, say, the
Middle West, will meet and *you first* each other into a virtual traffic
jam of hospitality, as exasperated locals on either side mutter *keep moving people* and *let's go already*, or words to that effect, behind them.) Add
to this the high rail to field-side, the concrete wall and odd fence grate
opposite, the uneven elevation of the walkway itself, and the fact that
typically there are SRO fans not only against the rail but packed into
the narrow space behind it (making the walkway more like ¾ the average adult width) and the whole stretch begins to take on a unmistakably *penal* feel. And on steamy August nights one half expects the
prison siren to sound out, the searchlights to come wheeling out onto
Ipswich, and all of us SRO inmates to turn clinging to the fence grates
for a look.

Certainly there is such a thing, particularly here in Ye Olde New
England, as charmingly small; otherwise referred to as quaint or intimate or (if you happen to be a real estate agent in the Greater Boston
area) *cozy*. But this is not it. What this is, is too damn tight. Best to
continue on—turning our shoulders and flashing crooked *hel-lo?*
glances at fans who insist on leaning against the rail with their not-

insubstantial backsides blocking all but a sliver of walkway, fans who ignore our repeated *pardon me*'s, and who pretend not to feel the various hip-checks and elbows applied to said not insubstantial backside as we finally squeeze past—up the first base line until the brick wall to our left gives way to a wide open deck, the clear night sky, and a soft breeze passing through. Amid which welcome comforts one almost feels moved to kneel down and say a quiet prayer of thanks to Janet Marie Smith, chief architect of the Boston Red Sox and Patron Saint of all Standing Room Only fans at Fenway Park.

Not long ago, pre-Janet Marie Smith, the narrow Late Cell Block motif along right field extended all the way up the first base line without widening so much as an inch until it emptied into the crowded delta around home plate (hardly a relief itself, as we shall see). All of this changed with the creation of the First Base Deck, the first display of New Fenway on our tour and an ingenious bit of addition by subtraction on the part of Janet Marie Smith (hereafter: St. Janet Marie) that involved nothing so much as the removal of one brick wall and incalculably improved the comfort level of all grandstand patrons, SRO in particular. Essentially the deck consists of the half dozen or so brick support columns left over from said wall, a wide concrete deck area which overlooks Ipswich on one side and is lined by a bank of two concession stands on another, with a wide staircase between them that empties directly onto street level at the corner of Ipswich and Yawkey, and a dozen elbow-high cocktail tables in Fenway Green scattered between the brick columns and field-side rail. So if nothing else the deck is a welcome oasis for fans nudging their way around the grandstand to restrooms and concessions and seats. Yet at the same time, by allowing the traffic of fans to flow out away from the seats, it has created a nice comfortable pocket for SRO. Granted there is no more lateral space here than elsewhere (even less so since the Standing Room areas tend to fill up quick around here) but what space there is, for those who are able to arrive early enough to secure a spot, is infinitely more comfortable than anywhere else on the right side of the field. The breeze alone is enough, and on a hot and humid night the cooling wisps from the deck behind are as welcome as Sox runs on the field ahead. (Weather permitting, of course, as in another month that same breeze can make itself decidedly un-welcome.) Plus the cocktail tables come in handy if one is eating, drinking, or scoring; and the concession stands are a quick *would you mind holding my spot for a second* away (ditto on the restrooms); and passing fans tend to steer wide of the columns and over the deck which means no elbow or hip checks or not-insubstantial backsides to worry about. All this, plus the light. And though we cannot confirm the rumor that St. Janet Marie was responsible for importing what we now know as "Natural Sunlight" to Fenway Park, it is a matter of record that her First Base Deck was the first to install it on the grandstand level; and whether standing for a day game with the sun on one's shoulders, or merely passing through out of a dark concourse and briefly into a soft summery twilight, all of Fenway is the better for it.

The view from this area, incidentally, is from just to the first base side of home plate and at a slight elevation, a fine angle from which to follow the essential pitcher v. batter matchup, clearly see the infield movements, and aside from the overhang and a post blocking second base, more or less par for the grandstand.

Yet there is always among fans that innate sense that closer to home plate is better, and the gravitational pull of the game's Alpha and Omega pulls us farther along, past the First Base Deck and back into the crowded, bustling, Downtown-Crossing-at-noon nexus that is the home plate concourse. And if Fenway Park has a belly button, this is it.

Here we find the only full-scale concession stand on the second level, with the grandstand's largest and busiest Women's and Men's rooms flanking it to either side, a large entranceway to the right where both the walkway ramp and Fenway's central elevator bank empty out onto the second level, and opposite this a new stairway coming up from Yawkey Way; all meeting directly behind the four keystone sections (Secs. 19-22) back of home plate. With fans coming from and going and in all directions at all times, traffic jams abound. For one thing the line to the Women's Room (and there always is a line) extends across the entranceway from the ramps and elevators, meaning those coming into the grandstand level are often greeted by a blockade of tightly bunched and mildly perturbed female Sox fans. Less mildly so towards the back. (It used to be even worse. Up until the 2007 season this was the only Women's Room on the grandstand level, creating interminable lines and causing more than a few men in the stands to wonder what the hell happened to their dates.) Whereas with the Men's Room the problem is not so much the entrance, where there are rarely lines, but the exit, from which sufficiently relieved male fans pour out without much paying attention to their surroundings (as sufficiently relieved male fans tend to do) and therefore cause all sorts of confusion with the fans on their way to and from the large, bustling, cafeteria-style concession stand situated directly between the two restrooms. So there are fans here, and lots of them, and most of them are moving in opposite directions in a hurried attempt to get either to or away from food, drink, or the lavatory. One can imagine, then, what the SRO must be like here along the back rows, where fans pack in two and three deep to begin the game and then deal with a more or less constant flow of passing fans stopping on their way to and fro for a quick look over the shoulder.

And perhaps here is as good a place as any to stop for a moment—among this packed-in, nudging over, inching-up crowd—and review a few of the basic principles of SRO etiquette. Or what that famously Enlightened philosopher (had he ever caught the back end of a day-night double-header) might have called, *Du Contrat SRO*.

PART TWO:

Principles of Standing Room Only Etiquette
(or, The SRO Contract)

Here as elsewhere, possession is nine-tenths of the law. This means that if you are standing on a parcel of concrete upon which SRO is allowed then that is *your spot*, and will remain so until you vacate said parcel. A simple enough premise which nonetheless forms the basis for nine-tenths of all Standing Room Only disputes. The problem being that few people are either willing or able to stand in the same spot without moving for the better part of three hours. (Nearer four in the better spots since they require laying claim to well before first pitch, and nearer *five* hours for the Yankees and in October.) Though the roaming vendors help out a great deal in this regard, one still finds the occasional reason (such as the fact that they do not vend beer) to visit the concession stand and, depending on how many similar visits are made, the restroom.

A practical amendment is needed then, and that amendment is the unwritten but universal law of Can You Hold My Spot For a Second. Which states that it is entirely acceptable for a fan in SRO to request of an adjacent fan the privilege of watching over their spot and assuring that it remains unoccupied for a minimal period of time, and that it is expected of the fellow fan under all but a few extreme circumstances to accept. This then is the social contract in action, a mutually beneficial agreement with both sides accepting a set of tacit responsibilities. For the spot-holder this means making sure the spot remains unoccupied, and is usually done by way of *spreading out*. This is something fans seem to do almost instinctively, as if somewhere along the fan evolutionary chart we developed it (along with an inclination to blame the umpire) for survival. When the departee leaves their spot vacant the spot-holder spreads out—like a blowfish expanding to protect itself—inching over with elbows out and stance widened, thus signaling to fans hovering in the area that this space is Not Open. (This move is exponentially more efficient when done by a group, where three or four fans can easily envelope an empty spot.) As in nature every fan has their own particular spread-out technique, and we have seen everything from a quick, darting spread, in which one stands completely still and then shoots out a blocking arm (*taken!*) at any approaching poacher (this the chameleon, blending in), to one with feet spread impossibly wide, chest puffed out, and fists planted on hips Yule-Brynner-style (this the peacock). Both equally effective. No matter the style in which it is held, when the departee returns with digestive system relieved and rations replenished the holder contracts back into a normal repose stance (the three fans fold back down), the empty spot opens up for the departee to step right back in. And the circle of life continues.

Of course it takes two to make a social contract. And the departee is responsible for upholding their end of the agreement as well. This becomes immediately clear when we consider that A) holding a *spread-out* pose is neither natural nor comfortable, and B) holding said pose for more than a half-inning while fending off the inevitable nudging-in from surrounding fans, while at the same time trying to keep an eye on the game one is ostensibly there to watch, is even less so. Which means the departee who has asked a complete stranger to hold a spot for them needs to hurry it up already. So no dawdling; no peeking in from other areas to watch an at bat or two; no deciding on your way back to go for a smoke on Yawkey. Do what you need to do and get back to your spot, or else you run the risk of hearing, when you return to a clogged knot of fans in what was previously your spot, an apologetic *sorry man, I didn't think you were coming back*. Exactly how long the social pact between departee and holder lasts depends on several independent variables. For one, how big a game is it? How crowded is the SRO section being held (and therefore how many encroaching fans need to be fended off)? How generous and/or patient a soul is the holder? How amicable or obnoxious has the departee been throughout the game? (Do not expect your spot to be held long, or at all, if the net result for the holder is that you will no longer be there to elbow him in the ribs.) (Conversely there should be little worry over the spot being held if there has been a little friendly repartee between fans beforehand.) What is the gender combination? (We are pleased to report that men tend to save spots for women almost without asking, and protect such spots with particularly chivalrous gusto.) And so on. All things being equal, you've got about an inning. After which the holder starts to fidget, starts to shake their head at the fifth or sixth *is anyone there* inquiry, and finally after an inning and a half has every right to answer the seventh inquiry with a shrug, a slide over, and an acquiescent *not sure what happened to that guy*.

Let's say you have your spot though. You've sought it out, claimed it, and have now successfully negotiated the social contract which allows you to leave freely and return unimposed. The rest is just common sense, fundamental manners, and the basic social courtesies we enjoy as members of a civil and presumably advanced society. Which of course is where the real problems begin.

Just as in all crowded public spaces (the T comes immediately to mind) the ballpark populous in general favors a respectful observance of personal space; but just as in all crowded public spaces (the T still firmly in mind), all it takes to throw the entire order into chaos is one who does not. And for that one to be stuck, inevitably, right next to you. It hardly matters if *on the whole* it is a polite, respectful crowd when a sweaty guy in a tank top keeps nudging over into your personal space (and you keep backing off to avoid his sweatiness until eventually you are pressed against a pole and more or less blocked from the game). Or if the guy to your left keeps turning to *his* left and thus thumping you in the ribs with his gigantic Expedition Grade backpack, apparently stuffed with doorknobs, which thumping he is of course completely oblivious to and continues for some time. Not even if the person next to you is a shockingly loud talker who throughout the first three innings practically shouts a minute-by-minute account of what-all happened today in his third grade classroom, despite the fact that this narrative overlaps a key second-and-third, two out situation with Big Papi up, so that the Loud Talker has to shout his anecdotes of pre-pubescent hijinks *over* the roaring crowd. (All despite the fact that he has earlier made several claims of being a *huge* Sox fan.) As elsewhere in life you are allowed a simple tap on the shoulder and an *excuse me*; and as elsewhere in life this gesture of civility will likely produce slightly underwhelming results. In general, rooted as you are to your spot, you are left to twist in the winds of the socially oblivious. Including the loud talker, the cell phone shouter (*no, I'm at the game... I don't know the score, I think we're winning...yeah, uh I think it's....hey, what inning are we in?...you know me, I'm a huge Sox fan!*), the chronic fidgeter, the flagrantly drunk, the ever-popular flagrantly drunk chronic fidgeter; the guy trying to start the *Let's-Go, Red-Sox* chant between innings; the inevitable Funny Comment Guy (who performs a kind of ersatz stand-up routine for the unsolicited benefit of the entire section, and to the deepening mortification of his visibly embarrassed wife); the pair of homely little New England aunts who consistently drop borderline racists comments into otherwise ordinary anecdotes of grocery shopping and knitting; the guy who between calls home to his wife and kids mutters uncouth comments about every female who passes by, including ones who frankly appear *uncomfortably* young in the context of such comments; those who practice less than stellar personal hygiene; those who apparently have little or no control over their limbs; those who inexplicably boo your favorite player as overrated; those who inexplicably boo your favorite player and then repeatedly confuse Brian Roberts (who is white) with Dave Roberts (who is not); those who shout *Get out!* at shallow infield pop ups and shout *Turn it!* with two outs; those who spill beer every time they move; those who flip peanut shells into other people's personal space; those who are rude, those who are obnoxious, those who are in every way intolerable. And Yankee fans.

This bleak portrait of life in SRO is of course skewed to point out its pitfalls, and in all likelihood you will avoid many if not all of the above and simply enjoy the game among good fans. The point is that one of these is enough to ruin the experience for everybody. And in order to make certain you are not, by simple naiveté, that one (and the mere fact that you are reading an essay on SRO etiquette is a fair indication that you are not) we hereby offer a few basic guidelines to standard SRO decorum which may help avoid some of the more common, and for the most part innocent, misunderstandings.

Nudging. This the gradual, almost imperceptible encroachment into another fan's space caused by an instinctual urge to move forward, or over, or around a pole and into a better sightline. You may not even know you're doing it. But the person next to you does. Because every one of us has different comfort levels when it comes to the their-elbow-is-totally-touching-me moment. And because each time you nudge over their elbow gets drawn in closer; then they are turning slightly;

next thing you know they are almost behind you. (Unless of course they are either socially oblivious or especially firm in holding their ground, in which you will know you are nudging by the fact that your shoulder is pressed flush against theirs.) The solution is simply to be aware of yourself and your surroundings. And if you feel a gentle little bump in the shoulder or back, recognize that you have drifted too far, and that your failure to kindly retract to your original space will likely result in further bumps which next time may not be so gentle.

Height Awareness. Let us assume that if you are, say, 6' 7", you are likely already aware of your height and the impositions it might cause in these situations. Yet even for those of more modest stature a certain awareness of its relativity to those around you is not only helpful, but absolutely essential to maintaining the often delicately balanced SRO social order. This means that whoever you are and wherever you are standing, when you take up a new spot in SRO a good old-fashioned courtesy check behind you is in order. Just a glance, perhaps a polite *am I in your way*, will do. Most of the time you will not be, but even if you slightly are the courtesy itself will endear you to your neighbors enough to let it slide. Also, it is not uncommon or unwelcome for a tall person to offer to switch places if a shorter person is stuck behind them (particularly if that shorter person is a child, an elderly person, or someone who would not be entirely unpleasant to look at should they occasionally block one's view).

Seat Poaching. This practice, typical and more or less accepted at other ballparks, is, at Fenway, both pointless and often needlessly disruptive. Here's how: a pair of fans have it in mind that they are going to find the two magically unoccupied seats in all of sold-out Fenway Park, and thereby turn their cheap SRO tickets into pricey grandstand views. Only each time they go to sit down they find out shortly thereafter that the legitimate seat holder was actually just at the restroom or concession stand or whatever. Causing our poachers to fall back into the general SRO pool, which of course is the disruptive part. The simple fact is that you should not expect a seat at Fenway out of an SRO ticket unless 1) it is in fact snowing; 2) it is the first game of a rescheduled double header on a Tuesday afternoon, and it is snowing; or 3) the Sox are seventeen games out of first, it is the first game of a rescheduled double header on a Tuesday afternoon, and it is snowing. Then you've got a shot. Otherwise, find a good SRO spot and leave the seats to those who paid for them.

Down in Front! Speaking of those who have paid for seats. Not only do they have a right to sit in them, but they have just as much right as anyone to stand up in a key situation and cheer. As all good fans should. Unfortunately for several swaths of SRO fans (behind home and down the third base line in particular) this means when Papelbon comes set for the final pitch and everybody stands, their view of the climactic moment is completely blotted out by the *crowd on its feet at Fenway*. Unfortunate, yes. But such is life in SRO. Which makes the random *down in front!* shouts leveled by certain SRO fans to those in the grandstand before them all the more inappropriate. And, given that these shouts almost always come from bullhorn-voiced, middle-aged men (often with children whom they shamelessly exploit as an excuse for such behavior), it comes off as a little desperate and more than a little bit pathetic. Though not nearly as pathetic as...

Everybody Up! Some mundane situation—let's say a runner on first with two outs in the second inning of a scoreless game—and as the grandstand quietly looks on, SuperFan, way back in SRO, is pounding out thick claps and barking over their heads, *Come on, everybody up!* Then, when nobody budges and a lazy fly ball ends the inning, an admonishing, *Come on people, get in the game!* Heads crane back, expressions clench, and the antagonistic relationship between section and fan that will likely continue all night has begun. (At least until the Sox actually produce a crucial situation and the crowd actually does stand up, at which point SuperFan shamelessly takes credit for having caused what is a natural sporting occurrence with a magnanimous, *Alright, that's more like it!*) Look, we wish all crowds stood more in key situations. We wish there wasn't that awkward half-standing hesitation when the bases are loaded and the count runs full. We wish Fenway stood on every two strike count like they do at the Stadium. Even so, baseball is often enough a leisurely game, a patient game, an untroubled game, and it is important to keep in mind that many people come to it and enjoy it for this very reason. That is to say they want to sit back, relax, have their Crackerjacks and watch the Red Sox without some nut-job shouting at them for nine innings. And they have every right to do so by buying a seat to sit in. (All of which is on top of the fact that it is more than a bit self-righteous to give fans grief for not standing when you yourself *have no choice but to stand*.) Not surprisingly all this is almost always done by male fans, typically young and muscle-bound and kind of jittery (the can't-sit-still type). And it is our purely speculative theory that the same nervy young men who shout *Everybody up!* in their twenties eventually grown into the bullhorn-voiced fathers who shout *Down in front!* in their forties. Lord only knows what they shout in their thirties.

Pardon Me. Excuse Me. Thank You. SRO space is tight and often difficult to move about within. And while the accepted Fenway Park means of moving oneself by an impasse of fans seems to be, by all observational data, to stand and roll one's eyes and silently brood while nudging a foot or elbow or shoulder forward until the person notices you and moves, the three little phrases above are not only acceptable, but surprisingly effective. Trust us.

Now, it may be observed that much of the above, particularly this last bit, is not only a matter of SRO etiquette but of basic everyday manners. This is true. The only difference is that in a crowded ballpark, particularly a crowded *old* ballpark, these practices which are mere niceties in the city at large become absolutely indispensable to the overall tone of the SRO experience. Three or four signs of poor manners—the tall guy who plants himself in front of the shorter girls, the guy shouting *down in front* when Ortiz comes up with the bases loaded, the girls who toddle off (without asking for any spot-saving privileges) for three innings only to come back and wedge their way into a too-small spot—and suddenly there is an irritated, confrontational tone in the air which can only lead to no good. We've seen it happen, and fast, and it can stain everything around it including a good game.

On the other hand the slight courtesy, the small neighborly gesture, the considerate look back to see if you are blocking someone's way (*no you're fine, thank you*) can all go a long way to making for a pleasant, communal, we're-all-in-this-together atmosphere that lasts the whole game. And we've seen this happen, too. (Nevermind which we've seen more of.)

What it comes down to in the end is awareness; simply being cognizant of the other human beings around you, and that your actions can have a discernable effect on the ballpark experience of others, good or bad. We all get in each other's way from time to time in SRO. The question is how we handle it, and the difference between a good atmosphere and a bad one, the difference between strangers shooting you nasty glances and newfound friends giving you a high five when the Sox score—and really in the end the difference between living in a civilized society and wallowing in a nasty Hobbesian anarchy—is nothing more terribly difficult than *pardon me, excuse me,* and *thank you.*

PART THREE:

Home to Left

Dense, active, loud, and aggressively social, the concourse levee behind home plate is Standing Room Only's version of the bleachers. Complete with all of its attendant pleasures and predicaments. The only real difference being that in the bleachers you can at least count on your seat being in the same spot all night and not, as it tends to do in SRO, drifting off a few feet to the right and/or narrowing significantly throughout the game until you are forced, out of discomfort and annoyance, to find another. This happens quite a bit in the area behind home plate; mostly because the rate of nudging (see above) per capita is greater here than any other area in SRO due to the sheer number of fans coming and going from the concession stands and restrooms, passing through on their way from one side of the grandstand to the other, coming off of and going towards the elevators, stopping on their way to lean in and see the next pitch, standing in the aisle to locate or relocate their row, and pacing back and forth with cell phone to ear shouting *where are you, section what, I don't see you, maybe you should stand up in the middle of a pitch and wave your arm like an imbecile and shout Jim! Hey Jim! Over here! so that when I get there everyone within a ten row radius will despise both of us.* All of which translates into a great deal of nudging and moving and excusing for the standee, who once moved never does quite return to the same spot as before. (Remember the science class video showing what happens when water molecules heat towards their boiling point, where at first they vibrate in place until they begin to bounce and weave about in a frantic, patternless scramble? It's like that. Only with cell phones.) Add to this the odd sensation of being at a major sporting event with thirty-five-thousand fans spread out before you and still having the majority of noise and commotion and activity going on *behind you*, and you get a section that is about as conducive to an evening of leisurely diversion as you might find at, say, Logan Airport the day before Thanksgiving (with a snow storm in the forecast and half the airlines on strike). On the plus side though, you *are* close to the restrooms.

All of which would be only a minor hindrance if putting up with it offered one a view of the game commensurate with the price of attaining it. But unless you have a really, really strong preference for geometric symmetry then the view is simply not worth the trouble. Yes there is something mildly pleasing about standing directly on the catcher-pitcher-center fielder axis and having the whole field spread harmoniously out before you from a single fixed point (though Fenway Park being asymmetrical this balance will never be exact); but the overhanging EMC Club seats trim the top half of the view down to a close panorama, and the newly added camera well hanging off its bottom edge narrows it even further. It is not a bad view, and in an empty ballpark it would do just fine. There is simply not enough to distinguish it beyond the considerable number of factors which can so easily spoil its charm; not the least of which is that:

As elsewhere, much depends upon the weather. So much so that these sections (much like the roof boxes) can either be among the best situated to cope with the weather or, depending on the forecast, a strong candidate for the very worst. This due to the fact that unlike the two newly created areas flanking it down either baseline (the afore-mentioned First Base Deck and the forthcoming Third Base Deck), the area directly behind home plate is blocked from the wind. Perhaps a slight cross-breeze might blow through the seats from time to time, and those seated farther down in the section will certainly feel a west-erly wind; but back in the back, and especially all the way back in SRO, the overhang blocks anything coming in and the concession stands and restrooms take care of the rest. The effects of which depend entirely on the weather.

Early and late in the season, when it is gray and drizzly and the wind a biting tormentor, the blocked-off levee, by holding the air in, creates an insulating effect on the sections before it. Add to this the bank of hot grills and frialators and pretzel warmers in the oversized concession stand directly behind, and of course all the people whose movement now emit welcome BTU's of body heat to the air, and on the whole this area becomes perhaps the warmest, most comfortable outdoor space in the ballpark—a welcome and hospitable shelter on a cold raw April night.

Other times...

Well, they don't turn those hot grills and boiling frialators and steamy pretzel warmers off in August you know. Not even when it's 95-degrees out; not even when the humidity is 85% and you break into a full sweat while making your morning coffee; not even when the crowd is packed with damp foreheads and glossy cheeks and people trying to fan themselves with their programs and picking their Sox shirts away from their bodies, and in general just looking miserable as they sit and wilt in the late summer heat. No, those grills keep crank-ing away, pumping heat into the already overheated levee. Heat that is only made worse by the BTU's coming from all those people who still crowd around the area, but whose arms and shoulders nudging and bumping against you are now sweaty arms and sweaty shoulders. Heat that will find no relief from even a slight breeze, the steamy air now trapped by the same obstacles which once provided shelter. In the heat and especially in the humidity, the area is a kiln. And there is no use disguising this fact, or that those packed into the SRO area on such nights will find their noisy, crowded, active, distracting experience now enhanced by the added discomforts of stifling humidity and dead air. If all this sounds appealing to you—if you are the type of person who likes the heat, who does not find the feeling of sweat trickling down your back unpleasant, and who is perfectly comfortable on a crowded subway car with the AC broken and everyone in sight appearing to have just run a mini-marathon before cramming in next to you, with their arms raised—then this is most definitely the Standing Room Only area for you. Otherwise, you might want to keep moving.

As you do be sure to keep an eye to the ground, for over the next several yards your best SRO guide will be the one right beneath your feet. This because as you move to the third base side of home the aisle immediately narrows, first to a small delta of space just left of center where a series of openings in the brick façade allow in both fresh air and light (making it a lovely spot to linger over prior to the game, lazily overlooking Yawkey Way as the grill smoke mixes with the brass band and the expectant, happily arriving crowd below), then quickly funnels into a narrow passageway that empties, after maybe twenty feet, onto the third base side proper and a long stretch of more or less unencumbered SRO space. But first the obstacle course.

In an effort on the Red Sox part to aide both fans and ushers in sorting out which areas were viable SRO grounds and which were not, a series of white rectangular boxes have been painted on the concrete behind each section, marked STANDING ALLOWED. There are boxes behind Sections 18-21, but none behind Section 22, the third base side delta where instead the white boxes are moved back to the terrace overlooking Yawkey Way and again marked STANDING ALLOWED. As the area narrows the markings change once more, this time to a series of cross-hatched yellow warning lines covering the width of the passageway. A clear, straightforward system of demarca-tion that is, for the most part, almost completely ignored by every fan who has ever passed over it.

Part of the problem is placement, in that very few fans go about a crowded ballpark checking the ground for useful signage. But a bigger part is the inconsistency of the marking itself. For starters, this is the only area of the ballpark thus marked. Every other SRO area is marked by its being a blank, unmarked piece of concrete from which no one asks you to move. So that by trying to regulate all the shifting behind home the Sox have attempted to direct fans who quite simply are not looking for direction. (What they are looking for is a good view; and when they see one they tend to stand in that spot until someone tells them they can't.) Which is why the STANDING ALLOWED signage mostly fails; because once it shifts fans do not recognize a blank spot as something they are not allowed to stand on. Better to tell fans where they cannot stand, and let them figure out the rest. (One theory is that the Sox would like to avoid the unpleasantly authoritative command of NO STANDING, despite the fact that it would probably be more effective.) Then again fans tend to have a way of conspicuously *not* see-ing signs that they do not want to see in the first place; and so in the end it may not matter, and the weary Fenway usher shooing people away would be no better served by a giant neon sign reading NO STANDING ALLOWED AT ANY TIME BY ANY FAN; NO, NOT EVEN FOR AN INNING; AND NO IT DOESN'T MATTER IF YOU HAVE A SMALL KID WHO CAN'T SEE, WE DON'T CARE THIS MEANS NO SO MOVE IT ALREADY.

(Sadly, one cannot help but notice this unpleasant pattern of child-as-excuse-to-break-clearly-stated-rules as it applies to SRO. And while no one would suggest that using one's child as a means of weaseling into SRO spots one otherwise would be shooed away from technically qualifies as child abuse, it is difficult to see how it could be anything less than a strain on the parent-child bond. If not now, perhaps later on. The scene is always the same. Aggressive father with reluctant son in tow finds a spot miraculously open during the middle of the game (*way to go Dad, this is great*), only to have an usher come by moments later to point out the yellow lines beneath their feet and inform them that standing is allowed over yonder, you know, where all those people are crammed in. Dad, not wanting to feel like an underage kid being ushered out of an R-rated movie in front of his own son, proceeds to make an impassioned argument, which argument typically consists of his repeating *oh come on!* over and over again in an increasingly whiny tone. Finally, when these and similar flourishes of oratory inevitably fail, he places a hand on the shoulder of his son, now suddenly and unknowingly Exhibit A in his father's plea bargain. *Come on,* the father implores, *he's just a kid, he can't see anywhere else, besides it's his first game; and it's his birthday; and he's partially blind in one eye and has one leg that's shorter than the other so he has to stand on this side of the field and in this exact spot or he'll never be able to see his beloved Red Sox play ever, and you don't want that on your conscience now do you, Mister Usher-man, I mean really, come on.* Unimpressed, the usher moves them along, the father now muttering words which are hardly appropriate for children no matter how many good eyes they have, and his son invariably looking embarrassed and surely wondering why, if Dad cared so much about him to shout in public, he didn't just spring for seats to begin with.)

Farther down the third base line things are simpler. Sections 24-27 offer a straight line of blue wooden seatbacks along a generous birth of concrete space. (Thanks largely to a fork in the concourse aisle where one branch continues along the grandstand and the other descends down a series of switchback ramps to ground level.) The area is straightforward and relatively low traffic (it is roughly equidistant to the two major concession/restroom areas), and the views nothing to complain about. Directly perpendicular to the third base line, one has an excellent ¾ view of both pitcher and batter as well as a very nice tableau of the infield. Because of its width there is almost always at least one pole blocking a column-wide patch of outfield, but this minor obstruction is negligible compared with the obstacles in other sections. The only real drawback along this stretch is its elevation, which is in fact slightly below the seats (they sit up on an odd concrete platform). This of course is not a problem so long as nothing particularly thrilling is going on in the game, but becomes a big problem once there is. For when the grandstand crowd stands up your view of the game disappears, and your field of vision instead becomes a case study in the misshapen backsides of baseball fans. A tough deal to strike, perhaps (you will be able to clearly see everything which is uninteresting, and very little of what is) but one that many fans would settle for in return for a bit of elbow room and a good view of the pitcher.

For those willing to seek out a bit more, there is the Third Base Deck.

Located closer to left field than third base and new to the ballpark as of the 2007 season, the Third Base Deck offers the same broad release on the third base side of the field as its older sibling the First Base Deck does across the way. Only more so. By removing a large block of office space and blowing out the wall which once separated it from the field, St. Janet Marie and the Red Sox were able to create not only a spacious retreat for crowded fans to congregate in but a long, three section wide stretch of green countertop that has quickly become the most valuable SRO real estate in all of Fenway. (The uplift was a dramatic one. In the past these sections were abutted by a wall so close that it made the crawlspace behind them one of the more uncomfortable passageways in a ballpark full of uncomfortable passageways. That it now hosts an oasis of creature comforts still strikes some older Fenway fans as something of a mirage. A year later, and they still can't believe it.) Structurally the area is not terribly complicated. There is a lower level with a full bank of concession stands along the back wall, an upper level with cocktail tables scattered about and the aforementioned green counter separating it from the grandstands, and a handicap ramp connecting the two levels. (With a smile we spy the signature St. Janet Marie touch of adding three wide window births along the back wall, which not only allow in light and a soft breeze but overlooks the always entertaining intersection of Lansdowne, Brookline, and the Cask n' Flagon.)

For SRO fans the focal point is obviously the counters. The very same counters used on the Monster and Roof Boxes, they provide the SRO fan with the very same luxurious sense of settlement. It is difficult to explain, but for whatever reason a SRO fan who has a small piece of hard plastic countertop to lean against feels as if they have, if not exactly a seat, at least something that is theirs. They have a space, and that space is physically grounded by something one can hold onto. (We have seen this same kind of demarcation-as-ownership dynamic enacted with everything from support beams to guard rails to aisle-ways, even a foot up on a seatback—all in one way or another laying claim.) It is essentially primal, we think, and for the most part deeply instinctual for us to try and block off this or that space with a piece of something hard and sturdy, even if that something is a fallen tree or cloth tent or rocky crevice carved out of a mountainside, so long as it is something we can lean on and call *ours*. Plus the countertop is really great for scorekeeping. And setting your beverage on without having to do any of the arm-to-side pinching maneuvers necessary elsewhere in non-countertop areas. Which means it's both deep-seated primal urge satiating, *and* practical.

Beyond these countertops the Third Base Deck is essentially a cocktail lounge. And a comfortable one at that. The lines are never long at either the concession stands or the brand new Women's room at the near end of the area, which happens to be (so we're told) one of the nicer facilities in the ballpark. (Here again the thanks goes to St. Janet Marie, for whom the longstanding restroom inequality on the third base side—there was a Men's, but no Women's—was an unacceptable arrangement which did not last long on her watch.) And overall the area is a pleasant enough place for those looking to linger over their beers, congregate around one of the cocktail tables for a bite, and watch the game (now taking place live over their left shoulder) on one of the large flatscreen televisions above.

However, two aspects set the area apart from even its first base counterpart.

One is sheer space, of which the Third Base Deck has more of than any other area with an open view from the concourse. It is big, and even when busy far from feeling crowded. This is not something fans at Fenway Park are terribly used to, and creates the odd sensation of watching the game with a packed crowd ahead and so much wide open, unfilled space stretching out behind. Particularly when that space is so brightly lit. Which this space emphatically is; and this the other distinguishing aspect. The entire area is lit from above by large hanging lamps blanketing every surface in clear white light, like a department store. Which would not be so terribly noticeable were it not for the fact that every other area in the ballpark besides the field itself is dimly lit at best. The contrast is sharp—with the Third Base Deck bright and open and active, and the grandstands a few feet away tightly packed, inert and shadowy beneath the low clearance overhang above. So that the combined effect creates, for fans used to being on the outside looking in, the odd sensation of being on the inside looking out. Almost as if one is leaning not on a ballpark countertop but on the top-deck rail of some immense luxury ocean liner, with the laughter of the brightly lit deck behind us, and the dark moving waves of grandstand below lapping against some curiously active foreign port. As the great ship, and us on its top rail looking out, drifts lazily by in the night.

A small stretch of brick wall (ancient ruins from the old third base crawlspace) extends out to the left of the Third Base Deck until it reaches the left field corner and the stairway up to the Monster; and that's it, really. That is Standing Room Only at Fenway Park. Not a great deal of space to choose from, but a great deal more than there used to be and overall a fair enough array of options. Particularly if one has a bit of sense about them, goes in with a little of that cavalier spirit and, most importantly of all, gets to the ballpark early.

For in every area of SRO, no matter how pleasant or disagreeable, time is a determining factor. And while there are no hard-set deadlines for reaching any one particular area, there is an undeniably systematic order to how those areas fill up. No secrets here: the good areas fill up first, the bad areas later on. More specifically you can expect the Third Base Deck rail to be occupied long before anything else (let's say a half-hour before first pitch, or an hour before Yankees and/or playoff games), then the First Base Deck, and from there spreading out from behind home plate to the corners. If you mess around and wait until game time or beyond to pick a spot you're going to be looking at either the right field corner or two-deep in a better section, where you will stand behind someone who had the sense to get there early.

This isn't altogether a bad thing. Often times the same cavalier spirit which allows someone to go in on SRO also allows them the patience to wait around until someone moves or leaves or otherwise vacates a good spot. And some fans simply prefer to stay in motion during the game. Some even like to spend several innings smoking on Yawkey Way while only vaguely keeping an eye on the flatscreens in the window, which is an excellent though not terribly economical way to simulate the experience of smoking on your front porch while listening to the game. Otherwise you're best bet is to spend a few minutes ahead of time formulating a plan, get there plenty early, polish up your common courtesies, and learn how to *spread out*.

It may not be for everyone. Some might find the entire Standing Room Only process overly involved, frustratingly haphazard, and in the end simply tiresome. For others, we'll take what we can get. Because, well...

Because what Standing Room Only is really about is being a fan. Not the kind of fan who says *oh yeah I'm a huge baseball fan* so long as the team is playing well and I have good seats and the conditions are to my liking (and I don't have anything particular going on that night), but rather the kind of fan who says *I love this game* enough to watch it anytime, any place, under any conditions, and am willing to put up with all *this* (see above) just to be able to do so. The kind of fan who understands that the game of baseball was never meant to be watched on television. The kind of fan who knows (at times intimately) that the crowd is a necessary part of the baseball experience. The kind of fan who takes real pleasure in watching the first and third basemen playing catch outside of the dugout before the game, or seeing the shortstop share a joke with a runner on second during a pitching change, or a starting pitcher lazily shagging fly balls during batting practice. The kind of fan for whom the treasures of the game are always well worth its trials. It is particularly for this fan, that Standing Room Only exists.

Overcast, cold, gray, windy, rainy? It is worth it. Hot, humid, cloudless, breezeless, blazing, sweaty? It is worth it. Late start, early start, game running late, had to be up early this morning, have to be up early next morning? It is worth it. Tired, headache, congested, coughing, told by multiple friends and a few strangers that *you might want to have that looked at*? It is worth it. Monday night, Tuesday afternoon, Wednesday very late after a rain delay? It is worth it. Sox in first by a half game, Sox in third by double digits, Sox in last place and mathematically eliminated and with every starter on the DL indefinitely? It is worth it. Buddies bailed, significant other busy, huge fan who is *definitely down to catch a game whenever absolutely* inexplicably occupied by a blind date? It is worth it. The prospect of overpriced hot dogs and yellow beer and sticky-sweet Crackerjack and salty neon popcorn, for dinner, again? It is worth it. The prospect of standing in the same spot for an hour before the game even begins for fear of losing the one viable SRO spot left? It is worth it. The prospect of being forced to hear about how he *like totally doesn't even listen he's just like always watching the game or whatever* while Mike Lowell stares out at a full count with the bases loaded? It is (just barely) worth it. Being nudged, elbowed, bumped, jostled, shifted, having beer spilt on one's shoes, having the beer on the ground between one's feet reached for (twice), and repeatedly having one's scorecard upset mid-notation, all while never once hearing any form of the phrase *excuse me*? It is worth it. Game sold out, scalpers criminally gouging prices, bleachers double and triple face value, grandstands a small fortune, box seats a large fortune, spare singles with obstructed view going for three figures, maybe a handful of Standing Room Only tickets left and even those overpriced? It is...well...

Whadda'ya say pal?

A pause, a glance to the ballpark, and then, *Alright, gimme one Standing.*

It is worth it. And it is worth it because the intrepid Standing Room Only fan knows with absolute certainty that there is a part of this game that is unconditionally enjoyable, and therefore may be unconditionally enjoyed. No matter the circumstances, no matter the viewpoint. It is somewhere at its very core, locked into the framework of the game, and can neither be obstructed nor altered. It is weatherproof. It is soundproof. It is corporation-proof. It is scandal-proof, spin-proof, marketing-proof. It does not adapt or erode or calcify with age. It transcends scores and standings and every statistical formulation ever invented. And it cares not for contracts. It can be seen by small children and studied by professors, and passed around a winter barbershop by storytellers of all ages. And it is there in some form— at times dim, at times dazzling—in every single baseball game ever played. Whatever it is (for it has no name), it lies somewhere deep within the unique combination of pattern and design and structure and rules which together make up the game as we know it, and is therefore both timeless and absolutely incorruptible. The intrepid Standing Room Only fan knows this (or intuits it in that glance to the ballpark), and therefore knows that it does not matters where one watches it from—for it will be there still. The moment *will* come. Large or small, subtle or striking, in an instant or stretching out long into the night. And when it does it will not matter if the Sox are in first place or last; will not matter what kind of day you had or what you have planned for the weekend; will not matter if it is sunny or drizzling cold rain; will not matter who you are, or where you come from, or what you do; and it will not matter one single bit whether you see it through the insulated glass of a luxury suite or through the crowded wildly waving arms of Standing Room Only; for it will be there nonetheless, amid that leaping shouting cheering spectacular panoramic floodlit actuality, full of life, and worth it all along.

The author wishes to thank

Mr. Jaimie Muehlausen of Bartlett Park; Mrs. Patricia Curtis, Mr. Jerry Remy, and Mr. John O'Rourke of The Remy Report; Mr. Brian Wilson of Three Islands Press; Mr. James House and the entire staff of Eau Claire Printing; Mrs. Elizabeth Prindle of the Boston Public Library; Mrs. Kerry Haggerty Elderkin, Mr. Christopher Serio, Mr. Robert Dougherty, Mr. Dennis O'Connor, Mr. Dennis DeLucca, and Mr. John T. Roosevelt, all of Fenway Park; Mr. Keith Edwards, Ms. Paula Munier, Mr. Byrd Leavell, Mr. Andrew Williams, and Ms. Andrea Calabretta; as well as the entire Longest family, the entire Robey family, and, in particular, that esteemed gentleman, writer, humorist, man of letters, patron of the arts, beloved uncle and dearly missed friend to whom this volume is inscribed.